Navigating Generative AI in Higher Education

Navigating Generative AI in Higher Education

Ethical, Theoretical and Practical Perspectives

Edited by

Soroush Sabbaghan

Associate Professor, Werklund School of Education, University of Calgary, Canada

Edward Elgar PUBLISHING

Cheltenham, UK • Northampton, MA, USA

Published by

Edward Elgar Publishing Limited
The Lypiatts
15 Lansdown Road
Cheltenham
Glos GL50 2JA
UK

Edward Elgar Publishing, Inc.
William Pratt House
9 Dewey Court
Northampton
Massachusetts 01060
USA

Authorised representative in the EU for GPSR queries only: Easy Access System Europe – Mustamäe tee 50, 10621 Tallinn, Estonia, gpsr.requests@easproject.com

A catalogue record for this book
is available from the British Library

Library of Congress Control Number: 2025939120

This book is available electronically in the Elgaronline
Sociology, Social Policy and Education subject collection
https://doi.org/10.4337/9781035337873

MIX
Paper | Supporting responsible forestry
FSC® C013056

ISBN 978 1 0353 3786 6 (cased)
ISBN 978 1 0353 3787 3 (eBook)
ISBN 978 1 0353 7140 2 (ePub)

Printed and bound in Great Britain by
TJ Books, Padstow, Cornwall

Contents

Contributors

Abbas, Muhammad National University of Computer and Emerging Sciences, Pakistan

Al-Zahrani, Abdulrahman M. University of Jeddah, Saudi Arabia

Asamoah, Daniel Basingstoke College of Technology, United Kingdom

Baidoo-Anu, David Conestoga College Institute of Technology and Advanced Learning, Canada

Brown, Barbara University of Calgary, Canada

Chiu, Thomas K. F. The Chinese University of Hong Kong, Hong Kong

Detrick, Rita Old Dominion University, United States

Eaton, Sarah Elaine University of Calgary, Canada

Farrokhnia, Mohammadreza University of Twente, the Netherlands

Keyhani, Mohammad University of Calgary, Canada

Kim, Jinhee Old Dominion University, United States

Kowch, Eugene G. University of Calgary, Canada

Kumar, Rahul Brock University, Canada

Lee, Alwyn Vwen Yen Nanyang Technological University, Singapore

Mohaghegh-Neyshabouri, Safaneh University of Calgary, Canada

Monsurat, Raji Conestoga College Institute of Technology and Advanced Learning, Canada

Noroozi, Omid Wageningen University and Research, the Netherlands

Roberts, Verena Thompson Rivers University, Canada

Sabbaghan, Soroush Werklund School of Education, University of Calgary, Canada

Sharmi, Shahneela Tasmin University of Calgary, Canada

Soleimani, Saba Interdisciplinary Transformation University, Austria

Tweedie, M. Gregory University of Calgary, Canada

1. Introduction to artificial intelligence and its relevance to academia

Soroush Sabbaghan

INTRODUCTION

Imagine a future in which your research assistant isn't a person, but an artificial intelligence capable of crafting new ideas, analyzing endless streams of data, and even drafting complete sections of your paper. This isn't something out of a science fiction novel; it's the reality of Generative Artificial Intelligence (GenAI) in academic circles during the mid-2020s.

As we begin this chapter, we're not just reading words on a page; we're stepping into a pivotal change in how knowledge is created and shared. GenAI isn't just another tool at our disposal; it's a spark for rethinking what it means to be a scholar, researcher, and educator today. We'll explore what GenAI is about, looking at its technology, its history, and how it's used in different fields. We'll question what it means for authorship, originality, and creativity.

But this chapter isn't just about what GenAI can do; it's a call for us to act. As educators, we have a duty not only to understand this technology but to shape how it grows and fits into our scholarship. We should look at GenAI with a critical mindset, recognizing its flaws and biases while using its strengths to expand our knowledge. Prepare for a journey that will make you question your beliefs, ignite your curiosity, and imagine the future of academia in this new age. The future is not something we merely encounter; it's something we must carve out with wisdom and a commitment to learning.

WHAT IS GENERATIVE AI?

GenAI represents a unique branch of Artificial Intelligence (AI) that focuses on generating new data or content, such as text, images, audio, and video. It taps into the patterns and connections it discovers in existing data (Ooi et al., 2023). Unlike the traditional AI systems that primarily categorize or predict based on current data, GenAI has the ability to produce entirely new content. This ability arises from its capacity to discern patterns and relationships within vast datasets and then employ this knowledge to craft new, coherent, and contextually relevant outputs (Chen et al., 2023). With this versatility, GenAI unlocks a multitude of possibilities across various fields. In education, for instance, it can be employed to create teaching materials, develop learning activities, design assessment criteria, and even create new educational tools and applications.

The underlying technologies that power GenAI make it not only a robust tool for invention but also an engine of creativity. At the core of GenAI models are neural networks, systems inspired by the human brain. These networks consist of layers of artificial neurons, processing incoming signals, recognizing patterns, and producing new outputs relevant to specific tasks (Chan & Colloton, 2024). Deep learning—a subset of machine learning—uses neural networks with several layers. This approach involves automatically extracting high-level, complex abstractions as data representations through a hierarchical learning process, and it allows models to master complex patterns and data representations. Take image recognition: An evolving deep learning model begins by identifying basic elements such as edges and textures, gradually recognizing more sophisticated features such as shapes and objects in its deeper layers. This layering equips the model to classify images with accuracy. Deep learning stands at the forefront of significant advances in GenAI, paving the way for the development of more refined models (Chan & Colloton, 2024).

At its core, Natural Language Processing (NLP) aims to teach machines the art of understanding, interpreting, and creating human language. Much like the narratives that shape our sense of self and community, NLP combines foundational rules that help decipher language structure with the aid of statistical methods and machine and deep learning models. These early strides have opened doors to more sophisticated systems, such as OpenAI's GPT-3. This model represents how large language models (LLMs) can grasp context and generate text that replicates human dialogue. Just as stories mold the identities and connections of social groups, these advanced AI models reshape our expectations of what artificial intelligence can achieve in language processing and generation, expanding the conversation between humans and machines. (Talha Junaid et al., 2024).

Think of GenAI as an elaborate, multi-tiered orchestra. The neural networks act like different sections of musicians—strings, brass, woodwinds—each processing part of the musical score (input data) to create harmonious sound (output). Deep learning is akin to adding more musicians and layers to each section, enriching the complexity and depth of the music. NLP functions like the conductor, orchestrating these sections to interpret and perform complex symphonies (human language) smoothly. Together, they perform beautifully coordinated pieces, from simple melodies to intricate compositions, demonstrating the power and creativity of GenAI. The synergy of these technologies, especially LLMs, culminates in powerful GenAI models capable of producing high-quality, contextually relevant, and creative content.

Historical Evolution of Artificial Intelligence Leading Up to GenAI

The concept of AI has been around since the 1950s. Initially, research aimed to create systems capable of tasks such as decision-making, problem-solving, and understanding language—tasks traditionally seen as requiring human intelligence (MacCann et al., 2003). The Dartmouth workshop in 1956 marks a pivotal moment in AI's history, setting the stage for its academic pursuit and outlining its primary goals: language use, abstraction, problem-solving, and self-improvement (Chan & Colloton, 2024). This workshop initiated what is sometimes called the "Genesis Phase" of AI, a time marked by eager optimism about technology's potential.

A key breakthrough came with natural language processing, exemplified by early chatbots such as ELIZA, designed by MIT's Joseph Weizenbaum in 1966. The broad spectrum of ideas behind ELIZA laid the groundwork for GenAI, which gained momentum through advancements such as deep neural networks, fundamental to modern AI. Today's Generative AI systems use these methods to create new texts, images, and other media, showcasing a clear progression from their early theoretical beginnings. The rise of Big Data and the Internet of Things (IoT) fueled further AI development by supplying large datasets for training AI models. Consequently, these advancements have allowed AI to better understand and generate human language, offering a more sophisticated evolution in its capabilities (Chan & Colloton, 2024).

The way we use language today is increasingly being shaped by new GenAI models such as OpenAI's o1, Claude 3.5 Sonnet, and Google's Gemini Flash 2.0. These models are part of a larger system aimed at improving how we understand and create text across a variety of platforms. Since the debut of OpenAI's first model, GPT-1, in June 2018, we've seen remarkable strides forward. These models leverage vast amounts of data to better mimic human-like communication. A major leap came with GPT-3, released in May 2020, which introduced few-shot learning. This advance marked a significant move in learning without extensive supervision, allowing the model to conduct multiple tasks. Later, an interim model, GPT-3.5, launched in March 2022, set the stage for the advent of ChatGPT in November 2022. ChatGPT enhanced our ability to interact and understand context within conversation.

Continuing this evolution, GPT-4 arrived in March 2023, offering improved text generation and problem-solving skills. After this, Claude 3 emerged in March 2024, focused on refining natural language processing and expanding domain expertise. In May of the same year, GPT-4o, which could do simple reasoning tasks across audio, image, and text in real time, made its debut.

Claude 3.5, unveiled in June 2024, was designed to be accurate and secure. Then came Gemini 1.5 in September 2024, enhancing multimodal capacities and user interactions. By December 5, 2024, OpenAI rolled out the full o1 and o1-mini models, pioneering strategizing task sequences and execution. On December 11, 2024, Gemini 2.0 Flash was released, paving the way for agentic GenAI. These models mostly operate on a *mixture of experts* architecture, as noted by Chan & Colloton (2024), which utilizes various specialized sub-models to manage different tasks efficiently. This method boosts overall performance, scalability, and flexibility, enriching the possibilities within complex natural language processing.

Types of GenAI

GenAI has evolved across many areas, largely due to advancements in machine learning and neural networks. It's important to understand the different forms of GenAI to fully appreciate its varied uses in academic contexts.

Generative pre-trained transformers

Multimodal generation is perhaps the most widely recognized application of GenAI, driven by models such as OpenAI's GPT-4o model, Anthropic's Claude 3.5 Sonnet, and Google's Gemini Flash 2.0. These models can generate text, images, audio, video, and possibly other types of data, allowing for richer interactions and more complex outputs based on prompts they receive. Moreover, they can perform an array of tasks, such as drafting, editing, and refining essays and research papers. They also offer translations and summaries, and aid in the synthesis of academic papers and research articles. Used this way, GenAI is not merely a technological advancement but a new narrative in how we learn and create, inviting us to consider what stories we might tell with these powerful tools at our disposal.

Generative Adversarial Networks (GANs)

Generative Adversarial Networks, or GANs, represent a significant advancement in GenAI, especially when it comes to crafting images. Developed by Goodfellow et al. (2014), GANs consist of two neural networks: the generator and the discriminator. These networks join forces to create images that can be remarkably lifelike. The generator's role is to produce images, while the discriminator's job is to assess these images by comparing them to real-world data. This interaction continues until the images produced are so refined that it becomes nearly impossible to tell them apart from genuine ones. In biomedical research, GANs contribute greatly by generating realistic medical images, which serve as a valuable resource for training and validating diagnostic algorithms. This proves particularly useful in areas such as radiology and pathology, where there's often a shortage of annotated medical images. By helping to craft diverse and representative datasets, GANs enable AI models to perform more reliably across varied clinical settings. The power of GANs thus lies in their ability to not just replicate reality but to enrich our understanding and application of it in critical fields (Yi et al., 2019).

Variational Autoencoders (VAEs)

Variational Autoencoders (VAEs) belong to an interesting category of AI technology that addresses the complexity of processing and generating data, such as images and text, by crafting and refining multimedia content through deep learning. These models take input data—be it a photo or a piece of text—and distill it into a simpler version known as a latent space. This process is somewhat similar to breaking down a book into a handful of key ideas. But this distillation is not just any summary; it adheres to a specific pattern, typically resembling a bell curve (Gaussian distribution). This aids the model in understanding the nuances and variations within the data. Once the data is compressed, the VAE tries to recreate the original content from this reduced form, as one might when developing those key ideas back into a complete book, striving to match the original as closely as possible. Yet, this process isn't entirely deterministic; it incorporates an element of randomness, granting the model the ability to concoct new, diverse, yet coherent data instances akin to what it has learned. By modeling the probability distributions of intricate datasets, VAEs open up new vistas for researchers to uncover hidden patterns and insights. Take chemistry, for example; VAEs can aid in crafting new molecules by traversing the latent space of chemical structures, potentially leading to breakthroughs in the discovery of new drugs or materials (Gozalo-Brizuela & Garrido-Merchán, 2023).

Other forms

GenAI is not just redefining text and images; it's also making significant marks in the worlds of music and art. Tools such as Udio and Sono compose music in various styles, learning from existing works (Marr, 2023). These advancements provide tools for creative minds and open up interactive ways for students to dive into music theory and composition. Meanwhile, OpenAI's Sora, an AI that turns text into video, offers a new pathway for creativity and educational content. Sora includes safety features such as watermarks and content limitations to help prevent misuse. Simulations present another exciting use of GenAI, enabling the creation of virtual scenarios for training and learning. These simulations mimic real-life conditions, offering a safe space for students to practice and refine their skills. For instance, some GenAI models can create 3D images of molecular structures and medical data, supporting research and diagnostics (Gozalo-Brizuela & Garrido-Merchán, 2023).

THE INTERSECTION OF GENAI AND ACADEMIA

GenAI isn't just a vision of the future; it's already becoming a part of various academic fields, bringing both clear benefits and new challenges. GenAI reshapes how research is conducted, offering models that help scholars keep up with fast-changing technology. This is important, as there's a massive amount of data and literature to handle in today's research landscape. In doing so, GenAI helps academics manage and review the vast sea of information effectively (Mishra et al., 2024). Furthermore, GenAI enhances both creativity and productivity in research. It reduces the time spent on repetitive academic tasks such as writing grant applications, formatting publications, and navigating the peer review process, which helps increase research efficiency (Boulus-Rødje et al., 2024). GenAI also brings new ways of approaching traditional research, encouraging transdisciplinary research and challenging established academic norms. For instance, GenAI tools streamline the process of literature reviews, which usually takes up a lot of a researcher's time. These tools quickly process large volumes of literature, spot main themes and trends, and even highlight missing areas in research (Al-Zahrani, 2025). This not only speeds up research but also enriches it by allowing a broader and deeper understanding of existing knowledge, encouraging collaboration across various disciplines (Mishra et al., 2024). These examples show how GenAI is already changing academia. As this technology keeps evolving, we can look forward to even more creative applications that will continue to blend human insight with machine intelligence in our quest for knowledge and learning.

Case Studies: GenAI in Action

Integrating GenAI into academia has brought a wide array of case studies to light, highlighting not only its potential advantages but also the obstacles it presents. These real-world examples give us a view of how GenAI is being used in various educational settings, showing its impact on students' learning experiences.

One of the most exciting uses of GenAI in education is in creating personalized learning and tutoring experiences. At a major university in Western Canada, the GPT-4 API (Application Programming Interface) helped develop personalized learning interactions that cater to each student's needs. This approach not only aligns with students' learning goals but also boosts their engagement and helps retain knowledge. By using AI-powered personas, like those in the PEARL system (Brown & Roberts, 2025; Sabbaghan & Brown, 2024), education becomes more engaging and effective.

Hennekeuser et al. (2024) used a GPT-4-based system integrated with a vector database to assist higher education lecturers. Participants in their study utilized the system for tasks such as generating exercises, summarizing content, and developing new lecture materials. The system was praised for saving time, offering well-formulated responses, and enhancing lecture preparation. However, participants noted issues such as response delays, knowledge base limitations, and difficulties handling ambiguous or misspelled queries.

In civil engineering education, learning is evolving with the help of ChatGPT, which plays a role in shaping personalized learning experiences. According to Talha Junaid et al. (2024), it can act like a human tutor and aid students in solving problems by adapting to their unique learning needs. By analyzing students' past work, the system can offer tailored advice suited to each person's learning path. This approach recognizes that education, much like history, is guided by narratives and can be customized rather than taking a one-size-fits-all approach (Talha Junaid et al., 2024).

ChatGPT's language processing capabilities have made it a valuable tool for language learning and translation. Hong (2023) explored the use of ChatGPT as a conversational partner for students learning English as a second language. Students could engage in text-based conversations with ChatGPT, practicing their language skills and receiving immediate feedback. The study found that students who used ChatGPT showed improvement in their fluency and confidence in speaking English.

THEORETICAL IMPLICATIONS

GenAI has sparked a wave of introspection among academics, leading us to rethink long-held beliefs about what we know, how we learn, and what defines human intelligence. This section looks at how GenAI is changing higher education by affecting how we produce knowledge. It also examines the challenges it brings to how we understand knowledge and considers the different viewpoints coming from various fields. In a world where our understanding of knowledge and intellect faces constant revision, these shifts pose both challenges and opportunities for dialogue and growth.

Impact on Knowledge Production

As GenAI has the ability to sift through massive amounts of data, propose hypotheses, and even help craft research papers, it makes us rethink what it means to contribute intellectually. Kasneci et al. (2023) assert that researchers can harness GenAI to uncover patterns that were once hidden, explore ideas that might seem unconventional, and come up with hypotheses that could have otherwise remained undiscovered. Rather than remaining on the old paths of research, GenAI challenges us to engage with our work in a dialogue of sorts, pushing research into new and unexplored territories.

The rise of GenAI tools in research raises important questions about who gets credit for ideas and inventions. When a GenAI tool plays a major role in a study, how do we acknowledge it? Is it right to name a machine as a co-author? Could AI even receive patents for its inventions? These are key issues in today's ethical debates in academia. Some argue that since AI, including GenAI, lacks awareness and intention, it can't be seen as an author in the traditional sense (Lund & Naheem, 2024; Nazarovets, 2024). Hosseini et al. (2023) propose that AI's contribution should be acknowledged, perhaps through a distinct category of AI-assisted authorship. Eaton and Keyhani (2025) suggest that authorship involves collaboration between humans and AI, requiring new frameworks that value critical thinking, decision-making, and ethical use, while maintaining accountability and learner agency. Kumar (2025) adds to this notion and calls for guidelines on attribution, transparency, and citation practices to address AI's integration into academic writing, balancing recognition of AI contributions with ethical responsibility. These new methods honor the role of AI while upholding ethical standards of authorship, which demand accountability.

Epistemological Considerations

GenAI challenges how we think about knowledge, leading us to reconsider what knowledge is, how it's formed, and how we share it. Traditional academic approaches, usually based on human thought and experience, now face a new kind of knowledge creation driven by algorithms and a lot of data. A key question is how GenAI affects our view of truth and objectivity. These AI systems, trained with enormous datasets, can spot patterns that humans might miss. But this reliance on data can also spread biases present in the original information, resulting in a distorted or incomplete picture of reality (Bender et al., 2021). This raises concerns about giving GenAI systems too much power in shaping our understanding while potentially neglecting the essential human aspects of knowledge creation. To address some of these challenges, Robertson et al. (2024) propose using constructivism to improve how we engage with GenAI tools. They argue that by incorporating constructivist ideas, individuals can actively work with GenAI, building on their existing knowledge. This method promotes a dynamic interaction with GenAI, encouraging users to not just absorb information but actively participate in creating knowledge. Perhaps we should advocate for a human-centered approach in knowledge creation, ensuring that learning stays interactive, thoughtful, and closely tied to human thinking and values.

The increasing reliance on GenAI insights poses questions about the role of human judgment in forming what we consider knowledge. GenAI can produce vast amounts of data and offer analysis, but it falls on us, humans, to make sense of this information (Eaton & Keyhani, 2025). If we lean too heavily on AI's output, we may find ourselves sidelining our own critical thinking skills, which are crucial for separating fact from fiction (Frank et al., 2019). There's also a risk that AI could muddy the waters of trust in knowledge and create confusion about our identities. Users might find it challenging to tell which content is generated by humans and which by AI, leading to a loss of control over our understanding and decisions (Mishra et al., 2024). This blurring of boundaries can lead to a loss of epistemic agency, as individuals become increasingly reliant on GenAI systems for knowledge and decision-making (Nie, 2024).

To address these challenges, we need to cultivate a critical stance on how GenAI fits into our lives (Feng et al., 2024). This means growing our understanding of what GenAI means for how we acquire knowledge and continuously working on managing the risks these systems present (Boulus-Rødje et al., 2024). One practical approach could be for educators to include AI-related case studies in their teaching. This would allow students to explore and discuss the ethical questions surrounding AI content and its impacts on our understanding and independence of thought (Brown & Roberts, 2025). Through these efforts, we can aim to enhance the partnership between humans and AI, aligning its use with the values and goals that matter to us (Robertson et al., 2024).

Ultimately, the epistemological questions raised by generative AI present complex challenges, yet they are not impossible to overcome. To address these issues effectively, we must adopt a forward-thinking and collaborative strategy. By encouraging critical thinking, promoting openness, and emphasizing human agency, we can unlock GenAI's potential, address its drawbacks, and safeguard the central role human insight plays in shaping what we know.

Disciplinary Perspectives

GenAI's influence is echoing through various areas within the humanities and social sciences, leading to new viewpoints and innovative uses. In languages and literature, for instance, GenAI is now part of examining text patterns, crafting creative writing, and translating works. This pushes us to rethink how we understand literary styles, pinpoint who wrote what, and even craft new stories (Tsao & Nogues, 2024).

In nursing education, GenAI tools such as ChatGPT are being employed to create simulation scenarios and backstories, providing students with realistic learning experiences (Reed & Dodson, 2023). GenAI is also being utilized to assist with tasks such as automatic coding and checking the accuracy of human coding processes (Yim et al., 2024). In clinical settings, it streamlines documenting the nursing process, embodying a new chapter for the nursing profession (Gosak et al., 2024).

In the field of history, we now find GenAI making its mark in interesting ways. One promising avenue is its role in education, where tools such as ChatGPT could shine a light on history from a critical perspective (Ali et al., 2024). Another application lies in art history. By harnessing GenAI, researchers propose a computational approach to map out and understand large-scale patterns in historical art. This could allow us to connect the dots across vast collections of art data, potentially offering fresh insights into the evolution of art throughout the ages (Hutson & Nichols, 2023).

In clinical psychology, new advancements in GenAI are reshaping the way we understand patients' mental health. GenAI can sift through large amounts of data, offering valuable insights to aid mental health professionals in their decision-making (Tortora, 2024). Moreover, GenAI is also used to craft psychological profiles of individuals. It does this by analyzing people's digital footprints, such as their social media posts and online activities. These profiles are then used by AI models to predict various psychological traits (Matz et al., 2024). By connecting these digital dots, GenAI not only supports clinicians in their work but also underscores the complex ways technology intertwines with the human psyche.

GenAI is starting to find its place in various disciplines. Each area, with its unique views and hurdles, contributes to a lively and changing conversation about the role and boundaries of GenAI in shaping how we see our world. By sharing and understanding these perspectives, we engage in an ongoing exchange of ideas.

ETHICAL CONSIDERATIONS

To bring GenAI into academia transcends the mere adoption of new technology; it marks a significant shift that demands careful reflection on its ethical implications. As we journey forward, we're faced with intricate questions about academic integrity, bias, fairness, transparency, and accountability. If we neglect these ethical concerns, we risk eroding the very foundations of knowledge-making and learning that academia seeks to protect and build upon.

The ease with which GenAI can generate text, code, and even creative works has raised serious concerns about academic integrity, particularly regarding plagiarism and originality. Students might be tempted by the ease of letting GenAI handle their assignments, missing out on actually learning and undermining the true aim of education. The value of academic qualifications might be undermined as well. Our traditional idea of plagiarism, focused on exact copying, may no longer be sufficient. AI-generated content, though not directly lifted from one source, still builds on existing data. So, when people turn in AI-created work as their own without acknowledging it, it's a new kind of plagiarism, which Chan and Colloton (2024) call "Aigiarism." Eaton (2023) argues that, as human and AI writing continue to blend, our old views on plagiarism might become outdated. Instead, we should think about the ethical issues these technologies bring up to keep academic honesty alive. Moreover, GenAI challenges how we think about originality. If AI crafts something new or creative, is it truly original? And who owns the rights to these creations? These questions touch on the ongoing debates about the legal and moral impacts of AI content. Using GenAI in research also brings ethical concerns. Researchers might be drawn to using GenAI to speed up their work, generating data or writing papers without enough human oversight. This could lead to flawed or dishonest research getting published, which damages trust in science.

Transparency and Accountability

The intricate nature of GenAI models often results in a lack of clarity regarding how they make decisions. Tweedie and Sharmi (2025) assert that the "black box" issue makes it challenging to comprehend the processes through which AI systems reach their conclusions, prompting concerns about who is responsible and how these systems might be misused. This problem of opacity means that the systems are so tangled in complexity that even their creators might not completely understand how these systems generate their outcomes. This lack of transparency makes it difficult to:

- **Identify and Correct Biases:** If we don't understand how an AI system is making decisions, it is challenging to identify and correct potential biases.
- **Explain AI Decisions:** When AI systems are used in high-stakes contexts, such as grading student work or making medical diagnoses, it is essential to be able to explain their decisions. The black box problem makes this difficult.
- **Hold AI Systems Accountable:** If an AI system makes a harmful decision, it is challenging to hold it accountable if we don't understand how it arrived at that decision.

To address the black box issue in AI, we must work together to create systems that are transparent and easier to understand (see Tweedie & Sharmi, 2025). One approach is to focus on Explainable AI (Longo et al., 2024), a research area dedicated to designing AI that can offer explanations of its decisions in a way humans can understand. By freely sharing our research, code, and data, we can promote transparency and responsibility in the development of GenAI. Additionally, setting ethical standards for using GenAI in academia will help ensure it is applied in a way that benefits everyone. This collaborative effort not only enhances AI but also aligns with our shared stories of progress and innovation.

PRACTICAL IMPLICATIONS

GenAI has the potential to transform the way we develop teaching materials, such as presentation slides, exams, and coursework. Acting as a knowledge broker, this technology can bridge the research–practice gap by providing university teachers with insights for the effective and ethical integration of GenAI tools (Farrokhnia et al., 2025). GenAI enables personalized education and inclusive pedagogy by tailoring content to students' learning needs, levels, and speeds. It supports diverse needs through adaptive instruction, real-time translations, and accessibility tools. This transformation necessitates redefining assessments and educators' roles to balance AI assistance with meaningful, independent learning outcomes (Keyhani & Mohaghegh-Neyshabouri, 2025). GenAI also facilitates diverse and personalized classroom assessments by automating question generation, providing tailored feedback, and assisting in grading, thereby enhancing efficiency and promoting adaptive, student-centered learning practices (Baidoo-Anu et al., 2025). GenAI can also streamline various administrative tasks by automating aspects such as feedback mechanisms. For example, GenAI can be employed to automatically provide personalized feedback to students. This automation leverages the machine's ability to analyze text content, understand grading rubrics, and apply them across multiple student submissions. This not only streamlines the feedback process, saving time for educators, but also ensures a level of uniformity in providing feedback to students, contributing significantly to the efficiency of assessment for learning (Al-Zahrani, 2025).

Skills and Training

To effectively engage with GenAI, we must develop more than just basic digital skills. Both academics and students need to understand AI concepts, ethical issues, and practical uses if we are to use GenAI wisely and effectively (Keyhani & Mohaghegh-Neyshabouri, 2025). It's clear that academics need to get comfortable with interactive activities and collaborating, especially with GenAI platforms such as ChatGPT, Claude, and Google AI Studio. We need to actively use these platforms to get better at them. As Hashmi and Bal (2024) point out in their research, becoming skilled with GenAI takes practice and hands-on experience. This practice shouldn't stop at knowing the basics; we need to understand the strengths and limits of different GenAI tools. Detrick and Kim (2025) suggest that academics can also improve their use of GenAI by engaging in professional growth opportunities, collaborating with others across different sectors, trying out AI tools, and joining learning communities where we can share knowledge and keep up with new developments.

In the academic world where multiple disciplines are coming together, educators are called to take on a role more similar to guides than keepers of all knowledge. This shift echoes Rancière's pedagogical philosophy, which proposes that everyone has the same intellectual potential and that learning thrives when learners are empowered to take charge of their own education. This approach promotes a learning environment where self-direction is key, with GenAI playing a role in nurturing equal access to knowledge and encouraging students to discover for themselves. In these contexts, the approach is less about providing direct instructions and more about fostering exploration, requiring a departure from conventional grading systems and evaluative practices (Tsao & Nogues, 2024).

To truly prepare individuals for the complex landscape of modern education, we must consider the interplay of digital skills, ethical thinking, and engaging pedagogy. These elements are crucial to navigating the ever-changing demands of academia, where the pressure to publish looms large and the presence of GenAI is more pronounced than ever. When we consider the evolving landscape of academia, it becomes apparent that mere adherence to traditional methods will no longer suffice.

CONCLUSION

As we navigate the brave new world of GenAI in academia, I hope that we realize that this technology is a significant shift that will change the landscape of higher education. It redefines research methods, influences how we acquire knowledge, and reshapes pedagogy while fostering collaboration across disciplines. The reach of GenAI is wide and meaningful.

However, along with the excitement generated by its potential, GenAI introduces complex ethical, intellectual, and practical dilemmas. Issues such as academic integrity, bias, transparency, and accountability demand careful consideration and proactive action from our academic community. As educators, scholars, and lifelong learners, our responsibility is twofold: to understand both the capabilities and constraints of GenAI and to guide its integration into our educational systems mindfully. We must equip ourselves and our students with the knowledge and skills to use GenAI wisely, staying open-minded and reflective.

The rise of GenAI in academia offers both opportunities and challenges. Our role is to approach this new landscape thoughtfully and fairly, with a steady commitment to the pursuit of knowledge in the age of AI.

REFERENCES

Ali, S., Ravi, P., Williams, R., DiPaola, D., & Breazeal, C. (2024). Constructing dreams using generative AI. *Proceedings of the AAAI Conference on Artificial Intelligence, 38*(21), 23268–23275. https://doi.org/10.1609/aaai.v38i21.30374.

Al-Zahrani, A. M. (2025). The future landscape: Predictions and prospects for generative AI in academia. In S. Sabbaghan (Ed.), *Navigating generative AI in higher education: Ethical, theoretical, and practical perspectives*. Edward Elgar.

Baidoo-Anu, D., Asamoah, D., & Monsurat, R. (2025). Innovative applications of generative artificial intelligence in classroom assessment: A scoping review. In S. Sabbaghan (Ed.), *Navigating generative AI in higher education: Ethical, theoretical, and practical perspectives*. Edward Elgar.

Bender, E. M., Gebru, T., McMillan-Major, A., & Shmitchell, S. (2021). On the dangers of stochastic parrots: Can language models be too big? *Proceedings of the 2021 ACM Conference on Fairness, Accountability, and Transparency*, 610–623. https://doi.org/10.1145/3442188.3445922.

Boulus-Rødje, N., Cranefield, J., Doyle, C., & Fleron, B. (2024). GenAI and me: The hidden work of building and maintaining an augmentative partnership. *Personal and Ubiquitous Computing*. https://doi.org/10.1007/s00779-024-01810-y.

Brown, B., & Roberts, V. (2025). Responsive instructional design using GenAI and digital skill development framework. In S. Sabbaghan (Ed.), *Navigating generative AI in higher education: Ethical, theoretical, and practical perspectives*. Edward Elgar.

Chan, C. K. Y., & Colloton, T. (2024). *Generative AI in higher education: The ChatGPT effect*. Routledge.

Chen, B., Zhu, X., & Díaz Del Castillo H. F. (2023). Integrating generative AI in knowledge building. *Computers and Education: Artificial Intelligence*, *5*, 100184. https://doi.org/10.1016/j.caeai.2023.100184.

Detrick, R., & Kim, J. (2025). Collaborative approaches: Bridging the gap between generative AI developers and educators. In S. Sabbaghan (Ed.), *Navigating generative AI in higher education: Ethical, theoretical, and practical perspectives*. Edward Elgar.

Eaton, S. E. (2023). Postplagiarism: Transdisciplinary ethics and integrity in the age of artificial intelligence and neurotechnology. *International Journal for Educational Integrity*, *19*(1), 23, s40979-023-00144–1. https://doi.org/10.1007/s40979-023-00144-1.

Eaton, S. E., & Keyhani, M. (2025). The pedagogical ethics: Navigating learning in a generative AI-augmented environment in a post-plagiarism era. In S. Sabbaghan (Ed.), *Navigating generative AI in higher education: Ethical, theoretical, and practical perspectives*. Edward Elgar.

Farrokhnia, M., Soleimani, S., & Noroozi, O. (2025). Generative AI in higher education: Transformative tools for research, teaching, and assessment. In S. Sabbaghan (Ed.), *Navigating generative AI in higher education: Ethical, theoretical, and practical perspectives*. Edward Elgar.

Feng, C. (Mitsu), Botha, E., & Pitt, L. (2024). From HAL to GenAI: Optimize chatbot impacts with CARE. *Business Horizons*, S0007681324000570. https://doi.org/10.1016/j.bushor.2024.04.012.

Frank, M. R., Autor, D., Bessen, J. E., Brynjolfsson, E., Cebrian, M., Deming, D. J., Feldman, M., Groh, M., Lobo, J., Moro, E., Wang, D., Youn, H., & Rahwan, I. (2019). Toward understanding the impact of artificial intelligence on labor. *Proceedings of the National Academy of Sciences*, *116*(14), 6531–6539. https://doi.org/10.1073/pnas.1900949116.

Goodfellow, I., Pouget-Abadie, J., Mirza, M., Xu, B., Warde-Farley, D., Ozair, S., Courville, A., & Bengio, Y. (2014). Generative adversarial nets. *Advances in Neural Information Processing Systems*, *27*.

Gosak, L., Pruinelli, L., Topaz, M., & Štiglic, G. (2024). The ChatGPT effect and transforming nursing education with generative AI: Discussion paper. *Nurse Education in Practice*, *75*, 103888. https://doi.org/10.1016/j.nepr.2024.103888.

Gozalo-Brizuela, R., & Garrido-Merchán, E. C. (2023). *A survey of generative AI applications*. arXiv. http://arxiv.org/abs/2306.02781.

Hashmi, N., & Bal, A. S. (2024). Generative AI in higher education and beyond. *Business Horizons*, *67*(5), 607–614. https://doi.org/10.1016/j.bushor.2024.05.005.

Hennekeuser, D., Vaziri, D. D., Golchinfar, D., Schreiber, D., & Stevens, G. (2024). Enlarged education – Exploring the use of generative AI to support lecturing in higher education. *International Journal of Artificial Intelligence in Education*. https://doi.org/10.1007/s40593-024-00424-y.

Hong, W. C. H. (2023). The impact of ChatGPT on foreign language teaching and learning: Opportunities in education and research. *Journal of Educational Technology and Innovation*, *5*(1). https://doi.org/10.61414/jeti.v5i1.103.

Hosseini, M., Resnik, D. B., & Holmes, K. (2023). The ethics of disclosing the use of artificial intelligence tools in writing scholarly manuscripts. *Research Ethics*, *19*(4), 449–465. https://doi.org/10.1177/17470161231180449.

Hutson, J., & Nichols, M. H. (2023). Generative AI and algorithmic art: Disrupting the framing of meaning and rethinking the subject-object dilemma. *Global Journal of Computer Science and Technology*, *23*(1), 55–61. https://doi.org/10.34257/GJCSTDVOL23IS1PG55.

Kasneci, E., Sessler, K., Küchemann, S., Bannert, M., Dementieva, D., Fischer, F., Gasser, U., Groh, G., Günnemann, S., Hüllermeier, E., Krusche, S., Kutyniok, G., Michaeli, T., Nerdel, C., Pfeffer, J., Poquet, O., Sailer, M., Schmidt, A., Seidel, T., … Kasneci, G. (2023). ChatGPT for good? On opportunities and challenges of large language models for education. *Learning and Individual Differences*, *103*, 102274. https://doi.org/10.1016/j.lindif.2023.102274.

Keyhani, M., & Mohaghegh-Neyshabouri, S. (2025). The rise of generative AI: Capabilities and potential for higher education. In S. Sabbaghan (Ed.), *Navigating generative AI in higher education: Ethical, theoretical, and practical perspectives*. Edward Elgar.

Kumar, R. (2025). Rethinking authorship in a generative AI-driven academic world. In S. Sabbaghan (Ed.), *Navigating generative AI in higher education: Ethical, theoretical, and practical perspectives*. Edward Elgar.

Longo, L., Brcic, M., Cabitza, F., Choi, J., Confalonieri, R., Ser, J. D., Guidotti, R., Hayashi, Y., Herrera, F., Holzinger, A., Jiang, R., Khosravi, H., Lecue, F., Malgieri, G., Páez, A., Samek, W., Schneider, J., Speith, T., & Stumpf, S. (2024). Explainable artificial intelligence (XAI) 2.0: A manifesto of open challenges and interdisciplinary research directions. *Information Fusion*, *106*, 102301. https://doi.org/10.1016/j.inffus.2024.102301.

Lund, B. D., & Naheem, K. T. (2024). Can ChatGPT be an author? A study of artificial intelligence authorship policies in top academic journals. *Learned Publishing*, *37*(1), 13–21. https://doi.org/10.1002/leap.1582.

MacCann, C., Matthews, G., Zeidner, M., & Roberts, R. D. (2003). Psychological assessment of emotional intelligence: A review of self-report and performance-based testing. *The International Journal of Organizational Analysis*, *11*(3), 247–274. https://doi.org/10.1108/eb028975.

Marr, B. (2023). *Data-driven HR: How to use AI, analytics and data to drive performance*. Kogan Page Publishers.

Matz, S. C., Teeny, J. D., Vaid, S. S., Peters, H., Harari, G. M., & Cerf, M. (2024). The potential of generative AI for personalized persuasion at scale. *Scientific Reports*, *14*(1), 4692. https://doi.org/10.1038/s41598-024-53755-0.

Mishra, P., Oster, N., & Henriksen, D. (2024). Generative AI, teacher knowledge and educational research: Bridging short- and long-term perspectives. *TechTrends*, *68*(2), 205–210. https://doi.org/10.1007/s11528-024-00938-1.

Nazarovets, S. (2024). Dealing with research paper mills, tortured phrases, and data fabrication and falsification in scientific papers. In P. B. Joshi, P. P. Churi, & M. Pandey (Eds.), *Scientific publishing ecosystem* (pp. 233–254). Springer Nature Singapore. https://doi.org/10.1007/978-981-97-4060-4_14.

Nie, M. (2024). Artificial intelligence: The biggest threat to democracy today? *Proceedings of the AAAI Symposium Series*, *3*(1), 376–379. https://doi.org/10.1609/aaaiss.v3i1.31239.

Ooi, K.-B., Tan, G. W.-H., Al-Emran, M., Al-Sharafi, M. A., Capatina, A., Chakraborty, A., Dwivedi, Y. K., Huang, T.-L., Kar, A. K., Lee, V.-H., Loh, X.-M., Micu, A., Mikalef, P., Mogaji, E., Pandey, N., Raman, R., Rana, N. P., Sarker, P., Sharma, A., … Wong, L.-W. (2023). The potential of generative artificial intelligence across disciplines: Perspectives and future directions. *Journal of Computer Information Systems*, *65*(1), 1–32. https://doi.org/10.1080/08874417.2023.2261010.

Reed, J. M., & Dodson, T. M. (2023). Generative AI backstories for simulation preparation. *Nurse Educator*, *49*(4), 184–188. https://doi.org/10.1097/NNE.0000000000001590.

Robertson, J., Ferreira, C., Botha, E., & Oosthuizen, K. (2024). Game changers: A generative AI prompt protocol to enhance human-AI knowledge co-construction. *Business Horizons*, 67(5), 499–510. S0007681324000533. https://doi.org/10.1016/j.bushor.2024.04.008.

Sabbaghan, S., & Brown, B. (2024). The role of AI-powered personas in developing graduate interviewing skills. *International Journal on Innovations in Online Education*, *8*(1). https://doi.org/10.1615/IntJInnovOnlineEdu.2024051770.

Talha Junaid, M., Barakat, S., Awad, R., & Anwar, N. (2024). Adopting the power of AI chatbots for enriching student learning in civil engineering education: A study on capabilities and limitations. In A. Al-Marzouqi, S. A. Salloum, M. Al-Saidat, A. Aburayya, & B. Gupta (Eds.), *Artificial intelligence in education: The power and dangers of ChatGPT in the classroom* (pp. 25–47). Springer Nature Switzerland. https://doi.org/10.1007/978-3-031-52280-2_3.

Tortora, L. (2024). Beyond discrimination: Generative AI applications and ethical challenges in forensic psychiatry. *Frontiers in Psychiatry*, *15*, 1346059. https://doi.org/10.3389/fpsyt.2024.1346059.

Tsao, J., & Nogues, C. (2024). Beyond the author: Artificial intelligence, creative writing and intellectual emancipation. *Poetics*, *102*, 101865. https://doi.org/10.1016/j.poetic.2024.101865.

Tweedie, M. G., & Sharmi, S. T. (2025). Transparency and the "black box" dilemma. In S. Sabbaghan (Ed.), *Navigating generative AI in higher education: Ethical, theoretical, and practical perspectives*. Edward Elgar.

Yi, X., Walia, E., & Babyn, P. (2019). Generative adversarial network in medical imaging: A review. *Medical Image Analysis*, *58*, 101552. https://doi.org/10.1016/j.media.2019.101552.

Yim, D., Khuntia, J., Parameswaran, V., & Meyers, A. (2024). Preliminary evidence of the use of generative AI in health care clinical services: Systematic narrative review. *JMIR Medical Informatics*, *12*, e52073. https://doi.org/10.2196/52073.

2. The rise of generative AI: Capabilities and potential for higher education

Mohammad Keyhani and Safaneh Mohaghegh-Neyshabouri

INTRODUCTION

The rapid advances in generative artificial intelligence (GenAI) mark the beginning of a new technological era and a defining moment in the history of higher education. We now have access to a never-tiring digital brain-on-demand that can assist us in any task that requires thinking and creativity (Mollick, 2024). Most if not all students and educators have access to some version of this technology free of charge or at affordable prices. The immense impact of this technology on education will forever delineate the post-GenAI era from the pre-GenAI one. As stated by Bowen and Watson (2024, p. 2), "if the internet changed our relationship with knowledge, AI is going to change our relationship with thinking."

We are already seeing students, faculty, and staff in higher education use GenAI in a variety of ways. While this is impressive, even arguably overwhelming, these are just the early applications we are seeing after only a couple of years since the technology has become widely available. To better grasp where the future is headed, we need to think from first principles: what do we know about the characteristics and capabilities of GenAI? And what does this mean for the future of higher education? These questions provide the main motivation and structure for this chapter.

This chapter argues that GenAI fundamentally transforms higher education by revolutionizing not just how we teach and learn but also how we conduct research and manage academic institutions. This transformation requires a strategic reimagining of educational practices, research methodologies, and administrative processes to harness AI's benefits while addressing its challenges. The impact of this technology is so profound that it necessitates a complete rethinking of assessment methods, educator roles, research processes, and institutional operations.

To support this argument, we examine three critical domains where GenAI is reshaping higher education. First, in teaching and learning, we demonstrate how AI is not only providing powerful tools for personalized education and inclusive pedagogy but also forcing us to fundamentally reimagine assessment methods and redefine educator roles. Second, in research and scholarship, we explore how GenAI serves as an invaluable thinking assistant, enabling new forms of scientific discovery and transforming traditional research processes. Third, in academic administration, we analyze how AI is streamlining operations, creating new institutional roles, and democratizing software development within educational institutions.

This chapter presents a conceptual overview of GenAI in higher education, synthesizing current literature and emerging trends in the field. Our approach involves a comprehensive review of recent academic publications, industry reports, and expert commentary on GenAI technologies and their applications in educational contexts. We have focused on identifying key themes and potential impacts across various aspects of higher education, drawing on both theoretical frameworks and practical examples where available.

Most of the arguments in this chapter are based on large language models (LLMs), which typically output text and are arguably the most important type of generative AI technology for higher education, because text is the standard way to communicate knowledge and reasoning. However, many of the arguments apply to other GenAI technologies, such as diffusion models used to create images, audio, or video. LLMs themselves are increasingly becoming multi-modal, capable of taking audio and video inputs in addition to text.

This chapter is structured as follows: First, we discuss the key capabilities and characteristics of GenAI, with a focus on LLMs. We then explore the implications and potential of this technology in three key areas of higher education: teaching and learning, research and scholarship, and academic administration. Finally, we conclude with a discussion of the broader implications for higher education institutions as they adapt to this rapidly evolving technological landscape.

CAPABILITIES AND CHARACTERISTICS OF GENERATIVE AI

The following is a non-exhaustive exposition of key characteristics of generative AI technology, particularly in the form of LLMs, that can aid our thinking in understanding this technology and assist us in educated speculation about the future of its impact on higher education.

LLMs Can Reason and Learn, Be Wrong and Creative, and Respond to Prompt Engineering

LLMs operate by predicting the next word or "token" in a sequence, transforming machine learning prediction into text generation (Wolfram, 2023). This process, while powerful, can sometimes lead to factual inaccuracies or "hallucinations" (Yao et al., 2023), which paradoxically also contribute to the model's creativity. The input we give an AI model is called a prompt, and the art of prompting is an important skill in learning how to work with AI (Pletnyova et al., 2024). When we use specialized techniques or systematic methods in prompting, we typically refer to it as prompt engineering. The effectiveness of LLMs often improves with longer inputs that provide better context, explaining the success of techniques like "Chain of Thought" prompting (Wei et al., 2022) because it helps the AI produce quality context for itself before giving the final answer.

LLMs can be enhanced with additional knowledge and skills through various methods. Retrieval-Augmented Generation (RAG) injects external information into the model's context window, potentially reducing hallucinations (Gao et al., 2024). Few-shot learning allows LLMs to adapt to specific styles or reasoning formats by providing examples in the prompt (Brown et al., 2020). For more extensive adaptations, fine-tuning the model with additional training data can be employed (Ding et al., 2023). These methods, combined with prompt engineering, can effectively mimic short-term and long-term memory functions in LLMs.

Despite their human-like conversational abilities, LLMs do not function exactly like human brains. They are often described as "alien brains" due to our limited understanding of their inner workings. This has given rise to the field of "machine psychology," which aims to study how LLMs think and behave (Hagendorff, 2023). Research in this area has led to unexpected discoveries in prompt engineering, such as the effectiveness of asking the AI to "take a deep breath" (Yang et al., 2024) or using prompts styled after Star Trek (the TV series) captain's logs (Battle & Gollapudi, 2024). These findings underscore the complexity and uniqueness of LLM behavior, highlighting the need for continued exploration in this field.

LLMs Are Both Enabled and Constrained by Their Training Data

The quantity and quality of data used to train an LLM define most of its capabilities and behaviors, and therefore determine many of its affordances and constraints. This is also why frontier LLMs seem to be converging in their capabilities, because it is not easy to go beyond a dataset that approximates the set of everything everyone has ever written. However, breakthroughs may emerge in various ways, such as if we learn new ways to use synthetic (AI-generated) data (Yu et al., 2023) or data from simulated virtual worlds for training, filter out lower-quality data, combine non-text data with text data, or find significantly better ways for the AI to learn from existing data.

Advances in data quality are necessary not just to improve the performance and accuracy of LLMs but also as a matter of social justice, fairness, and equity. LLM training data can contain explicit and implicit representations of all the biases, injustices, and dominant power structures that harm vulnerable and marginalized groups in society (Garg et al., 2018), thereby recreating these biases and injustices in the behavior of the trained models (Navigli et al., 2023). Studies have already found bias and discrimination in LLMs (in both explicit and subtle forms) based on age, gender, status or caste, geography or socioeconomic development, nationality, race and ethnicity, sexual orientation, physical appearance or disability, religion, and culture (Kamruzzaman et al., 2024; Navigli et al., 2023).

LLMs are Digital Artifacts that can Interface with Other Digital Artifacts

LLMs are digital artifacts that function as disembodied intelligence-as-a-service or digital brains-on-demand, free from biological constraints and capable of operating at scales beyond human capacity. As software products, they essentially follow the economics of information goods (Shapiro & Varian, 1999) and can be easily replicated and deployed at minimal cost. Their extensibility allows them to interface with various digital entities, enabling applications far beyond mimicking human brain functions. For instance, a single LLM can control multiple devices, or multiple LLMs can operate a single device (Wu et al., 2023), opening up possibilities for tasks that were previously impractical or impossible due to human limitations.

LLMs are not limited to generating unstructured text; they can produce structured outputs according to specific templates, including those required for function-calling other software tools (Chen et al., 2024). This capability allows LLMs to interact with various software and hardware tools through APIs, and they can reason about when to use these tools. The ability to generate structured outputs, such as JSON, is particularly valuable for integrating LLM results with other software systems and automating repetitive tasks (Qin et al., 2023). Moreover, LLMs can assist non-technical users by helping to write the necessary programming code for these operations (Cai et al., 2024).

When given the ability to prompt themselves, LLMs can function as autonomous agents, making independent decisions and taking actions to solve problems or achieve objectives (Wang et al., 2024). This autonomy, combined with access to tools, presents both opportunities and challenges, necessitating ongoing research into balancing autonomy with alignment to user intentions (Händler, 2023). Autonomous LLM agents can also interact with other AI agents and humans, leading to complex multi-agent architectures (Guo et al., 2024; Sharma et al., 2024). These systems can be employed for various purposes, including guiding, evaluating, or assisting humans and other AI agents, building software, simulating social structures, and facilitating collective decision-making processes (Chan et al., 2023).

IMPLICATIONS AND POTENTIAL OF GENERATIVE AI FOR HIGHER EDUCATION

In terms of the impact of GenAI on higher education, it is helpful to divide our discussion into three topics: a) teaching and learning, b) research and scholarship, and c) academic administration.

Implications of GenAI for Teaching and Learning

The availability of GenAI is leading to a fundamental rethinking of the nature of teaching and learning and the tasks required of teachers and learners. For students, tools such as ChatGPT can explain any concept at any desired level, write essays, write code, solve math problems, analyze cases and documents, analyze datasets, come up with creative ideas, and answer quiz questions (Samala et al., 2024), all at a level more advanced than most undergraduate students. While all this is useful, it also poses a threat of overreliance on AI and the gradual weakening of cognitive muscles (Mollick, 2024), similar to ways in which skills such as handwriting and horseback riding have experienced demise, but with more serious consequences for humanity.

For educators, ChatGPT can help with course design, curriculum design, lesson plan development, design of assessments and learning experiences, grading and rubric development, feedback provision, development of cases and illustrative examples, and the development of exercises, games, simulations, slides, graphics, and other educational materials (Bowen & Watson, 2024). A generative AI tool can also act as a custom tutor, helping the student learn almost anything at exactly their desired pace, customized to exactly their pre-existing competency, and in their exact preferred style in a manner that is personally interesting to them (Khan, 2024). These AI tutors can also be good at providing feedback, and do not have biological limits on their time, attention, and patience when it comes to providing feedback. Again, while this is all wonderful, it means that educators will need to redefine their role in order to adapt to the reality that much of their traditional tasks may now be handled by AI. For example, educators will increasingly use generative AI to create custom graphics, animations, or interactive software tools to address the learning needs of their students, and eventually to teach the students to do this themselves. The nature of the student–teacher relationship is likely to change, and new pedagogies are needed in the GenAI era. Chapter 4 of this volume (Brown & Roberts, 2025) showcases some ways in which universities are using GenAI in the design of learning experiences.

GenAI will provide us with a plethora of tools for inclusive pedagogy. Being equipped with AI can allow students facing various barriers and disadvantages to catch up with their peers and participate in educational activities in ways that were previously hindered by the barriers they faced. Custom AI tools have already been developed to help students with special needs (Mallory, 2024) or help educators better align their courses and lesson plans with the accessibility features required by these students (Sabbaghan, 2024).

GenAI can enhance inclusive pedagogy by providing real-time language translation for non-native speakers or by generating alternative explanations of complex concepts tailored to different learning styles or backgrounds (Samala et al., 2024). For personalized learning, AI could create custom practice problems or reading materials that adapt to each student's current level of understanding and learning pace (Khan, 2024).

At the same time, AI has the potential to exacerbate inequities in many ways. Given that the rich and privileged are likely to have access to better AI tools, this is likely to further increase the digital divide between young and old, rich and poor, and the Global South and the Global North (Capraro et al., 2024). If discriminatory biases in training data and AI behavior continue unmitigated, the increased use of this technology and the prevalence of AI-generated content are likely to further reinforce the discrimination against marginalized groups, communities, and cultures.

GenAI requires a fundamental rethinking of assessment methods. The take-home essay has suffered a major demise already, as have other open formats for exams that would allow students to use AI to answer the questions (Scarfe et al., 2024). Even in more closed or paper-based exams, a plethora of tools have become available to students that allow them to "cheat" in such exams with AI. While learning is becoming increasingly accessible and democratized, assessment is becoming increasingly specialized, which means that the learning community is likely to demand a more sophisticated quality assessment function from higher education institutions while reducing its reliance on them for learning, especially at less advanced levels. Chapter 9 of this volume focuses specifically on GenAI and assessment (Lee, 2025).

Approaches to assessment in the age of AI compel us to recognize that: a) in some cases, AI should likely be banned if the point of the learning is not to learn how to use AI; b) in cases where students are learning to achieve outcomes with the help of AI, there should be new standards for outcomes because students can now achieve things that were previously impossible or hard to accomplish at certain levels or in specific time frames, such as building software, conducting research, or creating media or art; and c) in cases where students can achieve something with AI so easily or quickly that it diminishes their sense of ownership and responsibility for the outcome, assessments and exercises need to promote the idea of doing the mental work of reading and revising the AI-generated output until students truly feel that they own the work and take responsibility for it (Eaton & Keyhani, 2025).

In terms of programming, there are two conflicting pressures that need to be balanced. On the one hand, universities face substantial pressure in the short term to adapt to the new reality of a GenAI-dominated world. Students demand courses that will help them learn to use this technology and prepare for the future that it ushers. Similarly, the job market demands graduates equipped with new skills such as prompt engineering, which are required to make productive use of GenAI in the workplace. On the other hand, as more people begin to rely on AI to assist in various tasks, we are likely to be faced with an influx of individuals who are over-reliant on AI and unable to conduct high-quality work in contexts without AI or where AI is not very helpful, or unable to surpass the quality of AI-generated work. The market will increasingly demand the training of talent that does not have these weaknesses from higher education institutions.

Implications of GenAI for Research and Scholarship

Research is one of the most thinking-intensive activities that humans do, so it is no surprise that researchers are already taking advantage of GenAI as a thinking assistant. The most low-hanging fruit is help with academic writing. Studies are showing massive adoption by researchers as evidenced by surveys (Prillaman, 2024) and by the changing style and terminology used in scientific writing, which increasingly includes words such as "delve," which are commonly used by the default writing style of ChatGPT and similar tools (Matsui, 2024). Worrying evidence seems to suggest that numerous papers have already been published that contain mindless copy-pasting from ChatGPT where the authors neglected to remove phrases such as "as an AI language model" when pasting the text (Schmidt & Meir, 2024), but these are of course only the obvious and detectable cases. Nevertheless, there are also real benefits for serious researchers, such as tools to improve grammar, translate, paraphrase, summarize, and interpret text, as well as overall reduced barriers to non-native English speakers (Rezaei et al., 2024).

But it is not just in writing that GenAI can help researchers. Both OpenAI's ChatGPT and Google's Gemini have been found to exhibit more informed views about the nature of science and academic research than are typically found in undergraduate students, graduates, and educators (Nyaaba, 2024).

Thus, it is no surprise that GenAI can assist in many different tasks in the research process. This includes idea generation for research questions and hypotheses, thinking through arguments and providing critiques, suggesting relevant theories and literature, generating simulated data and computational models, designing experiments, generating test cases, and exploring problem spaces, as well as thinking about implications and next steps for any given study. For relatively simple research goals, much of the research process in some domains can already be automated with LLMs, but complex research is best done with human–AI collaboration (Ifargan et al., 2024).

Researchers have been able to make new scientific discoveries by systematically using LLMs in the research process, typically in ways that involve using them to reason about specific sub-problems at a scale that would be difficult, if not impossible, for humans to do within a reasonable time frame. The trick with these automated discovery approaches is to have a systematic or algorithmic way to verify the knowledge claims suggested by the LLMs in the mass of sub-problems given to it. One of the most well-known applications of this method to date has been the work of Romera-Paredes et al. (2024), where they used LLMs to systematically search through function spaces to discover new solutions to mathematical problems and successfully found a number of solutions previously unknown to humans. The method of using LLMs for automated scientific discovery by systematically searching specific problem spaces is rapidly growing. One of the most important applications of this approach is in the discovery of chemicals and pharmaceutical drugs (Chakraborty et al., 2023; Vert, 2023). Similar approaches can be implemented in the social sciences by using LLMs to automatically generate and test hypotheses (Manning et al., 2024). For a review of scientific LLMs see Zhang et al. (2024).

Finally, an important implication of GenAI for research is that the technology itself raises a slew of new research questions and opens the path for entirely new fields of study about the nature of this technology, the ethical and philosophical conundrums it presents, and its various applications in society. For example, a domain of research is developing around the interpretability and explainability of neural networks in LLMs (Bills et al., 2023). As previously mentioned, at the intersection of psychology and AI a domain of research has opened up under the banner of "machine psychology" (Hagendorff, 2023) and similar research is developing in other fields. GenAI has opened an entirely new world for researchers in every field to explore.

Implications of GenAI for Academic Administration

As with any other organization, staff and administrators working in academic institutions will be more productive and effective in all knowledge work when equipped with GenAI assistants. Given the strength of LLMs in generating business ideas (Girotra et al., 2023), they could be used for ideation in programming and generating new course or activity suggestions and ideas for new initiatives or continuous improvement projects. They can be used as aids for strategic decision-making, in particular due to their strengths in being able to consider a large scope and scale of alternatives and perspectives compared with humans (Doshi et al., 2024). The ability of GenAI tools to assist in research processes such as data collection and analysis (Hassani & Silva, 2023) will also enable institutional research teams to automate processes involved in competitive research, such as the analysis of job-market demands and prospective applicants. If you have one descriptive PDF file for every competing program, you can easily use an LLM-powered tool such as *ottogrid.ai* or *petal.org* to complete a competitive analysis spreadsheet.

Given that for simpler tasks LLMs can be deployed to substitute for humans and even work at scales and scopes that would be impossible for humans, the calculations around the intelligence-hours allocated to various tasks in an organization will shift drastically. LLMs acting as customer service chatbots have been able to do the equivalent work of hundreds of human employees in ways that human employees would not have been able to do in the first place, for example, by being available 24/7 and speaking in all major world languages (Kolasani, 2023).

Faculty and staff at universities are often frustrated with the amount of busywork and repetitive bureaucratic tasks that take up their time when they could be doing more important and fulfilling work that builds on their deep expertise. GenAI will allow these knowledge workers to free up their time and attention by taking care of the more structured, repetitive, and mundane tasks in their day-to-day operations. For example, checking if a course outline or syllabus satisfies certain criteria, if the dates for class times align with the university calendar, if wording is in line with university policies, and if citations are in the correct format are all tasks that an LLM can easily handle after receiving the course outline as input.

Even when the AI cannot directly solve a problem or carry out a task, users may be able to use AI to build a software tool for themselves or their team to find a solution. Even if users are not comfortable handling code generated by AI, there are many no-code/low-code tools available to build AI-powered software with drag-and-drop visual programming (Binzer & Winkler, 2022). GenAI will result in rapidly increasing "citizen development" in organizations (whereby non-programmers and non-technical employees build their own software solutions), removing bottlenecks of software development, purchase, and maintenance, and already over-burdened IT departments (Simon, 2022). Furthermore, given how much easier it will be to develop software when programmers and entrepreneurs are equipped with GenAI (Dohmke et al., 2023), higher education institutions will enjoy a proliferation of third-party software and tools available to their students, staff, and faculty that will impact every aspect of their work.

Important new roles will be created for librarians and other staff and faculty involved in libraries and cultural resources, as well as teaching and learning centers at colleges and universities. These roles will include some more obvious and less obvious ones. For example, it is clear that we will expect these centers in our institutions to help students and instructors gain the knowledge, skills, and tools to use GenAI in various ways to ethically enhance the learning experience while preserving academic integrity. One potentially less obvious role that libraries and similar organizations in higher education can take on is the acquisition, curation, and dissemination of new knowledge products and digital artifacts needed for GenAI, such as prompt templates and fine-tuning datasets, as well as guides, frameworks, and other source materials that can be used as reference material or few-shot examples in prompt engineering (Svendsen & Garvey, 2023).

Given how much new GenAI-related research needs to be done in every domain and discipline, it may be helpful for universities to consider developing a shared applied GenAI research infrastructure. Such an infrastructure could aid in training and fine-tuning custom AI models, giving them senses, tools, knowledge, memories, or bodies, and deploying them as agents to perform tasks, solve problems, make discoveries, and interact with other AI and human agents, while observing and studying their performance. Researchers in a variety of faculties and domains could use the same shared infrastructure to ask research questions related to GenAI without having to spend resources on reinventing and building the underlying software tools and components every time.

CONCLUSION

The rise of GenAI will require a fundamental rethinking of many aspects of our higher education institutions. As we have explored throughout this chapter, the capabilities and characteristics of LLMs and other GenAI technologies are reshaping the landscape of teaching, learning, research, and academic administration.

In the realm of teaching and learning, GenAI offers powerful tools for personalized education, inclusive pedagogy, and enhanced content creation. However, it also necessitates a fundamental reimagining of assessment methods and raises concerns about potential over-reliance on AI assistance. Educators must navigate this new terrain by redefining their roles and developing strategies to harness AI's benefits while mitigating its risks.

For research and scholarship, GenAI serves as an invaluable thinking assistant, capable of aiding in various stages of the research process from ideation to analysis and writing. While we have yet to witness AI making novel scientific discoveries independently, the rapid progress in this field suggests that such breakthroughs may be on the horizon. The emergence of automated discovery approaches using LLMs opens up exciting new avenues for scientific exploration across disciplines.

In academic administration, GenAI promises to streamline operations, enhance decision-making processes, and free up valuable human resources for more complex and fulfilling tasks. Through citizen development initiatives, staff can leverage these AI capabilities to create innovative tools and solutions within higher education institutions.

As we stand at this technological crossroads, it is crucial for higher education institutions to proactively engage with GenAI technologies. This engagement should involve developing comprehensive strategies for integration, addressing ethical concerns, and fostering AI and digital literacy among students, faculty, and staff. Institutions should invest in professional development programs that equip faculty with the skills to effectively integrate GenAI into their teaching. These programs could include workshops on prompt engineering, AI ethics, and assessment design in the age of AI. Faculty should be encouraged to experiment with these tools and share best practices with their colleagues. Chapter 13 in this volume provides further insights into AI policy in academia (Kowch, 2025).

By embracing the transformative potential of GenAI while critically examining its implications, higher education can evolve to meet the needs of a rapidly changing world, fostering innovation, inclusivity, and intellectual growth in ways previously unimaginable.

REFERENCES

Battle, R., & Gollapudi, T. (2024). *The unreasonable effectiveness of eccentric automatic prompts*. arXiv. https://doi.org/10.48550/arXiv.2402.10949.

Bills, S., Cammarata, N., Mossing, D., Tillman, H., Gao, L., Goh, G., Sutskever, I., Leike, J., Wu, J., & Saunders, W. (2023). Language models can explain neurons in language models. OpenAI. *https://openaipublic.blob.core.windows.net/neuron-explainer/paper/index.html.*

Binzer, B., & Winkler, T. J. (2022). Democratizing software development: A systematic multivocal literature review and research agenda on citizen development. In N. Carroll, A. Nguyen-Duc, X. Wang, & V. Stray (Eds.), *Software business* (pp. 244–259). Springer International Publishing. https://doi.org/10.1007/978-3-031-20706-8_17.

Bowen, J. A., & Watson, C. E. (2024). *Teaching with AI: A practical guide to a new era of human learning*. Johns Hopkins University Press. https://www.amazon.ca/Teaching-AI-Practical-Guide-Learning/dp/1421449226.

Brown, B., & Roberts, V. (2025). Responsive instructional design using GenAI and digital skills development framework. In S. Sabbaghan (Ed.), *Navigating generative*

AI in higher education: Ethical, theoretical and practical perspectives. Edward Elgar.
Brown, T. B., Mann, B., Ryder, N., Subbiah, M., Kaplan, J., Dhariwal, P., Neelakantan, A., Shyam, P., Sastry, G., Askell, A., Agarwal, S., Herbert-Voss, A., Krueger, G., Henighan, T., Child, R., Ramesh, A., Ziegler, D. M., Wu, J., Winter, C., … Amodei, D. (2020). *Language models are few-shot learners*. arXiv. https://doi.org/10.48550/arXiv.2005.14165.
Cai, T., Wang, X., Ma, T., Chen, X., & Zhou, D. (2024). *Large language models as tool makers*. arXiv. https://doi.org/10.48550/arXiv.2305.17126.
Capraro, V., Lentsch, A., Acemoglu, D., Akgun, S., Akhmedova, A., Bilancini, E., Bonnefon, J.-F., Brañas-Garza, P., Butera, L., Douglas, K. M., Everett, J. A. C., Gigerenzer, G., Greenhow, C., Hashimoto, D. A., Holt-Lunstad, J., Jetten, J., Johnson, S., Kunz, W. H., Longoni, C., … Viale, R. (2024). The impact of generative artificial intelligence on socioeconomic inequalities and policy making. *PNAS Nexus*, *3*(6). https://doi.org/10.1093/pnasnexus/pgae191.
Chakraborty, C., Bhattacharya, M., & Lee, S.-S. (2023). Artificial intelligence enabled ChatGPT and large language models in drug target discovery, drug discovery, and development. *Molecular Therapy – Nucleic Acids*, *33*, 866–868. https://doi.org/10.1016/j.omtn.2023.08.009.
Chan, C.-M., Chen, W., Su, Y., Yu, J., Xue, W., Zhang, S., Fu, J., & Liu, Z. (2023). *ChatEval: Towards better LLM-based evaluators through multi-agent debate*. arXiv. https://doi.org/10.48550/arXiv.2308.07201.
Chen, W., Li, Z., & Ma, M. (2024). *Octopus: On-device language model for function calling of software APIs*. arXiv. https://doi.org/10.48550/arXiv.2404.01549.
Ding, N., Qin, Y., Yang, G., Wei, F., Yang, Z., Su, Y., Hu, S., Chen, Y., Chan, C.-M., Chen, W., Yi, J., Zhao, W., Wang, X., Liu, Z., Zheng, H.-T., Chen, J., Liu, Y., Tang, J., Li, J., & Sun, M. (2023). Parameter-efficient fine-tuning of large-scale pre-trained language models. *Nature Machine Intelligence*, *5*(3), 220–235. https://doi.org/10.1038/s42256-023-00626-4.
Dohmke, T., Iansiti, M., & Richards, G. (2023, June 26). *Sea change in software development: Economic and productivity analysis of the AI-powered developer lifecycle*. arXiv. https://arxiv.org/abs/2306.15033v1.
Doshi, A. R., Bell, J. J., Mirzayev, E., & Vanneste, B. (2024). *Generative artificial intelligence and evaluating strategic decisions*. SSRN. https://doi.org/10.2139/ssrn.4714776.
Eaton, S. E., & Keyhani, M. (2025). The pedagogical ethics: Navigating learning in a generative AI-augmented environment. In S. Sabbaghan (Ed.), *Navigating generative AI in higher education: Ethical, theoretical and practical perspectives*. Edward Elgar.
Gao, Y., Xiong, Y., Gao, X., Jia, K., Pan, J., Bi, Y., Dai, Y., Sun, J., Wang, M., & Wang, H. (2024). *Retrieval-augmented generation for large language models: a survey*. arXiv. https://doi.org/10.48550/arXiv.2312.10997.
Garg, N., Schiebinger, L., Jurafsky, D., & Zou, J. (2018). Word embeddings quantify 100 years of gender and ethnic stereotypes. *Proceedings of the National Academy of Sciences*, *115*(16), E3635–E3644. https://doi.org/10.1073/pnas.1720347115.
Girotra, K., Meincke, L., Terwiesch, C., & Ulrich, K. T. (2023). *Ideas are dimes a dozen: Large language models for idea generation in innovation*. SSRN. https://doi.org/10.2139/ssrn.4526071.

Guo, T., Chen, X., Wang, Y., Chang, R., Pei, S., Chawla, N. V., Wiest, O., & Zhang, X. (2024). *Large language model based multi-agents: A survey of progress and challenges*. arXiv. https://doi.org/10.48550/arXiv.2402.01680.

Hagendorff, T. (2023). *Machine psychology: Investigating emergent capabilities and behavior in large language models using psychological methods*. arXiv. https://doi.org/10.48550/arXiv.2303.13988.

Händler, T. (2023). *Balancing autonomy and alignment: a multi-dimensional taxonomy for autonomous LLM-powered multi-agent architectures*. arXiv. https://doi.org/10.48550/arXiv.2310.03659.

Hassani, H., & Silva, E. S. (2023). The role of ChatGPT in data science: How AI-assisted conversational interfaces are revolutionizing the field. *Big Data and Cognitive Computing*, *7*(2). https://doi.org/10.3390/bdcc7020062.

Ifargan, T., Hafner, L., Kern, M., Alcalay, O., & Kishony, R. (2024). *Autonomous LLM-driven research from data to human-verifiable research papers*. arXiv. https://doi.org/10.48550/arXiv.2404.17605.

Kamruzzaman, M., Shovon, M. M. I., & Kim, G. L. (2024). *Investigating subtler biases in LLMs: Ageism, beauty, institutional, and nationality bias in generative models*. arXiv. https://doi.org/10.48550/arXiv.2309.08902.

Khan, S. (2024). *Brave new words: How AI will revolutionize education (and why that's a good thing)*. Penguin Random House.

Kolasani, S. (2023). Optimizing natural language processing, large language models (LLMs) for efficient customer service, and hyper-personalization to enable sustainable growth and revenue. *Transactions on Latest Trends in Artificial Intelligence*, *4*(4). https://ijsdcs.com/index.php/TLAI/article/view/476.

Kowch, E. (2025). An innovation policy analysis for higher education generative AI leaders and researchers. In S. Sabbaghan (Ed.), *Navigating generative AI in higher education: Ethical, theoretical and practical perspectives*. Edward Elgar.

Lee, A. V. Y. (2025). The double-edged sword of generative AI for learning and assessment: efficiency versus homogenization. In S. Sabbaghan (Ed.), *Navigating generative AI in higher education: Ethical, theoretical and practical perspectives*. Edward Elgar.

Mallory, J. (2024). Empowering special needs STEM students through unique generative AI tools: A path to inclusive learning. In J. Cohen & G. Solano (Eds.), *Proceedings of Society for Information Technology & Teacher Education International Conference* (pp. 2156–2161). Las Vegas, NV: Association for the Advancement of Computing in Education (AACE).

Manning, B. S., Zhu, K., & Horton, J. J. (2024). *Automated social science: Language models as scientist and subjects*. arXiv. https://doi.org/10.48550/arXiv.2404.11794.

Matsui, K. (2024). *Delving into PubMed records: Some terms in medical writing have drastically changed after the arrival of ChatGPT*. medRxiv. https://doi.org/10.1101/2024.05.14.24307373.

Mollick, E. (2024). *Co-intelligence: Living and working with AI*. Portfolio.

Navigli, R., Conia, S., & Ross, B. (2023). Biases in large language models: Origins, inventory, and discussion. *Journal of Data and Information Quality*, *15*(2), 10:1–10:21. https://doi.org/10.1145/3597307.

Nyaaba, M. (2024). Generative AI conception of the nature of science. In J. Cohen & G. Solano (Eds.), *Proceedings of Society for Information Technology & Teacher Education International Conference* (pp. 1818–1827). Las Vegas, NV: Association for the Advancement of Computing in Education (AACE).

Pletnyova, A., Anselmo, L., & Keyhani, M. (2024). *Maximizing learning with effective GenAI prompt writing: An instructor's resource for students.* University of Calgary. https://taylor-institute.ucalgary.ca/resources/maximizing-learning-with-effective-genai-prompt-writing.

Prillaman, M. (2024). Is ChatGPT making scientists hyper-productive? The highs and lows of using AI. *Nature, 627*(8002), 16–17. https://doi.org/10.1038/d41586-024-00592-w.

Qin, Y., Liang, S., Ye, Y., Zhu, K., Yan, L., Lu, Y., Lin, Y., Cong, X., Tang, X., Qian, B., Zhao, S., Hong, L., Tian, R., Xie, R., Zhou, J., Gerstein, M., Li, D., Liu, Z., & Sun, M. (2023). *ToolLLM: Facilitating large language models to master 16,000+ real-world APIs.* arXiv. https://doi.org/10.48550/arXiv.2307.16789.

Rezaei, M., Salehi, H., & Tabatabaei, O. (2024, February). Uses and misuses of ChatGPT as an AI-language model in academic writing. In *2024 10th International Conference on Artificial Intelligence and Robotics (QICAR)* (pp. 256–260). IEEE.

Romera-Paredes, B., Barekatain, M., Novikov, A., Balog, M., Kumar, M. P., Dupont, E., Ruiz, F. J. R., Ellenberg, J. S., Wang, P., Fawzi, O., Kohli, P., & Fawzi, A. (2024). Mathematical discoveries from program search with large language models. *Nature, 625*(7995), 468–475. https://doi.org/10.1038/s41586-023-06924-6.

Sabbaghan, S. (2024). *Embracing inclusive education: The rise of SMARTIE, an AI-powered course design tool.* Technology and Teacher Education [Conference Presentation]. Canadian Society for the Study of Education, Montreal, QC, Canada.

Samala, A. D., Rawas, S., Wang, T., Reed, J. M., Kim, J., Howard, N.-J., & Ertz, M. (2024). Unveiling the landscape of generative artificial intelligence in education: A comprehensive taxonomy of applications, challenges, and future prospects. *Education and Information Technologies, 30*, 3239–3278. https://doi.org/10.1007/s10639-024-12936-0.

Scarfe, P., Watcham, K., Clarke, A., & Roesch, E. (2024). A real-world test of artificial intelligence infiltration of a university examinations system: A "Turing Test" case study. *PLOS ONE, 19*(6). https://doi.org/10.1371/journal.pone.0305354.

Schmidt, P. G., & Meir, A. J. (2024). Using generative AI for literature searches and scholarly writing: Is the integrity of the scientific discourse in jeopardy? *Notices of the American Mathematical Society, 71*(1), 93–104.

Shapiro, C., & Varian, H. R. (1999). *Information rules: A strategic guide to the network economy.* Harvard Business Press.

Sharma, A., Rao, S., Brockett, C., Malhotra, A., Jojic, N., & Dolan, B. (2024). Investigating agency of LLMs in human-AI collaboration tasks. In Y. Graham & M. Purver (Eds.), *Proceedings of the 18th Conference of the European Chapter of the Association for Computational Linguistics (Volume 1: Long Papers)* (pp. 1968–1987). Association for Computational Linguistics. https://aclanthology.org/2024.eacl-long.119.

Simon, P. (2022). *Low-code/no-code: Citizen developers and the surprising future of business applications.* Racket Publishing.

Svendsen, A., & Garvey, B. (2023). *An outline for an interrogative/prompt library to help improve output quality from generative-AI datasets.* SSRN. https://doi.org/10.2139/ssrn.4495319.

Vert, J.-P. (2023). How will generative AI disrupt data science in drug discovery? *Nature Biotechnology, 41*(6), 750–751. https://doi.org/10.1038/s41587-023-01789-6.

Wang, L., Ma, C., Feng, X., Zhang, Z., Yang, H., Zhang, J., Chen, Z., Tang, J., Chen, X., Lin, Y., Zhao, W. X., Wei, Z., & Wen, J. (2024). A survey on large language model based autonomous agents. *Frontiers of Computer Science, 18*(6), 186345. https://doi.org/10.1007/s11704-024-40231-1.

Wei, J., Wang, X., Schuurmans, D., Bosma, M., Ichter, B., Xia, F., Chi, E., Le, Q. V., & Zhou, D. (2022). Chain-of-thought prompting elicits reasoning in large language models. *Advances in Neural Information Processing Systems, 35*, 24824–24837.

Wolfram, S. (2023). *What is ChatGPT doing … and why does it work?* Wolfram Media.

Wu, Q., Bansal, G., Zhang, J., Wu, Y., Li, B., Zhu, E., Jiang, L., Zhang, X., Zhang, S., Liu, J., Awadallah, A. H., White, R. W., Burger, D., & Wang, C. (2023). *AutoGen: Enabling next-gen LLM applications via multi-agent conversation.* arXiv. https://doi.org/10.48550/arXiv.2308.08155.

Yang, C., Wang, X., Lu, Y., Liu, H., Le, Q. V., Zhou, D., & Chen, X. (2024). *Large language models as optimizers.* arXiv. https://doi.org/10.48550/arXiv.2309.03409.

Yao, J.-Y., Ning, K.-P., Liu, Z.-H., Ning, M.-N., & Yuan, L. (2023). *LLM lies: Hallucinations are not bugs, but features as adversarial examples.* arXiv. https://doi.org/10.48550/arXiv.2310.01469.

Yu, D., Backurs, A., Gopi, S., Inan, H., Kulkarni, J., Lin, Z., Xie, C., Zhang, H., & Zhang, W. (2023, November 28). *Training private and efficient language models with synthetic data from LLMs.* Socially Responsible Language Modelling Research. https://openreview.net/forum?id=FKwtKzglFb.

Zhang, Y., Chen, X., Jin, B., Wang, S., Ji, S., Wang, W., & Han, J. (2024). *A comprehensive survey of scientific large language models and their applications in scientific discovery.* arXiv. https://doi.org/10.48550/arXiv.2406.10833.

3. Generative AI in higher education: Transformative tools for research, teaching, and assessment

Mohammadreza Farrokhnia, Saba Soleimani and Omid Noroozi

INTRODUCTION

The advent of generative artificial intelligence (GenAI) tools has prompted considerable debate among educators and researchers regarding their impact on higher education (Jensen et al., 2024). The substantial benefits of these tools, combined with their ease of use, have encouraged many university teachers to integrate GenAI into their teaching practices (Brown and Roberts, 2025). Research findings underscore multiple benefits of integrating GenAI tools in educational practices. These tools can act as intelligent tutors to support university students' knowledge mastery and skills development (Liu et al., 2022). Moreover, GenAI's ability to deliver personalized instructional support has been shown to positively influence students' academic performance, motivation, and attitudes toward learning (Noroozi et al., 2024). Additionally, studies suggest that GenAI tools can substantially transform assessment practices in higher education by providing high-quality feedback on assignments (Banihashem et al., 2024) and transforming assessment methods across various academic disciplines (Xia et al., 2024).

Although GenAI has transformative potential for research, teaching, and assessment in higher education, its effective and ethical integration requires careful attention to pedagogical approaches, institutional policies, and faculty development (Jensen et al., 2024). Empirical studies on these tools' effectiveness and applications are critical for guiding informed and responsible use. However, the complexity of research presentations in scholarly articles can hinder educators and institutions from translating findings into practical teaching and policy decisions (Hering, 2016). Bridging this research–practice gap calls for "knowledge brokering" (Rycroft-Smith, 2022), which involves translating research into "comprehensible, plausible, and potentially fruitful" forms for practitioners (Hirschkorn & Geelan, 2008, p. 11). For GenAI, this includes accessible overviews of its effective use in higher education, informed by research and theory, along with guidance on ethical considerations for responsible integration.

This chapter addresses this need by acting as a knowledge broker, highlighting the transformative potential of GenAI in higher education alongside its limitations across various domains. It also presents a conceptual framework for understanding human–AI interaction and offers recommendations for professional development programs to enhance educators' proficiency and awareness of the benefits and risks of integrating GenAI into education.

IMPLICATIONS OF GENAI TOOLS IN HIGHER EDUCATION

As universities increasingly explore the integration of GenAI tools into formal education, understanding the various ways these tools can be implemented is essential. This section draws on empirical findings available at the time of writing, providing insights into the practical implications of GenAI in three key areas in higher education: *research*, *teaching*, and *assessment*. While this overview is not exhaustive, it highlights examples that are both valuable and broadly transferable across different GenAI tools.

It is important to note that the examples provided use GPT-4o, an advanced OpenAI language model with enhanced multimodal capabilities, including real-time voice interaction and image analysis (OpenAI, 2024a). As GenAI technologies evolve, future developments are expected to expand functionalities further, offering new opportunities and addressing existing challenges. For illustrative purposes, these examples employ a Zero-shot prompt engineering technique, which relies on the model's inherent capabilities with minimal pre-configuration. However, more sophisticated techniques, such as chain-of-thought prompting, may yield deeper and more goal-aligned results for research or education (Wang et al., 2023).

Using GenAI in Research

The research sphere is often characterized by complex and time-consuming processes, presenting significant challenges for researchers. They may not be well-acquainted with the most appropriate statistical tests for analyzing their data, or they may find it challenging to use data analytics tools effectively for quantitative analysis (Chudoba et al., 2010). In qualitative analysis, common research practices such as coding transcribed interviews have been particularly challenging, requiring creativity to choose the best possible terms in the coding scheme (Stuckey, 2015).

With the emergence of GenAI tools, many of the aforementioned challenges have been mitigated. For quantitative analysis, GenAI is able to suggest suitable statistical tests, simplify data analytics with automated preprocessing, and offer real-time guidance (Inala et al., 2024). In qualitative analysis, GenAI streamlines coding by suggesting themes, aiding in coding scheme development (Sun et al., 2025), and assessing inter-rater reliability (Noroozi et al., 2024). By doing so, GenAI reduces the cognitive load on researchers, allowing them to focus more on the interpretative aspects of qualitative analysis.

The following sub-sections illustrate key applications of GenAI in research, with examples of its effective use. This discussion will then transition to an overview of the possible limitations of GenAI when used in research.

Quantitative analysis of data

GenAI tools enable researchers to perform advanced quantitative analyses with greater efficiency and precision. They can handle large datasets, visualize results, and facilitate comparisons across studies. In 2024, customized versions of GPT-4o were introduced to enhance data analysis and reporting. These tools process diverse datasets, perform statistical analyses, and create visualizations (see OpenAI, 2024b).

As an example of ChatGPT's utilization for quantitative analysis, several studies have demonstrated its accuracy in generating results comparable to those produced by statistical software such as SAS, SPSS, and R when performing analyses such as t-tests and ANOVA (e.g., Y. Huang et al., 2024). To illustrate this capability, as shown in Figure 3.1, a dataset of students' grades from three experimental conditions across three courses was provided to GPT-4o. The model was prompted to conduct a one-way ANOVA to determine whether significant differences existed between any conditions. It was also asked to provide a detailed interpretation of the results.

GenAI's ability to visualize quantitative data is another remarkable capability. Studies have showcased its strengths in tasks such as data enhancement, visual mapping, stylization, and interaction (Ye et al., 2024). These features make data visualization more accessible to those with limited technical skills, allowing them to focus on interpreting findings and deriving insights.

Beyond performing analyses and visualizing data, GenAI tools can instruct users on conducting statistical tests in various software applications. This capability enhances statistics education by building statistical reasoning skills and fostering positive attitudes toward the subject (Wahba et al., 2024).

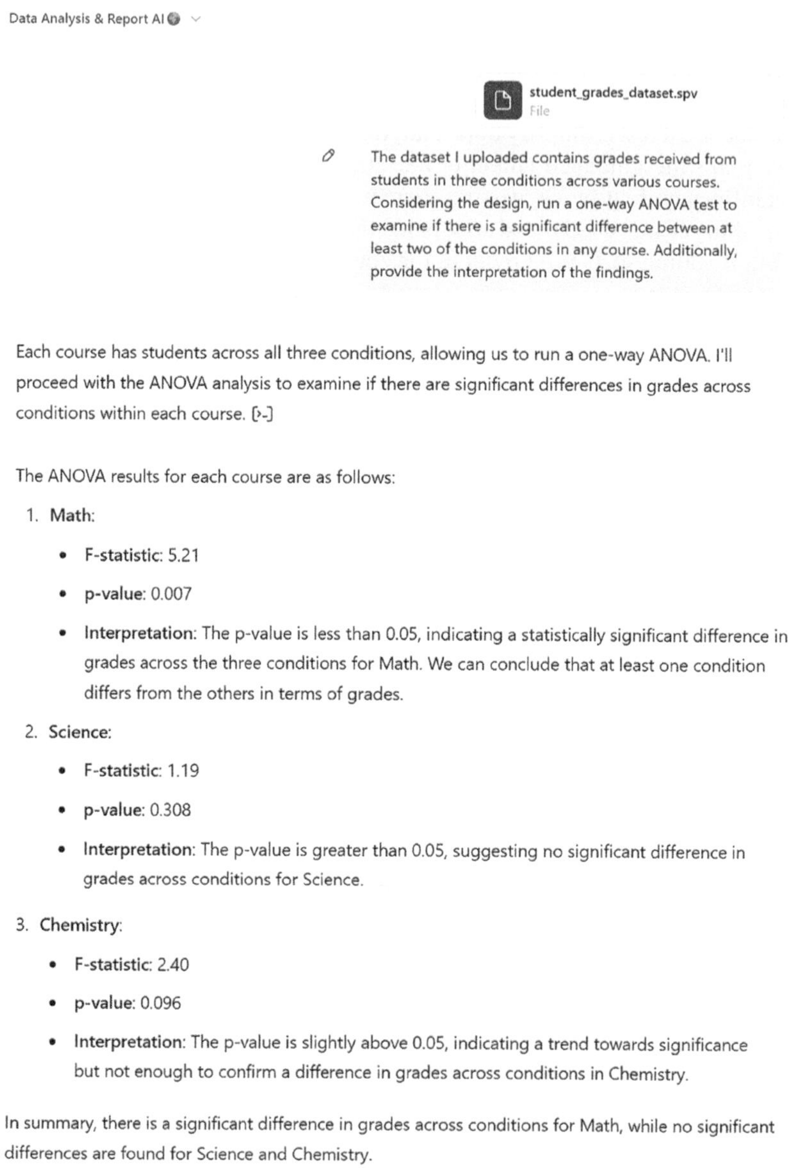

Source: Authors.

Figure 3.1 Using "Data Analysis & Report AI" for ANOVA test

Qualitative analysis of data

Qualitative analysis is a fundamental component of research for examining complex phenomena and understanding the subjective experiences and perspectives of individuals (Sabbaghan, 2024), offering profound insights into nuanced contexts and human interactions (Sun et al., 2025). However, traditional qualitative approaches can be time-intensive, particularly when analyzing large datasets, and are susceptible to researchers' biases, potentially leading to subjective interpretations of the data (Anderson, 2010). GenAI tools have been shown to effectively mitigate these challenges, offering abilities comparable to humans in generating themes and codes (Sun et al., 2025) as well as coding in-depth interviews through deductive and inductive approaches (Qiao et al., 2024). For example, as illustrated in Figure 3.2, GPT-4o was prompted to apply pre-defined codes to transcribed interview dialogues (i.e., deductive coding), identify codes with higher occurrence, and provide an interpretation of the findings.

GenAI tools can also assist in thematic analysis, helping researchers identify overarching themes within textual data (Sabbaghan, 2024; Sun et al., 2025). For instance, using a GenAI-powered tool leveraging GPT-4 for thematic analysis, Sabbaghan (2024) demonstrated that tasks requiring 20 days by a human team were completed by the tool and one researcher in just a few hours. The tool significantly streamlined the process, efficiently handled large volumes of data, and maintained consistency in theme identification.

Challenges and limitations

Despite the significant potential of GenAI tools in quantitative and qualitative analysis, several limitations persist. In quantitative analysis, Shahrul and Syed Mohamed (2024) found that, while ChatGPT-4 performs basic statistical tests as accurately as SPSS, it struggles with advanced tasks such as post-hoc tests, confidence interval estimations, and complex statistical procedures. Similarly, Ye et al. (2024) cautioned that GenAI-generated visualizations often lack the contextual understanding needed for precise data representation, with simple prompts proving insufficient for capturing data complexities. Furthermore, empirical studies have shown that GenAI, even when used as a tutor, may occasionally recommend inappropriate statistical tests, potentially leading to the misinterpretation of research findings (Ordak, 2023).

In qualitative analysis, reliability concerns persist. Prescott et al. (2024) reported that, while GenAI significantly reduces coding time, its reliability is lower than that of human coders. Similarly, Qiao et al. (2024) noted that, despite achieving over 80% accuracy, GenAI-generated codes sometimes contained systematic biases and inaccuracies, raising privacy concerns. Moreover, Sabbaghan (2024) highlighted that GenAI's ability to identify themes in text heavily depends on well-crafted prompts, with poorly designed prompts

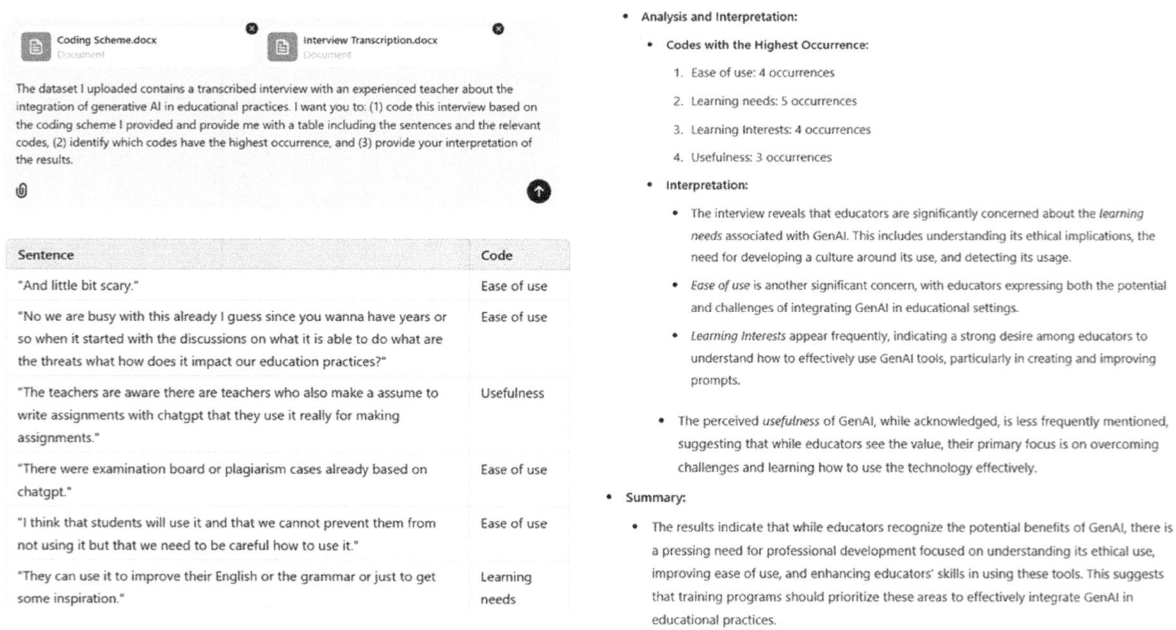

Coding Scheme.docx
Document

Interview Transcription.docx
Document

The dataset I uploaded contains a transcribed interview with an experienced teacher about the integration of generative AI in educational practices. I want you to: (1) code this interview based on the coding scheme I provided and provide me with a table including the sentences and the relevant codes, (2) identify which codes have the highest occurrence, and (3) provide your interpretation of the results.

Sentence	Code
"And little bit scary."	Ease of use
"No we are busy with this already I guess since you wanna have years or so when it started with the discussions on what it is able to do what are the threats what how does it impact our education practices?"	Ease of use
"The teachers are aware there are teachers who also make a assume to write assignments with chatgpt that they use it really for making assignments."	Usefulness
"There were examination board or plagiarism cases already based on chatgpt."	Ease of use
"I think that students will use it and that we cannot prevent them from not using it but that we need to be careful how to use it."	Ease of use
"They can use it to improve their English or the grammar or just to get some inspiration."	Learning needs

- **Analysis and Interpretation:**
  - **Codes with the Highest Occurrence:**
    1. Ease of use: 4 occurrences
    2. Learning needs: 5 occurrences
    3. Learning Interests: 4 occurrences
    4. Usefulness: 3 occurrences
  - **Interpretation:**
    - The interview reveals that educators are significantly concerned about the *learning needs* associated with GenAI. This includes understanding its ethical implications, the need for developing a culture around its use, and detecting its usage.
    - *Ease of use* is another significant concern, with educators expressing both the potential and challenges of integrating GenAI in educational settings.
    - *Learning Interests* appear frequently, indicating a strong desire among educators to understand how to effectively use GenAI tools, particularly in creating and improving prompts.
    - The perceived *usefulness* of GenAI, while acknowledged, is less frequently mentioned, suggesting that while educators see the value, their primary focus is on overcoming challenges and learning how to use the technology effectively.
- **Summary:**
  - The results indicate that while educators recognize the potential benefits of GenAI, there is a pressing need for professional development focused on understanding its ethical use, improving ease of use, and enhancing educators' skills in using these tools. This suggests that training programs should prioritize these areas to effectively integrate GenAI in educational practices.

Source: Authors.

Figure 3.2 Using "NVivo Data Analysis" for coding a transcribed interview

leading to missed or irrelevant themes. These limitations underscore that, while GenAI tools can streamline the research process, they cannot replace human cognition, which remains essential for critically evaluating the reliability and credibility of outcomes.

Using GenAI for Teaching

Teaching has always faced challenges due to students' diverse learning needs, which require personalized approaches (Walkington & Bernacki, 2020). Content creation and aligning lectures with learners' prior knowledge and learning outcomes add further complexity. The emergence of GenAI tools has introduced strategies to tackle these challenges. Systematic reviews suggest that GenAI has created new opportunities (e.g., Ansari et al., 2024; Jensen et al., 2024), with two key themes consistently emerging: (1) acting as a *teaching assistant* and (2) serving as a *personal tutor.*

Teaching assistant

GenAI tools stand out as a promising frontier, offering novel capabilities to autonomously generate new content, such as text, images, and even multimedia (Tlili et al., 2023), making them valuable teaching assistants in higher education. GenAI streamlines lesson preparation by automating time-consuming tasks, such as creating detailed lesson plans, designing activities, and generating assessment questions (Ansari et al., 2024). It also facilitates differentiated instruction by generating scenario-based tasks tailored to various student levels (Jensen et al., 2024). These capabilities reduce teachers' workload, allowing them to focus on tasks requiring human empathy, such as fostering meaningful interactions and supporting social–emotional and interpersonal skill development (Chan & Tsi, 2024).

To demonstrate how GenAI can be used as a teaching assistant, GPT-4o was asked to generate assessment questions for medical education (see Figure 3.3). The prompt was designed to meet specific requirements, such as following a particular exam format or aligning with frameworks such as Bloom's Taxonomy. This highlights GenAI's ability to create customized educational content for different subjects while meeting pedagogical goals.

When it comes to generating scenario-based tasks, the ability to take on any character role offers a unique opportunity to create authentic experiences that are crucial for developing professional skills, especially when access to real-life contexts is limited. For example, teachers can instruct GPT-4o to act as a patient, helping medical students enhance their diagnostic skills. These tasks have proven highly effective in improving not only students' theoretical knowledge but also their clinical skills and critical-thinking abilities (Zheng et al., 2024).

I want you to generate multiple-choice questions formatted in the style of USMLE Step 1, each containing a clinical vignette of about 5 to 6 sentences.

Sure, here are a few multiple-choice questions formatted in the style of USMLE Step 1:

Question 1

A 35-year-old woman presents to the clinic with complaints of progressive weakness and fatigue over the past three months. She reports having difficulty climbing stairs and rising from a seated position. Physical examination reveals proximal muscle weakness, but no sensory deficits. Laboratory studies show elevated creatine kinase levels. Electromyography shows decreased amplitude of motor potentials. A muscle biopsy demonstrates perifascicular atrophy and perimysial inflammation.

What is the most likely diagnosis?

A. Polymyositis
B. Dermatomyositis
C. Myasthenia Gravis
D. Lambert-Eaton Myasthenic Syndrome
E. Amyotrophic Lateral Sclerosis

Source: Authors.

Figure 3.3 Creating preparation questions for medical students

Personal tutor

Personalized learning tailors education to individual learners' unique needs, goals, and abilities (Shemshack et al., 2021), offering flexibility, choice, and opportunities for potential growth (Laak et al., 2024). Achieving this requires addressing cognitive factors such as prior knowledge and self-regulation, along with non-cognitive elements such as gender and emotions (Shemshack et al., 2021), guided by relevant theoretical frameworks (Bernacki et al., 2021). The complexity of delivering such customized learning experiences has driven the adoption of technology-based personalized learning solutions (Xie et al., 2019).

Developing technology-based personalized learning solutions is often challenging for educators due to limited technical expertise, insufficient resources, or the complexity of designing adaptive systems. The emergence of GenAI and its integration into intelligent tutoring systems offer promising solutions to these barriers. GenAI is increasingly used as a personal tutor, providing university students with tailored guidance, instant feedback, and adaptive learning experiences aligned with their unique needs and goals (Batsaikhan & Correia, 2024). Such personalized tutoring can generally be facilitated based on various building blocks of personalized (adaptive) instruction: *source*, which is what will be adapted; *target*, which is what is being adapted; and *pathway*, which is the translation from source to target (Vandewaetere et al., 2011).

For example, adapting the teaching approach to individual learner preferences is one possible target. GPT-4o can be prompted to act as a personal tutor, selecting a method that helps students achieve their intended learning outcomes. To enhance engagement, the ALACT Reflection Model (Korthagen & Vasalos, 2005) can be integrated, guiding students through action, reflection, awareness, exploration, and application. This structured reflection process encourages learners to re-evaluate their chosen approach, consider alternatives, and ultimately improve engagement and learning outcomes (Ribeiro et al., 2019).

Challenges and limitations

The use of GenAI in teaching also presents notable challenges, particularly the risk of generating inaccurate teaching materials. These risks stem from inherent limitations in GenAI models, which may lack the latest knowledge, and from educators' limited expertise in interacting with these tools (Ansari et al., 2024). The quality of GenAI outputs heavily depends on prompt design (Knoth et al., 2024), yet many teachers, like other people not expert in the use of AI, rely on trial-and-error methods, diminishing both the efficiency and reliability of the generated outputs (Lee et al., 2024). These issues are often overlooked by individuals with limited AI literacy, leading to the use of GenAI-generated materials without proper scrutiny or adaptation (Chu-ke & Dong, 2024), which increases the risk of misinformation, inaccuracies, and low-quality content (Barman et al., 2024).

Similarly, despite extensive research on fostering personalized learning with GenAI, critics argue that it cannot fully guarantee true personalization. Laak et al. (2024) note that GenAI often produces homogeneous outputs, failing to address learners' diverse abilities, cultural contexts, and cognitive needs, limiting its adaptability. Effective use of GenAI also requires self-regulation and critical thinking skills not inherently developed through its use. Without these, students risk over-relying on GenAI's confident but sometimes flawed outputs, undermining independent learning and academic performance (Ding et al., 2023). This issue may also explain negative findings in studies on its role in personalized learning. For example, Bastani et al. (2024) observed that students relying on GPT-based tutors as a "crutch" during practice problem sessions performed worse independently. This highlights that meaningful personalization in education requires not only technological advancements but also deliberate pedagogical strategies informed by theory to guide its use effectively and foster essential learning skills (Bernacki et al., 2021).

Using GenAI for Assessment

Assessment is a cornerstone of education, essential for evaluating quality and measuring learners' achievement of outcomes. It serves two main purposes: *summative* assessment summarizes achievements for certification and *formative* assessment provides ongoing feedback to support learning (Weurlander et al., 2012). However, both require significant expertise and time, often leading to less effective implementation and limiting their potential to fully support and accurately measure student learning (Taras, 2008).

With the advent of GenAI tools and their increasing support in the educational field, the assessment process has become more feasible and adaptive (Swiecki et al., 2022). Recent research highlights several affordances of GenAI tools, which have significantly transformed assessment practices in higher education (see Xia et al., 2024, for an overview). Building on these advancements, the following sections delve into the specific applications of GenAI in summative and formative assessments.

GenAI for summative assessment

A key potential of GenAI tools is their ability to facilitate summative assessment practices in higher education (Owoseni et al., 2024a). Their applications include generating assessment rubrics (Fernández-Sánchez et al., 2024), creating questions aligned with frameworks such as Bloom's Taxonomy (Hwang et al., 2024), and automating the grading of large volumes of text-based answers (Tobler, 2024). For instance, university instructors can use GenAI to design personalized rubrics guided by theoretical models. GPT-4o can be prompted to create a rubric for assessing argumentative essays based on the Toulmin Model, which analyzes arguments through key components such as claims, evidence, and warrants (Toulmin et al., 1979).

Another application of GenAI in summative assessment is grading textual assignments, which can save lecturers significant time, allowing them to focus on more critical teaching tasks and student engagement. As shown in Figure 3.4, GPT-4o was prompted to grade university students' assignments in an academic writing course, where they wrote discussion and limitations sections of a scientific article. A pre-defined rubric was uploaded, and the tool was instructed to grade assignments while providing specific suggestions for improvement on each evaluation criterion. Empirical studies have demonstrated internal consistency between expert tutors' scores and ChatGPT-generated grades using pre-defined rubrics (e.g., Awidi, 2024).

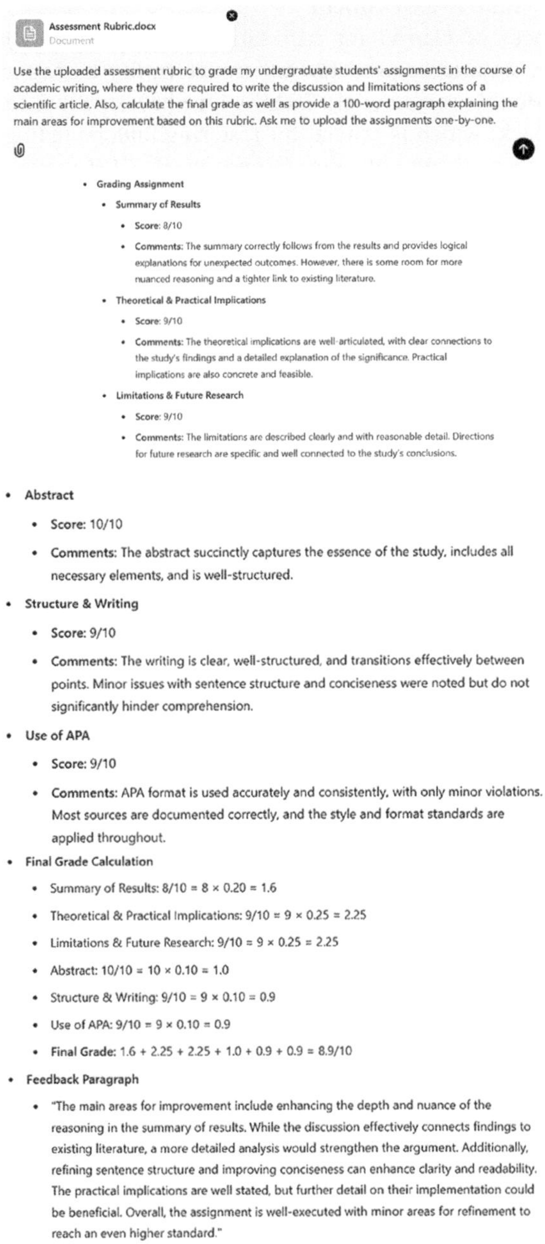
Assessment Rubric.docx
Document

Use the uploaded assessment rubric to grade my undergraduate students' assignments in the course of academic writing, where they were required to write the discussion and limitations sections of a scientific article. Also, calculate the final grade as well as provide a 100-word paragraph explaining the main areas for improvement based on this rubric. Ask me to upload the assignments one-by-one.

- **Grading Assignment**
  - **Summary of Results**
    - **Score:** 8/10
    - **Comments:** The summary correctly follows from the results and provides logical explanations for unexpected outcomes. However, there is some room for more nuanced reasoning and a tighter link to existing literature.
  - **Theoretical & Practical Implications**
    - **Score:** 9/10
    - **Comments:** The theoretical implications are well-articulated, with clear connections to the study's findings and a detailed explanation of the significance. Practical implications are also concrete and feasible.
  - **Limitations & Future Research**
    - **Score:** 9/10
    - **Comments:** The limitations are described clearly and with reasonable detail. Directions for future research are specific and well connected to the study's conclusions.

- **Abstract**
  - **Score:** 10/10
  - **Comments:** The abstract succinctly captures the essence of the study, includes all necessary elements, and is well-structured.
- **Structure & Writing**
  - **Score:** 9/10
  - **Comments:** The writing is clear, well-structured, and transitions effectively between points. Minor issues with sentence structure and conciseness were noted but do not significantly hinder comprehension.
- **Use of APA**
  - **Score:** 9/10
  - **Comments:** APA format is used accurately and consistently, with only minor violations. Most sources are documented correctly, and the style and format standards are applied throughout.
- **Final Grade Calculation**
  - Summary of Results: 8/10 = 8 × 0.20 = 1.6
  - Theoretical & Practical Implications: 9/10 = 9 × 0.25 = 2.25
  - Limitations & Future Research: 9/10 = 9 × 0.25 = 2.25
  - Abstract: 10/10 = 10 × 0.10 = 1.0
  - Structure & Writing: 9/10 = 9 × 0.10 = 0.9
  - Use of APA: 9/10 = 9 × 0.10 = 0.9
  - **Final Grade:** 1.6 + 2.25 + 2.25 + 1.0 + 0.9 + 0.9 = 8.9/10
- **Feedback Paragraph**
  - "The main areas for improvement include enhancing the depth and nuance of the reasoning in the summary of results. While the discussion effectively connects findings to existing literature, a more detailed analysis would strengthen the argument. Additionally, refining sentence structure and improving conciseness can enhance clarity and readability. The practical implications are well stated, but further detail on their implementation could be beneficial. Overall, the assignment is well-executed with minor areas for refinement to reach an even higher standard."

Source: Authors.

Figure 3.4 Using "GPT-4o" for grading assignments

GenAI for formative assessment

The affordances of GenAI for facilitating formative assessment have also emerged as a significant potential for transforming assessment practices in higher education (Owoseni et al., 2024b). One key aspect of formative assessment is feedback, which is crucial for fostering understanding and encouraging improvement among students (Pereira et al., 2016). However, providing detailed feedback is time-consuming, limiting teachers' ability to offer individualized, constructive comments (Nicol & Macfarlane-Dick, 2006). Peer feedback also faces challenges due to students' limited expertise and confidence, often resulting in inconsistent or superficial comments (Zong et al., 2021).

GenAI offers promising solutions for improving feedback provision in formative assessment. Guo and Wang (2023) found that ChatGPT generated significantly more feedback than teachers, distributing its attention evenly across content, organization, and language—unlike teacher feedback, which focused mainly on content and language. For peer feedback, Banihashem et al. (2024) highlighted ChatGPT's ability to provide detailed, descriptive comments on essay structure and writing quality, similar to expert feedback and independent of assignment quality. Additionally, Jürgensmeier and Skiera (2024) found that automated feedback provided by GenAI is significantly faster—typically requiring less than one minute per exam—and approximately one (GPT-4) to three (Gemini 1.0 Pro) orders of magnitude less expensive than human evaluators.

Challenges and limitations

Despite its potential, GenAI in summative and formative assessment faces significant challenges. In summative assessment, AI-generated rubrics, while consistent in structure and language, often lack the personalized touch of human tutors (X. Huang et al., 2024). Some students report misalignment between these rubrics and assignment objectives, reflecting limited contextual adaptability (Giannakos et al., 2024). In grading, discrepancies among GenAI models persist. ChatGPT-3.5 often awards higher scores than human graders, while GPT-4o provides more aligned evaluations. Both models, however, show biases—being lenient at lower performance levels and stricter at higher ones (Wetzler et al., 2024). Moreover, repetitive scoring by ChatGPT has shown a decline in consistency over time (Awidi, 2024).

In formative assessment, GenAI-generated feedback presents similar challenges. Students often find the feedback lacking the "human touch" typically provided by teachers or peers and sometimes difficult to understand (Teng, 2024). They also expressed concerns about ChatGPT potentially "making mistakes" or "not fully understanding their inquiries when seeking further clarification." Additionally, some teachers reported that the feedback was excessively lengthy, making it difficult for those with low language proficiency to read and comprehend, or that it included irrelevant comments (Guo & Wang, 2023). Research findings also associate feedback quality with the prompt technique used (Jürgensmeier & Skiera, 2024).

To address these challenges, scholars recommend combining GenAI with human oversight to ensure assessments are accurate and fair (X. Huang et al., 2024). This approach aligns with the European Union's AI Act, which classifies fully AI-based evaluations as high-risk, emphasizing AI's role as a supportive tool rather than a replacement for human judgment (EU AI Act, n.d.).

DISCUSSION

This chapter explores the key implications of GenAI tools in higher education, offering evidence-based examples of their applications—from performing statistical analyses and generating assessment rubrics to serving as intelligent tutors and facilitating professional skill development. While highlighting these potentials, it also addresses critical challenges stemming from the models' limitations and users' limited skills in effectively interacting with these tools. These challenges highlight the essential role of human cognition in human–AI interactions, emphasizing the need to transition from the passive implementation of GenAI tools to more active and informed applications. Building on this perspective, Figure 3.5 presents a conceptual framework that illustrates a continuum from passive to active engagement with GenAI tools across key dimensions of higher education—namely, research, teaching, and assessment.

On the left side of this framework, passive adoption corresponds to greater reliance on GenAI outputs without critical human intervention, thereby increasing the risk of incorporating low-quality or misleading results, as shown in previous sections. These vulnerabilities are closely tied to the inherent strengths and limitations of specific GenAI models. For instance, while some GPT models excel at handling complex tasks, domain-specific nuances, and context-sensitive queries, others struggle under similar conditions (Sallam et al., 2024). In a comprehensive study examining various large language models for essay scoring, Seßler et al. (2024) found that closed-source models, particularly OpenAI-o1, demonstrated higher reliability across multiple trials and produced ratings more closely aligned with human assessments. Conversely, open-source models such as LLaMA3 and Mixtral exhibited minimal to no correlation with human evaluations, often assigning scores near the midpoint with low variance, indicating a limited capacity to differentiate between varying levels of essay quality.

As we move to the right side of the framework, increased human oversight not only mitigates risks associated with GenAI outputs but also enhances human–AI interaction. This active approach is further supported by integrating

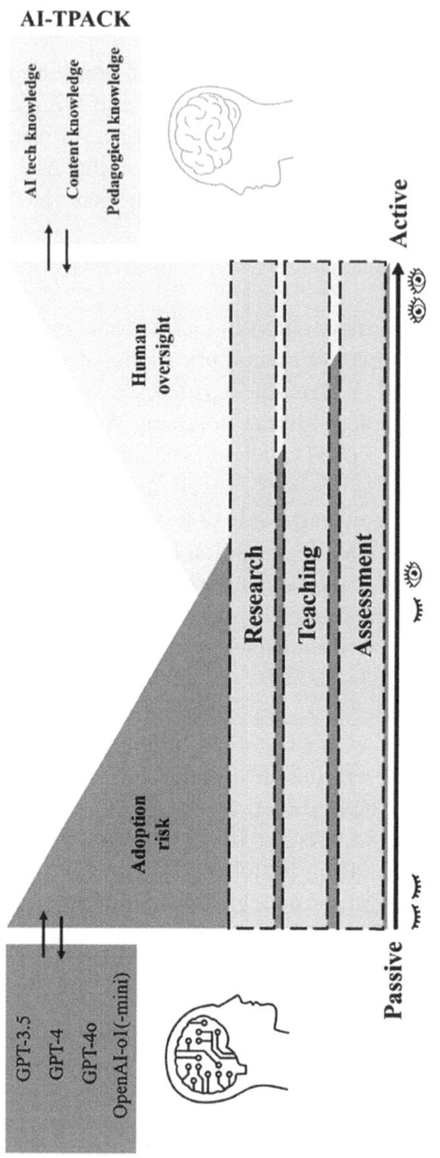

Source: Authors.

Figure 3.5 The GenAI integration in higher education framework

AI-TPACK (Technological Pedagogical Content Knowledge for AI), which provides the essential knowledge and skills to effectively use GenAI tools in education (Celik, 2023). AI technological knowledge equips educators and students with AI literacy, helping them identify model limitations (Hur, 2024) and craft meaningful, contextually appropriate prompts (Ansari et al., 2024). Content knowledge enables educators and researchers to critically assess the model's outputs against expert standards, improving the outcomes (van den Berg & du Plessis, 2023). Pedagogical knowledge guides the integration of GenAI into research, teaching, and assessment, grounded in relevant learning theories and instructional strategies. In short, the interplay of these knowledge domains fosters active application, reducing the risks associated with passive adoption and ensuring that GenAI tools are integrated thoughtfully and responsibly into higher education practices. Such informed practices can also address some of the major ethical issues associated with using GenAI in education—see Eaton and Keyhani (2025, Chapter 10).

CONCLUSION AND RECOMMENDATIONS FOR PRACTICE

This chapter introduced knowledge brokering as a critical mechanism for bridging the research–practice gap in the integration of GenAI tools in higher education. It provided a comprehensive, though not exhaustive, overview of key applications and challenges. By synthesizing these insights, the chapter highlighted the evolving nature of GenAI adoption, emphasizing a shift from passive reliance on automated outputs to more active, informed engagement. This transition was further illustrated through the proposed framework for GenAI integration in higher education (and, arguably, education more broadly). The framework underscores the importance of human oversight, supported by a deep understanding of AI functionalities and pedagogical applications (as exemplified by the AI-TPACK framework). Such informed oversight can mitigate risks while enhancing the quality of GenAI-driven outcomes in research, teaching, and assessment.

Building on these insights, the next step is translating them into practice. This requires deliberate, context-sensitive efforts from researchers, educators, and institutions to implement GenAI tools responsibly across higher education. To this end, this chapter concludes with specific recommendations for the key stakeholders involved.

For *researchers*, the focus should be on identifying large language models suited to specific educational contexts and objectives. This includes evaluating models based on their capacity to handle complex tasks and respond appropriately to contextual queries. Researchers should also engage in fine-tuning existing GenAI models to enhance their relevance and reliability in academic settings (e.g., Sabbaghan, 2024). Additionally, developing prompt-engineering techniques tailored to educational needs is crucial, as current methods are largely rooted in computer science and require adaptation for education (e.g., Lee et al., 2024).

For *educators*, active engagement with GenAI outputs is essential. This includes critically evaluating GenAI in teaching and assessment to ensure alignment with pedagogical objectives. Educators must also expand their knowledge and skills to adapt to the evolving GenAI landscape and adopt ethical, learner-centered approaches that enhance educational experiences while maintaining academic integrity.

Finally, for *higher education institutions*, banning GenAI tools outright is neither a sustainable nor effective response to their growing role in education (Farrokhnia et al., 2024). Instead, institutions should adopt a proactive stance, emphasizing transparent and responsible use. To achieve this, they must prioritize designing and disseminating professional development programs that serve as knowledge brokers, focusing on strengthening AI literacy and promoting evidence-informed applications of GenAI.

REFERENCES

Anderson, C. (2010). Presenting and evaluating qualitative research. *American Journal of Pharmaceutical Education*, *74*(8), 141.

Ansari, A. N., Ahmad, S., & Bhutta, S. M. (2024). Mapping the global evidence around the use of ChatGPT in higher education: A systematic scoping review. *Education and Information Technologies*, *29*(9), 11281–11321. https://doi.org/10.1007/s10639-023-12223-4.

Awidi, I. T. (2024). Comparing expert tutor evaluation of reflective essays with marking by generative artificial intelligence (AI) tool. *Computers and Education: Artificial Intelligence*, *6*, 100226. https://doi.org/10.1016/j.caeai.2024.100226.

Banihashem, S. K., Kerman, N. T., Noroozi, O., Moon, J., & Drachsler, H. (2024). Feedback sources in essay writing: peer-generated or AI-generated feedback? *International Journal of Educational Technology in Higher Education*, *21*(1), 23. https://doi.org/10.1186/s41239-024-00455-4.

Barman, D., Guo, Z., & Conlan, O. (2024). The dark side of language models: Exploring the potential of LLMs in multimedia disinformation generation and dissemination. *Machine Learning with Applications*, *16*, 100545. https://doi.org/10.1016/j.mlwa.2024.100545.

Bastani, H., Bastani, O., Sungu, A., Ge, H., Kabakcı, O., & Mariman, R. (2024). Generative AI can harm learning. *SSRN*, 4895486. http://dx.doi.org/10.2139/ssrn.4895486.

Batsaikhan, B. Z., & Correia, A. P. (2024). The effects of Generative Artificial Intelligence on Intelligent Tutoring Systems in higher education: A systematic review. *Studies in Technology Enhanced Learning*, *4*(1). https://doi.org/10.21428/8c225f6e.33570bb1.

Bernacki, M. L., Greene, M. J., & Lobczowski, N. G. (2021). A systematic review of research on personalized learning: Personalized by whom, to what, how, and for what purpose (s)? *Educational Psychology Review, 33*(4), 1675–1715. https://doi.org/10.1007/s10648-021-09615-8.

Brown, B., & Roberts, V. (2025). Responsive instructional design using GenAI and digital skill development framework. In S. Sabbaghan (Ed.), *Navigating generative AI in higher education: Ethical, theoretical, and practical perspectives.* Edward Elgar.

Celik, I. (2023). Towards Intelligent-TPACK: An empirical study on teachers' professional knowledge to ethically integrate artificial intelligence (AI)-based tools into education. *Computers in Human Behavior, 138*, 107468. https://doi.org/10.1016/j.chb.2022.107468.

Chan, C. K. Y., & Tsi, L. H. (2024). Will generative AI replace teachers in Higher Education? A study of teacher and student perceptions. *Studies in Educational Evaluation, 83*, 101395. https://doi.org/10.1016/j.stueduc.2024.101395.

Chudoba, K., Hauser, K., & Olsen, D. (2010). Teaching tools for data analysis. *International Journal of Management & Information Systems (IJMIS), 14*(3).

Chu-Ke, C., & Dong, Y. (2024). Misinformation and literacies in the era of generative artificial intelligence: A brief overview and a call for future research. *Emerging Media, 2*(1), 70–85.

Ding, L., Li, T., Jiang, S., & Gapud, A. (2023). Students' perceptions of using ChatGPT in a physics class as a virtual tutor. *International Journal of Educational Technology in Higher Education, 20*(1), 63. https://doi.org/10.1186/s41239-023-00434-1.

Eaton, S. E., & Keyhani, M. (2025). The pedagogical ethics: Navigating learning in a generative AI-augmented environment. In S. Sabbaghan (Ed.), *Navigating generative AI in higher education: Ethical, theoretical and practical perspectives.* Edward Elgar.

EU AI Act. (n.d.). Annex III. Retrieved from https://artificialintelligenceact.eu/annex/3/.

Farrokhnia, M., Banihashem, S. K., Noroozi, O., & Wals, A. (2024). A SWOT analysis of ChatGPT: Implications for educational practice and research. *Innovations in Education and Teaching International, 61*(3), 460–474. https://doi.org/10.1080/14703297.2023.2195846.

Fernández-Sánchez, A., Lorenzo-Castiñeiras, J. J., & Sánchez-Bello, A. (2024). Navigating the future of pedagogy: The integration of AI tools in developing educational assessment rubrics. *European Journal of Education*, e12826. https://doi.org/10.1111/ejed.12826.

Giannakos, M., Azevedo, R., Brusilovsky, P., Cukurova, M., Dimitriadis, Y., Hernandez-Leo, D., … & Rienties, B. (2024). The promise and challenges of generative AI in education. *Behaviour & Information Technology*, 1–27. https://doi.org/10.1080/0144929X.2024.2394886

Guo, K., & Wang, D. (2023). To resist it or to embrace it? Examining ChatGPT's potential to support teacher feedback in EFL writing. *Education and Information Technologies, 29*(7), 8435–8463. https://doi.org/10.1007/s10639-023-12146-0.

Hering, J. G. (2016). Do we need "more research" or better implementation through knowledge brokering? *Sustainability Science, 11*(2), 363–369. https://doi.org/10.1007/s11625-015-0314-8.

Hirschkorn, M., & Geelan, D. (2008). Bridging the research-practice gap: Research translation and/or research transformation. *Alberta Journal of Educational Research*, 54(1).

Huang, Y., Wu, R., He, J., & Xiang, Y. (2024). Evaluating ChatGPT-4.0's data analytic proficiency in epidemiological studies: A comparative analysis with SAS, SPSS, and R. *Journal of Global Health, 14*. https://doi.org/10.7189/jogh.14.04070.

Huang, X., Jen, F. L., Lian, Y., & Jiao, J. (2024). Can generative AI really empower teachers' professional practices? A quasi-experiment on human-GenAI collaborative rubric design. In *International Conference on Technology in Education* (pp. 124–133). Springer Nature Singapore. http://doi.org/10.1007/978-981-96-0205-6_8.

Hur, J. W. (2024). Fostering AI literacy: Overcoming concerns and nurturing confidence among preservice teachers. *Information and Learning Sciences*. https://doi.org/10.1108/ILS-11-2023-0170.

Hwang, K., Wang, K., Alomair, M., Choa, F. S., & Chen, L. K. (2024). Towards automated multiple choice question generation and evaluation: aligning with Bloom's taxonomy. In *International Conference on Artificial Intelligence in Education, 14830*, 389–396. Springer Nature Switzerland. https://doi.org/10.1007/978-3-031-64299-9_35.

Inala, J. P., Wang, C., Drucker, S., Ramos, G., Dibia, V., Riche, N., ... & Gao, J. (2024). *Data analysis in the era of generative AI*. arXiv. https://doi.org/10.48550/arXiv.2409.18475.

Jensen, L. X., Buhl, A., Sharma, A., & Bearman, M. (2024). Generative AI and higher education: a review of claims from the first months of ChatGPT. *Higher Education*, 1–17. https://doi.org/10.1007/s10734-024-01265-3.

Jürgensmeier, L., & Skiera, B. (2024). Generative AI for scalable feedback to multimodal exercises. *International Journal of Research in Marketing, 41*(3), 468–488. https://doi.org/10.1016/j.ijresmar.2024.05.005.

Knoth, N., Tolzin, A., Janson, A., & Leimeister, J. M. (2024). AI literacy and its implications for prompt engineering strategies. *Computers and Education: Artificial Intelligence, 6*, 100225. https://doi.org/10.1016/j.caeai.2024.100225.

Korthagen, F., & Vasalos, A. (2005). Levels in reflection: Core reflection as a means to enhance professional growth. *Teachers and Teaching, 11*(1), 47–71. https://doi.org/10.1080/1354060042000337093.

Laak, K. J., Abdelghani, R., & Aru, J. (2024). Personalisation is not guaranteed: The challenges of using generative AI for personalised learning. In *International Conference on Innovative Technologies and Learning, 14785* (pp. 40–49). Springer Nature Switzerland. https://doi.org/10.1007/978-3-031-65881-5_5.

Lee, U., Jung, H., Jeon, Y., Sohn, Y., Hwang, W., Moon, J., & Kim, H. (2024). Few-shot is enough: Exploring ChatGPT prompt engineering method for automatic question generation in English education. *Education and Information Technologies, 29*(9), 11483–11515. https://doi.org/10.1007/s10639-023-12249-8.

Liu, Y., Chen, L., & Yao, Z. (2022). The application of artificial intelligence assistant to deep learning in teachers' teaching and students' learning processes. *Frontiers in Psychology, 13*, 929175. https://doi.org/10.3389/fpsyg.2022.929175.

Nicol, D., & Macfarlane-Dick, D. (2006). Formative assessment and self-regulated learning: a model and seven principles of good feedback practice. *Studies in Higher Education, 31*(2), 199–218. https://doi.org/10.1080/03075070600572090.

Noroozi, O., Soleimani, S., Farrokhnia, M., & Banihashem, S. K. (2024). Generative AI in education: Pedagogical, theoretical, and methodological perspectives. *International Journal of Technology in Education, 7*(3), 373–385. https://doi.org/10.46328/ijte.845.

OpenAI. (2024a). *Hello GPT-4o*. https://openai.com/index/hello-gpt-4o/.

OpenAI. (2024b). *Improvements to data analysis in ChatGPT.* https://openai.com/index/improvements-to-data-analysis-in-chatgpt/.

Ordak, M. (2023). ChatGPT's skills in statistical analysis using the example of allergology: Do we have reason for concern? *Healthcare, 11*(18). https://doi.org/10.3390/healthcare11182554.

Owoseni, A., Kolade, O., & Egbetokun, A. (2024a). Applications of Generative AI in summative assessment. In *Generative AI in higher Education: Innovation strategies for teaching and learning* (pp. 97–122). Springer Nature Switzerland. http://dx.doi.org/10.1007/978-3-031-60179-8_4.

Owoseni, A., Kolade, O., & Egbetokun, A. (2024b). Applications of Generative AI in formative learning and assessment. In *Generative AI in higher education: Innovation strategies for teaching and learning* (pp. 63–95). Palgrave Macmillan. https://doi.org/10.1007/978-3-031-60179-8_3.

Pereira, D., Flores, M. A., Simão, A. M. V., & Barros, A. (2016). Effectiveness and relevance of feedback in higher education: A study of undergraduate students. *Studies in Educational Evaluation, 49*, 7–14. https://doi.org/10.1016/j.stueduc.2016.03.004.

Prescott, M. R., Yeager, S., Ham, L., et al. (2024). Comparing the efficacy and efficiency of human and generative AI: Qualitative thematic analyses. *JMIR AI, 3*, e54482. https://doi.org/10.2196/54482.

Qiao, S., Fang, X., Garrett, C., Zhang, R., Li, X., & Kang, Y. (2024). Generative AI for qualitative analysis in a maternal health study: Coding in-depth interviews using large language models (LLMs). *medRxiv.* https://doi.org/10.1101/2024.09.16.24313707.

Ribeiro, L. M. C., Mamede, S., de Brito, E. M., Moura, A. S., de Faria, R. M. D., & Schmidt, H. G. (2019). Effects of deliberate reflection on students' engagement in learning and learning outcomes. *Medical Education, 53*(4), 390–397. https://doi.org/10.1111/medu.13798.

Rycroft-Smith, L. (2022). Knowledge brokering to bridge the research-practice gap in education: Where are we now? *Review of Education, 10*(1), e3341. https://doi.org/10.1002/rev3.3341.

Sabbaghan, S. (2024). Exploring the synergy of human and AI-driven approaches in thematic analysis for qualitative educational research. *Journal of Applied Learning and Teaching, 7*(2). https://doi.org/10.37074/jalt.2024.7.2.32.

Sallam, M., Al-Salahat, K., Eid, H., Egger, J., & Puladi, B. (2024). Human versus artificial intelligence: ChatGPT-4 outperforming Bing, Bard, ChatGPT-3.5, and humans in clinical chemistry multiple-choice questions. *medRxiv.* https://doi.org/10.1101/2024.01.08.24300995.

Seßler, K., Fürstenberg, M., Bühler, B., & Kasneci, E. (2024). *Can AI grade your essays? A comparative analysis of large language models and teacher ratings in multidimensional essay scoring.* arXiv. https://doi.org/10.48550/arXiv.2411.16337.

Shahrul, A., & Syed Mohamed, A. F. (2024). A comparative evaluation of statistical product and service solutions (SPSS) and ChatGPT-4 in statistical analyses. *Cureus, 16*(10), e72581. https://doi.org/10.7759/cureus.72581.

Shemshack, A., Kinshuk, & Spector, J. M. (2021). A comprehensive analysis of personalized learning components. *Journal of Computers in Education, 8*(4), 485–503.https://doi.org/10.1007/s40692-021-00188-7.

Stuckey, H. L. (2015). The second step in data analysis: Coding qualitative research data. *Journal of Social Health and Diabetes, 3*(01), 007–010. http://dx.doi.org/10.4103/2321-0656.140875.

Sun, H., Kim, M., Kim, S., & Choi, L. (2025). A methodological exploration of generative artificial intelligence (AI) for efficient qualitative analysis on hotel guests' delightful experiences. *International Journal of Hospitality Management, 124*, 103974. https://doi.org/10.1016/j.ijhm.2024.103974.

Swiecki, Z., Khosravi, H., Chen, G., Martinez-Maldonado, R., Lodge, J. M., Milligan, S., Selwyn, N., & Gašević, D. (2022). Assessment in the age of artificial intelligence. *Computers and Education: Artificial Intelligence, 3*, 100075. https://doi.org/10.1016/j.caeai.2022.100075.

Taras, M. (2008). Summative and formative assessment: Perceptions and realities. *Active Learning in Higher Education, 9*(2), 172–192. https://doi.org/10.1177/1469787408091655.

Teng, M. F. (2024). "ChatGPT is the companion, not enemies": EFL learners' perceptions and experiences in using ChatGPT for feedback in writing. *Computers and Education: Artificial Intelligence, 7*, 100270. https://doi.org/10.1016/j.caeai.2024.100270.

Tlili, A., Shehata, B., Agyemang, M., Bozkurt, A., Hickey, D. T., Huang, R., & Agyemang, B. (2023). What if the devil is my guardian angel: ChatGPT as a case study of using chatbots in education. *Smart Learning Environments, 10*(15). https://doi.org/10.1186/s40561-023-00237-x.

Tobler, S. (2024). Smart grading: A generative AI-based tool for knowledge-grounded answer evaluation in educational assessments. *MethodsX, 12*, 102531. https://doi.org/10.1016/j.mex.2023.102531.

Toulmin, S., Rieke, R. D., & Janik, A. (1979). *An introduction to reasoning* (2nd ed.). Pearson.

van den Berg, G., & du Plessis, E. (2023). ChatGPT and generative AI: Possibilities for its contribution to lesson planning, critical thinking and openness in teacher education. *Education Sciences, 13*(10), 998. https://doi.org/10.3390/educsci13100998.

Vandewaetere, M., Desmet, P., & Clarebout, G. (2011). The contribution of learner characteristics in the development of computer-based adaptive learning environments. *Computers in Human Behavior, 27*(1), 118–130. https://doi.org/10.1016/j.chb.2010.07.038.

Wahba, F., Ajlouni, A. O., & Abumosa, M. A. (2024). The impact of ChatGPT-based learning statistics on undergraduates' statistical reasoning and attitudes toward statistics. *Eurasia Journal of Mathematics, Science and Technology Education, 20*(7), em2468. https://doi.org/10.29333/ejmste/14726.

Walkington, C., & Bernacki, M. L. (2020). Appraising research on personalized learning: Definitions, theoretical alignment, advancements, and future directions. *Journal of Research on Technology in Education, 52*(3), 235–252. https://doi.org/10.1080/15391523.2020.1747757.

Wang, H., Wang, R., Mi, F., Deng, Y., Wang, Z., Liang, B., … & Wong, K. F. (2023). *Cue-CoT: Chain-of-thought prompting for responding to in-depth dialogue questions with LLMs*. ACL Anthology. https://doi.org/10.18653/v1/2023.findings-emnlp.806.

Wetzler, E. L., Cassidy, K. S., Jones, M. J., Frazier, C. R., Korbut, N. A., Sims, C. M., … & Wood, M. (2024). Grading the graders: Comparing generative AI and human assessment in essay evaluation. *Teaching of Psychology, 20*(7), em2468. https://doi.org/10.29333/ejmste/14726.

Weurlander, M., Söderberg, M., Scheja, M., Hult, H., & Wernerson, A. (2012). Exploring formative assessment as a tool for learning: students' experiences of

different methods of formative assessment. *Assessment & Evaluation in Higher Education*, *37*(6), 747–760. https://doi.org/10.1080/02602938.2011.572153.
Xia, Q., Weng, X., Ouyang, F., Lin, T. J., & Chiu, T. K. (2024). A scoping review on how generative artificial intelligence transforms assessment in higher education. *International Journal of Educational Technology in Higher Education*, *21*(1), 40. https://doi.org/10.1186/s41239-024-00468-z.
Xie, H., Chu, H. C., Hwang, G. J., & Wang, C. C. (2019). Trends and development in technology-enhanced adaptive/personalized learning: A systematic review of journal publications from 2007 to 2017. *Computers & Education*, *140*(C), 103599. https://doi.org/10.1016/j.compedu.2019.103599.
Ye, Y., Hao, J., Hou, Y., Wang, Z., Xiao, S., Luo, Y., & Zeng, W. (2024). Generative AI for visualization: State of the art and future directions. *Visual Informatics*, *8*(2), 43–66. https://doi.org/10.1016/j.visinf.2024.04.003.
Zheng, K., Shen, Z., Chen, Z., Che, C., & Zhu, H. (2024). Application of AI-empowered scenario-based simulation teaching mode in cardiovascular disease education. *BMC Medical Education*, *24*(1), 1003. https://doi.org/10.1186/s12909-024-05977-z.
Zong, Z., Schunn, C. D., & Wang, Y. (2021). Learning to improve the quality peer feedback through experience with peer feedback. *Assessment & Evaluation in Higher Education*, *46*(6), 973–992. https://doi.org/10.1080/02602938.2020.1833179.

4. Responsive instructional design using GenAI and digital skill development framework

Barbara Brown and Verena Roberts

INTRODUCTION

In this chapter, we describe a responsive instructional design approach embedding generative artificial intelligence (GenAI) in the context of teaching and learning in post-secondary settings. Drawing on our experiences, we reflect on our learning designs using a Digital Skill Development Framework (Torres et al., 2018) from the perspectives of course instructor/program coordinator (Barb) and an educational developer/instructional designer (Verena). We teach in two Canadian post-secondary institutions and provide some contextual background to help situate our pedagogical underpinnings for learning designs in online courses using a responsive instructional design approach. This chapter argues that a responsive instructional design approach, guided by the Digital Skill Development (DSD) framework, is one method for effectively integrating GenAI into post-secondary education while addressing ethical considerations and fostering student agency. It offers a novel integration of the DSD Framework with GenAI, provides practical examples from diverse learning contexts, and explores the implications of GenAI for experiential learning and open educational practices.

BACKGROUND AND CONTEXT

(Barb) As an instructor and program coordinator for a fully online master's certificate in education, I integrate experiential learning with participatory and technology-mediated approaches in my teaching practice. My pedagogical strategy leverages Kolb's (1984) experiential learning cycle—incorporating concrete experience, abstract conceptualization, active experimentation, and reflection—into the design of online courses to engage students actively and collaboratively. Utilizing learning technologies, I design graduate education courses that encourage active engagement, critical thinking, synthesis, and co-creation, including optional GenAI applications, to support experiential learning in a fully online environment.

(Verena) As an educational developer and instructional designer, I focus on creating community-based and inclusive learning environments with supportive networks. My educational philosophy is rooted in Vygotsky's (1978) sociocultural theory, emphasizing relationship-based, community-driven approaches. I design interactive asynchronous online courses for a diverse range of academic disciplines, prioritizing flexible, student-centered learning opportunities and integrating GenAI tools to adapt to the evolving educational landscape. So, unlike courses that are designed to be updated and changed every time they are offered, the undergraduate courses that I design might not be updated for up to five years.

We both embrace a learner-centered approach that encourages active engagement, collaboration, and the co-creation of knowledge in digital learning environments. We advocate for integrating technology to enhance learning experiences and emphasize the use of open educational resources (OER) and participatory learning opportunities. We have a shared commitment to designing learning that is experiential, collaborative, and community-driven, ensuring that education is responsive to the needs of all learners and critical thinking is enriched by the possibilities of new technologies.

LITERATURE

We consider ourselves responsive in our approaches, as described by Willison (2024, p. 11): "Responsive teachers perceive and understand the interconnectivity of the different components of the learning enterprise and so do not make changes without considering the broader context and interactions." Our pedagogical underpinnings include learning designs rooted in experiential learning theory and open education practices, and in the next section we consider the literature in these areas through the lens of technology-mediated learning with GenAI.

GenAI in Learning Designs

Artificial intelligence is not a new learning technology. However, in recent years, there has been increased attention on the use of GenAI, a subset of AI capable of generating text, images, audio-media, and other types of output, in educational contexts (Chan & Hu, 2023). It is not surprising that there are both advocates and critics of the incorporation of GenAI into teaching and learning practices and instructional design. According to McLeod and Richardson

(2023, p. 77), there are benefits to the explicit teaching of ChatGPT and the development of students' AI literacy skills:

1. Digital literacy, in terms of understanding how AI works in order to create useful prompts.
2. Critical media literacy, in terms of evaluating the products of GenAI within a critical framework.
3. Academic literacy, in terms of understanding the format and style expected in an academic assessment, particularly the ability to synthesize ideas from ChatGPT in their writing.

Berg (2023) provided a case for using GenAI in research practice, suggesting this can support students as a mentor and as an analytic and writing tool. In a review of the literature, Baidoo-Anu and Ansah (2023) described benefits in teaching and learning, such as designing personalized and interactive learning and generating prompts for assessment activities. Similarly, Bahroun et al. (2023) found these types of application can support assessment and personalized learning and provide intelligent tutoring systems. Authors have also examined the use of GenAI to generate personas and simulate interviews with fictional actors (Kocaballi, 2023; Sabbaghan & Brown, 2024). However, Williamson (2024) provided a list of 21 arguments against AI in education, noting issues such as unproven benefits, operational opacity, mental diminishment, outsourcing responsibility, and bias, to name a few. Despite these arguments, the Walton Family Foundation research found that instructors and their students are using GenAI applications such as ChatGPT (Walton Family Foundation 2023). In a study with secondary students (grades 10–12), one third (33%) of students said they have used ChatGPT for school (2023), so, as these students transition to post-secondary learning contexts, many will have experience using GenAI for learning activities. In Chan and Lee's (2023) study, which explored the intentions of students and teachers, they highlighted that Generation Z students (born between 1995 and 2012) have grown up with constant access to technology, and this can shape their learning preferences, including their affinity for interactions with GenAI tools.

In a study in Hong Kong, 399 undergraduate and graduate students were surveyed across various disciplines to explore their familiarity with and attitudes towards using GenAI such as ChatGPT, and they found a significant level of engagement among students (Chan & Hu, 2023). Students reported using GenAI for "personalized learning support, writing and brainstorming assistance, and research and analysis capabilities" (p. 1). In a crowdsourced collection of AI uses in education, instructor examples included connections to productivity, such as developing lesson plans, assessments, and cases/

problems, as well as for skill development (Nerantzi et al., 2023). This collection could be used to speculate that GenAI in education can serve to reduce the workload of the instructor. While instructors are using GenAI for productivity, they also fear their students are submitting AI-generated work (Ofgang, 2024). There is certainly a need to develop an understanding of the human–AI interface (Darvishi et al., 2024). In other words, it is necessary to understand the way people interact with AI systems and how technology and human input come together. In this chapter, we aim to provide a description of the human–AI interface in higher education by drawing on our practical experiences as two post-secondary instructors who are tinkering with the use of GenAI for instructional design and at the same time encouraging our students to use GenAI for learning purposes.

GenAI in Experiential Learning

Experiential learning theory amplifies learning through *experience* with *reflection* (Kolb, 1984). Experiential learning (EL) is considered a high-impact pedagogical approach and involves designing authentic learning experiences for students through an iterative learning cycle of embedding concrete experience, abstract conceptualization, active experimentation, and reflective observation in the design (Kolb, 1984; Kolb & Kolb, 2017). Concrete experience provides the learner with an opportunity to be actively involved in learning that might cause disruption to previous understanding. Through abstract conceptualization, the learner makes sense of the learning experience and, through active experimentation, the learner puts learning into action. Finally, the learner resolves the disruptions to previous understanding through reflection. High-quality experiential learning has evidence of pedagogy that supports students in connecting experience to learning, engagement in meaningful experiences that involve students in contributing to the discipline, continuous assessment to advance learning, and ongoing reflection to support learning and growth (Kolb & Kolb, 2017).

The foundation of EL is authenticity in the learning design. Examples of experiential learning include service learning, problem-based learning, action learning, simulation, and gaming (Kolb, 1984). Experiential learning does not require the use of technology; however, when technology is used, Mayer and Schwemmle (2023) describe this as technology-mediated experiential learning and argue this requires an expanded role for educators. GenAI can simulate real-world experiences and provide an authentic and experiential learning opportunity (Dogru, 2023). Authors also argue these experiential learning opportunities may not have been previously attainable (Bahroun et al., 2023). The success of technology-mediated experiential learning "relies not only on technological components, but also on educators' willingness and capability to align their teaching" (Mayer & Schwemmle, 2023, p. 12). In this chapter, we aim to share how our thinking underpins the learning designs for technology-mediated experiential learning.

GenAI in Open Educational Practices

Open educational practices (OEP) can be described as "collaborative practices that include the creation, use, and reuse of open educational resources as well as pedagogical practices employing participatory technologies and social networks for interaction, peer-learning, knowledge creation, and empowerment of learners" (Cronin, 2017, p. 18). An open learning design framework can further describe open educational practices: (a) clarify the co-design process and negotiate each learner's personal learning pathway; (b) build and share knowledge through learners choosing how to communicate their learning and make thinking visible; (c) build learning relationships; and (d) sustain the learning beyond the learning design by developing and expanding upon personal learning networks (Roberts, 2019). This type of participatory pedagogy can foster student empowerment in digital contexts and situate learners as active agents in the knowledge-building process.

OEP has been shown to help students engage in authentic learning through co-design and participatory pedagogy in technology-enhanced learning environments (Brown et al., 2024) and could also inform open learning designs using GenAI. Tlili and Burgos (2022) suggest that current projects connecting OEP and GenAI have generally focused on workshops that promote the potential use of open educational resources (OER). Although OEP has often been included in discussions of the future of education, the ways in which GenAI can assess and track openly created digital learning artifacts continue to be a concern (Jivet et al., 2020) and there is also the fear of biased understanding of cultural competencies and misuse of open student data (Liu et al., 2016). However, Tlili and Burgos (2022) also suggest some potential benefits of connecting open learning and GenAI, which include harnessing the power to complete time-consuming tasks and focus on learning, developing open digital tutors to help with more timely feedback and possibly more varied and supportive OER recommendations for course content. The connections between GenAI and open learning present multiple areas of potential growth as an emerging area of interest. In this chapter, we hope to expand upon the responsive open learning design as an integral part when considering pedagogical connections to GenAI.

Theoretical Framework

Educators and learners require digital competencies related to artificial intelligence use in education (Ng et al., 2023). There are many frameworks that can be used to support instructors when determining pedagogies and approaches. In this chapter, we used the DSD framework for technology-mediated learning (Torres et al., 2018) as this framework connects to our shared philosophical approaches to teaching with an aim to integrate digital tools to achieve educational goals and to support students' developmental learning through active learning. The DSD is connected to models of engaged learning and teaching and the research skill development continuum (Willison, 2024), with six digital facets and descriptors with a developmental view of learning, as shown in Table 4.1.

The framework emphasizes continuous learning and adaptability to new technologies; however, there are also criticisms of the use of this framework. Critics argue that focusing on predefined skills may not keep pace with new technologies and students' prior learning and experiences (Pilz et al., 2021). Another criticism is the assumption of equal access to digital tools, overlooking the digital divide and challenges faced by students with limited or no access to new technologies. In the following section, we illustrate our learning designs and help identify the interconnected facets of the DSD (Torres et al., 2018). In the first example, Barb provides a description of a learning design that incorporates the use of a custom GenAI tool to simulate interview participants (persona simulator) and uses bold font to identify the terms that connect to the DSD framework. In the second example, Verena reflects on the key design elements that align with the DSD framework and provides questions that help guide her incorporation of AI tools into online courses.

Example 1: Graduate online course design with a custom GenAI persona simulator

During Spring 2023, I (Barb) taught a course that included a learning outcome for students to develop research skills in analyzing publicly accessible data to help develop an action plan for solving a "wicked" problem identified in their workplace context. One of the challenges of a condensed term course (six weeks) is the short timeframe for students to develop an authentic inquiry, collect data to help inform the problem, and analyze results to develop an action plan. As I was reflecting on one of my goals to increase opportunities for students to be situated as partners in the course, I decided to reach out to students prior to the commencement of the course to **explore and clarify** the learning outcomes. I provided students with an option to meet with me prior to the term in an online video conference session to discuss the design of the course. As another option, I also offered to send the draft syllabus so students could

Table 4.1 *Digital Skills Development framework*

DSD Facets	Descriptors
Explore & Clarify	*Curious* What is my/our Purpose? Determine the purpose for using digital technology, taking into account digital practices (i.e., e-safety, digital wellbeing, digital profile, and footprint).
Select & Use	*Experimental* What will I/we use? Choose appropriate digital technology to use for the purpose.
Evaluate & Reflect	*Discerning* Will this suit my/our purpose, and how will I/we know? Critically assess and reflect on the suitability of digital technology and practices in a changing digital environment.
Organize & Manage	*Harmonizing* How will I/we plan my approach? Organize and manage processes, self, and team function using digital strategies and systems.
Synthesize & Create	*Creative* What can I/we make? Synthesize using digital techniques to create new products, understandings, and solutions.
Collaborate & Communicate	*Connected* How do I/we relate? Collaborate and communicate using digital practices in digital settings, accounting for e-protocols, e-safety, digital wellbeing, profile, and footprint.

Note: This table outlines six facets of the Digital Skills (DSD) framework, which focuses on integrating digital tools to achieve educational goals. Each facet has descriptors: 1. Explore & Clarify: Involves determining the purpose for using digital technology while considering digital practices such as e-safety and wellbeing. 2. Select & Use: Focuses on choosing appropriate digital tools for specific purposes. 3. Evaluate & Reflect: Entails assessing and reflecting on the suitability of digital tools in a dynamic environment. 4. Organise & Manage: Involves planning approaches using digital strategies. 5. Synthesise & Create: Encourages creating new products or solutions through digital techniques. 6. Collaborate & Communicate: Highlights using digital practices for collaboration and communication, considering digital etiquette and safety.

review independently and then send me their input via email. Approximately half of the students enrolled in the class opted to send me feedback via email or meet with me and a small group of their peers in a video conference to discuss the syllabus prior to the beginning of the term. I appreciated their questions, which helped clarify the learning intentions, and, as a result, I made some changes to the design of the course based on their input.

A benefit of having these discussions prior to the course was to get a sense of how students would respond to the **selection and use** of a GenAI persona simulator in the course. Some students were excited about the opportunity to learn how to incorporate GenAI use in the learning tasks, while other students were not keen to do this. As a result of the consultation with students, I **evaluated and reflected**, and this led to the provision of an optional pathway for completing the inquiry. One option included the use of the GenAI persona simulator, and the other pathway included the use of publicly accessible data sources for completing the inquiry.

In this example, I focus on describing how I **organized and managed** the option for using a customized persona simulator called PEARL (Persona Emulating Adaptive Research and Learning Bot: https://pearl-mcl4.onrender.com/) to complete the inquiry assignment. I organized a synchronous session where I invited my colleague, who developed PEARL, to meet with students and share how the application works (see Figure 4.1). While sharing the screen during the seminar, we illustrated how to enter information about the persona, similar to the example provided in PEARL about Katarina, a 40-year-old math teacher.

After entering the description of the persona, the application prompts the user to begin the interview. Figure 4.2 provides an example of the output after entering the persona description provided as an example and typing the first interview question, "How would you describe your teaching practice and use of technology in teaching?"

During this session, the developer described some of the ethical considerations when using AI applications and explained the importance of entering persona information without any identifiers of real people (e.g., real names, school locations, etc.). We also discussed how students could **collaborate and communicate** with each other to complete the learning activity. For example, students could develop their personas and meet synchronously online to share screens, collaborate, and work together to refine questions or develop follow-up questions. Students recognized that PEARL could serve as a safe platform to conduct participant interviews with mock research participants. Students quickly realized that this tool could provide a means to practice asking research questions and provide interview transcripts at the conclusion of the mock interview. When conducting multiple mock interviews, the efficient output of transcripts provided a rich data source that could be analyzed and interpreted for the inquiry. PEARL provided a digital tool that helped students practice their interview skills, test their interview questions, and generate a data source to practice analysis and interpretation.

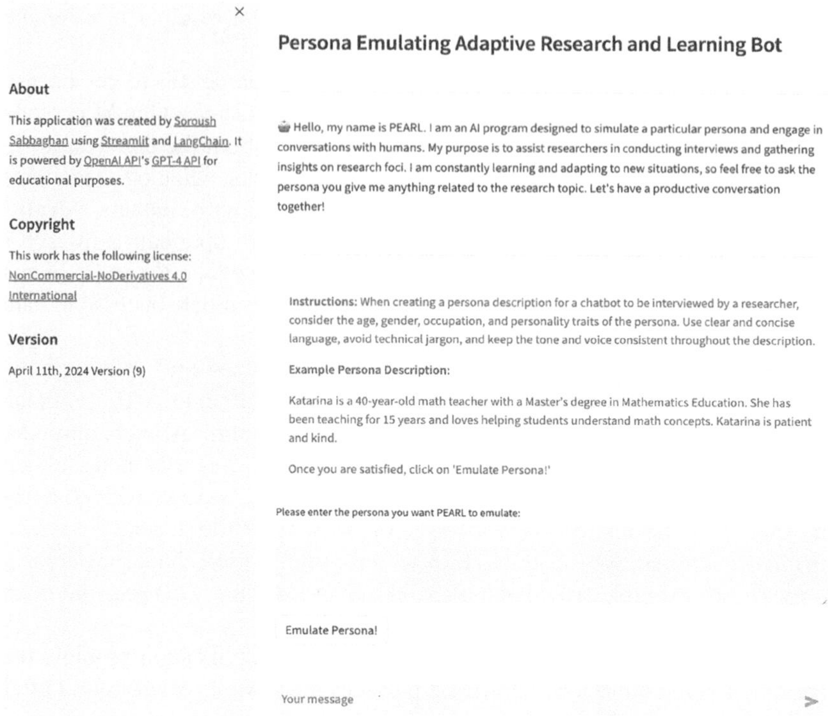

Source: Authors.

Figure 4.1 *Visual of PEARL interface*

Students who used the chatbot reflected on their experiences synthesizing information from the transcripts, reported the benefits in quickly creating a data set to practice analyzing qualitative data, and reflected on how this process helped them improve their interview questions and skills (see Sabbaghan & Brown, 2024). Adding contextual information about the mock participant when running the questions through PEARL generated a unique data set for each of the students to **synthesize and create** a report for their inquiry. Developing interview questions is a challenge many graduate students face when conducting research, and PEARL provided students with an application that could support the development of research-based skills that would otherwise not be possible during the timeframe of the course (Sabbaghan & Brown, 2024).

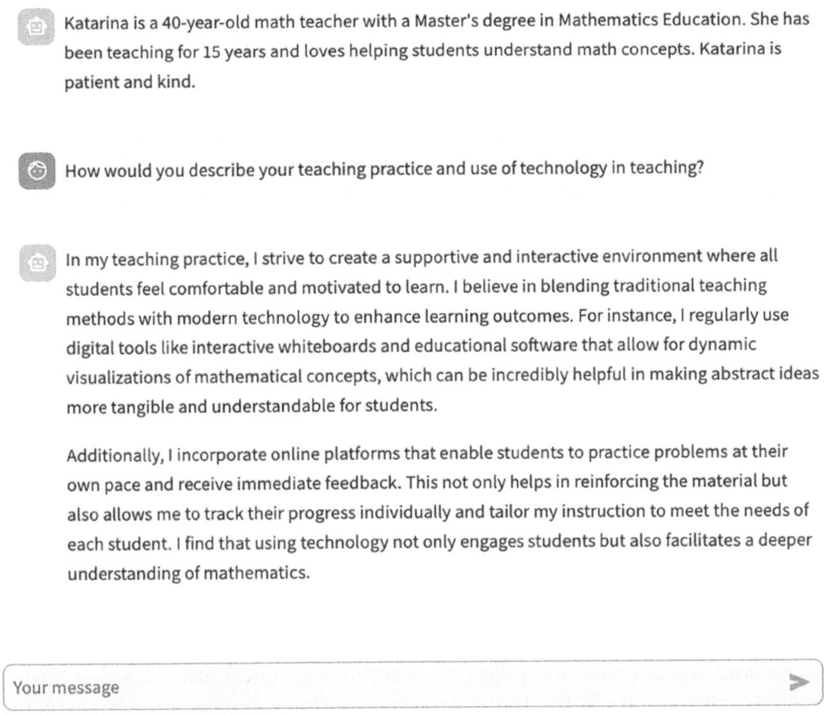

Source: Authors.

Figure 4.2 *Visual of PEARL response to interview question*

Example 2: Reflection on key design elements and questions to guide learning designs using GenAI

In my role as an educational developer, when GenAI applications became known and more commonly used by students, I (Verena) began to work to mitigate potential breaches of academic integrity. Instructors raised concerns about students copying information directly from GenAI applications for their assignments. This fear seemed to stem primarily from the instructional design pattern that concludes with a final essay that is heavily weighted as the major assignment in the course. Faculty were approaching me daily to ask about how they could prevent students from using GenAI (e.g., ChatGPT) to write their course essays. After considering this issue, I turned to my own course designs in undergraduate and graduate education courses to reflect on my design approach. Upon reflection, I realized I consider key elements and questions in my learning design process as summarized in Table 4.2, which aligns with the facets (bold terms) of the DSD Framework (Torres et al., 2018).

Intersection of Learning Designs with GenAI and DSD Facets

Sharing our reflections about learning designs and key considerations for designing courses and learning tasks using GenAI tools helped us recognize the intersections with the DSD facets. We recognized that a common feature is that we use a responsive instructional design approach to integrate GenAI in our courses, aligning with the DSD framework. In this section, we provide a description of each of the six DSD facets in connection with our reflections and the intersections with literature related to experiential learning and open education.

Facet 1—curious

We noted that a key element of our learning designs is to explore and clarify the purpose, and how the learning design is authentic and responsive to learners in the course. Experiential learning provides opportunities for active experimentation and includes a reflective component (Kolb, 1984). When designing experiential learning opportunities with GenAI, referred to as technology-mediated experiential learning (Mayer & Schwemmle, 2023), it is important to consider the purpose and take into account the digital practices that will be needed (Torres et al., 2018). In the persona simulator example, the learners had a choice to use the customized simulator, or they could select an alternative tool or type of inquiry. It was up to the learner to initiate engagement with the GenAI tools. It is also up to the learner to understand what the GenAI tool expectations are for the course, and to clearly communicate how and why they used a tool.

Facet 2—experimental

We recognized that selecting and using appropriate technologies for the learning task is as important as providing students with choice. The persona simulator provides an example of a customized tool that is safe to use and accessible to the students at no cost. Even so, there were students who were not comfortable using the tool. In a study by Sabbaghan and Brown (2024), students were surveyed after using the persona simulator, and results showed that using a GenAI-powered tool provided students with an experiential learning opportunity to practice conducting research interviews. However, some students did not find the AI-generated personas were able to adequately replicate an interview with a human participant, while other students perceived the interviews as providing an authentic and concrete experience. As shown in Figure 4.2, the responses from the personas provided transcripts with clearly articulated

Table 4.2 Design considerations for assignments using GenAI

Consideration	Descriptor
Authentic learning design: **Explore & Clarify**	I consider how the assignments provide opportunities to connect to real-life and student interest-driven topics. How does the learning design provide opportunities for assessment and opportunities for self-reflection, feedback that is peer-driven, and feedback provided by instructors?
Ethical considerations: **Select & Use**	a. I consider what kind of data I am sharing with the tool and what kind of data is being shared with others. Where is the data coming from and what kind of bias does the data have? b. Who has access to the GenAI tool? Is it openly accessible to all, or only those who can pay for it? c. I consider who I could I hurt by using this tool. If I am using this tool to reduce my cognitive function in some way, how am I doing that and will that hurt or help me and why? For example, will the outcome be biased and have no evidence of critical thinking, or will it help me in that the outcome will offer me a draft from which to expand from and save me hours of work?
Accessibility: **Evaluate & Reflect**	I consider what features the GenAI tool can offer me that will help a student or myself in terms of making my learning easier. For example, how does the tool consider and offer support for Universal Design for Learning (UDL) (CAST, 2018)? Is there a summary tool that can help me understand a difficult topic? Will this tool help me save time in my teaching?
Participatory practices: **Organize & Manage**	There must be some element of co-design. How do the learner and instructor add data and then respond, expand upon, or suggest options? How does the GenAI tool create choices in how students complete a task or follow directions?
Layered Assignments: **Synthesize & Create**	In addition, I consider scaffolding assignments in steps or stages. Each of the assignments builds upon one another in order to build knowledge throughout the course. How might OEP support flexible designs that are responsive and offer experiential learning opportunities to students?

Consideration	Descriptor
Flexibility: **Communicate & Collaborate**	I aim to communicate learning outcomes that focus on the evidence of student learning and provide a scaffolded framework that clearly describes the activities and assignments needed to be completed throughout an entire course in order for the students to demonstrate evidence of their learning. How can GenAI contribute to reflective and experiential assignments to ensure that students can present evidence of their learning? How can GenAI help provide flexibility and choice for students within the activity and assignment expectations to ensure that the students have multiple ways to demonstrate their learning?

Note: This table presents considerations for incorporating GenAI into assignment designs, aligning with the DSD framework. Key points include: 1. Ensuring authentic learning design by connecting assignments to real-life topics and providing opportunities for reflection and feedback. 2. Addressing ethical considerations such as data privacy, bias, and accessibility of GenAI tools. 3. Evaluating accessibility features for diverse learner needs, including Universal Design for Learning (UDL) principles. 4. Promoting participatory practices by involving students in co-design and creating flexible, scaffolded assignments. 5. Emphasizing collaboration and communication through clear frameworks that allow multiple ways to demonstrate learning.

sentences, unlike human conversation, which may not be as coherent during an interview. Perhaps engagement with GenAI applications will continue to rise as students become more familiar and adept at experimenting with the tools and as simulated tools become more realistic. This is where student and instructor digital literacy experience is essential, and the opportunity to experiment with and have access to multiple GenAI tools is needed to understand how to use different tools and why to choose them.

Facet 3—discerning

It is important to critically assess and reflect on the suitability of the digital tool. An important design consideration is the accessibility of a tool for all learners. As more GenAI tools are created and used for teaching and learning, authors are reporting benefits of uses (Bahroun et al., 2023; Chan & Hu, 2023; Kocaballi, 2023). Likewise, there are authors reporting issues with integrating GenAI applications in teaching and learning (Chan & Hu, 2023; Williamson, 2024). Evaluating and reflecting on the benefits and implications of using digital tools is a key facet when integrating digital tools in learning designs (Torres et al., 2018). Instructors and students will need to be critical of the tools used for learning and develop the skills to evaluate AI-generated content, identify biases, and develop responsible AI-use practices.

Facet 4—harmonizing

Organizing and managing how instructors and students will use the tools needs to be considered. Consider how students will work alone and with others when using the GenAI tools. Inviting a guest speaker to introduce a tool or providing customized resources for students to learn about unfamiliar technologies can be ways to support students. Instructors may need to prepare in advance of the course and work alongside educational developers or other sources of support on campus to explore unfamiliar technologies. The willingness of the instructor to develop technological fluency becomes particularly important when technology-mediated experiential learning offers learning opportunities to students that were not previously attainable (Bahroun et al., 2023). In addition, using GenAI tools that can save time can encourage students and instructors to focus on collaboration, comparison, and critique, as well as balancing task completion with the potential for new learning.

Facet 5—creative

Understanding how the information will be synthesized and that new products can be created using digital techniques is another key consideration when constructing a learning design. Working together with students to explore the development of new products can involve OEP (Cronin, 2017), for example, and can provide students with opportunities to create innovative solutions to complex problems (Torres et al., 2018).

Facet 6—connected

Collaborating and communicating using AI tools is another key facet of the learning design. This facet also connects to OEP (Cronin, 2017). The DSD framework calls on educators to "transform, innovate, and repurpose digital technologies to optimize collaboration and communication" (Torres et al., 2018, p. 1).

CONCLUSION

In this chapter, we provided insights into our responsive approach to designing learning activities with GenAI in higher education courses. We recognize that a limitation of this chapter is the absence of student perspectives on the instructional designs and see this as a next step in our research, building on earlier work (e.g., Brown & Sabbaghan, 2025). We offer recommendations for instructors to leverage GenAI in pedagogical approaches. First, we recommend instructors reflect on their epistemological underpinnings and consider frameworks that inform their instructional designs. DSD is a flexible framework that shows promise in keeping pace with continually changing technologies. DSD provided us with a useful framework that we plan to continue using when planning courses or lessons using GenAI-powered tools. Second, we recommend instructors apply technology-mediated experiential learning and OEP in the instructional design process for designing authentic learning experiences. Intersections with experiential learning and OEP aligned well with our philosophies of teaching and the ways we approach our technology-mediated learning designs. Third, we recommend considering how human input and technology can come together in the learning process. We concur with Siemens (2024) and recognize there is a need to develop an understanding of the human–AI interface in instructional design, so further research in this area is recommended. The responsive instructional design frame discussed in this chapter could provide a conceptual framework and lens for analysis in future study.

REFERENCES

Bahroun, Z., Anane, C., Ahmed, V., & Zacca, A. (2023). Transforming education: A comprehensive review of generative artificial intelligence in educational settings through bibliometric and content analysis. *Sustainability, 15*(17). https://doi.org/10.3390/su151712983.

Baidoo-Anu, D., & Ansah, L. O. (2023). Education in the era of generative artificial intelligence (AI): Understanding the potential benefits of ChatGPT in promoting teaching and learning. *Journal of AI*, *7*(1), 52–62.

Berg, C. (2023). *The case for generative AI in scholarly practice.* SSRN. https://doi.org/10.2139/ssrn.4407587.

Brown, B., & Sabbaghan, S. (2025). Applying interview-research methods using generative AI technology: An action research study with graduate students in mock research teams. *The Canadian Journal of Action Research, 25*(1), 53-70.

Brown, B., Jacobsen, M., Roberts, V., Hurrell, C., Travers, M., & Neutzling, N. (2024). Open educational practices (OEPs) for research skill development with in-service school teachers. In J. Willison (Ed.), *Research thinking for responsive teaching: Research skill development with in-service and preservice educators* (pp. 33–47). Springer Nature. https://doi.org/10.1007/978-981-99-6679-0_3.

CAST. (2018). *Universal Design for Learning Guidelines version 2.2.* Retrieved May 22, 2024, from https://udlguidelines.cast.org/.

Chan, C. K. Y., & Hu, W. (2023). Students' voices on generative AI: Perceptions, benefits, and challenges in higher education. *International Journal of Educational Technology in Higher Education, 20*(1), 43. https://doi.org/10.1186/s41239-023-00411-8.

Chan, C. K. Y., & Lee, K. K. W. (2023). The AI generation gap: Are Gen Z students more interested in adopting generative AI such as ChatGPT in teaching and learning than their Gen X and millennial generation teachers? *Smart Learning Environments, 10*(1), 60. https://doi.org/10.1186/s40561-023-00269-3.

Cronin, C. (2017). Openness and praxis: Exploring the use of open educational practices in higher education. *The International Review of Research in Open and Distributed Learning, 18*(5). https://doi.org/10.19173/irrodl.v18i5.3096.

Darvishi, A., Khosravi, H., Sadiq, S., Gašević, D., & Siemens, G. (2024). Impact of AI assistance on student agency. *Computers & Education, 210*, 104967. https://doi.org/10.1016/j.compedu.2023.104967.

Dogru, T., Line, N., Hanks, L., Acikgoz, F., Abbott, J., Bakir, S., Berbekova, A., Bilgihan, A., Iskender, A., Kizildag, M., Lee, M., Lee, W., McGinley, S., Mody, M., Onder, I., Ozdemir, O., & Suess, C. (2023). The implications of generative artificial intelligence in academic research and higher education in tourism and hospitality. *Tourism Economics, 30*(5), 1083–1094. https://doi.org/10.1177/13548166231204065.

Jivet, I., Scheffel, M., Schmitz, M., Robbers, S., Specht, M., & Drachsler, H. (2020). From students with love: An empirical study on learner goals, self-regulated learning and sense-making of learning analytics in higher education. *The Internet and Higher Education, 47*, 100758. https://doi.org/10.1016/j.iheduc.2020.100758.

Kocaballi, A. B. (2023). *Conversational AI-powered design: ChatGPT as designer, user, and product.* arXiv. https://doi.org/10.48550/arXiv.2302.07406.

Kolb, D. A. (1984). *Experiential learning: Experience as the source of learning and development.* Prentice-Hall.

Kolb, A., & Kolb, D. (2017). Experiential learning theory as a guide for experiential educators in higher education. *Experiential Learning & Teaching in Higher Education, 1*(1), 7–44.

Liu, Z., Brown, R., Lynch, C. F., Barnes, T., Baker, R., Bergner, Y., & McNamara, D. (2016). *MOOC learner behaviors by country and culture: An exploratory analysis: 9th International Conference on Educational Data Mining, EDM 2016* (pp. 127–134). In the proceedings of the 9th International Conference on Educational Data

Mining (EDM). Raleigh, NC. https://asu.elsevierpure.com/en/publications/mooc-learner-behaviors-by-country-and-culture-an-exploratory-anal.
McLeod, A., & Richardson, H. (2023). Co-constructing skills for ChatGPT at university. *Journal of Academic Language and Learning*, *17*(1), T70-T80. https://journal.aall.org.au/index.php/jall/article/view/929.
Mayer, S., & Schwemmle, M. (2023). Teaching university students through technology-mediated experiential learning: Educators' perspectives and roles. *Computers & Education*, *207*, 104923. https://doi.org/10.1016/j.compedu.2023.104923.
Nerantzi, C., Abegglen, S., Karatsiori, M., & Martinez-Arboleda, A. (Eds.). (2023). 101 creative ideas to use AI in education. https://creativehecommunity.wordpress.com/2023/06/23/oa-book-101-creative-ideas-to-use-ai-in-education/.
Ng, D. T. K., Leung, J. K. L., Su, J., Ng, R. C. W., & Chu, S. K. W. (2023). Teachers' AI digital competencies and twenty-first century skills in the post-pandemic world. *Educational Technology Research and Development*, *71*(1), 137–161. https://doi.org/10.1007/s11423-023-10203-6.
Ofgang, Erik. (2024, January 22). *7 Ways to detect AI writing without technology*. Tech & Learning. https://www.techlearning.com/news/7-ways-to-detect-ai-writing-without-technology.
Pilz, S., McLeod, A., & Yazbeck, B. (2021). Transforming practice through digital skill development. In L. Torres, F. Salisbury, B. Yazbeck, S. Karasmanis, J. Pinder, & C. Ondracek (Eds.), *Connecting the library to the curriculum: Transformative approaches that enhance skills for learning* (pp. 211–228). Springer Nature. https://doi.org/10.1007/978-981-16-3868-8.
Roberts, V. (2019). *Open Educational Practices (OEP): Design-based research on expanded high school learning environments, spaces, and experiences*. University of Calgary.http://hdl.handle.net/1880/110926.
Sabbaghan, S., & Brown, B. (2024). The role of AI-powered personas in developing graduate interviewing skills. *International Journal on Innovations in Online Education*, *8*(1), 1–27. https://doi.org/10.1615/IntJInnovOnlineEdu.2024051770.
Siemens, G. (2024, February 22). *10 minute chats on Generative AI*. Learning and Teaching: Teach HQ. https://www.monash.edu/learning-teaching/TeachHQ/Teaching-practices/artificial-intelligence/10-minute-chats-on-generative-ai.
Tlili, A., & Burgos, D. (2022). Unleashing the power of Open Educational Practices (OEP) through Artificial Intelligence (AI): Where to begin? *Interactive Learning Environments*, 1–8. https://doi.org/10.1080/10494820.2022.2101595.
Torres, L., McLeod, A., Yazbeck, B., Rayner, G., Yates, S., Skrbis, M., Dickson, N., & Fulton, H. (2018). *Digital skill development (DSD) framework*. Monash University. https://www.monash.edu/__data/assets/pdf_file/0010/1652437/DSD-22.05.20.pdf.
Vygotsky, L. (1978). Mind and society: The development of higher psychological processes. In V. Cole, S. John-Steiner, S. Scribner, & E. Souberman (Eds.), *Interaction between learning and development* (pp. 79–91). Harvard University Press.
Walton Family Foundation. (2023, March 1). *Teachers and students embrace ChatGPT for education*. https://www.waltonfamilyfoundation.org/learning/teachers-and-students-embrace-chatgpt-for-education.

Williamson, B. (2024, February 22). AI in education is a public problem. *Code Acts in Education*. https://codeactsineducation.wordpress.com/2024/02/22/ai-in-education-is-a-public-problem/.
Willison, J. (2024). Teachers' research thinking. In J. Willison (Ed.), *Research thinking for responsive teaching: Research skill development with in-service and preservice educators* (pp. 1–15). Springer. https://doi.org/10.1007/978-981-99-6679-0_3.

5. Innovative applications of generative artificial intelligence in classroom assessment: A scoping review

David Baidoo-Anu, Daniel Asamoah and Raji Monsurat

INTRODUCTION

Artificial Intelligence (AI), defined as the capacity of machines and software to emulate human intelligence, is significantly transforming various industries, including healthcare, finance, transportation, entertainment, and education (Pham & Davies, 2024). Within the realm of AI, Generative AI (GenAI) stands out for its innovative capabilities in creating diverse data types, such as text, images, audio, and 3D models. GenAI operates by analyzing existing data patterns to generate new content, including code and synthetic data (Kanbach et al., 2024). Language models, such as ChatGPT, exemplify the capabilities of GenAI. However, it is essential to note that AI and GenAI differ in their functionality, data utilization, creativity, and applications, as discussed by scholars such as Grech et al. (2023) and Holmes (2020). Given these distinctions, this chapter specifically emphasizes GenAI's role in assessment, with a particular focus on ChatGPT.

In educational settings, especially in assessment practices, AI and GenAI are demonstrating transformative potential. Traditional assessments, which typically include essays, multiple-choice questions (MCQs), and short-answer formats, have been the longstanding standard for evaluating student learning (Kaipa, 2021). However, these traditional methods present significant challenges: they often burden educators, do not promote deep learning effectively, and adopt a one-size-fits-all approach that overlooks the diverse backgrounds and learning styles of students (Mislevy et al., 2012; Rudolph et al., 2023; Swiecki et al., 2022). As a result, traditional assessments may offer limited insight into a student's true comprehension and learning process.

The introduction of AI into assessment practices has led to the development of tools that extend beyond conventional methods, enabling more adaptive and personalized evaluations. Cope et al. (2021) assert that AI has the potential to radically transform assessments, a perspective that has evoked a range of responses within the educational community. Although some educators express concerns about the potential for misuse and over-reliance on technology in assessment, others recognize AI as a valuable resource that enhances learning experiences through more efficient assessment tools and feedback mechanisms (Baidoo-Anu & Ansah, 2023). This division is evident, with some institutions, such as the New York City Department of Education, opting to block tools such as ChatGPT-3.5 due to concerns regarding academic integrity and the possibility of undermining traditional learning processes (Elsen-Rooney, 2023). However, as GenAI continues to advance, future iterations such as ChatGPT-5 may pose further challenges to these restrictive measures.

Despite these apprehensions, an increasing number of educators advocate for the integration of AI, highlighting its advantages for teaching and assessment. Proponents contend that AI streamlines assessment design by automating the generation of both open-ended and multiple-choice questions, thereby reducing the workload for educators and creating a more dynamic assessment environment (Chen & See, 2020; Jia et al., 2023). AI platforms also promote peer assessment, allowing students to provide feedback to one another, which fosters collaborative learning (Purchase & Hamer, 2018).

Another significant area of advancement is in writing analytics, where tools such as MI Write utilize regression and classification models to automate essay scoring, facilitating rapid and standardized evaluations (Graham et al., 2015). Furthermore, AI-supported electronic platforms personalize assessments by randomizing question order, integrating multimedia, and delivering immediate, individualized feedback, particularly beneficial for online courses and Massive Open Online Courses (MOOCs) (Baidoo-Anu & Ansah, 2023).

Discussions surrounding the role of AI in classroom assessment often seem to be driven more by speculation than by empirical evidence. As the popularity of ChatGPT and similar models continues to rise, the educational sector requires an objective, data-driven analysis of how GenAI tools can effectively support learning outcomes. Kocon et al. (2023) emphasize the broad appeal and user-friendliness of ChatGPT in comparison to other models, highlighting the necessity of adopting an evidence-based approach to guide its integration into assessment practices. This chapter seeks to clarify the innovative, practical, and effective application of ChatGPT in assessments, addressing both opportunities and concerns to better inform educational policy and practice. As AI and GenAI continue to reshape assessment practices, they offer educators a valuable opportunity to transition from traditional methods toward more adaptive, student-centered approaches.

The next sections will involve exploring methodology, presenting findings, and discussing the recommendations and implications for educational practices, thereby providing actionable insights for the responsible incorporation of GenAI such as ChatGPT to enhance assessment, teaching, and learning.

METHODOLOGY

We adopted a scoping review methodology to collate, organize, and summarize research on the innovative use of ChatGPT for promoting assessment practices (Arksey & O'Malley, 2005). This methodology was deemed appropriate to collect and analyze extant theoretical and empirical literature to provide a conceptual understanding of how ChatGPT can support assessment practices. The review followed the five framework stages proposed by Arksey and O'Malley (2005). These stages include: (i) identifying a research question and the core constructs, (ii) identifying relevant studies, (iii) selecting studies, inclusion, and exclusion criteria, (iv) charting the data, and (v) summarizing and reporting the results.

Stage One: Identification of the Research Questions and the Core Constructs

Research questions must be clearly identified and defined to establish the core concepts or constructs (Arksey & O'Malley, 2005). Clearly defining the research questions in advance enables informed decision-making regarding the most appropriate methodological approach for article selection and data extraction. The following research questions guided this review:

1. What innovative methods are being employed to utilize ChatGPT in enhancing assessment practices?
2. What challenges are associated with the use of ChatGPT as an assessment tool within the classroom?

Stage Two: Identification of Relevant Studies

Based on our research questions, we conducted a comprehensive keyword search utilizing the EBSCO search engine, the largest full-text research database globally (Stapleton et al., 2020). Additionally, we included four other major electronic databases: ERIC (via EBSCO), Scopus, PsycINFO (via ProQuest), and Web of Science. Table 5.1 provides a summary of the search terms used across each database.

Table 5.1 Scoping review search strategy

Database	Interface	Search terms	Term search location
Education Source	EBSCO host	ChatGPT* AND assessment* ChatGPT assessment* AND Education* ChatGPT assessment* AND classroom*	Title, abstract, and keyword
ERIC	EBSCO host	ChatGPT * AND schools* ChatGPT* AND education* ChatGPT* AND classroom assessment*	Title, abstract, and keyword
PsycINFO	ProQuest	ChatGPT * AND assessment* ChatGPT assessment* AND Education* ChatGPT assessment* AND classroom*	Title, abstract, and keyword
Web of Science	Web of Science	ChatGPT* AND assessment* ChatGPT assessment* AND Education* ChatGPT assessment* AND classroom*	Title, abstract, and keyword

Stage Three: Selecting Studies—Inclusion and Exclusion Criteria

The authors conducted a collaborative review of study abstracts identified through the search process. In instances where the abstracts did not provide adequate information on relevant themes, we investigated the full texts of the articles to evaluate their relevance. Our search was confined to peer-reviewed articles, preprints, and essential documents in the field of education, published in English between 2022 and 2024. We selected 2022 as the starting year because it coincided with the public release of ChatGPT in November (OpenAI, 2022).

Our review concentrated on studies examining the use of ChatGPT in classroom assessment, specifically its applications in assessment practices, innovative classroom methodologies, challenges associated with using ChatGPT for assessment, and strategies for addressing these challenges to improve assessment practices. Table 5.2 presents the inclusion and exclusion criteria, and Figure 5.1 illustrates the selection process.

Table 5.2 Inclusion and Exclusion Criteria

Criterion	Inclusion	Exclusion
Timeframe	2022–2024	Before 2022
Language	English	Non-English
Access	Full-text availability	Only titles or abstracts Available
Type of publication	Peer-reviewed articles, occasional papers	Non-peer review, unpublished articles
Sample	Education setting only (PreK-Higher Ed)	Non-education setting
Focus of literature	Studies that addressed the use of ChatGPT in assessment.	Studies that did not address the use of ChatGPT in assessment

Note: This table defines the criteria used to include or exclude studies in the scoping review: Inclusion: Studies published between 2022 and 2024, written in English, available in full text, peer-reviewed, and focused on education settings (PreK-Higher Ed). Exclusion: Studies published before 2022, in non-English languages, only abstracts or titles available, non-peer-reviewed publications, or not focused on ChatGPT in assessment.

Due to the limited research available on ChatGPT in the context of assessment, only about 65% of the studies reviewed provided empirical evidence of its application in this area. Other language models were excluded from consideration, as current research does not offer sufficient insights into their roles in supporting assessment practices based on our established criteria.

Stage Four: Charting the Data

After the selection process, each article included in the review was systematically organized according to key findings and thematic elements. The information collected from the 37 articles, preprints, and other relevant documents was categorized based on the purpose of assessment (formative, summative, diagnostic, self, and peer assessment), functionality (question generation, automated grading, feedback provision, and plagiarism detection), and level of involvement (GenAI-assisted, GenAI-augmented, and GenAI-driven assessment). This structured framework provided the foundation for the findings and conclusions.

FINDINGS AND DISCUSSION

The findings are organized into five key themes: a) creating diverse assessment tasks to support students' learning, b) quality of feedback provided by GenAI

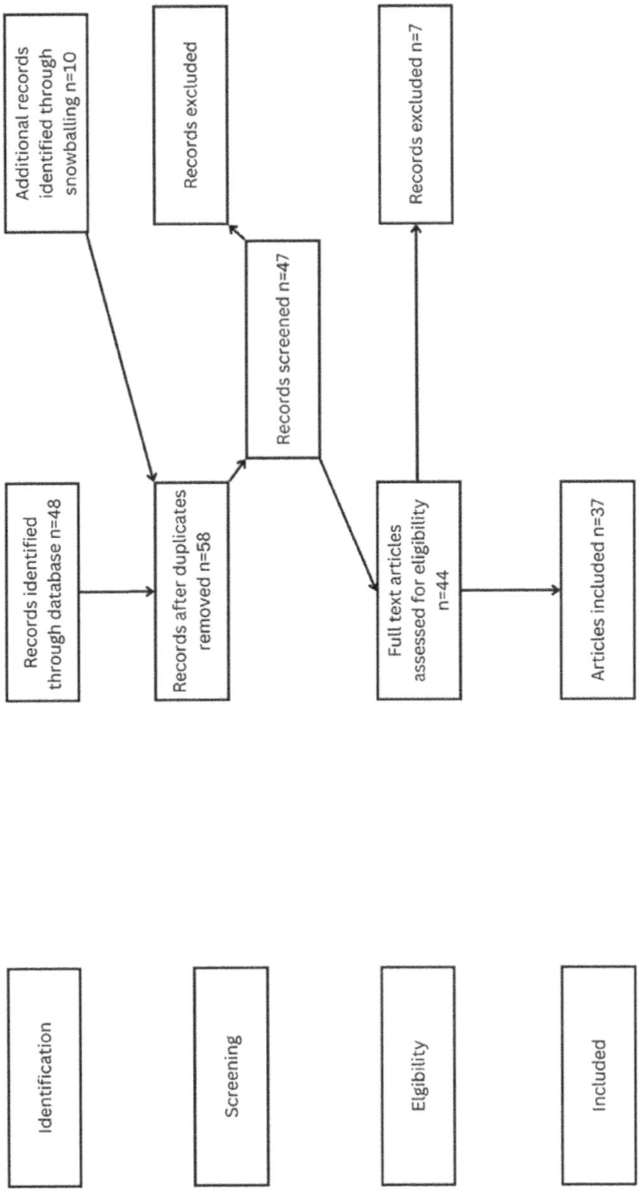

Source: Authors.

Figure 5.1 *Publication selection process*

versus humans, c) student-generated questions and feedback to promote autonomous learning, d) accuracy in grading students' written submissions, and e) challenges in using ChatGPT for assessment. We also discuss in this chapter the framework for integrating GenAI in assessment, resources for effective assessment prompts, and emerging trends in GenAI and assessment, as well as providing recommendations and best GenAI practices.

Creating Diverse Assessment Tasks to Support Students' Learning

The studies reviewed here have revealed that ChatGPT could be used to create diverse assessment tasks that support students' learning (e.g., Moore et al., 2022; Indran et al., 2023; Bernal, 2024; Ni et al., 2024; O'Cain et al., 2023; Schaper, 2024). For example, Indran et al. (2023) leveraged ChatGPT to create MCQs for diverse students in medical education in Singapore. They argued that, in medical education, students need to be prepared to handle a diverse range of patients, each with unique backgrounds and needs. Therefore, when creating instructions for generating MCQs, it is vital to incorporate elements of diversity into patient scenarios. This inclusion of diverse patient scenarios helps students gain a better understanding of and respect for the variations in patient presentation and management. Although AI lacks real-world experience, it generated a wide array of hypothetical clinical scenarios based on the data it was trained on (Han et al., 2024; Qi et al., 2023; Ni et al., 2024). This capability greatly benefits medical education, where exposure to various clinical cases is essential.

Using ChatGPT to generate diverse assessment questions fits with modern education's focus on personalized, inclusive, and interdisciplinary learning. It helps create personalized learning experiences, quickly builds diverse question sets for different learning levels, and integrates extensive knowledge, providing a well-rounded educational experience (Nisar & Aslam, 2023; Bernal, 2024; Schaper, 2024). In supportive assessment tasks, Schaper (2024) highlighted that the generated tasks accurately reflect the cognitive demands of the targeted learning objectives. That is, using ChatGPT for task generation in specific teaching areas requires careful consideration. To effectively prompt ChatGPT, Schaper (2024) further recommended that educators specify the desired number of examination tasks and the format (e.g., written exam), along with the learning outcome for which tasks are needed. Additionally, it is important to define the target group and any prerequisites candidates should meet (e.g., prerequisite skills or knowledge).

Moreover, relevant contextual references or desired levels of realism should be communicated to ensure task authenticity. Additionally, if specific task difficulties or requirements are desired (e.g., requiring justifications), these should be clearly articulated. By considering these factors when formulating prompts, educators can effectively leverage ChatGPT's capabilities to design assessment tasks that align with their educational objectives while supporting students' learning.

Quality of Feedback: GenAI versus Human Educators

The review found differences in the quality of feedback provided by ChatGPT and humans (e.g., Baidoo-Anu & Ansah, 2023; Herft, 2023; Bernal, 2024; Steiss et al., 2024). Compared with ChatGPT, human educators are able to provide higher-quality feedback. For example, Steiss et al. (2024) conducted a study comparing the feedback provided by human evaluators and ChatGPT on students' writing. The study found that well-trained, compensated, and time-rich human evaluators excelled in offering quality feedback in key areas such as providing clear guidance for improvement, ensuring accuracy, prioritizing important elements, and maintaining a supportive tone. The study highlighted the impressive capabilities of experienced human educators in delivering valuable formative feedback. The review found limitations in the ability of current GenAIs, such as ChatGPT, to offer personalized feedback. However, integration in interactive e-learning platforms can offer personalized feedback. For instance, in Bernal's (2024) Learnix project, GPT-4 was used to enhance interactive learning in e-learning platforms by generating diverse MCQs and providing tailored feedback for Python coding problems and short-answer questions. The integration of GPT-4 significantly improves the e-learning experience by offering diverse and up-to-date content, personalized feedback to students, and adaptability to different educational contexts. Bernal's findings emphasize the effectiveness of personalized feedback in reinforcing learning concepts and addressing individual learning needs. By leveraging the GPT-4 language model, the Learnix platform provides tailored feedback to users, enhancing their understanding and retention of educational material.

Students-generated Questions and Feedback to Promote Autonomous Learning

The research reviewed in this study has also shown that ChatGPT can be a valuable tool for students in receiving immediate feedback on their learning, allowing them to track their progress and become independent learners (Herft, 2023; Qi et al., 2023; Ni et al., 2024). Herft (2023) suggests that ChatGPT enables students to develop self-assessment tools such as rubrics or checklists, empowering them to evaluate their own work. For instance, a prompt such as "Develop a rubric for self-assessment of [assignment or task]" can encourage students to take ownership of their learning. ChatGPT can also help students enhance their self-assessment skills by assisting them in creating questions that test their comprehension of the material. For example, students can use ChatGPT to formulate questions on various algebra problems after studying a section on the subject, including equations and word problems.

In the nursing field, Qi et al. (2023) have argued that ChatGPT can provide students with a convenient way to access information and practice clinical skills. It can offer immediate responses to clinical inquiries, simplify complex concepts, and provide current guidelines. ChatGPT can simulate patient interactions, present case studies, and assist with clinical decision-making. It can provide feedback on clinical reasoning, offer guidance on procedures, and help improve communication skills. Additionally, ChatGPT supports ongoing learning by generating quizzes, suggesting personalized learning materials, and recommending educational resources. This can improve knowledge, clinical skills, and communication abilities, assisting students in their growth as healthcare professionals. The inclusion of student-generated questions and feedback is essential in the learning process, encouraging deeper engagement with the educational content's objectives and criteria for success.

By encouraging students to formulate their own questions, they are prompted to engage in critical thinking and reflection on their learning, which helps them internalize key concepts and objectives. This approach not only reinforces their understanding but also helps align their efforts with the intended learning outcomes. Moreover, student-generated questions and feedback offer valuable opportunities for self-assessment and peer-assessment. When students assess their own questions and responses, they participate in metacognitive practices that improve their ability to identify strengths and areas for improvement. Similarly, exchanging questions and feedback with peers enables students to gain varied perspectives, collaborate on learning, and deepen their understanding of the subject matter. This interactive process cultivates a supportive learning environment where students can continuously enhance their knowledge and skills.

Accuracy in Grading Students' Written Submissions

This review has highlighted inconsistencies in literature around the accuracy of ChatGPT in grading students' written submissions. Although some studies found ChatGPT to be unreliable in grading students' written submissions (e.g., Fuller & Bixby, 2024; Jackaria et al., 2024; Morjaria et al., 2024), other studies found otherwise (e.g., Alnajashi, 2024; Chang & Ginter, 2024; Li et al., 2024). For instance, analysis of the data collected by Fuller and Bixby (2024) using ChatGPT-3.5 revealed significant variations in grading patterns, feedback justifications, and response formats. ChatGPT exhibited a 24-point gap between the lowest and highest scores (ranging from 74% to 98%) for the same assignment. The feedback provided by ChatGPT-3.5 lacked consistency in rationale per rubric item, which may hinder learning. Fuller and Bixby (2024) recommended that educators should be cautious when employing ChatGPT for grading and feedback purposes. Contrarily, Alnajashi (2024) used data from a high-stakes end-of-year exam administered and graded by human instructors at the university level. These assignments were fed into ChatGPT-4 along with the corresponding rubric, which was then used to grade 40 paragraphs based on the same criteria. A precision test was conducted to assess the machine's grading accuracy. The results of the precision test demonstrated a high level of accuracy, highlighting the effectiveness of ChatGPT-4 in grading assignments based on a rubric.

One noteworthy finding among these studies is the impact of the version of ChatGPT used. The studies that did not consider ChatGPT a reliable grading tool typically used the older version (i.e., 3.5), whereas those that deemed ChatGPT reliable for accurately grading students' written assignments used the current advanced version (i.e., 4). This correlation was supported by Li et al. (2024), who highlighted ChatGPT-4's enhanced grading consistency with experts compared with GPT-3.5 in terms of topic relevance, clarity of expression, answerability, and difficulty level. The studies that reported a high level of accuracy with ChatGPT-4 used the tool only to grade different assignments and then compared the outcomes. What would have been more insightful is using ChatGPT to grade the same assignment multiple times, observing the consistency of its grading with the same rubric at different times. This approach was used in studies involving ChatGPT-3.5. Therefore, it cannot be conclusively stated that ChatGPT-4 can consistently grade student submissions. Both versions have limited consistency when used for grading.

Challenges in Using ChatGPT for Assessment

Employing ChatGPT for assessments reveals notable inconsistencies that may complicate teachers' responsibilities rather than simplify them (Crompton & Burke, 2024; Tlili et al., 2023). Although the review proposes several strategies to address these inconsistencies in the concluding section of this chapter, a significant concern is the risk of plagiarism. AI essay-writing systems can create essays based on defined parameters or prompts, which may enable students to bypass academic integrity by submitting work that is not their own (Scaria et al., 2024; Dehouche, 2021; Kung et al., 2023). This undermines the fundamental objective of assessments in education, which is to evaluate students' attainment of specified learning outcomes.

Another challenge lies in the susceptibility of students when using GenAI. Many students may accept the outputs generated by ChatGPT without applying critical analysis to them. This issue is further compounded by the absence of clear institutional guidelines that would assist students in utilizing ChatGPT safely and effectively to enhance their learning experiences (Atlas, 2023; Gilson et al., 2023; Kung et al., 2023).

Additionally, there is a potential for ChatGPT to create inequitable advantages for some students. Those with access to GenAI tools may produce higher-quality written assignments, granting them an edge over peers who lack such resources, thereby contributing to disparities in the assessment process (O'Connor, 2023; Mogali, 2023). Moreover, differentiating between a student's original work and a response generated by a chatbot can be challenging, which may compromise the validity and reliability of assessment results (Choi et al., 2023; Cotton et al., 2023).

Furthermore, the use of ChatGPT in assessment, especially in grading, also raises concerns regarding continuous human oversight, potential bias, and inconsistencies in grading (Carrasco et al., 2023; Kasneci et al., 2023; Fuller & Bixby, 2024; Jackaria et al., 2024; Morjaria et al., 2024). For instance, the discrepancies in grading and feedback pointed out by Fuller and Bixby (2024) support the notion that the feedback given by ChatGPT-3.5 lacked consistency in explaining the rationale for each criterion, which could hinder the educational experience. ChatGPT may favor certain cultural norms or fluency in English, disadvantaging students from diverse backgrounds who may encounter cultural and linguistic biases. It may also favor traditional, formal writing styles, potentially undervaluing creative or unique expressions. Students equipped with GenAI tools may find themselves at an advantage over those without access, resulting in an inequitable situation stemming from socioeconomic biases. As ChatGPT is trained on historical data, it may produce outdated or biased responses, particularly concerning emerging topics or progressive ideas, thus reflecting the underlying biases present in its data and algorithms (Zheng, 2024).

FRAMEWORK FOR INTEGRATING GENAI IN ASSESSMENT

The review suggests that GenAI tools such as ChatGPT can be effectively integrated into classroom assessments. Formative assessments aim to provide feedback for guiding learning and identifying areas for improvement. ChatGPT can generate low-stakes, quick questions to assess understanding in the form of quizzes and quick checks, with prompts such as "Generate five multiple-choice questions on the causes of the French Revolution suitable for a quick knowledge check," exit tickets with prompts like "Create three exit ticket questions that prompt students to reflect on today's lesson on photosynthesis," or Socratic questions for discussion using prompts like "Generate five questions that encourage students to debate different viewpoints on climate change."

Summative assessment evaluates cumulative learning at the end of an instructional period. ChatGPT can create comprehensive assessments, including essay prompts with examples such as "Generate a comprehensive essay prompt for high school students on the impact of the Industrial Revolution," project-based tasks using prompts like "Develop a project prompt and rubric criteria for students to create a presentation on renewable energy sources," or case studies and scenario questions with prompts like "Write a case study prompt on supply and demand, including questions that ask students to apply economic concepts."

ChatGPT can also support open-ended assessments to promote student creativity and critical thinking. This may involve developing reflection questions with prompts like "Create reflection questions for students who have completed a unit on ecosystems, encouraging them to discuss personal takeaways and remaining questions," research questions with a prompt like "Generate five research questions for a high school history class studying World War II," or analysis and interpretation tasks with a prompt like "Write a prompt that asks students to analyze a character's motives in *To Kill a Mockingbird* and discuss their development throughout the story."

Closed-ended questions are also beneficial for quickly assessing recall, comprehension, and application skills. ChatGPT can generate MCQs and true/false questions using prompts like "Generate ten multiple-choice questions on basic algebra concepts," as well as matching and fill-in-the-blank questions with prompts like "Create a fill-in-the-blank quiz on the scientific method" or short-answer questions with prompts like "Write five short-answer questions on the causes and effects of the Civil Rights Movement."

Students with diverse needs can also benefit from adaptive and differentiated assessments through GenAI. In ChatGPT, educators can create tiered questions with prompts like "Generate a set of tiered questions on fractions that progress from basic to advanced for a 5th-grade maths class," or personalized assessments using prompts like "Create simpler, personalized questions about ecosystems for students with a basic understanding of the topic."

ChatGPT can help develop oral presentations. It can generate assessment rubrics for evaluating speaking skills, presentation structure, and content depth, along with offering tips for effective delivery. One could use the prompt: "Create an oral presentation for students to explain a key scientific discovery and its impact on society, along with an assessment rubric that evaluates clarity, organization, engagement, and understanding of the topic." ChatGPT can also be used to create peer and self-assessment forms. It can assist in developing questions based on learning objectives to enhance student self-awareness regarding their progress. An appropriate prompt might be: "Create a self-assessment form for a group project, where students rate their contributions, teamwork, understanding of the project, and areas for improvement."

Resources for Effective Assessment Prompts

Creating effective prompts for assessments is essential for GenAI assessment practices. Online tools and resources are available for developing impactful assessment prompts, including the Understanding by Design (UbD) framework by Wiggins and McTighe, Bloom's Taxonomy, Marzano's New Taxonomy, and Edutopia's assessment articles. Practical guides for writing assessments can also be found, such as Classroom Assessment Techniques (CATs) by Angelo and Cross and resources on creating effective classroom assessment prompts from Education.com. Additionally, rubric creation tools such as Rubistar and Quick Rubric are valuable tools.

Additionally, the University of Illinois Center for Innovation in Teaching and Learning, Conestoga College in Canada's Teaching and Learning Department, and the National Academies Press offer free online prompts and templates for diverse assessment formats, including MCQs, essays, and evaluation criteria. Professional development courses and webinars, such as Coursera's Assessment for Learning and FutureLearn's Assessment for Learning in STEM, cover essential formative and summative assessment prompts. With well-developed prompts, GenAI applications—ChatGPT (OpenAI), Google's Bard, Microsoft Copilot, Perplexity AI, Khanmigo, Quillionz, Eduaide.AI, and Curipod—can be leveraged to support assessment practices.

Emerging Trends in GenAI and Assessment

The review highlights key emerging trends in GenAI and assessment. One significant trend is the use of automated feedback and personalized assessments, where GenAI delivers instant, customized feedback on assignments and quizzes. Rajabi et al. (2024) argue that GenAI can enhance personalized learning by providing timely feedback and facilitating self-assessment. This represents a valuable opportunity, as personalized feedback aids students in developing specific skills while enabling educators to address individual learning needs in real time.

Another notable advancement is adaptive testing. GenAI can adjust question difficulty based on student responses, allowing educators to accurately assess each student's skill level and comprehension. This identifies areas where additional instruction may be necessary. Adaptive tests also save time by concentrating on relevant questions, resulting in more efficient assessments for both students and educators.

Data-driven insights from GenAI provide educators with a deeper understanding of student progress. By analyzing performance data, GenAI can identify learning patterns, such as common areas of difficulty or students who may be at risk of falling behind. These insights enable educators to implement timely interventions to support students in succeeding.

GenAI is also facilitating interactive and immersive assessments through simulations, allowing students to critically engage with AI-generated information. Kerber (2024) advocates for assessment methods that encourage students to question the validity of GenAI content, fostering awareness of potential biases in GenAI tools. Simulations can create realistic scenarios, enabling students to apply their knowledge in practical contexts. Such assessments enhance engagement and reinforce critical-thinking and problem-solving skills relevant to real-world situations. Additionally, natural language processing (NLP) within GenAI is enabling the development of content-specific assessments, which is beneficial in language learning. AI tools can offer immediate feedback on grammar, style, and pronunciation, allowing students to refine their language skills.

As GenAI becomes more integrated into education, students should be educated on GenAI ethics and responsible technology usage. For instance, Tan and Maravilla (2024) emphasize the need to maintain academic integrity in assessments. They discuss how GenAI can identify trends in student responses, thereby enhancing formative assessments without overshadowing educator oversight. Incorporating lessons on data privacy and bias in GenAI will equip students to navigate and use technology responsibly (Konnelly & Sanders, 2024; Morris et al., 2024). These advancements not only enhance the educational experience but also prepare students for a technology-driven future, positioning GenAI, especially current versions with optimal performance, as a valuable tool for improving classroom assessment and educational practices.

RECOMMENDATIONS AND BEST GENAI PRACTICES

Using GenAI, particularly ChatGPT, in assessment comes with the risks of plagiarism, student vulnerability and lack of critical analysis, inequality, and validity and reliability issues, requiring best practices for GenAI implementation. To address the potential risk of plagiarism, clear academic integrity policies should be established, utilizing GenAI detection and originality tools, and designing assessments that are less susceptible to GenAI intervention (Atlas, 2023; Baidoo-Anu et al., 2024; Baidoo-Anu & Ansah, 2023). Additionally, incorporating critical-thinking and media-literacy education, providing explicit guidelines for responsible GenAI use, and offering instructor-led demonstrations can help mitigate student vulnerability and promote critical analysis in the use of GenAI. Facilitating institutional access to GenAI tools, particularly in underprivileged areas, offering a variety of assessment options, and emphasizing digital literacy and responsible usage can help ensure equitable access and address disparities in the use of GenAI.

Although ChatGPT offers opportunities to advance educational assessment, educators using ChatGPT-3 for assessment purposes, especially ChatGPT for grading, should be aware of its potential inconsistency in grading. For example, the results showed that using ChatGPT for grading and feedback resulted in inconsistencies. Given that grading student work can have high-stakes consequences, ensuring consistency and validity of the assigned grades and the quality of feedback is crucial. Key qualities of useful and high-quality feedback include providing clear guidance for improvement, ensuring accuracy, highlighting important elements, and maintaining a supportive tone (Dawson et al., 2019; Feeney, 2007; Richards et al., 2017). The older version of ChatGPT, like most GenAI tools, has limitations in providing such quality feedback. Therefore, educators using ChatGPT and other GenAI should exercise caution when employing these tools for grading students' written submissions. By understanding the limitations of ChatGPT and other GenAIs in grading and feedback, educators can mitigate potential unfair and inconsistent assessments to optimize student success and learning outcomes.

To optimize the use of ChatGPT and other GenAI tools, educational institutions could prioritize developing and providing clear guidelines to help educators and students use GenAI safely and constructively. Educating students and educators on the appropriate use of ChatGPT is helpful in ensuring both teachers and students use it safely to support their learning. This can be accomplished through workshops, training sessions, or integrating content related to academic integrity and plagiarism into the curriculum (Atlas, 2023; Baidoo-Anu & Ansah, 2023)

Moreover, our analysis indicates that acquiring the most recent version of ChatGPT may offer improved accuracy and reliability compared with the earlier versions. Although older versions such as ChatGPT-3.5 may be available for free access, upgrading to the latest AI tools can lead to enhanced output quality and increased user engagement. It is essential for stakeholders to regularly update AI models to ensure optimal performance. However, accessing the full capabilities of the latest versions of AI tools, such as ChatGPT-4, may require a financial cost. This can be a significant barrier for individuals in lower-income countries or those with limited socio-economic status. As a result, they may face challenges in accessing these tools, which could potentially impact the reliability of their work if they choose to use ChatGPT or similar AI tools.

REFERENCES

Alnajashi, A. (2024). Investigating the accuracy of large language models 'chatgpt-4' in grading students' writing according to a specific rubric. Available at SSRN: https://ssrn.com/abstract=4691198 or http://dx.doi.org/10.2139/ssrn.4691198

Arksey, H., & O'Malley, L. (2005). Scoping studies: Towards a methodological framework. *International Journal of Social Research Methodology: Theory & Practice, 8*(1), 19–32. https://doi.org/10.1080/1364557032000119616

Atlas, S. (2023). ChatGPT for higher education and professional development: A guide to conversational AI. https://digitalcommons.uri.edu/cba_facpubs/548

Baidoo-Anu, D., & Ansah, L. O. (2023). Education in the era of generative artificial intelligence (AI): Understanding the potential benefits of ChatGPT in promoting teaching and learning. *Journal of AI, 7*(1), 52–62. https://dergipark.org.tr/en/pub/jai/issue/77844/1337500

Baidoo-Anu, D., Asamoah, D., Amoako, I., & Mahama, I. (2024). Exploring student perspectives on generative artificial intelligence in higher education learning. *Discover Education, 3*(1), 98. https://link.springer.com/article/10.1007/s44217-024-00173-z

Bernal, M. E. (2024). Revolutionizing eLearning assessments: The role of GPT in crafting dynamic content and feedback. *Journal of Artificial Intelligence and Technology, 4*(3), 188–199. https://doi.org/10.37965/jait.2024.0513

Carrasco, J. P., García, E., Sánchez, D. A., Porter, E., De La Puente, L., Navarro, J., & Cerame, A. (2023). ¿ Es capaz "ChatGPT" de aprobar el examen MIR de 2022? Implicaciones de la inteligencia artificial en la educación médica en España. Revista española de educación médica, 4(1).

Chang, L.-H., & Ginter, F. (2024). Automatic short answer grading for Finnish with ChatGPT. *Proceedings of the AAAI Conference on Artificial Intelligence, 38*(21), 23173–23181. https://doi.org/10.1609/aaai.v38i21.30363

Chen, J., & See, K. C. (2020). Artificial Intelligence for COVID-19: Rapid review. *Journal of Medical Internet Research, 22*(10), e21476. https://doi.org/10.2196/21476

Choi, E. P. H., Lee, J. J., Ho, M. H., Kwok, J. Y. Y., & Lok, K. Y. W. (2023). Chatting or cheating? The impacts of ChatGPT and other artificial intelligence language models on nurse education. *Nurse Education Today, 125*(2), 105796. https://doi.org/10.1016/j.nedt.2023.105796

Cope, B., Kalantzis, M., & Searsmith, D. (2021). Artificial intelligence for education: Knowledge and its assessment in AI-enabled learning ecologies. *Educational Philosophy and Theory*. https://doi.org/10.1080/00131857.2020.1728732

Cotton, D. R. E., Cotton, P. A., & Shipway, J. R. (2023). Chatting and cheating: Ensuring academic integrity in the era of ChatGPT. *Innovations in Education and Teaching International, 61*(2), 228–239. https://doi.org/10.1080/14703297.2023.2190148

Crompton, H., & Burke, D. (2024). The educational affordances and challenges of ChatGPT: State of the field. *TechTrends, 68*, 380–392. https://doi.org/10.1007/s11528-024-00939-0

Dawson, P., Henderson, M., Mahoney, P., Phillips, M., Ryan, T., Boud, D., & Molloy, E. (2019). What makes for effective feedback: Staff and student perspectives? *Assessment & Evaluation in Higher Education, 44*(1), 25–36. https://doi.org/10.1080/02602938.2018.1467877

Dehouche, N. (2021). Plagiarism in the age of massive Generative Pre-trained Transformers (GPT-3). *Ethics in Science and Environmental Politics*, *21*, 17–23. https://doi.org/10.3354/esep00195

Elsen-Rooney, M. (2023). NYC education department blocks ChatGPT on school devices, networks. Chalkbeat. https://ny.chalkbeat.org/2023/1/3/23537987/nyc-schools-ban-chatgpt-writingartificial-intelligence

Feeney, E. J. (2007). Quality feedback: The essential ingredient for teacher success. *The Clearing House: A Journal of Educational Strategies, Issues and Ideas,* 80(4), 191-198.

Fuller, L. P., & Bixby, C. (2024). The theoretical and practical implications of OpenAI system rubric assessment and feedback on higher education written assignments. *American Journal of Educational Research*, *12*(4), 147–158. http://dx.doi.org/10.12691/education-12-4-4

Gilson, A., Safranek, C. W., Huang, T., Socrates, V., Chi, L., Taylor, R. A., & Chartash, D. (2023). How does ChatGPT perform on the United States medical licensing examination? The implications of large language models for medical education and knowledge assessment. *JMIR medical education*, *9*, e45312. https://doi.org/10.2196/45312

Graham, S., Hebert, M., & Harris, K. R. (2015). Formative assessment and writing: A meta-analysis. *The Elementary School Journal*, *115*(4), 523–547. https://doi.org/10.1086/681947

Grech, A., Mehnen, J., & Wodehouse, A. (2023). An extended AI-Experience: Industry 5.0 in creative product innovation. *Sensors*, *23*(6), 3009. https://doi.org/10.3390/s23063009

Han, Z., Battaglia, F., Udaiyar, A., Fooks, A., & Terlecky, S. R. (2024). An explorative assessment of ChatGPT as an aid in medical education: Use it with caution. *Medical Teacher*, *46*(5), 657–664. https://doi.org/10.1080/0142159X.2023.2271159

Herft, A. (2023). *A teacher's prompt guide to ChatGPT: Aligned with 'what works best'.* CESE NSW.

Holmes, W. (2020). Artificial intelligence in education. In A. Tatnall (Ed.), *Encyclopedia of Education and Information Technologies.* Springer. https://doi.org/10.1007/978-3-030-10576-1_107

Indran, I. R., Paranthaman, P., Gupta, N., & Mustafa, N. (2023). Twelve tips to leverage AI for efficient and effective medical question generation: A guide for educators using Chat GPT. *Medical Teacher*, 1–6. https://doi.org/10.1080/0142159X.2023.2294703

Jackaria, P. M., Hajan, B. H., & Mastul, A. R. H. (2024). A comparative analysis of the rating of college students' essays by ChatGPT versus human raters. *International Journal of Learning, Teaching and Educational Research*, *23*(2), 478–492. http://dx.doi.org/10.26803/ijlter.23.2.23

Jia, Z., Chen, J., Xu, X., … Shi, Y. (2023). The importance of resource awareness in artificial intelligence for healthcare. *Nature Machine Intelligence*, *5*, 687–698. https://doi.org/10.1038/s42256-023-00670-0

Kaipa, R. M. (2021). Multiple choice questions and essay questions in curriculum. *Journal of Applied Research in Higher Education*, *13*(1), 16–32. https://doi.org/10.1108/JARHE-01-2020-0011

Kanbach, D. K., Heiduk, L., Blueher, G., Schreiter, M., & Lahmann, A. (2024). The GenAI is out of the bottle: Generative artificial intelligence from a business model innovation perspective. *Review of Managerial Science*, *18*, 1189–1220. https://doi.org/10.1007/s11846-023-00696-z

Kasneci, E., Sessler, K., Küchemann, S., Bannert, M., Dementieva, D., Fischer, F., Gasser, U., Groh, G., Günnemann, S., Hüllermeier, E., Krusche, S., Kutyniok, G., Michaeli, T., Nerdel, C., Pfeffer, J., Poquet, O., Sailer, M., Schmidt, A., Seidel, T., … Kasneci, G. (2023). ChatGPT for good? On opportunities and challenges of large language models for education. *Learning and Individual Differences*, *103*(2), 102274. https://doi.org/10.1016/j.lindif.2023.102274

Kerber, A. (2024). Failure to contain or failure of imagination? Exploring artificial intelligence's implications for feminist pedagogy. *Feminist Pedagogy*, *4*(5). https://digitalcommons.calpoly.edu/feministpedagogy/vol4/iss5/6

Kocon, J., Cichecki, I., Kaszyca, O., Kochanek, M., Szydlo, D., Baran, J., … (2023). ChatGPT: Jack of all trades, master of none. *Information Fusion*, *99*, 101861. https://doi.org/10.1016/j.inffus.2023.101861

Konnelly, L., & Sanders, N. (2024). AI hype in the classroom. *Proceedings of the Linguistic Society of America*, *9*(3), 5852. https://doi.org/10.3765/plsa.v9i3.5852

Kung, T. H., Cheatham, M., Medenilla, A., Sillos, C., De Leon, L., Elepaño, C., Madriaga, M., Aggabao, R., Diaz-Candido, G., Maningo, J., & Tseng, V. (2023). Performance of ChatGPT on USMLE: Potential for AI-assisted medical education using large language models. *PLOS Digital Health*, *2*(2), e0000198. https://doi.org/10.1371/journal.pdig.0000198

Li, K., Yang, Q., & Yang, X. (2024). Can autograding of student-generated questions quality by ChatGPT match human experts? *IEEE Transactions on Learning Technologies*, *17*, 1600–1610. https://doi.org/10.1109/TLT.2024.3394807

Mislevy, R. J., Behrens, J. T., Dicerbo, K. E., & Levy, R. (2012). Design and discovery in educational assessment: Evidence-centered design, psychometrics, and educational data mining. *Journal of educational data mining*, *4*(1), 11–48. https://doi.org/10.5281/zenodo.3554641

Mogali, S. R. (2023). Initial impressions of ChatGPT for anatomy education. *Anatomical sciences education*, *17*, 444–447. https://doi.org/10.1002/ase.2261

Moore, S., Nguyen, H. A., Bier, N., Domadia, T., & Stamper, J. (2022). Assessing the quality of student-generated short answer questions using GPT-3. In I. Hilliger, P. J. Muñoz-Merino, T. De Laet, A. Ortega-Arranz, & T. Farrell (Eds.), *Educating for a new future: Making sense of technology-enhanced learning adoption*. EC-TEL 2022. Lecture notes in Computer Science, vol. 13450. Springer. https://doi.org/10.1007/978-3-031-16290-9_18

Morjaria, L., Burns, L., Bracken, K., Levinson, A. J., Ngo, Q. N., Lee, M., & Sibbald, M. (2024). Examining the efficacy of ChatGPT in marking short-answer assessments in an undergraduate medical program. *International Medical Education*, *3*(1), 32–43. https://doi.org/10.3390/ime3010004

Morris, W., Holmes, L., Choi, J. S., & Crossley, S. (2024). Automated scoring of constructed response items in math assessment using large language models. *International Journal of Artificial Intelligence in Education*. https://doi.org/10.1007/s40593-024-00418-w

Nisar, S., & Aslam, M. S. (2023). Is ChatGPT a good tool for T&CM students in studying pharmacology?. Aslam, M. & Nisar, S.(2023). *Artificial Intelligence Applications Using ChatGPT in Education: Case Studies and Practices*. IGI Global. https://doi.org/10.4018/978-1-6684-9300-7.

Ni, Z., Peng, R., Zheng, X., & Xie, P. (2024). Embracing the future: Integrating ChatGPT into China's nursing education system. *International Journal of Nursing Sciences*, *11*(2), 295–299. https://doi.org/10.1016/j.ijnss.2024.03.006

O'Cain, A., Fedoruk, B. D., Masri, Z., Frost, R., & Alahmar, A. (2023). A System for the improvement of educational assessment using intelligent conversational agents. SSRN Electronic Journal, 1–9. https://doi.org/10.2139/ssrn.4393234
O'Connor, S. (2023). Open artificial intelligence platforms in nursing education: Tools for academic progress or abuse? *Nurse Education in Practice*, *66*, 103537. https://doi.org/10.1016/j.nepr.2022.103537
OpenAI. (2022, November 30). ChatGTP: Optimizing language models for dialogue. https://openai.com/blog/chatgpt/
Pham, B. C., & Davies, S. R. (2024). What problems is the AI act solving? Technological solutionism, fundamental rights, and trustworthiness in European AI policy. *Critical Policy Studies*, 1–19. https://doi.org/10.1080/19460171.2024.2373786
Purchase, H., & Hamer, J. (2018). Peer-review in practice: Eight years of Aropä. *Assessment and Evaluation in Higher Education*, *43*(7), 1146–1165. https://doi.org/10.1080/02602938.2018.1435776
Qi, X., Zhu, Z., & Wu, B. (2023). The promise and peril of ChatGPT in geriatric nursing education: What we know and do not know. *Aging and Health Research*, *3*(2), 10–12. https://doi.org/10.1016/j.ahr.2023.100136
Rajabi, P., Taghipour, P., Cukierman, D., & Doleck, T. (2024). Unleashing ChatGPT's impact in higher education: Student and faculty perspectives. *Computer in Human Behaviour: Artificial Humans*, *2*(2), 100090. https://doi.org/10.1016/j.chbah.2024.100090
Richards, K., Bell, T., & Dwyer, A. (2017). Training sessional academic staff to provide quality feedback on university students' assessment: Lessons from a faculty of law learning and teaching project. *The Journal of Continuing Higher Education*, 65(1), 25-34.
Rudolph, J., Tan, S., & Tan, S. (2023). ChatGPT: Bullshit spewer or the end of traditional assessments in higher education? *Journal of Applied Learning and Teaching*, *6*(1), 342–363. https://doi.org/10.37074/jalt.2023.6.1.9
Scaria, N., Dharani Chenna, S., & Subramani, D. (2024). Automated educational question generation at different Bloom's skill levels using large language models: Strategies and evaluation. In A. M. Olney, I. A. Chounta, Z. Liu, O. C. Santos, & I. I. Bittencourt (Eds.), Artificial intelligence in education. AIED 2024. *Lecture notes in computer science*, 14830. Springer. https://doi.org/10.1007/978-3-031-64299-9_12
Schaper, N. (2024). Using ChatGPT to create constructively aligned assessment tasks and criteria in the context of higher education teaching. *IntechOpen*. http://doi.10.5772/intechopen.1005129
Stapleton, J., Carter, C., & Bredhal, L. (2020). Developing systematic search methods for the library literature: Method and analysis. *The Journal of Academic Librarianship*, *46*(5), 102190. https://doi.org/10.1016/j.acalib.2020.102190
Steiss, J., Tate, T., Graham, S., Cruz, J., Hebert, M., Wang, J., … & Olson, C. B. (2024). Comparing the quality of human and ChatGPT feedback of students' writing. *Learning and Instruction*, *91*, 101894. https://doi.org/10.1016/j.learninstruc.2024.101894
Swiecki, Z., Khosravi, H., Chen, G., Martinez-Maldonado, R., Lodge, J. M., Milligan, S., Selwyn, N., & Gašević, D. (2022). Assessment in the age of artificial intelligence. *Computers and Education: Artificial Intelligence*, *3*(8). https://doi.org/10.1016/j.caeai.2022.100075
Tan, T. J. M., & Maravilla, T. A. M. N. (2024). Shaping integrity: Why generative artificial intelligence does not have to undermine education. *Frontiers in Artificial Intelligence*, *7*, 1471224. https://doi.org/10.3389/frai.2024.1471224

Tlili, A., Shehata, B., Adarkwah, M. A., Bozkurt, A., Hickey, D. T., Huang, R., & Agyemang, B. (2023). What if the devil is my guardian angel: ChatGPT as a case study of using chatbots in education? *Smart Learning Environments, 10*(1). https://doi.org/10.1186/s40561-023-00237-x

Zheng, A. (2024). Dissecting bias of ChatGPT in college major recommendations. *Information Technology and Management.* https://doi.org/10.1007/s10799-024-00430-5

6. The future landscape: Predictions and prospects for generative AI in academia

Abdulrahman M. Al-Zahrani

INTRODUCTION

Generative artificial intelligence (GenAI) is rapidly transforming the landscape of academia, offering revolutionary potential in both educational practices and scientific research (Al-Zahrani & Alasmari, 2024). With its ability to generate, analyze, and synthesize complex data, GenAI is reshaping how knowledge is imparted and acquired, enabling educators and researchers to innovate in ways previously unimaginable (Bozkurt, 2023). This transformative power positions GenAI as a cornerstone of modern educational strategies, where it promises to tailor learning experiences to individual needs and create adaptive environments that foster student engagement and achievement (Machado et al., 2024).

GenAI is a catalyst for redefining educational paradigms. Advances in AI-driven technologies are revolutionizing content generation, offering new ways to personalize learning paths and provide real-time feedback to students (Pellas, 2023). This integration of GenAI in education opens a wealth of opportunities for educators to address diverse learning needs and presents significant challenges that demand thoughtful navigation (Al-Zahrani, 2024c).

Beyond education, GenAI is making remarkable strides in scientific research, serving as a powerful catalyst for innovation across various disciplines. From computational biology and materials science to environmental studies, GenAI enables researchers to delve deeper into complex problems and uncover insights that drive scientific progress (Al-Zahrani, 2023). By facilitating interdisciplinary collaboration, GenAI not only enhances our understanding of scientific phenomena but also aids in developing integrated solutions to pressing global challenges.

However, the transformative potential of GenAI comes with its own set of challenges. The ethical implications of AI in academia, including issues of bias, data privacy, and the over-reliance on automated systems, present significant hurdles that must be addressed to ensure responsible use (Potter et al., 2023). GenAI has the potential to revolutionize academia by enabling personalized learning and accelerating research, but its ethical implications must be carefully addressed to ensure responsible integration, complementing rather than replacing pedagogical innovation.

This chapter begins with an introduction that establishes the transformative role of GenAI in academia. It then explores GenAI's transformative potential through two main subsections: personalized learning and enhanced research capabilities. The third section examines the dynamic evolution of pedagogy, focusing on three key areas: the reconceptualization of teaching roles, the cultivation of creativity and analytical skills, and the evolution of assessment methods. The fourth section addresses the ethical implications of GenAI integration in academia. The fifth section provides recommendations and pathways forward, organized into three subsections: crafting transparent guidelines, fostering ethical GenAI utilization, and embracing human–AI collaboration. The chapter concludes with a summary of key points and includes a comprehensive table outlining the major areas of GenAI's impact and future trends in academia.

THE TRANSFORMATIVE POTENTIAL OF GENAI

Personalized Learning: Embracing the Uniqueness of Every Learner

GenAI is transforming the educational landscape by focusing on personalized learning (Al-Zahrani & Alasmari, 2024). By recognizing the uniqueness of every learner, GenAI provides customized support, particularly in enhancing skills such as writing and ideation (Al-Zahrani, 2024a). A key benefit of GenAI-infused personalized learning is the creation of tailor-made educational experiences that boost student engagement (Karpouzis et al., 2024).

For instance, GenAI is forecasted to catalyze a pivot toward student-centered teaching methods by creating personalized learning paths, offering instant automated feedback, and providing interactive learning tools (Aksoy & Kursun, 2024). For example, the Open University has implemented AI-powered writing assistants and virtual tutors to support students' learning experiences. Additionally, GenAI facilitates collaborative learning environments and ensures accessibility for all students, thus fostering an inclusive and engaging educational atmosphere (Aksoy & Kursun, 2024; Jung, 2024).

Moreover, GenAI's prowess in generating bespoke instructional content is set to enrich traditional teaching methods, leading to dynamic and individualized student interactions (Alier et al., 2024). In higher education, tools such as ChatGPT show impressive capabilities in tracking and supporting individual learning journeys (Escotet, 2023). The utility of GenAI spans crucial areas such as learning support systems, adaptive methodologies, accessibility efforts, and instructional design, benefiting learners and institutions alike (Bozkurt, 2023).

However, it's important to remain aware of potential issues, such as not fully accommodating students' learning preferences (Michel-Villarreal et al., 2023). Despite these caveats, the revolutionary impact of GenAI on education is clear, as ongoing research and improvements promise to enrich how we learn and teach (Chan & Hu, 2023).

The future of GenAI in academia seems destined for significant advancements, including the emergence of GenAI-powered adaptive learning systems. These systems are revolutionizing personalized education by catering to individual learning styles and performance levels (Al-Zahrani & Alasmari, 2024). They analyze vast amounts of data on student behavior and progress, identifying areas where a student struggles and adjusting the difficulty level of tasks in real time. This approach ensures that learning is timely, personalized, and continuously evolving based on the learner's needs.

GenAI's influence on instructional design is projected to be profound, enabling the creation of content that is highly adaptable to diverse learning preferences and needs. For instance, GenAI can generate customized lesson plans incorporating multimedia elements suited to different learning needs. Moreover, it can develop interactive simulations and virtual labs that offer hands-on learning experiences, making complex concepts more accessible and engaging. By continuously analyzing student interactions and feedback, GenAI can refine these instructional materials to ensure they remain effective and relevant.

GenAI applications are also poised to introduce advanced simulations that provide immersive and interactive ways to understand complex concepts, thereby improving comprehension and memory retention. Imagine a future where students can step into a virtual reality environment created by GenAI to explore historical events or scientific phenomena firsthand. For example, history students might walk through ancient cities, observing and interacting with the environment and historical figures to gain a deeper understanding of the past. Similarly, biology students could conduct virtual dissections or explore the inside of a cell at a molecular level, observing processes such as protein synthesis in real time. These simulations make learning more engaging and enable experiential learning, which is often challenging to achieve through traditional methods. In essence, GenAI can help solidify complex concepts in students' minds, enhancing both comprehension and retention.

Enhanced Research: The Power of GenAI as a Research Catalyst

GenAI is reshaping research through advanced data analysis, simulation, and knowledge discovery (Al-Zahrani, 2023). Its capabilities are ushering in new avenues for innovation, enhancing the scope and efficiency of scholarly investigations, and contributing to social progress within frameworks such as the Sustainable Development Goals (SDGs) (Rane, 2023).

GenAI's ability to process and analyze vast datasets quickly and accurately is reshaping research. In public health, for example, GenAI integrates data from epidemiology, genetics, and social sciences to devise effective interventions for disease prevention and health promotion. By combining insights from diverse fields, GenAI enables researchers to create comprehensive, data-driven strategies for global challenges (Canal-Alonso et al., 2021). Similarly, tools such as ChatGPT assist researchers in summarizing studies and identifying research gaps, making literature reviews faster and more effective, while tools such as the Transcript Analysis and Concept Extraction Resource (TRACER) enhance thematic analysis in educational research, ensuring consistency in theme identification and improving the quality of qualitative analysis (Sabbaghan, 2024).

GenAI also excels in simulation, as demonstrated by AlphaFold's impact on computational biology. By accurately predicting protein structures, AlphaFold has accelerated drug discovery and protein engineering (Hatch, 2021). In materials science, GenAI supports the design and simulation of catalytic complexes, enhancing research in industrial catalysis (Schilter et al., 2023). Computational catalysis, boosted by GenAI, facilitates the simulation and testing of complex catalytic reactions, providing essential data that informs the development of advanced materials and catalysts for various applications (Novo Diaz, 2023). These simulations help researchers explore hypothetical scenarios, optimize experimental designs, and develop new materials and compounds at unprecedented speeds.

GenAI's role as a research companion extends into academic settings, offering real-time feedback on writing, generating research ideas, and supporting the drafting process. Tools such as ChatGPT analyze writing style, suggest improvements, and aid in argument refinement, making it a valuable asset in academic writing (Wachter & Brynjolfsson, 2024). GenAI also assists in academic publishing by streamlining the peer review process. Its Natural Language Processing (NLP) capabilities improve review precision and minimize biases, enhancing the reliability of scholarly communication (Al-Zahrani, 2023). For instance, GenAI can detect language biases, check for plagiarism, and ensure proper citation, thus reinforcing the quality and integrity of published research.

Looking forward, GenAI's interdisciplinary applications are poised to address complex, global challenges collaboratively. In environmental science,

GenAI could analyze data to predict climate impacts, suggest sustainable agricultural practices, and optimize renewable energy distribution across regions. By fostering collaboration among experts from various fields, GenAI supports holistic solutions that promote sustainability and social equity (Bozkurt et al., 2023). This interdisciplinary approach accelerates progress toward the SDGs, ensuring that advancements are inclusive and beneficial across sectors.

THE DYNAMIC EVOLUTION OF PEDAGOGY: FOSTERING A SYNERGISTIC COALESCENCE OF HUMAN EXPERTISE AND GENAI ADVANCEMENTS

Reconceptualizing Roles: Transitioning from Disseminators of Knowledge to Catalysts of Learning Facilitation

The adoption of GenAI in education marks a substantial departure from conventional teaching roles towards ones that prioritize facilitation (Al-Zahrani, 2024a; Al-Zahrani & Alasmari, 2024). Educators, once viewed primarily as key distributors of knowledge, are evolving into facilitators of learning due to GenAI's integration (Bozkurt et al., 2023; Rane et al., 2023). Driven by GenAI's capabilities in content creation and learning facilitation, this shift is evident. AI-powered chatbots, for instance, offer dynamic experiences through adaptive interaction with students (Jeon & Lee, 2023). In response, educators are refocusing their roles to nurture critical thinking, mentorship, and effective learning environments rather than simply imparting knowledge (Rane et al., 2023).

The introduction of GenAI in education calls for a reassessment of the human–AI relationship. Human educators are expected to manage and supervise GenAI applications, further supporting this facilitative educational approach (Walczak & Cellary, 2023). This shift in roles encourages educators to adapt their pedagogical approaches to align with the rapid development of GenAI technologies, focusing on fostering critical-thinking and problem-solving skills in students.

Despite the adjustments required, GenAI is best seen as a complement to, not a replacement for, human educators. Mishra et al. (2024) recommend a balanced approach, with GenAI enhancing educational experiences for both novice and experienced teachers. They envision these tools as augmenting productivity, creativity, and critical thinking, thereby empowering educators to effectively leverage GenAI. Echoing this outlook, Salinas-Navarro et al. (2024) discuss how GenAI can enrich non-traditional educational settings by strengthening experiential learning, encouraging advanced skill acquisition, and promoting knowledge mastery.

Looking to the future, GenAI is anticipated to act as a catalyst for learning facilitation by creating highly interactive and immersive learning environments. Imagine virtual classrooms where GenAI avatars guide students through complex simulations of real-world scenarios, providing instant feedback and personalized support. These GenAI systems could facilitate peer collaboration by grouping students based on complementary skill sets and learning styles, fostering a more dynamic and cooperative learning experience. Furthermore, GenAI could harness augmented reality (AR) and virtual reality (VR) to create lifelike training environments for hands-on skills such as medical procedures, engineering tasks, or artistic endeavors, offering realistic practice opportunities without the constraints of physical resources or risks.

Additionally, GenAI could enhance learning facilitation by using advanced NLP to provide nuanced feedback on students' progress, identifying areas for improvement, and suggesting targeted resources. This personalized guidance would help students develop critical-thinking and problem-solving skills more effectively. These perspectives underscore the imperative role of educators in customizing GenAI tools to maximize their potential, ensuring that they elevate the quality and effectiveness of education. As GenAI continues to evolve, its integration into educational frameworks promises to transform how we approach teaching and learning, making education more accessible, engaging, and tailored to individual needs.

Cultivating Creativity and Analytical Aptitude: Empowering Educators for Tomorrow's Mindscape

As the teaching and learning landscape continuously evolves within the GenAI framework, a new emphasis is placed on the growing significance of creativity and analytical skills. This forward-looking paradigm equips educators with the means to shape future minds through the introduction of fresh ideas and teaching strategies that drive innovation and creativity in education (Liu et al., 2023).

Within educational settings, GenAI's integration takes multifaceted forms through its varied applications, ranging from creative assessments of student performance to promising educational advancements (Husain, 2023). As a catalyst for change, GenAI is notably effective in devising adaptive and personalized examinations designed for each student's unique learning journey (Al-Zahrani, 2024a). It further enhances learning with automated feedback systems that provide detailed critiques of written work and sophisticated algorithms that maintain academic integrity by identifying possible signs of misconduct. Predictive analytics driven by GenAI also offer forecasts of student performance, informing strategic educational interventions. These applications highlight GenAI's pivotal role in shaping a dynamic, tailored educational experience.

Moreover, GenAI is at the heart of advancing critical thinking and creativity, providing educators with the means to harness its transformative influence (Al-Zahrani, 2024b). It signals a transition in pedagogical practices, preparing educators to cultivate a future workforce skilled for an inevitably changing world. An example application for this is Strategic Module Assistant for Rubrics, Tasks, and Inclusive Education (SMARTIE), which is a tool designed to assist educators in creating comprehensive and inclusive course structures (University of Saskatchewan, n.d.). Beyond traditional applications, GenAI's convergence with literary creativity illustrates the harmonious blend of human creativity and machine ability (Husain, 2023).

Further, GenAI can recreate intricate real-world dilemmas within highly detailed and interactive simulations, challenging students to develop groundbreaking solutions (Al-Zahrani, 2024a). These simulations could mimic complex scenarios, such as managing a public health crisis, addressing climate change impacts, or navigating international diplomatic negotiations. For example, CaseCraft is an innovative legal research tool powered by GenAI, designed to streamline legal research and drafting. It enables users to quickly sort through millions of cases, statutes, and regulations to generate precise, tailored legal responses (CaseCraft, 2024).

By immersing students in these realistic environments, GenAI can provide opportunities to apply theoretical knowledge in practical settings, encouraging critical thinking, problem-solving, and decision-making skills. Such experiences would not only enhance students' understanding of the subject matter but also prepare them to tackle similar challenges in their professional lives (Al-Zahrani, 2024b).

These scenarios offer a platform for educators to advance essential problem-solving abilities, which are imperative for future job markets. In literature studies, GenAI's ability to produce new compositions inspired by classic texts presents students with opportunities for unique analysis and discussions on the fusion of technology and the arts (Marchena Sekli et al., 2024). This method enriches their understanding of literature and enhances their aptitude for engaging with the increasingly prevalent interplay between these domains.

Evolving Assessment Methods: Measuring the Nuances of Learning in the GenAI Age

The trajectory of teaching and learning is evolving rapidly, driven by the integration of GenAI. This shift has transformed traditional assessment paradigms, marking a considerable change within educational systems. GenAI tools are reshaping higher education by offering innovative assessment methodologies that complement the learning process (Dai et al., 2023). GenAI is not only transforming how students learn but also redefining how educational outcomes are assessed and validated.

GenAI-powered feedback tools, for instance, are revolutionizing personalized feedback by analyzing student submissions and providing targeted suggestions for improvement. These tools can examine aspects such as writing quality, argument structure, and language use, giving students immediate, constructive feedback that helps them refine their skills progressively (Lee & Moore, 2024). Such automated feedback tools are particularly valuable in courses that require frequent written submissions, allowing instructors to focus on more complex, individualized guidance while the AI handles routine feedback.

Adaptive testing platforms are another prominent example of GenAI's role in assessment. These platforms adjust the difficulty of questions based on a student's performance, providing a customized testing experience that accurately reflects each learner's knowledge level. Adaptive assessments are especially beneficial in large courses where a one-size-fits-all approach is less effective. By continuously adjusting the difficulty level, these tools can challenge advanced learners while offering support to those who may need it, creating a balanced, responsive assessment environment (Khine, 2024).

Automated grading systems further exemplify GenAI's potential in handling complex assessments. These systems can evaluate tasks such as coding assignments or mathematical problem-solving exercises by analyzing the accuracy, efficiency, and logic of student solutions. In coding education, for instance, GenAI can review code syntax and logic to provide detailed feedback, helping students correct errors and optimize their solutions progressively (Lee & Moore, 2024). This approach extends to other fields, such as engineering and data science, where GenAI-driven assessments can evaluate complex, open-ended tasks that require critical thinking and problem-solving skills.

However, the integration of GenAI in assessment introduces challenges, especially concerning academic integrity, as these tools become more pervasive in academia (Michel-Villarreal et al., 2023). Considering the rapid advancement of GenAI technologies, the development and implementation of robust risk-mitigation strategies are crucial to maintaining fairness and reliability in assessments (Alier et al., 2024).

As GenAI and data science continue to mature, assessment methods are anticipated to evolve into continuous and individualized processes driven by real-time data analytics. The use of stealth assessment strategies, subtly embedded within learning activities, could monitor student performance seamlessly without the added pressure of traditional exams (Verma et al., 2021). GenAI will likely enable more nuanced assessment methods that encourage critical thinking and real-world application, marking a significant departure from conventional testing models.

ETHICAL IMPLICATIONS OF GENAI INTEGRATION: BALANCING INNOVATION AND INTEGRITY

As GenAI gains traction in academia, addressing its ethical challenges is crucial to uphold fairness, privacy, and human judgment. Rapid AI adoption brings issues such as algorithmic bias, data privacy, and reliance on automated systems, which call for robust ethical frameworks that emphasize inclusivity, data protection, and the retention of human skills such as creativity and judgment.

GenAI's potential for algorithmic bias remains a primary concern, as models trained on biased data can lead to discriminatory outcomes (Al-Zahrani, 2024c). In educational settings, this may result in inequitable support across diverse student backgrounds. To combat bias, it's vital to train AI on representative datasets, conduct bias audits, and utilize bias detection tools regularly (Michel-Villarreal et al., 2023). Transparency in AI processes allows educators and students to understand and challenge AI-generated recommendations, while engaging marginalized communities ensures the inclusivity of AI tools (Bozkurt et al., 2023).

GenAI's reliance on sensitive data for personalized learning and research insights introduces privacy and security concerns. Institutions must adopt stringent privacy protocols, such as GDPR compliance, encryption, and transparent data practices (Michel-Villarreal et al., 2023). Empowering users with control over their data and conducting regular security audits further strengthens data protection (Slimi & Carballido, 2023). Effective data governance should balance individual privacy rights with educational innovation.

As GenAI systems become more capable, there is a risk of over-reliance on AI in academia, potentially diminishing critical human skills such as creativity and analytical thinking (Al-Zahrani, 2024b). Educators should encourage students to critically evaluate AI-generated content and use AI as a complement to human insight, not a replacement. In research, AI should support, rather than replace, human inquiry, with policies emphasizing human collaboration and training in AI literacy (Walczak & Cellary, 2023; Bozkurt et al., 2023). By integrating AI thoughtfully, institutions can foster a balanced environment where technology and human expertise coexist productively.

RECOMMENDATIONS AND PATHWAYS FORWARD: FORGING A TRAJECTORY TOWARDS ETHICAL GENAI INTEGRATION

Crafting Transparent Guidelines: Navigating Novel Realms with Clarity

The integration of GenAI requires clear and transparent guidelines that uphold responsibility and explicability. Given the complexities of GenAI's development and deployment, transparency and clarity are essential from start to finish (Slimi & Carballido, 2023). This includes refining data collection, labeling practices, and algorithmic documentation to avoid ambiguities (Bogina et al., 2022). Additionally, offering clear governance frameworks is crucial for navigating the intricate GenAI landscape (Johnson et al., 2023).

Implementing Responsible AI (RAI) frameworks is a practical measure to enhance transparency. These frameworks guide the documentation of GenAI systems, identify biases, and introduce risk mitigation and ethical deployment strategies (Lu et al., 2024). For example, the University of Cambridge's RAI toolkit aids researchers with detailed guidelines and impact assessment strategies for the responsible use of GenAI (University of Cambridge, 2022). Standardizing dataset documentation further clarifies the transparency of GenAI systems (Szabo et al., 2022). Additionally, clear source code documentation sheds light on code functionality, which is vital for user transparency.

Prioritizing human welfare is imperative while formulating guidelines for GenAI use (Le-Nguyen & Tran, 2024). Users should clearly understand GenAI application scenarios to avoid potential threats to human welfare. For instance, the misuse of GenAI could lead to privacy violations through unauthorized access to sensitive personal data. Biased algorithms could perpetuate existing inequalities, leading to unfair treatment of certain groups. The lack of transparency in GenAI systems might result in decisions that are difficult to challenge or understand, potentially causing harm to individuals affected by these decisions. Therefore, addressing fairness, bias, and transparency in academic GenAI research is non-negotiable and includes tools to help navigate GenAI technologies, ensuring they are used ethically and responsibly (Al-Zahrani, 2023).

The EU AI Act, passed by the European Parliament on August 1, 2024, illustrates a major step toward global RAI integration. This act classifies GenAI applications by risk, stressing transparency and accountability across all stages of GenAI's development (McCallum et al., 2024). Hence, these guidelines should address societal values and individual rights, incorporating data protection, accountability in GenAI decision-making, user-oriented transparency, operational security, bias mitigation, human-centric GenAI development, and environmental standards for GenAI sustainability. Such regulations are necessary to balance GenAI's benefits with the public interest and sustainable development.

Fostering Ethical GenAI Utilization: Nurturing a Culture of Critical Inquiry

Establishing a culture deeply rooted in critical inquiry is essential for navigating the path of RAI integration and ensuring its ethical use. This requires instilling principles of RAI practice throughout various procedural areas, emphasizing thorough documentation of data and models (Rakova et al., 2021). Fundamental in these steps is the integration of ethical considerations, which should be clearly articulated in the rigorous documentation outlining the moral facets of datasets (Peters et al., 2020).

On March 28, 2024, the US government took a significant step by instructing its agencies to assign Chief GenAI Officers (CAIOs) to supervise the ethical application of GenAI within their domains. These CAIOs are tasked with counseling agency leaders and maintaining adherence to ethical guidelines regarding GenAI's deployment (OMB, 2024). Implementing this model worldwide could prove beneficial, leading to harmonized GenAI ethical standards and policymaking. CAIOs ensure dedicated responsibility and refined expertise in the governance of GenAI, from planning to execution.

Adopting this model, other nations might tailor their approach in line with their cultural, legal, and economic frameworks. The advantages of such positions are globally applicable, and appointing CAIOs internationally could unite GenAI policies and foster cross-border cooperation. This uniform high-level ethical oversight could enhance public trust in GenAI management. Additionally, it paves the way for nations to promptly respond to the rapidly changing GenAI space and positions them as frontrunners in ethical GenAI practices.

Despite the challenges of a universal mandate due to diverse governance systems, international GenAI policy collaboration could be pursued, mirroring the Paris Agreement on climate change or the General Data Protection Regulation (GDPR) on data privacy (United Nations Climate Change, 2021; Wolford, 2023). Such cooperation could establish core principles while allowing localized execution flexibility, ensuring ethically grounded GenAI applications.

Furthering the pursuit of ethical GenAI use, the implementation of Data Cards presents a structured method for conveying ethical considerations and potential societal impacts of GenAI systems, supported by detailed case studies (Pushkarna et al., 2022). It is also vital to scrutinize the ethics of designing GenAI entities with human-like traits. This effort should be multidisciplinary, assessing risks such as deception and dependency while involving stakeholders in creating guiding ethical frameworks (Davison et al., 2024). A careful balance must be maintained between innovation and responsibility to preserve GenAI's role as a societal asset.

Lastly, championing a robust RAI framework with standardized processes and documentation is critical. This approach not only enhances GenAI project outcomes but also promotes ethical standards and ensures transparency and consistency among both academic and industry participants (Tutun et al., 2023). This becomes central to managing documentation across the GenAI maturation (Siala & Wang, 2022).

Embracing Human–AI Collaboration: A Symphony of Human Ingenuity and Machine Intelligence

Human–AI collaboration is not only inevitable but essential. For GenAI technology to be integrated responsibly, we must utilize it judiciously and ethically across various sectors. Achieving a balance between GenAI capabilities and human needs is critical for GenAI to benefit society sustainably (Borsci et al., 2023). At the heart of this integration is the creation of GenAI systems characterized by transparency, accountability, and adherence to ethical principles (Subramonyam et al., 2022).

The way humans interact with GenAI is essential. Adopting a model where GenAI shares tasks with humans can enhance collaboration, creating more equal partnerships and improving our understanding of GenAI systems (Venkat, 2023). In healthcare, for example, GenAI can process clinical documentation, charts, and notes, which facilitates its integration into organizational structures. This reshapes the roles of healthcare professionals, increasingly focusing them on interpreting GenAI insights, managing ethical standards, and advancing patient-focused care (Borsci et al., 2023).

While advocating for GenAI adoption is crucial, we must also consider that those unfamiliar with GenAI collaboration might struggle, potentially leading to unemployment (Fui-Hoon Nah et al., 2023). Therefore, it's vital to foster human–AI cooperation to address human needs. This goal is attainable through comprehensive education and training programs, awareness campaigns, interdisciplinary collaboration, inclusive policies, and the development of user-friendly GenAI tools. Implementing such measures will equip people to coexist with GenAI while also protecting them from job displacement.

CONCLUSION

GenAI has transformative potential in academia, offering personalized learning and advanced research capabilities that can elevate student engagement and foster innovation across disciplines. Through applications such as adaptive learning and immersive simulations, GenAI enhances educational experiences and research quality. However, its integration poses challenges, including risks of over-reliance that may weaken critical-thinking skills, as well as ethical concerns such as algorithmic bias and data privacy. Addressing these requires transparent, responsible AI frameworks, such as the EU AI Act and RAI standards, to ensure fair, ethical deployment.

This chapter proposes a balanced human–AI collaboration framework that promotes transparency, accountability, and ethical integrity. By positioning GenAI as a tool to complement, rather than replace, human expertise, institutions can encourage educators to transition into roles as mentors and critical-thinking facilitators. Comprehensive training, digital literacy programs, and inclusive policies will support both students and educators in navigating a GenAI-enhanced landscape responsibly.

Table 6.1 outlines key areas of GenAI's impact and future trends in academia, such as adaptive learning systems, academic companionship, instructional design, advanced simulations, and interdisciplinary research. This collaborative approach to AI integration upholds human values, promotes sustainable progress, and emphasizes ethical considerations to fully harness GenAI's potential in academic settings.

Table 6.1 *Key areas of impact and future trends of GenAI in academia*

Area of impact	Future trends and predictions
Adaptive learning systems	GenAI-powered systems will cater to individual learning styles and performance levels by analyzing vast amounts of student data, providing personalized content and real-time adjustments.
Academic companionship	Advanced tools such as ChatGPT will become essential in academic settings, offering real-time feedback, generating research ideas, and assisting in drafting research papers, enhancing productivity and creativity.
Instructional design	GenAI will enable the creation of highly adaptable content, incorporating multimedia elements suited to different learning styles and continuously refining instructional materials based on student interactions.
Advanced simulations	GenAI will create immersive simulations for experiential learning, such as virtual-reality environments for exploring historical events, scientific phenomena, and complex real-world scenarios.
Interdisciplinary synchronization	GenAI will integrate knowledge from diverse fields to develop comprehensive strategies for global issues, facilitating collaboration among experts and accelerating progress toward SDGs.
Academic publishing and peer review	GenAI will streamline publication processes, improve review precision, and minimize biases, but will also present risks, such as over-reliance on AI, perpetuation of biases, and potential ethical issues, including plagiarism.
Human–AI relationships	Human educators will oversee GenAI applications, focusing on critical thinking, mentorship, and ethical considerations while addressing challenges such as bias, data privacy, and maintaining meaningful human interaction.
Non-traditional educational settings	GenAI will enhance practical learning and authentic evaluation in non-traditional educational settings, leveraging advanced simulations and personalized feedback to promote advanced skill acquisition and knowledge mastery.
Ethical guidelines and human welfare	Clear and transparent ethical guidelines are needed to address potential threats to human welfare, such as privacy violations, biased algorithms, and lack of transparency, ensuring responsible and fair use of GenAI.

Note: This table outlines the significant impacts of generative AI (GenAI) on academia and its future potential:• Adaptive Learning Systems: GenAI-powered systems provide personalized content and real-time adjustments based on individual learning styles and performance levels.• Academic Companionship: Advanced tools such as ChatGPT support academic tasks, offering real-time feedback, research ideas, and assistance in drafting research papers.• Instructional Design: GenAI enables adaptable content creation tailored to diverse learning needs, refining materials based on student interaction.• Advanced Simulations: Immersive virtual environments for experiential learning, such as exploring historical events or scientific phenomena in real-time.• Interdisciplinary Synchronization: Facilitates collaboration across fields to address global challenges such as climate change and sustainability.• Academic Publishing and Peer Review: Streamlines the publishing process, improves precision in reviews, and minimizes biases.• Human-AI Relationship: Human educators oversee GenAI applications, focusing on fostering critical thinking, mentorship, and ethical oversight.• Non-Traditional Educational Settings: Enhances experiential learning through simulations and personalized feedback for advanced skills.• Ethical Guidelines and Human Welfare: Stresses the need for transparent, fair, and ethical frameworks for GenAI application.

REFERENCES

Aksoy, D. A., & Kursun, E. (2024). Behind the scenes: A critical perspective on GenAI and Open Educational practices. *Open Praxis*, *16*(3), 457–470. https://doi.org/10.55982/openpraxis.16.3.674.

Alier, M., García-Peñalvo, F.-J., & Camba, J. D. (2024). Generative artificial intelligence in education: From deceptive to disruptive. *International Journal of Interactive Multimedia and Artificial Intelligence*, *8*(5), 5. https://doi.org/10.9781/ijimai.2024.02.011.

Al-Zahrani, A. M. (2023). The impact of generative AI tools on researchers and research: Implications for academia in higher education. *Innovations in Education and Teaching International*, 1–15. https://doi.org/10.1080/14703297.2023.2271445.

Al-Zahrani, A. M. (2024a). The impact of generative AI tools on researchers and research: Implications for academia in higher education. *IgMin*, *2*(2), 102–112. https://doi.org/10.61927/igmin151.

Al-Zahrani, A. M. (2024b). From traditionalism to algorithms: Embracing artificial intelligence for effective university teaching and learning. *IgMin*, *2*(3), 145–158. https://doi.org/10.61927/igmin158.

Al-Zahrani, A. M. (2024c). Unveiling the shadows: Beyond the hype of AI in education. *Heliyon*, *10*(9), e30696. https://doi.org/10.1016/j.heliyon.2024.e30696.

Al-Zahrani, A. M., & Alasmari, T. M. (2024). Exploring the impact of artificial intelligence on higher education: The dynamics of ethical, social, and educational implications. *Humanities and Social Sciences Communications*, *11*(1), 912. https://doi.org/10.1057/s41599-024-03432-4.

Bogina, V., Hartman, A., Kuflik, T., & Shulner-Tal, A. (2022). Educating software and GenAI stakeholders about algorithmic fairness, accountability, transparency and ethics. *International Journal of Artificial Intelligence in Education*, *32*(3), 808–833. https://doi.org/10.1007/s40593-021-00248-0.

Borsci, S., Lehtola, V. V., Nex, F., Yang, M. Y., Augustijn, E.-W., Bagheriye, L., … Zurita-Milla, R. (2023). Embedding artificial intelligence in society: Looking beyond the EU GenAI master plan using the culture cycle. *AI & Society*, *38*(4), 1465–1484. https://doi.org/10.1007/s00146-021-01383-x.

Bozkurt, A. (2023). Unleashing the potential of generative AI, conversational agents and chatbots in educational praxis: A systematic review and bibliometric analysis of GenAI in education. *Open Praxis*, *15*(4), 261–270. https://doi.org/10.55982/openpraxis.15.4.609.

Bozkurt, A., Junhong, X., Lambert, S., Pazurek, A., Crompton, H., Koseoglu, S., … Romero-Hall, E. (2023). Speculative futures on ChatGPT and generative artificial intelligence (AI): A collective reflection from the educational landscape. *Asian Journal of Distance Education*, *18*(1), 53–130. https://doi.org/10.5281/zenodo.7636568.

Canal-Alonso, Á., Egido, N., Jiménez, P., & Corchado Rodriguez, J. M. (2021). Revolutionizing pharmaceuticals: Generative artificial intelligence as a bibliographic assistant. Retrieved from: http://hdl.handle.net/10366/153110.

CaseCraft. (2024). Custom Adaptive Scenario Education Creation and Resource Adaptation Facility Tool. https://casecraft.dev.

Chan, C. K. Y., & Hu, W. (2023). Students' voices on generative AI: perceptions, benefits, and challenges in higher education. *International Journal of Educational*

Technology in Higher Education, *20*(1), 43. https://doi.org/10.1186/s41239-023-00411-8.

Dai, Y., Liu, A., & Lim, C. P. (2023). Reconceptualizing ChatGPT and generative AI as a student-driven innovation in higher education. *Procedia CIRP*, *119*, 84–90. https://doi.org/10.1016/j.procir.2023.05.002.

Davison, R. M., Chughtai, H., Nielsen, P., Marabelli, M., Iannacci, F., van Offenbeek, M., … & Panteli, N. (2024). The ethics of using generative AI for qualitative data analysis. *Information Systems Journal*, *34*, 1433–1439. https://doi.org/10.1111/isj.12504.

Escotet, M. Á. (2023). The optimistic future of Artificial Intelligence in higher education. *Prospects*. https://doi.org/10.1007/s11125-023-09642-z.

Fui-Hoon Nah, F., Zheng, R., Cai, J., Siau, K., & Chen, L. (2023). Generative AI and ChatGPT: Applications, challenges, and AI-human collaboration. *Journal of Information Technology Case and Application Research*, *25*(3), 277–304. https://doi.org/10.1080/15228053.2023.2233814.

Hatch, V. (2021, July 22). DeepMind and EMBL release the most complete database of predicted 3D structures of human proteins. *EMBL*. https://www.embl.org/news/science/alphafold-database-launch/.

Husain, N. (2023). Educational renaissance: Unleashing the potential of interdisciplinary GenAI integration. *Journal of Environmental Sciences and Technology*, *2*(1), 159–166. https://jest.com.pk/index.php/jest/article/view/25.

Jeon, J., & Lee, S. (2023). Large language models in education: A focus on the complementary relationship between human teachers and ChatGPT. *Education and Information Technologies*, *28*(12), 15873–15892. https://doi.org/10.1007/s10639-023-11834-1.

Johnson, M., Albizri, A., & Harfouche, A. (2023). Responsible artificial intelligence in healthcare: Predicting and preventing insurance claim denials for economic and social wellbeing. *Information Systems Frontiers*, *25*(6), 2179–2195. https://doi.org/10.1007/s10796-021-10137-5.

Jung, I. (2024). Personalized education for all: The future of open universities. *Open Praxis*, *16*(1), 24–36. https://doi.org/10.55982/openpraxis.16.1.612.

Karpouzis, K., Pantazatos, D., Taouki, J., & Meli, K. (2024). *Tailoring education with GenAI: A new horizon in lesson planning*. arXiv. https://doi.org/10.48550/arXiv.2403.12071.

Khine, M. S. (2024). Using AI for adaptive learning and adaptive assessment. In M. S. Khine (Ed.), *Artificial Intelligence in Education*. Springer, Singapore. https://doi.org/10.1007/978-981-97-9350-1_3.

Lee, S. S., & Moore, R. L. (2024). Harnessing Generative AI (GenAI) for automated feedback in higher education: A systematic review. *Online Learning*, *28*(3). https://doi.org/10.24059/olj.v28i3.4593.

Le-Nguyen, H., & Tran, T. (2024). Charting the ethical course: Navigating GenAI advancements in communication education. In S. Elmoudden & J. Wrench (Eds.), *The role of Generative AI in the communication classroom* (pp. 214–261). IGI Global. https://doi.org/10.4018/979-8-3693-0831-8.ch011.

Liu, M., Ren, Y., Nyagoga, L. M., Stonier, F., Wu, Z., & Yu, L. (2023). Future of education in the era of generative artificial intelligence: Consensus among Chinese scholars on applications of ChatGPT in schools. *Future in Educational Research*, *1*(1), 72–101. https://doi.org/https://doi.org/10.1002/fer3.10.

Lu, Q., Zhu, L., Xu, X., Whittle, J., Zowghi, D., & Jacquet, A. (2024). Responsible AI pattern catalogue: A collection of best practices for AI governance and engineering. *ACM Computer Surveys*, *56*(7), Article 173. https://doi.org/10.1145/3626234.

McCallum, S., McMahon, L., & Singleton, T. (2024, March 13). MEPs approve world's first comprehensive GenAI law. BBC. https://www.bbc.com/news/technology-68546450.

Machado, A. B., dos Santos, J. R., Sacavém, A., Sharma, R., & Cruz, R. N. (2024). Transforming education: Generative AI and immediate engineering in synthetic content creation. In R. Sharma & A. Bozkurt (Eds.), *Transforming education with generative AI: Prompt engineering and synthetic content creation* (pp. 368–387). IGI Global. https://doi.org/10.4018/979-8-3693-1351-0.ch018.

Marchena Sekli, G. F., Godo, A., & Véliz, J. C. (2024). Generative AI solutions for faculty and students: A review of literature and roadmap for future research. *Journal of Information Technology Education: Research*, *23*, Article 14. https://doi.org/10.28945/5304.

Michel-Villarreal, R., Vilalta-Perdomo, E., Salinas-Navarro, D. E., Thierry-Aguilera, R., & Gerardou, F. S. (2023). Challenges and opportunities of generative AI for higher education as explained by ChatGPT. *Education Sciences*, *13*(9), 856. https://doi.org/10.3390/educsci13090856.

Mishra, P., Oster, N., & Henriksen, D. (2024). Generative AI, teacher knowledge and educational research: Bridging short- and long-term perspectives. *TechTrends*, *68*(2), 205–210.

Novo Diaz, O. (2023). *Exploring the quantum frontiers of generative adversarial networks in chemical catalysis*. [Unpublished doctoral dissertation]. ETSI_Sistemas_Infor. Retrieved from: https://oa.upm.es/76810/.

Office of Management and Budget. (2024, March 28). *Advancing governance, innovation, and risk management for agency use of artificial intelligence*. https://www.whitehouse.gov/wp-content/uploads/2024/03/M-24-10-Advancing-Governance-Innovation-and-Risk-Management-for-Agency-Use-of-Artificial-Intelligence.pdf.

Pellas, N. (2023). The influence of sociodemographic factors on students' attitudes toward AI-generated video content creation. *Smart Learning Environments*, *10*(1), 57. https://doi.org/10.1186/s40561-023-00276-4.

Peters, D., Vold, K., Robinson, D., & Calvo, R. A. (2020). Responsible AI—Two frameworks for ethical design practice. *IEEE Transactions on Technology and Society*, *1*(1), 34–47. https://doi.org/10.1109/TTS.2020.2974991.

Potter, J., Welsh, K., & Milne, L. (2023). Evaluating an institutional response to generative artificial intelligence (GenAI): Applying Kotter's change model and sharing lessons learned for educational development. *Journal of Perspectives in Applied Academic Practice*, *11*(3). https://doi.org/10.56433/jpaap.v11i3.582.

Pushkarna, M., Zaldivar, A., & Kjartansson, O. (2022). Data cards: Purposeful and transparent dataset documentation for responsible GenAI. *Proceedings of the 2022 ACM Conference on Fairness, Accountability, and Transparency, Seoul, Republic of Korea*. https://doi.org/10.1145/3531146.3533231.

Rakova, B., Yang, J., Cramer, H., & Chowdhury, R. (2021). Where responsible GenAI meets reality: Practitioner perspectives on enablers for shifting organizational practices. *Proceedings of the ACM on Human-Computer Interaction*, *5*(CSC). https://doi.org/10.1145/3449081.

Rane, N. (2023). Contribution of ChatGPT and other generative artificial intelligence (AI) in renewable and sustainable energy. *Journal of Advances in Artificial Intelligence, (2)*1, 1–26. http://dx.doi.org/10.2139/ssrn.4597674.

Rane, N. L., Choudhary, S. P., Tawde, A., & Rane, J. (2023). ChatGPT is not capable of serving as an author: ethical concerns and challenges of large language models in education. *International Research Journal of Modernization in Engineering Technology and Science*, *5*(10), 851–874. https://www.doi.org/10.56726/IRJMETS45212.

Sabbaghan, S. (2024). Exploring the synergy of human and AI-driven approaches in thematic analysis for qualitative educational research. *Journal of Applied Learning & Teaching*, *7*(2). https://doi.org/10.37074/jalt.2024.7.2.32.

Salinas-Navarro, D. E., Vilalta-Perdomo, E., Michel-Villarreal, R., & Montesinos, L. (2024). Using generative artificial intelligence tools to explain and enhance experiential learning for authentic assessment. *Education Sciences*, *14*(1), 83. https://www.mdpi.com/2227-7102/14/1/83.

Schilter, O., Vaucher, A., Schwaller, P., & Laino, T. (2023). Designing catalysts with deep generative models and computational data. A case study for Suzuki cross coupling reactions. *Digital Discovery*, *2*(3), 728–735. https://doi.org/10.1039/D2DD00125J.

Siala, H., & Wang, Y. (2022). Shifting artificial intelligence to be responsible in healthcare: A systematic review. *Social Science & Medicine*, *296*, 114782. https://doi.org/10.1016/j.socscimed.2022.114782.

Slimi, Z., & Carballido, B. V. (2023). Navigating the ethical challenges of artificial intelligence in higher education: An analysis of seven global GenAI ethics policies. *TEM Journal*, *12*(2). 590–602. Retrieved from: https://www.ceeol.com/search/article-detail?id=1122977.

Subramonyam, H., Im, J., Seifert, C., & Adar, E. (2022). *Human–AI guidelines in practice: Leaky abstractions as an enabler in collaborative software teams.* arXiv. https://doi.org/10.48550/arXiv.2207.01749.

Szabo, L., Raisi-Estabragh, Z., Salih, A., McCracken, C., Ruiz Pujadas, E., Gkontra, P., … Petersen, S. E. (2022). Clinician's guide to trustworthy and responsible artificial intelligence in cardiovascular imaging. *Frontiers in Cardiovascular Medicine*, *9*. https://doi.org/10.3389/fcvm.2022.1016032.

Tutun, S., Harfouche, A., Albizri, A., Johnson, M. E., & He, H. (2023). A responsible GenAI framework for mitigating the ramifications of the organ donation crisis. *Information Systems Frontiers*, *25*(6), 2301–2316. https://doi.org/10.1007/s10796-022-10340-y.

United Nations Climate Change. (2021). *The Paris agreement: What is the Paris agreement? United Nations.* https://unfccc.int/process-and-meetings/the-paris-agreement/what-is-the-paris-agreement.

University of Cambridge. (2022). *Generative AI tool guidelines.* University of Cambridge. https://www.communications.cam.ac.uk/generative-ai-tool-guidelines.

University of Saskatchewan. (n.d.). *SMARTIE.DEV: Strategic module assistant for rubrics, tasks, and inclusive education.* Teaching & Learning Technologies. https://teaching.usask.ca/learning-technology/tools/smartie.php.

Venkat, S. (2023). Exploring shared understandings of future GenAI systems through design [Master's dissertation]. TU Delft. https://repository.tudelft.nl/islandora/object/uuid:c161d380-4f3b-4f4d-8f9b-dee48b764031.

Verma, V., Amresh, A., Craig, S. D., & Bansal, A. (2021). Validity of a content agnostic game based stealth assessment. In F. de Rosa, I. Marfisi Schottman, J. Baalsrud

Hauge, F. Bellotti, P. Dondio, & M. Romero (Eds.), *Games and Learning Alliance* (pp. 121–130). Springer. https://doi.org/10.1007/978-3-030-92182-8_12.

Wachter, R. M., & Brynjolfsson, E. (2024). Will generative artificial intelligence deliver on its promise in health care? *JAMA*, *331*(1), 65–69. https://doi.org/10.1001/jama.2023.25054.

Walczak, K., & Cellary, W. (2023). Challenges for higher education in the era of widespread access to Generative AI. *Economics and Business Review*, 9(2), 71–100. https://doi.org/10.18559/ebr.2023.2.743

Wolford, B. (2023, September 14). What is GDPR, the EU's new data protection law? Retrieved May 12, 2024, from: https://gdpr.eu/what-is-gdpr/

7. Rethinking authorship in a generative AI-driven academic world

Rahul Kumar

INTRODUCTION

The emergence of generative artificial intelligence (GenAI) has disrupted the traditional concept of authorship in the academic world. Depending on their ideological stance on the role of GenAI in academia, people either want to preserve authorship in its current configuration or reimagine what authorship might mean. This chapter explores alternative possibilities of authorship in the context of GenAI-driven academic writing. More precisely, it argues for a shift towards collaborative authorship models that acknowledge and value human and AI contributions, necessitating the re-evaluation of traditional long-standing notions of originality, attribution, and responsibility. To achieve these objectives, the chapter provides a brief background of authorship and then introduces the concept of postplagiarism (PPM) proposed by Eaton (2023), which offers a new framework for understanding authorship in the age of AI.

Following this theoretical foundation, the chapter reports the findings from a study conducted to gauge public sentiment about authorship and creativity in academia regarding AI. The study involved a quantitative survey designed to assess attitudes toward AI's role in authorship and the principles of PPM. The chapter's Research Design section will briefly describe salient elements of this study, which received ethics board clearance. The chapter analyzes the study's survey findings in depth, highlighting key trends and insights into public perceptions of AI and authorship, and discusses the implications of these findings for academic practices and the future of authorship.

Finally, the chapter concludes by reimagining authorship's forms in a GenAI-driven academic world, advocating for new models that ensure fair recognition and attribution for all contributors. These conclusions address the necessity of clear guidelines and frameworks to navigate the evolving landscape of authorship.

BACKGROUND

Authorship

Authorship had been a contested concept even before the advent of GenAI. While, historically, single-author articles were typical, a trend towards collaborative authorship has occurred. This shift is reflected in the fact that multi-author articles tend to be cited more frequently than single-author articles, indicating a perceived higher impact (Campbell & Simberloff, 2022; Nawaz, 2016). The rise in multi-authorship has brought about various challenges: the recognition of contributors to scholarly works (Vasilevsky et al., 2020); the acknowledgment that authorship emerges from collaboration (Rojas, 2021); and the traditional notions of authorship, ownership, and control prevalent in the contemporary publishing industry (Bold, 2018). There are also contested issues of scholarship, such as the sequence of authorship in collaborative scholarly work (Zutshi et al., 2012), working with students and establishing correct author attribution (Zutshi et al., 2012), honorary and ghost authorships (Zutshi et al., 2012), increased number of authors (Lin, 2023), and ethical responsibilities associated with authorship (Ebrahimi & Ebrahimi, 2021). Additionally, disputes over authorship have led to conflicts in determining rightful authors (Lemmens & Srinivasan, 2022) and challenges in attributing authorship to short text streams, which emerge from evolving language and writing styles (Azarbonyad et al., 2015). In short, many issues concerning authorship were contested before GenAI became popular.

The underlying assumption of authorship is that the writer is presumed to have created the text as presented and that the ideas expressed in the writing belong solely to the author(s). As Rojas (2021) and Vasilevsky et al. (2020) have asserted, ideas are often built upon each other through formal and informal collaborations, resulting in the creation of the final output. However, authorship seldom reflects these nuances.

The introduction of GenAI in academia has further complicated the arena of authorship, raising questions about the origins of ideas and the contributions of AI systems to scholarly works. The inference of authorship is problematized; a reader can no longer be certain if the text is authored by a human being, by a human being aided by AI, or by AI entirely. This problem is compounded by two factors: First, automated detection systems are not always readily available unless in a highly formalized system such as postsecondary institutions (PSEs), where text-matching software technology is available for assignment submissions. Although such software platforms have been incorporating (and improving) AI detection mechanisms, the technology is not infallible; AI-generated text has been interpreted as being written by human beings (false negatives), and human-generated text has been deemed to be generated by AI (false positives) (Kobis & Mossink, 2021; Kumar & Mindzak, 2024). Both false positives and false negatives undermine the accuracy of the detection mechanism. Proponents of this technology and idea claim that the accuracy is improving persistently.

However, another significant segment of authorship does not have the same level of recognition and focus as formal writing for assessment in courses. This category includes email exchanges, website posts, and social media content. Text parsing tools are not commonly used in these cases due to their lack of integration into the software, the inconvenience of using the tools separately, and the associated costs and restricted access to the lay public.

If automated detection mechanisms are flawed, manual or human detection is the obvious recourse. But human detection, too, is woefully flawed. A study by Kumar and Mindzak (2024) showed that humans are worse at detecting passages written by AI than those written by humans.

There are two ways to address the problem of authorship under these circumstances. One is to try to arrest the use of AI, which is a futile enterprise (Zawacki-Richter et al., 2019), and there is growing literature to suggest that AI use in education has the potential to be transformative (Castro et al., 2023; Schumpeter, 2024; Spurrier & Kulesa, 2023). Furthermore, Kumar and McGray (2024) reported that the use of AI to do academic work was already at 73% among PSE students globally (n = 1021) in the 2022–2023 academic year. Given the extent of use, AI's role in education, and hence authorship, cannot be ignored or dismissed. An emerging trend being adopted in parts of the world includes acknowledging the use of AI in student submissions, but these are not yet recognized by the Committee on Publication Ethics (COPE, 2023), which states that "AI tools cannot meet the requirements for authorship as they cannot take responsibility for the submitted work" (para. 2). While these positions are evolving rapidly, co-authorship with AI has not been accepted yet.

Another approach to deal with the uncertainty of authorship is to accept that the use of AI is going to continue to grow. In fact, Eaton (2023) proposed the idea of PPM, which contends that there will be a time when human writing will be presumed to have some element of AI in it. Embracing the collaborative nature of AI engagement in writing will require a fundamental shift in how authorship is perceived and attributed. It will necessitate the development of new models that acknowledge the unique contributions of both humans and AI systems in academic writing. As we move into an era where AI's role in academic writing becomes increasingly significant, it is critical to establish clear guidelines and frameworks that reflect the evolving landscape of authorship. These new models will not only address the complexities introduced by AI but also ensure fair recognition and attribution for all contributors involved in the creation of scholarly works.

Postplagiarism

If we dispense with a punitive approach toward the use of AI in academic writing and instead accede to it as an evolving domain, the idea of PPM proposed by Eaton (2021, 2023) becomes particularly relevant. PPM is comprised of six tenets, and they propose how human creativity and AI's production will coexist and how the responsibility among human beings and AI will be redistributed. Specifically, Eaton's (2023, pp. 3–6) six tenets of postplagiarism are:

1. "Hybrid human–AI writing will become normal"
2. "Human creativity is enhanced"
3. "Language barriers disappear"
4. "Humans can relinquish control, but not responsibility"
5. "Attribution remains important"
6. "Historical definitions of plagiarism no longer apply"

The tenets of PPM are an invitation to reconceptualize the current concepts of authorship, attribution, and plagiarism. The first two tenets directly relate to authorship and creativity, which is what reimagining authorship is about, and the scope of this chapter.

An analogy illustrates how the concepts evolve: About 40 years ago, proper spelling was considered essential. Misspelled words in a letter or memo reflected poorly on the author. Then, with the widespread use of computers and word processors equipped with spell-checking tools, spelling errors could be easily corrected through suggestions by these programs. Nowadays, if an electronic message contains spelling errors, it is assumed that the writer did not take the time to run a spell check. On the other hand, if there are no spelling mistakes, judgment is not cast upon the sender for using a spell-checker; instead, it is simply expected that they utilized this tool as part of their writing process. In short, utilizing a spell-checker has become normalized and expected in modern communication. This could be dubbed the *post-spelling* era. Similarly, in the realm of academic writing, as AI becomes an integral part of the writing process, it is crucial to shift our perception and embrace the concept of PPM.

Implications of Postplagiarism for Academic Authorship

Eaton's (2023) PPM framework presents a novel perspective for understanding the intersection of human creativity and AI-generated content, particularly in academic writing. The framework provides a forward-looking approach to managing the inevitable integration of AI into authorship practices. However, the application of the PPM framework to GenAI-generated text in academic contexts brings strengths and challenges that must be carefully considered.

One of the key strengths of PPM is its acknowledgment of the collaborative nature of human–AI interaction in the writing process. By framing hybrid human–AI writing as normal, Eaton recognizes that AI tools will increasingly co-create content with human authors. This perspective moves away from punitive approaches and instead promotes an inclusive view of authorship that embraces GenAI as a legitimate contributor. Current temperaments and attitudes do not permit such collaboration (COPE, 2023). This is particularly relevant in an academic context, where the contribution of AI can significantly enhance research output, both in speed and in scope.

However, a significant challenge is how responsibility and accountability are attributed in academic settings. While PPM emphasizes that humans retain ultimate responsibility for the work, it does not fully address the complexities of attributing intellectual ownership when a GenAI tool generates a substantial portion of content. Is attribution relevant only because of human egos, or is something else central to it? This ambiguity raises questions about authorship ethics, particularly concerning GenAI's role in generating text that extends beyond mere editorial assistance to producing substantive content. Additionally, the framework does not sufficiently tackle the issue of originality, especially in cases where GenAI tools are trained on existing academic literature. Does the human-generated content that was used in training the first generation of LLMs remain key, or, after a certain number of iterations of *synthetic data* (content generated by GenAI and used to train subsequent models of LLMs/AIs), can the creativity can be said to be exclusively GenAI's? As GenAI-generated content evolves, it becomes increasingly difficult to determine the true origin of ideas, potentially complicating authorship attribution. This problem will likely exacerbate when synthetic data usage to train subsequent AI models increases.

Another point of concern is referencing GenAI-generated content. As AI models continue to update and generate content that is not static and not necessarily reproducible in subsequent iterations, traditional referencing methods, which rely on the static and searchable features of knowledge repositories, may be insufficient and need substantial reform. It is unclear to what extent PPM recognizes and addresses this issue. It leaves room for further exploration of how to establish a reliable system for referencing AI-generated material.

Examples of PPM Applied to GenAI Content

Eaton's (2023) six tenets provide a framework for rethinking authorship, and each tenet can be applied to GenAI content in the academic setting. These hypothetical examples are presented in Table 7.1.

Table 7.1 PPM examples by each tenet

Tenet of PPM	Example
Hybrid human–AI writing will become normal	A professor uses GenAI to generate basic formatting and a bibliography for a research article. The GenAI helps organize citations according to the required style guide, while the professor focuses on content quality.
Human creativity is enhanced	A scholar submits a draft introduction and asks GenAI to generate various ways to phrase the introduction of a research paper, selecting the most effective version. The GenAI acts as a stylistic aid, refining the human draft.
Language barriers disappear	A researcher working in a multilingual team uses GenAI to generate summaries of research articles in different languages, ensuring that the core insights are accessible to all team members, regardless of their language proficiency. The GenAI helps create consistent, readable summaries across various languages, facilitating smoother collaboration without perfect translations.
Humans can relinquish control, but not responsibility	A professor uses GenAI to suggest potential improvements to the structure of a research paper's discussion section. While the GenAI proposes changes to the flow of arguments, the professor carefully reviews and revises only those suggestions that align with the research's intent and ensures accuracy before submission, thereby retaining responsibility.
Attribution remains important	A researcher uses GenAI to draft a portion of a literature review by generating summaries of key articles. In the final paper, the researcher includes a note specifying that the GenAI was used to assist in summarizing these sources while ensuring that all cited works are properly referenced according to academic standards.
Historical definitions of plagiarism no longer apply	A research team uses GenAI to synthesize data from open-access publications. While the GenAI aggregates information, the team ensures that proper citations are included for all referenced studies, maintaining scholarly standards.

Note: These are arbitrary examples. The author is unaware of the extent to which GenAI is being used in these ways. This table provides practical examples of Eaton's six tenets of postplagiarism (PPM) in the context of Generative AI (GenAI):Hybrid human–AI writing will become normal: A professor uses GenAI to format and create bibliographies while focusing on content quality.Human creativity is enhanced: A scholar refines an introduction draft with GenAI-generated phrasing options.Language barriers disappear: GenAI generates multilingual summaries for research articles, facilitating collaboration.Humans can relinquish control, but not responsibility: A professor revises GenAI-suggested structural changes to align with research goals.Attribution remains important: A researcher uses GenAI to summarize articles and acknowledges its assistance.Historical definitions of plagiarism no longer apply: GenAI synthesizes data from open-access publications while maintaining proper citations.

But for these ideas to take hold, people must accept them. Their attitudes toward GenAI in academic writing and the concept of PPM will play a crucial role. Whether that is happening or not is reported here to contribute to the ongoing discourse on rethinking authorship in a GenAI-driven academic world.

RESEARCH DESIGN

This chapter is founded upon a quantitative study that investigated public sentiment regarding the concept of authorship and the principles of postplagiarism in the age of AI, drawing on Eaton's (2023) PPM framework. The study recruited participants from Canada and the US through Amazon's Mechanical Turk (MTurk) service. The only requirement was that participants were proficient in the English language and had completed an undergraduate degree in any discipline.

A structured survey instrument was developed, comprising three sections: demographic information, AI usage scenarios, and gauging participant impressions on postplagiarism elements through a Likert scale. The survey began by gathering demographic information about participants (age, gender, primary language). This section ensured the collection of basic participant characteristics to facilitate demographic analysis. Subsequently, participants were asked whether they had utilized GenAI before being presented with a scenario to assess their views on authorship. The scenario-based questions were designed to elicit participants' opinions on the attribution of authorship when GenAI is involved. Finally, participants were provided with 18 statements related to the six tenets of postplagiarism and were requested to rate each using a Likert scale. These statements were constructed to measure participants' agreement or disagreement with various aspects of postplagiarism.

Data analysis involved descriptive statistics to summarize the demographic information and the frequency of responses to the survey questions. Correlation analyses were performed to explore the relationships between agreement with postplagiarism elements and demographic/AI usage variables. Statistical significance was determined using appropriate tests, such as Pearson's correlation coefficient, with a *p-value* threshold set at 0.01.

FINDINGS AND DISCUSSION

In this section, I present the findings from the survey and discuss their implications. In total, there were 155 survey respondents, of whom 49% ($n = 76$) were male and 48.4% ($n = 75$) were female (two respondents did not disclose their gender, one identified as two-spirited, and one identified as non-binary); 78.7% ($n = 122$) of the respondents used GenAI, and only 20% ($n = 31$) did not (two did not disclose). A noteworthy point is that the current advanced models available to us were not available when the data were collected. All the participants reported English as their primary language. Their ages ranged from 21 to 72, with a median age of 42 and a mean age of 44.6 ± 0.87 years.

The participants were asked the following question:

> Imagine you have a document written by you or someone else. You upload this document to a GenAI tool (similar to ChatGPT, Gemini, or Meta) and request that it be summarized in a specific way. After several iterations, you are satisfied with the generated summary. In this case, who do you believe should be credited as the author?

The responses are summarized in Table 7.2.

The largest proportion of participants (*n* = 43, 29.05%) believed that authorship should be credited solely to the original author of the piece. These individuals valued and highlighted the importance of recognizing the work of the original author, regardless of the extent of changes made and the role the prompter and AI had in the revised text.

The co-authorship attributed to the original author, the prompter, and the GenAI (*n* = 37, 25%) indicates evolving attitudes toward what authorship might mean. The original author provides the initial idea; the prompter tailors the idea within the context where they apply the initial idea; and the GenAI lends its linguistic prowess to compose a grammatically correct amalgam.

Table 7.2 Responses to the scenario concerning authorship

Option	No. of responses (***n*** =)	Percentage (%)
Original author (A)	43	29.05
Prompter (P)	33	22.30
AI tool used (AI)	20	13.51
Unattributed	6	4.05
Prompter and AI (P & AI)	9	6.08
Original author, prompter, and AI (A, P, & AI)	37	25.00
Total	148	100.00

Note: Prompter (P) = the human assessing the AI-generated output and giving prompts to revise. AI tool used (AI) is the program used (such as ChatGPT). Unattributed = participants did not know to whom to attribute authorship. Seven of the 155 survey respondents did not respond, and hence n = 148. This table shows survey participants' views on who should receive authorship credit when GenAI aids in document revision:29.05% attributed credit solely to the original author.25% supported shared authorship among the original author, prompter, and AI.13.51% believed authorship should go solely to GenAI.

The shift towards collaborative efforts and shared credit within creative processes, where expertise from various sources is put together, is a recognition of Woodmansee and Jaszi's (1994) sentiment quoted at the beginning of the chapter. This approach values each contributor's role and recognizes their unique contributions while emphasizing the collective effort that brings it all together.

Only 20 of the 148 participants (13.51%) expressed the belief that authorship should be credited solely to GenAI, implying that, while the role of AI is increasing, it is not yet prominent in influencing authorship credit. Whether this sentiment will ever evolve will need to be tested periodically in the coming years. A question was posed to the participants to gauge their attitudes towards AI: Do you think *the impressions on the use of GenAI will evolve to be more permissible?* Responses are summarized in Figure 7.1.

The general attitude was that public sentiments would evolve to become more permissive towards GenAI use for various kinds of work. In fact, 102 out of 121 (84.3%) participants predicted that the attitudes towards AI use would change towards being more accepted. Only 19 participants (15.7%) were unsure or predicted that attitudes would not be permissible. Within the permissible prediction category, a significant number of participants (n = 41, 40.2%) thought this attitude change would happen in the next five to ten years. If and when that change in attitude among the general public occurs, the idea of

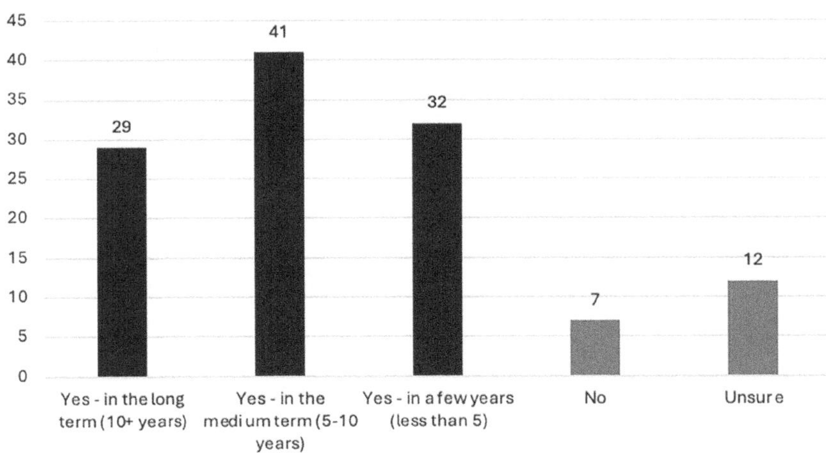

Source: Authors.

Figure 7.1 *Responses to AI permissibility*

authorship would matter less if the ideas generated are serviceable or if the attribution can be made to the AI tool.

These findings suggest that attitudes towards postplagiarism tenets related to authorship are relevant here. The first tenet of PPM concerns issues of authorship, and the second tenet is about creativity. These two tenets are then deconstructed into elements or statements, as Eaton (2023) described. Each participant was asked to react to these statements (PPM followed by the number), and they are referred to here as PPM1 through PPM8, spanning the first two tenets.

The research instrument assessed these principles by obtaining participant feedback using a Likert scale based on three statements from Tenet 1 and five statements constituting Tenet 3. Table 7.3 summarizes participants' feedback regarding the first tenet of postplagiarism surrounding authorship.

The first tenet is composed of three statements that address the issue of authorship. The first statement of a partnership between humans and AI is gaining traction, with 91.8% agreeing or strongly agreeing with the idea. The agreement with the idea that hybrid writing will soon become normalized was less prominent but still commanded a majority (66.9%). The third statement, which questions the futility of investing resources in determining the author between AI and humans, was rejected: 59.5% of participants either strongly disagreed or disagreed with avoiding detection; only 30.2% agreed with dispensing with detection. This indicates that there are elements of Tenet

Table 7.3 Responses to hybrid human–AI writing will become normal (in %)

Statement	SD	D	No Op	A	SA
PPM1: *Hybrid writing, co-created by human and artificial intelligence together, is becoming prevalent.*	0.8	2.5	5.0	61.2	30.6
PPM2: *Hybrid writing will soon become the norm.*	2.5	14.9	15.7	43.8	23.1
PPM3: *Trying to determine where the human ends and where the AI begins is pointless and futile.*	23.1	36.4	9.9	20.7	9.9

Note: SD = strongly disagree; D = disagree; No Op = no opinion (or neutral); A = agree; SA = strongly agree. All numbers are percentages. PPM1 through PPM3 are the statements that comprise Tenet 1. PPM is the acronym for the postplagiarism statement; the number following it is a separate sentence. This table shows participant agreement, with statements about the normalization of hybrid human–AI writing:91.8% agree that hybrid writing is becoming prevalent.66.9% agree it will soon be normalized.59.5% disagree that differentiating between human and AI authorship is pointless.

1 (PPM1 and PPM2) that participants are more agreeable towards, while the opposite is true with PPM3. Overall, the agreement with Tenet 1 was low (average response 3.55), indicating a weaker or neutral response to the tenet.

The weaker response to Tenet 1 indicates distrust in AI-generated material and, hence, in attributing author status to AI. This is consistent with the findings on the attribution of authorship indicated in Table 7.2 (rows 3 and 5). However, there is hope among the same participants that attitudes towards GenAI acceptance will continue to rise. Whether that means co-authorship will be endorsed or AI will be granted solo authorship is still unknown.

Since creativity is a central component of writing activity (Göçen, 2019), examining public sentiments towards creativity is imperative to understand the subtleties associated with authorship. Table 7.4 summarizes participants' feedback regarding the second tenet of post-plagiarism related to creativity.

The second tenet comprises five elements represented by each of the five statements (PPM4 to PPM8). Of the participants, 54.6% agreed or strongly agreed that AI enhances human creativity, while 30.6% disagreed. This split is indicative of the wide disparity among the general population. AI was not seen as a hindrance to human creativity, as 45.4% of the respondents indicated, compared to 39.7% who thought it hinders human creativity. There was a high degree of agreement (99.2%) with the sentiment that humans can be inspired

Table 7.4 *Responses to human creativity are enhanced (in %)*

Statement	SD	D	No Op	A	SA
PPM4: *Human creativity is enhanced by AI.*	9.9	20.7	14.9	33.9	20.7
PPM5: *Human creativity is not threatened by AI.*	16.5	28.9	14.9	27.3	12.4
PPM6: *Humans can be inspired and inspire others.*	0.0	0.0	0.8	22.3	76.9
PPM7: *Human creativity may be inspired by AI.*	4.1	9.9	12.4	43.8	29.8
PPM8: *Humans' ability to imagine, inspire, and create remains boundless and inexhaustible.*	0.8	5.8	5.8	37.2	50.4

Note: SD = strongly disagree; D = disagree; No Op = no opinion (or neutral); A = agree; SA = strongly agree. All numbers are percentages. PPM4 through PPM8 are the statements that comprise Tenet 2. PPM is the acronym for the postplagiarism statement; the number following it is a separate sentence. This table summarizes participant views on the impact of AI on human creativity:54.6% agree AI enhances creativity.99.2% agree humans can inspire and be inspired by others.87.4% believe human creativity remains boundless despite AI's role.

and inspire others. There was also considerable agreement (73.6%) that AI can inspire human creativity, with only 14% disagreeing with the sentiment. Finally, 87.4% of the participants agreed that humans' ability to inspire and imagine remains boundless and inexhaustible.

Like Göçen (2019), Wise and Van Luyn (2020) propose that all forms of writing involve creativity, as writing entails the creation of new texts. This act leads the author to ascribe their name to the produced text. If that premise is true, ideas about creativity are inextricably linked with writing and, hence, authorship. Overall, Tenet 2 garnered moderate agreement (average response 3.99), indicating tepid agreement, which was marginally above Tenet 1. The relatively low standard deviation for Tenet 2 (0.72) shows some response variability.

The study also explored whether there was any relationship between the elements of postplagiarism on the one hand and age, gender, and AI usage on the other. This was accomplished by examining the correlation between postplagiarism statements (PPM1 to PPM8) against age, gender, and whether participants used AI. The findings are shown in Tables 7.5a and 7.5b.

Table 7.5a Correlations between agreement with postplagiarism items and demographic/AI usage variables: Tenet 1

PPMs	n	Age (r, ***p***)	Gender (r, ***p***)	AI use (r, ***p***)
PPM1	141	+0.033, *p = 0.694*	–0.104, *p = 0.220*	–0.080, *p = 0.346*
PPM2	107	**–0.319, *p = 0.001***	+0.221, *p = 0.022*	–0.118, *p = 0.227*
PPM3	44	–0.199, *p = 0.196*	–0.188, *p = 0.223*	+0.194, *p = 0.206*

Table 7.5b Correlations between agreement with postplagiarism items and demographic/AI usage variables: Tenet 2

PPMs	n	Age (r, ***p***)	Gender (r, ***p***)	AI use (r, ***p***)
PPM4	83	–0.138, *p = 0.213*	–0.121, *p = 0.274*	+0.218, *p = 0.048*
PPM5	62	–0.132, *p = 0.308*	**+0.273, *p = 0.032***	+0.089, *p = 0.492*
PPM6	153	–0.114, *p = 0.162*	+0.091, *p = 0.265*	**–0.276, *p = 0.001***
PPM7	114	–0.042, *p = 0.660*	–0.061, *p = 0.518*	+0.120, *p = 0.204*
PPM8	138	–0.039, *p = 0.649*	–0.049, *p = 0.568*	+0.013, *p = 0.884*

Note: PPM1 to PPM3 represent elements of Tenet 1, and PPM4 to PPM8 represent elements of Tenet 2. $p < .01$ indicates significant entries (marked in bold). PPM is the acronym for the postplagiarism statement; the number following it is a separate sentence. This table presents correlations between participants' agreemen with PPM principles and demographic variables (age, gender, and AI usage):Younger participants showed slightly higher agreement with hybrid writing becoming normalized.AI users displayed more agreement with statements about AI enhancing creativity.

Overall, in this dataset, the correlations between agreement with postplagiarism elements and the demographic variables (age and gender) and AI usage (AI use) were generally weak. The strongest correlation was between PPM2 and age ($r = -0.319$, $p = 0.001$), indicating a slight tendency for younger participants to agree or strongly agree with this element. Similarly, the correlation between PPM5 and gender ($r = +0.273$, $p = 0.032$) suggests a mild gender-related difference in agreement. The correlation between PPM6 and AI use ($r = -0.276$, $p = 0.001$) indicates a slight difference in agreement patterns between AI users and non-users. This means that gender, age, or whether people use AI had an insignificant correlation with postplagiarism elements related to authorship and creativity.

The differing opinions on GenAI authorship and PPM reflect the complexity of integrating AI into academic writing. On the one hand, the gradual acceptance of hybrid human–AI authorship suggests an openness to collaboration with AI, particularly in enhancing creativity and efficiency. However, the hesitation to fully attribute authorship to GenAI reveals deep-seated concerns about the implications for originality, accountability, and intellectual integrity. Even conceptually, Eaton (2023) does not permit it, and neither does COPE (2023). These mixed sentiments highlight the challenges of navigating authorship in an AI-driven world, where traditional frameworks may no longer fully apply. They suggest that overcoming this reluctance will take much longer than enthusiasts expect or want. At the same time, the openness expressed by participants in this study presents opportunities for academia to rethink and redefine authorship, potentially fostering a more inclusive and dynamic scholarly landscape. Establishing clear guidelines, maintaining transparency, discovering new ways to cite dynamic content, and developing new ethical models will be crucial in addressing these challenges while embracing the opportunities that GenAI brings to academic authorship.

CONCLUSION

Exploring authorship in a GenAI-driven academic world reveals a complex and evolving landscape. Traditional notions of authorship—which the chapter identified as already being challenged before the proliferation of GenAI—are further complicated by AI systems' collaborative and often indistinguishable contributions. As discussed in the Introduction, survey findings indicate a shifting public sentiment toward recognizing AI's role in academic writing, with most respondents predicting increased acceptance of AI in the medium term (five–ten years). Hybrid human–AI writing is becoming normalized, reflecting a growing acceptance of the collaborative nature of AI engagement. Certain disciplines and personalities are more accepting of AI adoption than others. But this mumpsimus attitude will have to be overcome if there are to be gains in this arena. Yet, while there is a burgeoning acceptance of AI's role in enhancing human creativity, there remains a degree of skepticism about attributing authorship to AI. This skepticism will likely diminish as public attitudes evolve and AI technology becomes more integrated into everyday academic practices.

The concept of postplagiarism proposed by Eaton (2021, 2023) provides a framework for navigating these changes. Embracing this concept requires a fundamental shift in our perception of authorship, moving from a punitive approach to recognizing the unique contributions of both human and AI collaborators. This shift is not without challenges, as evidenced by mixed responses to postplagiarism's elements related to creativity and authorship.

To navigate the complexities of authorship in a GenAI-driven world, new models of attribution are essential. Attribution and citation models must account for the evolving roles that AI plays in creating scholarly work. One concrete recommendation is to establish clear guidelines for when and how to cite AI-generated content. If AI is used to assist in generating text, it should be acknowledged in a transparent manner, with appropriate citation practices that reflect AI's contributions without blurring the lines of human authorship. However, the dynamic nature of AI-generated content presents challenges: AI tools do not always produce identical outputs when prompted repeatedly, making traditional citation practices inadequate because no verification of the citation can be made. Developing technical standards that allow for the proper citation of fleeting, evolving AI content will be essential.

Another impediment concerns the acceptance of AI contribution. While the Committee on Publication Ethics (COPE) currently does not recognize AI as a co-author, new frameworks could differentiate between human and AI contributions, perhaps labeling AI as an *assistant* or *partner* rather than a co-author. Such models would ensure that human creators retain responsibility for the final product while recognizing the AI's role in content generation.

Educational strategies will also need to be developed to help students and faculty understand AI's ethical and practical implications. This includes understanding the capabilities and limitations of AI tools and cultivating critical thinking skills to evaluate AI-generated content. Training on responsibly using and citing AI tools will need to become a core component of academic education. However, for that to happen, the faculty must develop their competencies and skills first. Presently, this is not occurring systematically on a large scale.

As AI becomes more integral to writing processes, it is essential that we redefine intellectual ownership in ways that balance technological assistance with human creativity. Authorship might evolve into a spectrum, with human contributions and AI-generated content coexisting, but where humans are ultimately responsible for curating, verifying, and endorsing the final work.

The evolution of authorship models to accommodate AI contributions will likely include flexible attribution systems, where AI contributions are transparently acknowledged and human authorship remains accountable. This evolution also requires the development of new skills and competencies for researchers and students in a GenAI-driven world:

1. Effective and Responsible Use of GenAI: Understanding how to prompt, evaluate, and refine AI-generated content will be crucial for academic success. Knowing when and how to integrate AI into the writing process without sacrificing originality will become a key skill.
2. Learning from AI Responses: By observing how GenAI generates text, students and researchers can develop better writing strategies. AI tools can serve as educational aids, allowing individuals to explore alternative phrasings or structures.
3. Citing Dynamic Content: Given that AI-generated text can vary each time a prompt is entered, researchers will need to develop new citation practices that account for this fluidity. Technical standards, perhaps requiring version control or timestamps, will need to be adopted to ensure that AI-generated content can be accurately referenced.
4. Evolving Academic Integrity Standards: AI's increasing role in writing will likely lead to new academic integrity standards. This will require cultivating not only technical skills but also attitudes and values associated with using AI ethically. Students and faculty will need to be educated on how to responsibly integrate AI into their work without crossing ethical boundaries.
5. Public Acceptance and Human–AI Collaboration: The greatest challenge may be public acceptance of hybrid authorship. As demonstrated in this study, people are keen to know what proportion of text is human-generated versus AI-generated. A cultural shift will be needed to prioritize the substance of academic work over the authorship source, recognizing that both human intellect and AI tools can contribute to the scholarly process.

In conclusion, rethinking authorship in a GenAI-driven academic world is necessary and inevitable. Clear guidelines and frameworks must be developed to reflect the evolving landscape of authorship. These guidelines and ideas should address a new set of questions: To what extent and for which tasks will AI usage be accepted? How would referencing change? In AI-cited work, referencing AI models with version numbers and dates might be inadequate, as AI could produce different references at another time. The question then arises: How will references be cross-checked if they emerge from an ever-evolving (non-static) AI model? In such a scenario, more robust interpretations of academic integrity will need to be devised.

These questions will linger and require systematic study, exploration, and creative solutions that will need to be accredited in terms of their pragmatic serviceability. Consequently, our concepts of what constitutes fair recognition and attribution for all contributors in creating scholarly works and fostering a more inclusive and collaborative academic environment will need to be reimagined and developed. Significant solutions will have to emerge from within academia.

REFERENCES

Azarbonyad, H., Dehghani, M., Marx, M., & Kamps, J. (2015, August 9). Time-aware authorship attribution for short text streams. In *SIGIR 2015: Proceedings of the 38th international ACM SIGIR conference on research and development in information* (pp. 727–730). Association for Computing Machinery. https://doi.org/10.1145/2766462.2767799.

Bold, M. R. (2018). The return of the social author: Negotiating authority and influence on Wattpad. *Convergence*, *24*(2), 117–136. https://doi.org/10.1177/1354856516654459.

Campbell, S. E., & Simberloff, D. (2022). Forty years of invasion research: More papers, more collaboration … bigger impact? *NeoBiota*, *75*, 57–77. https://doi.org/10.3897/neobiota.75.86949.

Castro, E., Sinha, S., & Moran, C. (2023, December 18). How artificial intelligence can personalize education. *IEEE Spectrum*. https://spectrum.ieee.org/how-ai-can-personalize-education.

Committee on Publication Ethics (COPE). (2023, February 13). Authorship and AI tools: COPE position statement. https://publicationethics.org/cope-position-statements/ai-author.

Eaton, S. E. (2021). *Plagiarism in higher education: Tackling tough topics in academic integrity*. Bloomsbury.

Eaton, S. E. (2023). Postplagiarism: Transdisciplinary ethics and integrity in the age of artificial intelligence and neurotechnology. *International Journal of Educational Integrity*, *19*, Article 23. https://doi.org/10.1007/s40979-023-00144-1.

Ebrahimi, S., & Ebrahimi, A. (2021). Ethical challenges around multiple authorship in journal articles. *Journal of Archives in Military Medicine*, *8*(4), Article e111263. https://doi.org/10.5812/jamm.111263.

Göçen, G. (2019). The effect of creative writing activities on elementary school students' creative writing achievement, writing attitude and motivation. *Journal of Language and Linguistic Studies*, *15*(3), 1032–1044. https://doi.org/10.17263/jlls.631547.

Kobis, N., & Mossink, L. D. (2021). Artificial intelligence versus Maya Angelou: Experimental evidence that people cannot differentiate AI-generated from human-written poetry. *Computers in Human Behavior*, *114*, Article 106553. https://doi.org/10.1016/j.chb.2020.106553.

Kumar, R., & McGray, R. (2024, August 15). Global trends in generative artificial intelligence adoption: A quantitative survey of postsecondary students on the adoption of generative AI technologies [Paper presentation]. 10th annual Digital

Pedagogy Institute conference, Waterloo, ON, Canada. http://hdl.handle.net/10464/18633.
Kumar, R., & Mindzak, M. (2024). Who wrote this? Detecting artificial intelligence-generated text from human-written text. *Canadian Perspectives on Academic Integrity*, *7*(1), 1–9. https://doi.org/10.55016/ojs/cpai.v7i1.77675.
Lemmens, T., & Srinivasan, S. (2022). Authorship controversies in academic publication: Implications for science and the research environment. *Indian Journal of Medical Ethics*, *7*(3), 179–183. https://doi.org/10.20529/ijme.2022.051.
Lin, Z. (2023, January 30). *Modernizing authorship criteria and transparency practices to facilitate honest, open, and equitable team science*. PsyArXiv. https://doi.org/10.31234/osf.io/s6h58.
Nawaz, S. (2016). Authorship and content analysis of engineering education research: A case study. *International Journal of Engineering Pedagogy*, *6*(2), 39. https://doi.org/10.3991/ijep.v6i2.5577.
Rojas, L I. (2021). On conversation and authorship: Legal frameworks for collaborative methodologies. *International Journal of Qualitative Methods*, *20*. https://doi.org/10.1177/1609406921993289.
Schumpeter. (2024, January 11). AI can transform education for the better. *The Economist*. https://www.economist.com/business/2024/01/11/ai-can-transform-education-for-the-better.
Spurrier, A., & Kulesa, A. (2023, November 16). Reimagined: AI can be a catalyst for a more learner-centered system of education, if done right. Thomas B. Fordham Institute. https://fordhaminstitute.org/national/commentary/reimagined-ai-can-be-catalyst-more-learner-centered-system-education-if-done.
Vasilevsky, N., Hosseini, M., Teplitzky, S., Ilik, V., Mohammadi, E., Schneider, J., Kern, B., Colomb, J., Edmunds, S., Gutzman, K. E., Himmelstein, D., White, M., Smith, B., O'Keefe, L. L., Haendel, M., & Holmes, K. (2020). Is authorship sufficient for today's collaborative research? A call for contributor roles. *Accountability in Research*, *28*(1), 23–43. https://doi.org/10.1080/08989621.2020.1779591.
Wise, B., & Van Luyn, A. (2020). Not "all writing is creative writing" and that's OK: Inter/disciplinary collaboration in writing and writing studies. *Text*, *24*(59). https://doi.org/10.52086/001c.23485.
Woodmansee, M., & Jaszi, P. (1994). *The construction of authorship: Textual ownership in the modern world*. Duke University Press.
Zawacki-Richter, O., Marin, V. I., Bond, M., & Gouverneur, F. (2019). Systematic review of research on artificial intelligence applications in higher education – where are the educators? *International Journal of Educational Technology in Higher Education*, *16*, Article 39. https://doi.org/10.1186/s41239-019-0171-0.
Zutshi, A., McDonald, G., & Kalejs, L. (2012, January 6). Challenges in collaborative writing: Addressing authorship attribution. *European Business Review*, *24*(1), 28–46. https://doi.org/10.1108/09555341211191535.

8. The double-edged sword of generative AI for assessment: Efficiency versus homogenization

Alwyn Vwen Yen Lee

INTRODUCTION

Generative artificial intelligence (GenAI) has emerged as a powerful force that has reshaped various aspects of our lives, and its impact on education is no exception. While GenAI offers unprecedented efficiency in learning and assessment, its potential to homogenize learning experiences in content and thought processes means that educators must grapple with the tensions that emerge with the use of GenAI in classrooms and learning environments (Alasadi & Baiz, 2023). This chapter explores this double-edged sword, examining how educators can navigate this dynamic landscape via a balanced approach and through the concept of retuning assessment strategies and practices (Lee, 2024) in the face of technological disruptions such as GenAI.

Traditionally, assessment lies at the center of student experience and strongly influences student learning (Ramsden, 2003), and the need to get assessment right—whatever 'right' means in various contexts—is itself a tricky task (O'Donovan et al., 2004). Hence, educators have relied heavily on summative assessments such as written assignments to gauge student learning, and these methods have served their purpose in capturing snapshots of what a student has interpreted, applied, and explained while working on assigned tasks (Brown & Race, 2012).

As students used to copy from library books and now leverage alternative internet resources to construct their writing, the rise of anti-plagiarism software such as Turnitin has been helpful in mitigating blatant plagiarism, with a primary focus on identifying text similarity against databases of existing content. With students gaining easier access to GenAI tools, Turnitin (2024) reports that about 11% of over 200 million papers from worldwide educational institutions have been reviewed since 2023, with AI writing present in about 20% of the papers. This is done using its AI writing detection feature, which has shown high accuracy in distinguishing AI-generated papers and human-generated papers (Walters, 2023). To further highlight the growing concern and prevalence of AI writing in the classroom, Shaw et al. (2023) found that nearly half of surveyed students from a wide range of higher education institutions across the United States have used GenAI tools on a frequent daily and weekly basis for their work. This number is expected to grow and presents a cause for concern, as trusting relationships between teachers and students have deteriorated due to the use of GenAI (Luo, 2024).

Furthermore, when tools such as ChatGPT can readily generate seemingly original content, the integrity of traditional assessments is jeopardized. Imagine this: a student submits a GenAI-generated essay that demonstrates a flawless grasp of vocabulary and grammar but lacks real depth of understanding. The assessment by AI-aided assessment tools may not detect any writing issues, but the essay does not pass the scrutiny of a trained teacher who also has prior knowledge of the student's actual writing capabilities. Should the teacher penalize the student based on personal suspicions and experience, or should they mark the essay as it stands as the student's best work, and hope that it does not happen again? This scenario, sadly, is no longer a hypothetical concern, considering the ease with which GenAI can synthesize information and mimic human writing (Ferrara, 2024), therefore eroding educators' trust in traditional assessment methods and demanding a critical re-evaluation of our practices.

The solution lies not in abandoning assessment altogether, but rather in *retuning* our approach and adapting to the evolving educational landscape (Lee, 2024). Retuning requires educators to be flexible and adaptable, constantly re-evaluating and refining assessment strategies in light of technological advancements. When considering retuning in the age of AI, educators should explore alternative strategies appropriate for AI-enabled contexts and scenarios, with the realization that AI-powered tools may already have automated and replaced certain assessment functions. Thus, educators should look for areas that AI has not been able to replicate thus far and retune accordingly to students' needs. The onus is also on educators to switch up the format of students' assessment artifacts, ensuring a mixture of components that truly reflect students' efforts and can be blended for assessment and assessed regardless of AI's presence, while ensuring that the results of the assessment are valuable, meaningful, and actionable, and that the assessment will lead to future student learning and improvement.

In essence, educators may be faced with assessment tasks that already work to a certain extent but may require some modification to fit a given learning scenario. This does not imply that a complete overhaul is always required; there is still a need to retain certain aspects of traditional assessment. For example, assessing mastery of key concepts can still be valuable. On the whole, retuning necessitates a shift towards a more multi-faceted approach that emphasizes not just content knowledge but also higher-order thinking skills such as critical analysis, adaptive problem-solving, and independent thought.

This chapter builds upon the foundation laid in the proceeding chapters and delves deeper into the theoretical implications of GenAI, with a specific focus on the practical implications for assessment and learning. By exploring a range of retuned assessment strategies, educators can adapt their practices to different subjects and learning objectives. Alternative assessment methods that are less susceptible to GenAI manipulation can also be incorporated—such as interactive presentations that assess real-time communication skills, portfolios that track individual progress over time, and project-based learning that emphasizes process and collaboration—can also be incorporated, alongside their respective benefits. Further, by understanding the limitations of traditional assessment and embracing the concept of retuning, educators will be able to leverage GenAI's efficiencies while safeguarding against the homogenization of learning.

In essence, this chapter champions a balanced approach to GenAI in education, arguing that, by retuning assessment and learning practices, educators can create a dynamic and engaging learning environment that fosters critical thinking, problem-solving, and a love for lifelong learning, as it harnesses the efficiency and diversifying potential of GenAI. As GenAI continues to evolve at a rapid pace, educators who embrace the art of retuning will be best positioned to guide their students toward success in this ever-changing digital age.

THE EFFICIENCY PROMISE OF GENAI IN ASSESSMENT

We should not forget the purpose of classroom assessment in the pre-GenAI era but also be cognizant of its strengths and limitations. For decades, the cornerstone of classroom assessment has been summative evaluations such as written assignments and standardized tests, which offer a structured approach to gauging student learning and often provide a snapshot of a student's knowledge retention and big-picture learning outcomes (Kibble, 2017). Educators could assess a student's grasp of key concepts by evaluating their ability to recall and apply information in these assessments, but these traditional methods have inherent limitations when it comes to measuring a student's deeper understanding and critical-thinking skills (Behar-Horenstein & Niu, 2011). Traditional summative assessments often prioritize the *what*—memorization of facts and figures—over *how*, resulting in students excelling at regurgitation of information that helps them achieve high scores but without truly comprehending the underlying concepts. These assessments also do not readily reveal a student's ability to analyze information, synthesize ideas, or even apply knowledge to solve real-world problems.

The gaming of traditional assessment systems by students is becoming more prevalent—increasingly with GenAI tools—which has negative correlations with learning (Cocea et al., 2009), and is likely due to the difficulty and length of questions during assessments, the rigidity of the structure of assignments and tests that are topic-specific, and the lack of options for students to skip (Baker et al., 2008). Even then, these are also discrete snapshots of performance rather than nuanced views of learning over the longer term (Swiecki et al., 2022). These kinds of assessment also limit the opportunity for students to showcase their understanding in a broader context and fail to incentivize genuine curiosity in students. It has also become more critical to note that students' past ability to memorise enough information to succeed in traditional tests has now been superseded by the affordances offered by GenAI, which enable students to achieve short-term success in answering questions but cause them to also lose out in the long term, as they may achieve success in assessments without fostering knowledge retention or critical-thinking skills (Lee et al., 2023).

As a result of the rise of GenAI-based technologies, tools, and platforms, the effectiveness of traditional assessment methods is challenged, especially when such tools can synthesize and generate seemingly accurate, original content. This jeopardizes the integrity of assessments based on content recall and standardized tests. Recent studies (Huang et al., 2024) show that students use GenAI to confirm or challenge their responses, often relying on it to bypass the deeper cognitive effort required for learning. This behavior reduces assessments to surface-level checks of knowledge rather than encouraging deeper conceptual engagement.

With GenAI's capacity to rapidly generate essays, research papers, and answers, issues such as self-plagiarism and academic misconduct have become more prominent (Lim et al., 2023), making assessment outputs less reliable. This necessitates a shift toward process-based assessment methods such as open-ended questions, project-based learning, and peer-reviewed assignments, which focus on students' ongoing demonstration of understanding and application of concepts. As Porayska-Pomsta et al. (2023) suggest, this shift requires a reconsideration of the pedagogical approach that is appropriate for the target group and that incorporates more formative assessments that emphasize feedback and reflection, rather than relying solely on summative assessments that test only final outputs.

GenAI can streamline grading by automating tasks such as scoring multiple-choice tests, thus reducing educators' workloads and allowing more time for student interactions. However, over-reliance on automation risks simplifying assessments, limiting complex cognitive engagement. Silvestrone and Rubman (2024) warn that over-dependence on AI-driven systems may encourage educators to design assessments that prioritize machine-readability over genuine learning engagement, resulting in formulaic feedback that hinders students' strategic thinking. While automation boosts efficiency, it must be used thoughtfully to support, not replace, deep learning strategies.

In short, the limitations of summative assessments, the ease of GenAI-facilitated plagiarism, and the potential for students taking shortcuts that lead to superficial learning all contribute to the need for a more nuanced and adaptable approach to assessment.

The Homogenization Threat

The potential efficiency gains offered by GenAI are undeniable. However, alongside this potential lurks a significant threat: the homogenization of learning. This refers to the increasing global consensus that education reforms are required to meet the challenges of the 21st century, but has unfortunately led most educational systems to instead focus on a narrow set of cognitive skills in a limited number of subjects that achieve academic success and efficiency (Zhao & Gearin, 2016). This tendency also limits students' educational experiences in terms of curriculum, pedagogy, and assessment, leading to a global homogenization and standardization of learning experiences (Zhao, 2015).

With the proliferation of GenAI-based technologies and tools, efficiency is easily achieved via the facilitation of access to information trained with a large language model (LLM), and certain aspects of learning (e.g., summarization of textual works; Lee, 2024) are streamlined as a result. Europol (2022) has reported that up to 90% of online content may soon be synthetically generated by 2026. This has also led to concerns about whether a growing over-reliance on GenAI-generated content may impact and stifle critical thinking due to existing and inherent risks from a *copy–paste* culture, which originated from copy–paste syndrome (Weber, 2006) but has now re-emerged due to the use cases of GenAI for learning.

An example of such an instance is where students become more reliant on a wide range of easily available LLM-generated content and use it for completing assignments and work without considering the underlying rationale or the purpose of the assignment for which they will use it. Students therefore become passive consumers of information, accepting pre-packaged responses without questioning their validity, analyzing the underlying evidence, or formulating their own arguments. Efficient as it may be, this "copy–paste" approach to learning results in standardized thinking patterns and a possible decline in the ability to critically evaluate information, identify biases, and construct arguments. Learning also becomes a routine exercise of replicating correct answers that diminishes the joy of learning, rather than a journey of discovery and intellectual growth.

However, GenAI does not have to be the antithesis of rich and diverse learning. Some strategies can assist educators in harnessing GenAI to create a more diverse learning environment for students. For example, history education, which traditionally relied on textbooks and lectures to convey complex narratives of the past, is struggling to capture the attention of today's students. GenAI can be used to generate and work with a range of writing prompts (e.g., Steiss et al., 2024), scenarios, or research questions from vast databases of historical information that challenge students' thinking and encourage them to explore topics from new angles (e.g., Ballón Cusirramos et al., 2023). Imagine a history class where GenAI, as a chatbot, strikes up meaningful conversations with students over historical scenarios, prompting them to analyze primary sources, devise potential solutions, and defend their arguments. This approach, as seen from use in prior literature (Guo & Lee, 2023; Parsakia, 2023), can foster critical thinking, problem-solving skills, and the ability to analyze complex historical situations.

GenAI can also be leveraged to personalize learning experiences, catering to different student needs. Educators can provide LLMs with detailed classroom specifics, such as learning objectives and preferred teaching styles, alongside student demographics and the targeted educational outcomes from the series of lessons (e.g., Karpouzis et al., 2024). Tailored lesson plans using personalized dialogues or prompts can be guided by frameworks (e.g., Kong & Yang, 2024) and written based on a student's individual strengths and weaknesses, opening up the possibility of differentiated and individualized instruction that enhances student engagement, caters to diverse learning needs, and accelerates language acquisition.

While GenAI can generate factual information, it can also create conflicting or intentionally ambiguous content. What ambiguous content refers to is not the commonly known "hallucinations"—inaccurate or misleading by-products of GenAI—but rather the intentional creation of experiences that appear real yet are initially unrecognizable, offering the potential for multiple meanings that cannot be easily resolved though context. This will facilitate the capacity and opportunities for vital learning and intelligent action (Nicolaides, 2015). Further, ambiguity can compensate for semantic differences that remain a gap within human–computer interactions, and with some ambiguity built into GenAI designs, there is potential to use such designs to achieve the goal of seeking appropriate answers without propagating mistruths.

By embracing these strategies, educators can harness GenAI's potential to create a more diverse and intellectually stimulating learning environment, where GenAI becomes a reliable tool that educators and students can use to foster deeper analysis, critical evaluation, and achieve nuanced learning outcomes. GenAI can be a powerful tool for efficiency and access to information, but it should not replace the critical-thinking skills and intellectual curiosity that are essential for lifelong learning. The following section will explore how educators can retune their practices to leverage the benefits of GenAI while mitigating the risks of homogenization, ensuring a dynamic and engaging learning environment that fosters critical thinking, problem-solving, and a love for lifelong learning.

The Retuning Imperative: Rethinking Assessment

The limitations of traditional assessment methods and the homogenization threat posed by GenAI necessitate a fundamental shift in our approach to evaluating student learning. The concept of retuning is about assessing student work and development to match emergent needs (Lee, 2024), akin to a multi-faceted approach that deviates from traditional assessment methods, including memorization. While traditional methods are still important for learning (Hoque, 2018; Yusuf, 2010), they primarily measure factual knowledge and focus on rote memorization and regurgitation of information, which is of value but largely does not align with the skills and competencies required in the emergent GenAI landscape. Instead, the approach should be an ongoing process that involves re-evaluating and refining assessments to ensure they accurately reflect student understanding and promote critical-thinking skills in the face of evolving technologies.

Principles of retuned assessment

This multi-faceted approach, surprisingly, does not abandon current assessment methods and tools, but rather encourages building upon existing instruments and remodeling them to go beyond tried-and-tested tools and examinations. This approach respects that students have diverse learning styles, strengths, and interests. Existing assessments, which are already able to capture their unique capabilities and potential, should continue to do so. What the retuning approach calls for are "tuning deviations" from working assessment models or frameworks for students. This will be similar to how a musical instrument may be tuned perfectly using a machine, but not every guitar or violin around the world will be found to be perfectly tuned.

Likewise, by viewing every student as a unique learner with different needs, there can never be assessment processes or models that are perfect for every student. There should, however, be variants of assessment models, frameworks, and processes that can fairly assess students to identify performances of all qualities with minimal prejudices or biases. These variants will remain acceptable models that do not defy the recognized purpose of assessment—to diagnose, monitor, and direct student learning—in the current education landscape. Possibly, they can act as extensions to prepare students for sustainable assessment, encompassing the knowledge, skills, and predispositions required to underpin lifelong learning activities (Boud, 2000), especially within the emergent AI age.

The retuning of assessment also follows along the traditional summative–formative divide. While summative assessment remains important, it is vital to retune it to assess students' higher-order thinking skills, involving tasks that require students to analyze emergent information, synthesize content generated via GenAI, defend against GenAI-generated arguments, or even use evidence from GenAI appropriately to debate. The retuning of assessment using GenAI should involve the generation of plausible responses that educators can leverage and include in more complex and authentic summative assessments. These tasks (e.g., Salinas-Navarro et al., 2024) should move beyond simple recall by incorporating real-world problem-solving, case studies, or interdisciplinary projects that require deep analysis, critical thinking, creativity, and even multi-step problem-solving that GenAI has difficulty replicating or responding to in a convincing and humane manner.

In terms of formative assessment, AI-powered tools can provide immediate and personalized feedback, allowing students to track their progress over time. These tools analyze individual student performance and adapt feedback to target specific areas of weakness or misunderstanding, facilitating continuous improvement and deeper engagement with learning material. For example, AI-driven platforms such as Peerceptiv were used in studies (Li, 2023) to support AI-based online writing assessment across disciplines, using algorithms to evaluate student responses, generate tailored feedback, and suggest next steps, thus promoting an iterative learning process. In short, formative tools using GenAI not only enhance personalized learning experiences but also empower teachers to focus on higher-order feedback that is more insightful than students' original responses, which tend to be limited in scope (Lee et al., 2024), and are able to support student growth through targeted interventions at critical learning junctures. Alternative strategies include devising project-based assessments to incorporate digital-free components and involve varying levels of group work over time, or request students to build up personal portfolios and engage each other via interactive presentations and collaborative activities.

Implementation concerns

However, several impediments exist in implementing these strategies. The implementation of GenAI systems may boost productivity in some studies but can also work ineffectively and inadvertently increase user workload, as found in recent GenAI studies and demonstrated by Simkute et al. (2024). Suggested design solutions include the need for GenAI designs to provide continuous relevant feedback to users and to enable clear task allocation between users and systems as part of system personalization and flexibility.

Additionally, there are costs associated with acquiring and maintaining necessary resources, while additional time is required for both educators and students to adapt to new assessment methods, and challenges are posed by large class sizes that limit personalized feedback. Moreover, issues of academic integrity will arise: students may find new ways to circumvent assessment protocols and the issue of ensuring fair and consistent evaluation across diverse student groups is a complex one. The maintenance of such efforts requires institutional support, which should not be limited to the revision of pedagogical approaches that become burdensome to all stakeholders (McDonald et al., 2024). Rather, addressing these challenges will require thoughtful planning and adequate funding throughout the institution, as well as ongoing support for educators and students alike.

Despite these challenges, the proposed strategies are crucial for fostering dynamic and interactive assessment environments. All of the proposed strategies that are purposefully included in current assessments share a common trait: the need for students to be involved in ongoing work, producing continuous interactions with various stakeholders such as teachers and peers, and engaging with feedback while being supported in their growth and development. This course of action ensures that students can be better assessed via alternate forms of presentations and expressions of work, and are given opportunities to show how they were able to synergize and drive the work that they have supposedly developed and worked on. This also allows educators to verify that students completed their own work without significant reliance on GenAI tools and technologies.

Advantages of retuning assessment

For one, it is essential to maintain the authenticity of what educators are attempting to assess in the current age, by, for example, scaffolding GenAI curricula to promote authenticity and collaborative knowledge construction (Sabbaghan & Brown, 2024). In addition, by deploying alternative assessment methods, more opportunities are made available for students to engage with real-world tasks and demonstrate their skills and knowledge in meaningful contexts, mirroring the challenges they may encounter in their future careers. Educators will be able to conduct meaningful measurements of students' learning, and it is also critical to note that accuracy or correctness is likely not the main criterion, but rather the way in which appropriate modes of assessment can be implemented for evaluating student work that may or may not be assisted by GenAI technologies.

The abovementioned method may also be suited to assess higher-order thinking skills, focusing on assessing critical thinking, problem-solving, creativity, and innovation, which are all essential skills for success in the GenAI era, thus negating the possible decline in higher-order cognitive skills that some studies have found with over-dependence on AI use (e.g., Farrokhnia et al., 2023).

The retuning of assessment to allow for personalized and differentiated evaluation will also consider students' unique strengths, interests, and learning behaviors. However, some may argue that personalized learning systems, including those powered by GenAI, risk reinforcing existing inequalities or creating echo chambers that limit students' exposure to diverse perspectives. For example, more well-off learners may have greater access to refined AI-driven resources and high-quality data or learning platforms (Addy et al., 2023), while underprivileged students might receive less accurate or helpful feedback, exacerbating educational inequities and widening the digital divide (Giannini, 2023).

Still, it is critical to note that the benefits of GenAI alongside the incorporation of multiple assessment methods may help educators gain a more holistic view of student learning and also enable students to achieve a comprehensive understanding of their abilities, progress, and potential areas for improvement. Given the continued propensity of GenAI to hallucinate despite best efforts (Béchard & Ayala, 2024), there is potential for educators to design and use alternative assessments to address ethical concerns related to the design and implementation of GenAI for learning, such as plagiarism and the potential for deceit and the propagation of misleading information.

Retuned assessment methods and strategies in action

The incorporation of retuned assessment methods alongside traditional assignments can offer a more comprehensive picture of student learning and critical-thinking abilities. Below are some examples of retuned assessment methods, followed by possible strategies for using them in different disciplines:

- **Interactive hybrid presentations:** By instilling expectations for students to conduct well-designed oral presentations that contain digital (e.g., slides) and digital-free (e.g., skits, role-play) elements, these presentation types provide students with the opportunity to demonstrate content understanding through clear communication, effective organization, and the ability to answer follow-up questions. This format not only assesses knowledge retention but also reveals the extent to which students understand the material and can think on their feet, with little need to be concerned as to whether GenAI was involved in the generation of the slides or skit content. Although some students may potentially choose to memorize and stick to GenAI-generated scripts (e.g., classic acting), the difference from sincere performances generated by identifying with and understanding characters (e.g., method acting) will be clear.

- **Projects with varying levels of multi-party involvement:** Project-based learning allows students to delve into a topic in depth, encouraging research, critical analysis, and the application of knowledge to solve real-world problems. While GenAI will allow students to generate content that fulfills a project's requirements, students will still need to showcase their creativity, problem-solving skills, and ability to collaborate effectively through group presentations, demonstrations, or collaboratively written reports. It is also important to vary the number and types of participants within the project at different stages of the project's development trajectory. For example, educators can consciously encourage individual ideation at the start, followed by pair-work sharing and review, and allow groups to rise to a new level of understanding via constructive arguments that build on each other's knowledge and understanding.
- Personal and customized portfolios: Portfolios serve as both physical and digital collections of student work over time, demonstrating their growth, progress, and mastery of specific skills. However, the capabilities of GenAI in generating artistic artifacts should not be underestimated. Images generated en masse by GenAI cannot be effectively utilized by students curating portfolios designed to showcase their best, personalized work. Such portfolios allow educators to authentically assess students' understanding and track the evolution of their learning journey. For example, a student who started from scratch will be able to explain the important underlying designs that were considered before producing an art piece and turning it into a finished artifact.

A critical takeaway from these examples is that these alternative assessment methods are less susceptible to GenAI manipulation because they require students to actively engage with the materials, demonstrate their understanding in diverse ways, and apply their knowledge to novel situations. It is also pertinent to explore how educators can retune assessment practices across different disciplines. For example:

- **Understanding the human world via history:** Instead of solely relying on essays and the regurgitation of information to fulfill knowledge requirements, educators can incorporate oral debates where students argue from different historical perspectives. This can be supplemented with the use of GenAI tools and technologies. Educators can then assess critical analysis, historical reasoning, and students' ability to construct well-supported arguments.
- **Engaging in authentic science-based inquiries:** Rather than traditional means of examinations, educators can design projects where students will need to plan and conduct experiments based on research questions they

have formulated and improved using GenAI technologies. This mode of learning also encourages students to think critically and engage in problem-solving skills, and leverages students' ability to analyze scientific data for making claims, evidencing, and reasoning, all of which are critical for science education (Jiménez-Aleixandre & Erduran, 2007).

- **Appreciation of literature:** Instead of book reports, designs, or character interviews, students could be tasked with creating multi-media presentations that analyze a character's motivations, incorporating character profiles generated by GenAI to explore different interpretations. The use of interviews with characters from literature, as demonstrated by Yi and Shi (2016) in non-AI contexts, can be conducted using synthetic character generation to take on a persona from literature, therefore increasing authenticity and students' active engagement with the task, while allowing educators to critically analyze close reading skills and students' ability to construct a well-supported literary argument. With the emergence of newer bots and conversational GenAI as competent argumentative peers, it is highly likely that such interactions will become multi-modal and provide additional realism.

The above are several exemplifications of methods and strategies in action, but the possibilities for retuned assessment strategies are vast. Educators can adapt some of these methods for their specific disciplines and for varying learning objectives while ensuring assessment practices remain engaging, thought-provoking, and effective in fostering critical-thinking skills.

CASE STUDIES: SUCCESS STORIES IN RETUNING ASSESSMENT

Real-world examples have emerged to show the potential and effectiveness of retuned assessment practices. For instance, a study by Wu and Chang (2023) implemented GenAI for assessment and curriculum design for a project-based learning approach in higher education, allowing for the integration of GenAI into project-based learning. The innovative framework within the study focused on developing students' skills in applying GenAI as an effective problem-solving tool by understanding algorithmic mechanisms, identifying biases, and using AI tools to address real-world problems.

Another case study (Zhou & Lee, 2024) details the analysis of an art database of over four million artworks, where text-to-image AI significantly enhanced human creative productivity by 25% and increased the likelihood of receiving a favorite per view by 50%, but suffers from a drop in average content novelty. This suggests that artists' idea space is expanding but inefficient, and peer assessment of AI-assisted artists who can successfully explore more novel ideas is evaluated more favorably. Ideation and filtering are considered necessary skills in the text-to-image generation process. The resulting rise in "generative synesthesia" (Zhou & Lee, 2024) within the arts scene—the harmonious blending of human exploration and AI exploitation—lends credibility to the feasible notion of balanced efficiency and homogenization proposed through this piece.

GenAI-based technologies have also revolutionized once-traditional educational technologies such as word clouds (Koh et al., 2024), transforming them into efficient, accurate, creative, and accessible tools. This is important, as traditional word clouds are difficult to implement and use for learning and assessment. As a result, GenAI has enhanced existing capabilities of scaffolding teaching and learning for reflection, critical thinking, and content learning, and, in this study, has expanded the use cases of GenAI-generated word clouds to be used across international boundaries in China and Singapore.

These case studies demonstrate the power of retuned assessment strategies in promoting deeper learning and critical-thinking skills in the GenAI era. By moving beyond a reliance on a traditional combination of formative and summative assessments and adopting alternative methods such as projects, presentations, and portfolios, educators can ensure their assessments accurately reflect student understanding, encourage critical thinking, and foster a love for lifelong learning, all while navigating the evolving landscape of GenAI.

CONCLUSION

The emergence of GenAI tools and technologies presents both challenges and opportunities for learning and assessment in education. By embracing the concept of retuning, educators can adapt their practices to ensure a balanced approach. This involves moving beyond a reliance on traditional written assignments, incorporating alternative assessment methods, and strategically leveraging technology to create engaging and thought-provoking assessments. By prioritizing critical thinking and deeper understanding, and fostering a love for learning, educators can empower students to thrive in the GenAI era and become lifelong learners equipped with the skills to navigate a dynamic and ever-changing world.

REFERENCES

Addy, T., Kang, T., Laquintano, T., & Dietrich, V. (2023). Who benefits and who is excluded?: Transformative learning, equity, and generative artificial intelligence. *Journal of Transformative Learning*, *10*(2), 92–103.

Alasadi, E. A., & Baiz, C. R. (2023). Generative AI in education and research: Opportunities, concerns, and solutions. *Journal of Chemical Education*, *100*(8), 2965–2971. https://doi.org/10.1021/acs.jchemed.3c00323.

Baker, R., Walonoski, J., Heffernan, N., Roll, I., Corbett, A., & Koedinger, K. (2008). Why students engage in "gaming the system" behavior in interactive learning environments. *Journal of Interactive Learning Research*, *19*(2), 185–224.

Ballón Cusirramos, J. R., Higueras Matos, M. M., Lazarte Vera, E. A., & Del Carpio León, A. P. (2023). New technologies and the role of CHATGPT in teaching history. *Migration Letters*, *20*(S2), 1103–1112. https://doi.org/10.59670/ml.v20iS2.4594.

Béchard, P., & Ayala, O. M. (2024). *Reducing hallucination in structured outputs via Retrieval-Augmented Generation*. arXiv. https://arxiv.org/pdf/2404.08189.

Behar-Horenstein, L. S., & Niu, L. (2011). Teaching critical thinking skills in higher education: A review of the literature. *Journal of College Teaching & Learning (TLC)*, *8*(2). https://doi.org/10.19030/TLC.V8I2.3554.

Boud, D. (2000). Sustainable assessment: rethinking assessment for the learning society. *Studies in Continuing Education*, *22*(2), 151–167. https://doi.org/10.1080/713695728.

Brown, S., & Race, P. (2012). Using effective assessment to promote learning. In L. Hunt & D. Chalmers (Eds.), *University teaching in focus* (pp. 74–91). Routledge.

Cocea, M., Hershkovitz, A., & Baker, R. S. (2009). The impact of off-task and gaming behaviors on learning: immediate or aggregate? In *Artificial Intelligence in Education* (pp. 507–514). Ios Press.

Europol. (2022). *Facing reality? Law enforcement and the challenge of deepfakes*. https://www.europol.europa.eu/cms/sites/default/files/documents/Europol_Innovation_Lab_Facing_Reality_Law_Enforcement_And_The_Challenge_Of_Deepfakes.pdf.

Farrokhnia, M., Banihashem, S. K., Noroozi, O., & Wals, A. (2023). A SWOT analysis of ChatGPT: Implications for educational practice and research. *Innovations in Education and Teaching International*, 1–15. https://doi.org/10.1080/14703297.2023.2195846.

Ferrara, E. (2024). GenAI against humanity: Nefarious applications of generative artificial intelligence and large language models. *Journal of Computational Social Science*, 1–21. https://doi.org/10.1007/s42001-024-00250-1.

Giannini, S. (2023). *Generative AI and the future of education*. UNESCO.

Guo, Y., & Lee, D. (2023). Leveraging chatgpt for enhancing critical thinking skills. *Journal of Chemical Education*, *100*(12), 4876-4883.

Hoque, E. (2018). Memorization: A proven method of learning. *International Journal of Applied Research*, *22*(3), 142–150.

Huang, D., Huang, Y., & Cummings, J. J. (2024). Exploring the integration and utilisation of generative AI in formative e-assessments: A case study in higher education. *Australasian Journal of Educational Technology*. https://doi.org/10.14742/ajet.9467.

Jiménez-Aleixandre, M. P., & Erduran, S. (2007). Argumentation in science education: An overview. In S. Erduran and M. P. Jiménez-Aleixandre (Eds.), *Argumentation in science education: Perspectives from classroom-based research* (pp. 3–27). Springer Link. https://doi.org/10.1007/978-1-4020-6670-2.

Karpouzis, K., Pantazatos, D., Taouki, J., & Meli, K. (2024). *Tailoring education with GenAI: A new horizon in lesson planning*. arXiv. https://arxiv.org/pdf/2403.12071.

Kibble, J. D. (2017). Best practices in summative assessment. *Advances in Physiology Education*, *41*(1), 110–119. https://doi.org/10.1152/advan.00116.2016.

Koh, E., Zhang, L., Lee, A. V. Y., & Wang, H. (2024). Revolutionizing word clouds for teaching and learning with generative artificial intelligence: Cases from China and

Singapore. *IEEE Transactions on Learning Technologies*. https://doi.org/10.1109/TLT.2024.3385009.
Kong, S. C., & Yang, Y. (2024). A human-centred learning and teaching framework using generative artificial intelligence for self-regulated learning development through domain knowledge learning in K–12 Settings. *IEEE Transactions on Learning Technologies*, *17*, 1588–1599. https://doi.org/10.1109/TLT.2024.3392830.
Lee, A. V. Y. (2024). Staying ahead with generative artificial intelligence for learning: navigating challenges and opportunities with 5Ts and 3Rs. *Asia Pacific Journal of Education*, *44*(1), 81–93. https://doi.org/10.1080/02188791.2024.2305171.
Lee, A. V. Y., Tan, S. C., & Teo, C. L. (2023). Designs and practices using generative AI for sustainable student discourse and knowledge creation. *Smart Learning Environments*, *10*(1), 59. https://doi.org/10.1186/s40561-023-00279-1.
Lee, A. V. Y., Teo, C. L., & Tan, S. C. (2024). Prompt engineering for knowledge creation: Using chain-of-thought to support students' improvable ideas. *AI*, *5*(3), 1446–1461. https://doi.org/10.3390/ai5030069.
Li, A. W. (2023). Using Peerceptiv to support AI-based online writing assessment across the disciplines. *Assessing Writing*, *57*, 100746. https://doi.org/10.1016/j.asw.2023.100746.
Lim, W. M., Gunasekara, A., Pallant, J. L., Pallant, J. I., & Pechenkina, E. (2023). Generative AI and the future of education: Ragnarök or reformation? A paradoxical perspective from management educators. *The International Journal of Management Education*, *21*(2), 100790. https://doi.org/10.1016/j.ijme.2023.100790.
Luo, J. (2024). How does GenAI affect trust in teacher–student relationships? Insights from students' assessment experiences. *Teaching in Higher Education*, 1–16. https://doi.org/10.1080/13562517.2024.2341005.
McDonald, N., Johri, A., Ali, A., & Hingle, A. (2024). *Generative artificial intelligence in higher education: Evidence from an analysis of institutional policies and guidelines*. arXiv. https://arxiv.org/pdf/2402.01659.
Nicolaides, A. (2015). Generative learning: Adults learning within ambiguity. *Adult Education Quarterly*, *65*(3), 179–195. https://doi.org/10.1177/0741713614568887.
O'Donovan, B., Price, M., & Rust, C. (2004). Know what I mean? Enhancing student understanding of assessment standards and criteria. *Teaching in Higher Education*, *9*(3), 325–335. https://doi.org/10.1080/1356251042000216642.
Parsakia, K. (2023). The effect of chatbots and AI on the self-efficacy, self-esteem, problem-solving and critical thinking of students. *Health Nexus*, *1*(1), 71-76.
Porayska-Pomsta, K., Holmes, W., & Nemorin, S. (2023). The ethics of AI in education. In B. du Boulay, A. Mitrovic, & K. Yacef (Eds.). *Handbook of artificial intelligence in education* (pp. 571–604). Edward Elgar Publishing. https://doi.org/10.4337/9781800375413.00038.
Ramsden, P. (2003). *Learning to teach in higher education*. Routledge.
Sabbaghan, S., & Brown, B. (2024). Beyond conventional teaching towards networked learning: The role of generative AI chatbots in enhancing program evaluation skills. *Proceedings of the International Conference on Networked Learning*, *14*(1). https://doi.org/10.54337/nlc.v14i1.8003.
Salinas-Navarro, D. E., Vilalta-Perdomo, E., Michel-Villarreal, R., & Montesinos, L. (2024). Designing experiential learning activities with generative artificial intelligence tools for authentic assessment. *Interactive Technology and Smart Education*, *21*(4), 708–734. https://doi.org/10.1108/ITSE-12-2023-0236.

Shaw, C., Yuan, L., Brennan, D., Martin, S., Janson, N., Fox, K., & Bryant, G. (2023). *GenAI in higher education: Fall 2023 update time for class study*. Tyton Partners. http://www.tytonpartners.com/time-for-class-2023/GenAI-Update.

Silvestrone, S., & Rubman, J. (2024). *AI-assisted grading: A magic wand or a Pandora's Box?* MIT Sloan Teaching & Learning Technologies. https://mitsloanedtech.mit.edu/2024/05/09/ai-assisted-grading-a-magic-wand-or-a-pandoras-box/.

Simkute, A., Tankelevitch, L., Kewenig, V., Scott, A. E., Sellen, A., & Rintel, S. (2024). *Ironies of Generative AI: Understanding and mitigating productivity loss in human–AI interactions*. arXiv. https://arxiv.org/pdf/2402.11364.

Steiss, J., Tate, T., Graham, S., Cruz, J., Hebert, M., Wang, J., Moon, Y., Tseng, W., Warschauer, M., & Olson, C. B. (2024). Comparing the quality of human and ChatGPT feedback of students' writing. Learning and Instruction, 91, Article 101894. https://doi.org/10.1016/j.learninstruc.2024.101894.

Swiecki, Z., Khosravi, H., Chen, G., Martinez-Maldonado, R., Lodge, J. M., Milligan, S., … & Gašević, D. (2022). Assessment in the age of artificial intelligence. *Computers and Education: Artificial Intelligence*, *3*, 100075. https://doi.org/10.1016/j.caeai.2022.100075.

Turnitin. (2024, April 9). *Turnitin marks one year anniversary of its AI writing detector with millions of papers reviewed globally* [press release]. https://www.turnitin.com/press/press-detail_17793.

Walters, W. H. (2023). The effectiveness of software designed to detect AI-generated writing: A comparison of 16 AI text detectors. *Open Information Science*, *7*(1), 20220158. https://doi.org/10.1515/opis-2022-0158.

Weber, S. (2006). *Das Google-copy-paste-syndrom. Wie Netzplagiate Ausbildung und Wissen gefährden*. Heise.

Wu, T., & Chang, M. (2023, October). Application of generative artificial intelligence to assessment and curriculum design for project-based learning. *Proceedings of the 2023 International Conference on Engineering and Emerging Technologies (ICEET), Istanbul, Turkiye*, (pp. 1–6). https://doi.org/10.1109/ICEET60227.2023.10525933.

Yi, J. H., & Shi, C.-K. (2016). Synthetic character generation strategies: Character design through the application of novel conceptual combination strategies. *International Journal of Arts and Technology*, *9*(4), 346–379. https://dx.doi.org/10.1504/IJART.2016.081332.

Yusuf, M. (2010). Memorization as a learning style: A balance approach to academic excellence. *OIDA International Journal of Sustainable Development*, *1*(6), 49–58. https://ssrn.com/abstract=1672306.

Zhao, Y. (2015). Globalization in education. In J. D. Wright (Ed.), *International encyclopedia of the social & behavioral sciences*, 2nd ed. (pp. 247–253). Elsevier.

Zhao, Y., & Gearin, B. (2016). Squeezed out: the threat of global homogenization of education to creativity. In D. Ambrose & R. Sternberg (Eds.), *Creative intelligence in the 21st century* (pp. 119–138). Brill. https://doi.org/10.1163/9789463005067_009.

Zhou, E., & Lee, D. (2024). Generative artificial intelligence, human creativity, and art. *PNAS Nexus*, *3*(3), pgae052. https://doi.org/10.1093/pnasnexus/pgae052.

9. Transparency, assessment and the "Black Box" dilemma

M. Gregory Tweedie and Shahneela Tasmin Sharmi

BLACK BOXES – NOTHING NEW

This chapter will argue that the so-called black box problem of generative artificial intelligence (GenAI) in educational assessment, while certainly a challenging problem to solve, does not present an insurmountable one. As will be shown in the section that follows, educational assessment itself has been plagued by the black box problem, perhaps since its inception, and it may even be that AI represents a unique and timely opportunity to right a historical wrong. After defining the notion of black box in computing and GenAI, this opening section will make the case that opacity is evident not just in the realm of artificial intelligence but in educational assessment, particularly in higher education. This backdrop sets the stage for our central question: Are there ways GenAI might contribute to transparency in educational assessment?

First things first, by way of introduction: The black box problem of AI – it's a thing.[1] The present usage of the term *black box*, denoting something unknowable, is said to have originated during World War II, when military secrets and hardware were passed between Britain and America, quite literally, in a black box (Bucher, 2018; Von Hilgers, 2011). As traditionally understood in computing, the notion of black box approximates that of an interface: programmers being able to see into a system's functioning without knowledge of its inner workings (Tanenbaum, 1988). The term has expanded to a wide range of contexts, within the field of computer science and without, in broad categories and narrow, to denote opacity and inscrutability: for instance, the black box of cancer research (Campbell, 2023), of race and ethnicity (Guzzo

---

1 *be a thing* (idiom): to exist, especially when this is surprising. *Cambridge Advanced Learner's Dictionary & Thesaurus* (n.d.). Retrieved May 26, 2024, from https://dictionary.cambridge.org/dictionary/english/be-a-thing.

et al., 2015), of candidate selection in politics (Kenny & Verge, 2016), of academic degree classification for tertiary admission (Smith et al., 2024), to name only a randomly selected few. With GenAI, the black box metaphor usually describes systems that produce results without the need, or even the ability, to understand how they work. This recognition has led to calls for transparency in its use in higher education (Hillier, 2023), and has become a significant concern. While traditional assessment practices have long grappled with similar issues of transparency (as discussed in the next section), the increasing complexity of GenAI algorithms raises new challenges and opportunities. This chapter explores the potential of GenAI to either exacerbate or mitigate the black box dilemma in educational assessment, asking: Can GenAI contribute to a more transparent and explainable assessment process?

Second, by way of introduction: The black box problem in educational assessment – it's also a thing. Perhaps most famously, Black and Wiliam (1998) deployed the black box metaphor to describe classroom assessment, and their nomenclature gave rise to wide usage for critiques of inscrutability, from the classroom level to educational policy (Taras, 2009). Others acknowledge the black box of educational assessment, but view it unproblematically: Hattie (2009), for example, appears dismissive in discussing the opacity of tertiary assessment, sounding a lot like AI enthusiasts who emphasize the system results over understanding of the system.

> There is nothing wrong with black boxes: a ball-point pen is one and it works well – I do not want to know what is inside nor do I need to know, but it works fine. We have, in large part, a black box of assessment in tertiary education – it has worked for us for many years. We implicitly trust our academics to know what they value in their subjects, to set examinations and assignments, to mark reliably and validly, and then to record these marks, while the students move on, upwards, and/or out (p. 259).

To illustrate some of the negative results of the educational assessment black box, we take the case of Maisha, a secondary school student in Bangladesh,[2] for whom, as in many countries around the world, the impact of assessment represents significant educational and social consequences (Al Amin & Greenwood, 2018; Zumbo & Hubley, 2016). Maisha's written work will often be graded from unvalidated rubrics, which she may not really understand (Shaw,

[2] We have selected Bangladesh both because of its personal familiarity (one of the authors received the bulk of her formal education in this nation's school system) and because it represents one example (among many) of an education system where examinations heavily impact teaching, learning, and curriculum practices, and where the results from such assessments hold significant consequences for students' life trajectories (Al Amin & Greenwood, 2018).

2004), and likely without consideration of intra- or even inter-rater reliability (Jonsson & Svingby, 2007). Her performance on monthly, also unvalidated, grade-level-wide examinations determines classroom allocation; classes are, in turn resourced according to performance. Maisha's results on education-system-wide standardized tests have significant life-trajectory consequences, but may be more dependent on where she lives than the quality of instruction received (Au, 2022). Success in this exam-driven environment is critically dependent on the shadow education system (Lee et al., 2009), so Maisha draws heavily upon assistance from private tutors (when her parents can afford them). Past question papers are solved for practice until perfection is reached, yet the exact assessment parameters remain mysterious.

In an education system in another part of the world, perhaps less exam-focused but where assessment practices are still frustratingly opaque, Tinney describes an experience with a student (recounted in Anderson, 2018, p. 7) which is far from atypical.

> I leaned over the student's shoulder … and asked him if he could show me his teacher's feedback on his work and his current marks. He opened his electronic folder of social studies on his laptop and there was a list of assignments. … Besides [*sic*] one of the assignments, it said 100%. I asked him what that meant – "well I handed that in on time," he said.

"Good grades" are generally of significant import to students, their parents, teachers, school administrators, education ministries, universities, and employers. But the above example highlights the crux of the matter: grades are very often a black box. To the teacher of the social studies student described above, completing a learning task punctually warranted a grade of 100%. To another teacher, the same assignment might need to demonstrate critical analysis in order to score a high grade, and yet another teacher might require an accurate recount of facts. As Anderson (2018) asserts, grades can represent markedly different contrasting attributes,[3] distinctions which are often opaque to stakeholders viewing only a numerical or letter grade – even if used for highly consequential decisions. Grading practices vary considerably from teacher to teacher, school to school, region to region, and country to country, yet stakeholders usually see only a "final grade": A through F, a percentage score, or a Grade Point Average (GPA).

---

[3] Anderson (2018, pp. 7–8) helpfully suggests four contrasting ways grades might be presented: performance on a single task vs. multiple tasks; achievement at one point in time vs. achievements over time; achievement only vs. achievement plus other factors such as effort, attendance, and participation; and achievement of learning outcomes vs. achievement in comparison with peers.

Our point thus far is that, while GenAI certainly presents the possibility of a black box for educational assessment, opacity in educational assessment, as Jadakiss lyrically opined, "ain't nothin' new."[4] Students, teachers, and other stakeholders are often in the dark about how grades are arrived at and what they actually represent. The query at the heart of this chapter is whether AI/GenAI will make the existing black box of educational assessment even *more* inscrutable. If the answer is yes, we would perhaps do better to avoid it altogether. Are there any benefits to its implementation in education, and higher education specifically?

BENEFITS OF GENAI IN EDUCATION

There is a growing body of evidence regarding the benefits of AI/GenAI in teaching and learning in general (e.g., Ahmad et al., 2023; du Boulay, 2016; Kulik & Fletcher, 2016; Zhang & Aslan, 2021), and in higher education in particular (Chan & Hu, 2023; Meyer et al., 2023). Our assertion, based upon this evidence, is that higher education's students and faculty both stand to benefit: GenAI offers customized, immediate, and adaptive support in writing, in research and analysis, in research project administration, in the creation of multimedia materials, in grant proposal writing, in software coding, in the development of scholarly papers, in test question construction and preparation, and in literature reviews, while, for university administration, there are a multitude of ways in which GenAI can increase efficiency in administrative processes. A common advantage for all stakeholders involved is the presence of transparency: AI/GenAI can simplify complex decisions and break down illustratively the process by which decisions are taken. This might mean, for instance, that students clearly see the mark breakdown of their assessments and how it was arrived at; educators receive real-time access to data that helps to understand areas where students are struggling; and administration can view student and teacher modules through LMS interactions that can be used internally to gauge performance. For all three parties, we see exponential benefits to productivity, and even to overall quality of study and work life.

In terms of benefits to research in teaching and learning, the case of medicine is instructive: it is in this field that (Gen)AI offers exciting new possibilities for research aimed at improving human health (e.g., Libbrecht & Noble, 2015; Yu & Helwig, 2022). In such instances, it may be, as Samek and Müller (2019, p. 9) argue, that understanding and explaining *how* the AI made its

---

[4] *Ain't Nothin New.* Written by Shaffer Smith, Jason Phillips, Ermias Asghedom, Eliot Dubock, Dan Garcia, Francis Ubiera. From the 2015 album *Top 5 Dead or Alive.* Jadakiss. https://lyrics.lyricfind.com/lyrics/jadakiss-aint-nothin-new

prediction may actually be "more important than the prediction itself, because it unveils information about the biological, chemical or neural mechanisms and may lead to new scientific insights." A similar case may be made for insights gleaned through AI in educational research, since such systems can increasingly help us understand not just what was learnt, but *how* it was learnt (Zhang & Aslan, 2021). If the ultimate goal of education is more just and egalitarian societies (Dewey, 1916), then understanding how AI arrived at its conclusions may play a pivotal role in uncovering information to guide educationalists toward this objective.

In the view of the authors, a most significant benefit of GenAI is its ability to enhance *personalized learning*. Bloom's (1968) conception of mastery learning pointed out the variance between individual students' entry knowledge of a subject, as well as their individual capacities; logically, then, varying amounts of instruction are required to reach equivalent mastery. Bloom's well-known "2 sigma effect" (1984) demonstrated how personalized tutoring outperformed classroom teaching by two standard deviations, a finding that has inspired much work in artificial intelligence in education (AIED) (Holmes & Tuomi, 2022).

Similarly, educational theorists and policy-makers have called upon teachers to provide differentiated instruction (DI), a competency widely viewed as central to effective instruction (van Geel et al., 2019). At the same time as policy-makers call for DI, they simultaneously extol the virtues of diverse student populations; strikingly, policy-makers' practical guidance on *how* to deliver individualized learning to increasingly diverse classrooms is far less forthcoming. We envision GenAI as a solution.

To illustrate, we revisit Maisha, now a freshman engineering student struggling to master the content of an introductory course on Engineering Statics. Maisha, the first member of her family to attend university, is now a single parent of a young child, and working 20 hours per week in addition to her studies to meet basic living expenses. As with many traditional models for the delivery of higher education, the course content is delivered in one-hour lectures, thrice weekly, and attended by large numbers of students: in this course, more than 400. A tutorial conducted by an inexperienced graduate student is offered once a week, but these sessions are crowded, and Maisha struggles to have her questions answered. The professor's "office hours" are limited to three hours per week, and available time slots are often quickly booked.

In contrast, we envision a GenAI-enhanced learning environment which presents promising learning opportunities for Maisha's success.[5] Imagine that

[5] This particular example is fictitious, but all of the technologies listed are in existence at the time of writing and all have been shown in published empirical

the university's Learning Management System (LMS) models Maisha's interactions with it, customizing its performance as she accesses course materials (see Figure 9.1). An intelligent AI tutor designed specifically for the first-year engineering curriculum identifies Maisha's learning gaps and personalizes the course material in response; the intelligent tutor then provides her professor and tutorial leader with an anonymized aggregate report of the cohort's learning gaps, highlighting areas for whole-class review. The university's student success department uses machine learning models to predict struggling students through their interactions with the LMS, and reaches out to Maisha by email at critical points in the semester with a list of relevant supports. A virtual reality lab visualizes for Maisha key conceptual learning points of engineering

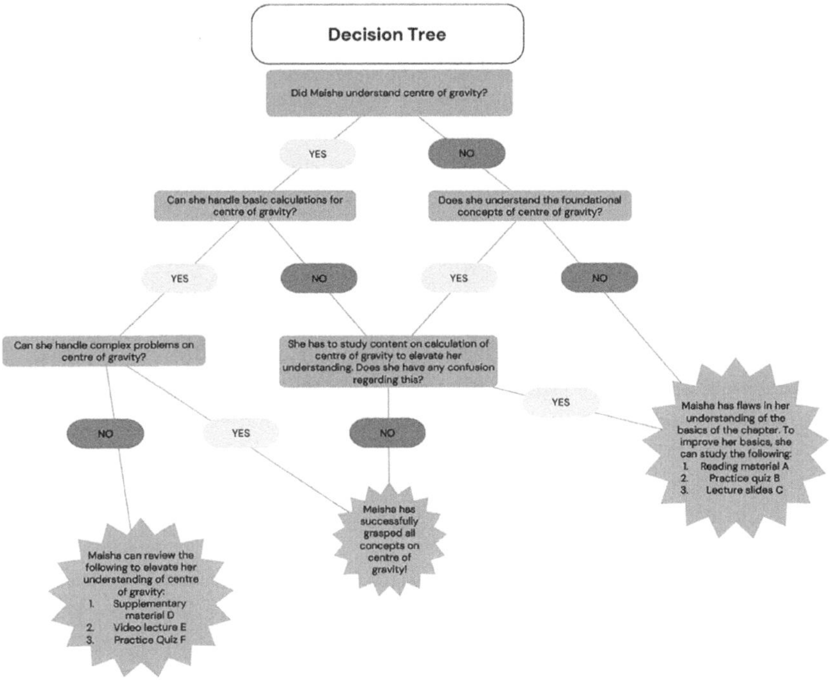

Source: Authors.

Figure 9.1 *Decision tree*

studies to positively impact teaching and learning (see Zhang & Aslan, 2021).

courses, delivering personalized gamification experiences for content mastery and increasing in difficulty as she interacts with it.

From our standpoint, the latter scenario offers vast advantages for personalized (and more socially just) learning and teaching compared with the former. Yet, the adoption and implementation of such a GenAI-enhanced learning environment pose significant challenges, chief among which are cost, scalability, matters of privacy, lack of institutional buy-in, educators' laggard adoption, and other factors (e.g., see Zhang & Aslan, 2021).

But what of the black box, the subject of this chapter? Can it be said to be *true* content mastery if Maisha interacts with an utterly opaque personalized learning system?

In one sense, yes, we suppose it can be. After all, as we pointed out previously, the higher education system as currently construed produces graduates with "final grades" assumed by stakeholders to represent content mastery. These largely unexplained "grades," of course, conceal multidimensional contrasting attributes that students, instructors, and institutions are hard-pressed to explain. Precise articulations of what these numerical or letter representations mean in terms of what a student actually "knows" or "can do" are thin on the ground. But this black box system, as Hattie reassures us (above), "works." These opaque representations move students up and out, factor in employer decisions for hiring, and are chief considerations in acceptance or rejection by graduate programs and scholarship committees. It seems all stakeholders are either largely content to implicitly trust academics who assign these black box representations called "grades" (or perhaps stakeholders are discontent, but accept the status quo in the absence of a viable alternative).

While this current state of affairs may indeed "work," we think it is far from ideal. We do not think there can be said to be real content mastery if learners like Maisha are interacting with completely unexplainable personalized learning systems.

The question, then, is whether the affordances of GenAI for personalized learning as described above can be offered as more of a *glass box* than the existing alternative – the subject of our next section.

GENAI AND THE GLASS BOX: HOW CAN EDUCATIONAL GENAI BE MORE EXPLAINABLE?

Addressing this multidimensional question requires multidimensional answers. The most obvious first consideration is that of the *audience* for the GenAI explanation. Imagine a decision made by AI on transcript equivalency for admission. A student with an unsuccessful application to the university may want to know something about how the decision was made, but likely in much less technical detail than the admissions officer who received the AI recommendation to reject this student's application; and the admissions officer even less than the AI researcher who is trying to improve the model (Khosravi et al., 2022).[6]

A second consideration is that of the *benefits* of an explanation. After all, adding an explanatory layer to a GenAI system, differentiated for the various stakeholders listed above, adds more costs to what is surely an already expensive proposition. In response, we reiterate the point made above. AI systems can uncover not only what was learnt, but *how* it was learned (OpenAI, 2024),[7] and understanding how learning takes place supports what (in our view) is the overall aim of education: namely, more just societies.

Our goal, then, is to provide the various audiences of higher education (students, instructors, researchers, administrators) with an *interpretable* or *explainable* GenAI system (Palacio et al., 2021).[8]

But what is it that makes a GenAI system interpretable? We put forward two often utilized explainability methods that we do not view as helpful. To begin with, we do not see the presentation of probabilities or statistical relationships as particularly useful for explaining a GenAI outcome. This is a generalization, of course, but we observe that, for many people, hearing the mathematically *most likely* cause of something, numerically presented, is less than fulfilling. Rather, the underlying cause of what is being displayed in statistical relationships seems to be preferred by most (Miller, 2019).

Second, we do not find it helpful to list *all* the potential causes for a particular GenAI result. Miller (2019) illustrates this point impactfully in discussing causal chains in Explainable AI (XAI). Ultimately, explanations of causation "can refer back to events that occurred during the Big Bang, but nonetheless, most adults can explain to a child why a bouncing ball eventually stops" (p. 5). The point being: it is not necessary to detail the entire chain of causation in order to provide a satisfying explanation. Of course, selecting *which* events

---

6 Khosravi et al. (2022) propose a useful six-part framework for considering XAI in education, encompassing stakeholders, advantages, drawbacks, tool design, approaches to explanations, and models.

7 Open AI's o1 Large Language Model, though in an experimental stage at the time of writing (Open AI, 2024), utilizes new methods for complex chain-of-thought reasoning and thus holds considerable promise for advancing our understanding of not just what was learned, but how.

8 Though acknowledging the shortcomings of doing so, for the limited scope of this chapter, we use *interpretable* and *explainable* interchangeably, following Miller (2019). For more precise definitions of both terms in XAI, we refer the reader to the very thorough discussion in Palacio et al. (2021).

among multiple to present as explanatory inevitably involves human bias, but "this an everyday thing"[9] – not at all unique to GenAI.

Following Miller (2019), we find *contrastive explanations* (CEs) to be of particular utility in making GenAI systems interpretable. The authors of this chapter are applied linguists by training and, in our field, a contrastive approach to language teaching has a long history (Lado, 1957). In a contrastive method of language instruction, teachers consider what structural differences exist between students' first language and the one they are attempting to learn, and provide explanations of grammar, vocabulary, pronunciation, and so on in both languages, highlighting the contrasts. In our experience, bi-/multilingual language teachers around the globe attest to the usefulness of this approach when effectively deployed in the classroom. In the field of philosophy, CEs are those which clarify "not only why some event A occurred, but why A occurred as opposed to some alternative event B" (Elzein, 2019, p. 1325). Insights from cognitive psychology have shown us why humans may in fact require these explanations (Lombrozo, 2006).

We envision (Box 9.1) how a contrastive explanation might be delivered to Maisha.

BOX 9.1 MAISHA'S CONVERSATION WITH XAI

Maisha: I don't understand the differences between trusses, frames and machines. Aren't they the same?

XAI: You can take a look at this table to see how truss, frame and machine can be similar and different in terms of their definition, applications, examples, and dynamic analysis.

Maisha: OK. How can scaffolding be an example of a frame? I know a different meaning of scaffolding.

XAI: I have been specifically trained to deal with queries in Engineering Statics. In engineering, scaffolding refers to a temporary structure used to support work crews and materials during the construction, maintenance, and repair of buildings, bridges, and other large structures. The primary purpose of scaffolding is to provide a safe and stable platform for workers to perform tasks at heights that would otherwise be inaccessible. Would you like some examples of scaffolding?

Maisha: No, that's fine. Can you please tell me why manufacturing equipment is a machine and not a truss?

XAI: Machinery is not classified as a truss because it involves complex assemblies with moving parts designed for dynamic tasks, whereas trusses are static structures composed of straight members primarily experiencing

[9] *Ain't Nothin New*. Written by Shaffer Smith, Jason Phillips, Ermias Asghedom, Eliot Dubock, Dan Garcia, Francis Ubiera. From the 2015 album *Top 5 Dead or Alive*. Jadakiss.

	axial forces. The fundamental differences in function, structural configuration, types of forces, and dynamic behavior distinguish machinery from trusses.
Maisha:	Axial forces?
XAI:	An internal or external force exerts pressure on a structure, causing it to experience tension. For example, pulling on both ends of a rope will exert axial force on the rope.
Maisha:	OK. A crane has moving parts as well. So it should be classified as machinery, right?
XAI:	Cranes have moving parts and mechanisms that allow them to lift and move loads, which might superficially suggest a similarity to machinery. However, the primary structural components and functions of cranes align more closely with those of frames and trusses. The main distinction lies in the nature of the structural elements (truss/frame) that provide the necessary support and rigidity for the crane's lifting operations. Therefore, while cranes have mechanical aspects, they are typically classified as structural systems (frames or trusses) rather than machinery.

Table 9.1 Maisha's conversation with XAI

Characteristic	Truss	Frame	Machine
Definition	A structure composed of straight members connected at joints, primarily experiencing axial forces (tension/compression).	A structure consisting of multiple members designed to support loads, experiencing axial forces, bending moments, and shear forces.	A structure designed to transmit and alter the direction or magnitude of forces, involving moving parts.
Applications	Bridges, towers, roof supports, cranes.	Building frames, bridges, support structures in civil engineering.	Machinery, vehicles, manufacturing equipment.
Examples	Warren truss, Pratt truss, Howe truss.	Building frames, crane structures, scaffolding.	Gear systems, hydraulic presses, engines.
Dynamic analysis	Primarily static analysis in basic applications; dynamic analysis possible for vibrations and dynamic loading.	Both static and dynamic analysis, considering vibrations, wind, and seismic forces.	Requires dynamic analysis due to moving parts and the need to study forces during operation and motion.

Miller terms this extra layer of elucidation, performing simultaneously alongside the algorithms that produced the result, an "explanatory model of self" (2019, p. 12). This explanatory layer is visually illustrated in Figure 9.2, below (adapted from Clement et al., 2023). Such *explanatory models* (EMs) are constructed solely for the purpose of providing explanations of the machine's decision. While acknowledging that EMs may in actuality be only approximations of the decision's complexity – with accompanying limitations (see, e.g., Slack et al., 2020) – explanatory approximations have been elicited in more easily interpretable forms such as decision trees (e.g., Frosst & Hinton, 2017).

With a contrastive explanation, the contrasts are drawn between two seemingly similar elements and differences are presented in simple terms. As depicted in the conversation in Box 9.1, the XAI draws a contrast between machinery and truss while explaining the main differences between the two. Readers will note that the contrastive explanation, though delivered by a machine, is done so in a social, conversational manner. There are many compelling reasons for providing XAI explanatory agents that simulate features of everyday human-to-human interactions, such as politeness, social etiquette, social face (cf. Goffman, 1967), and the like (Ribino, 2023). The idea that our interactions with computers parallel our everyday, real-world social relations is asserted by the notion of computers as social actors (CASA; Reeves & Nass, 1996), and a large body of research has accumulated investigating this paradigm (e.g., Gambino et al., 2020; Ribino, 2023). Since the importance of social dimensions of learning is widely acknowledged, and indeed underpins much influential educational theory (e.g., Bandura, 1986; Vygotsky, 1978), it is perhaps unsurprising that social aspects of knowledge acquisition would also apply to our learning from machines (Vygotsky, 1978).

CONCLUSION

We have acknowledged in this chapter that the black box problem of GenAI in higher education is a challenging one indeed. Lest higher education decision-makers be hasty in dismissing the use of GenAI altogether (if that were possible), we have been at pains here to remind readers that the black box of GenAI runs parallel with yet another black box problem in education: that of the assessment of learning in general. Yet, there is a possible solution: there exists a strong potential for leveraging the glass box of XAI to make the black box of educational assessment transparent.

Further research avenues, such as the development of new explainability techniques and avant-garde designs to simplify the complex procedures involved, can further demystify the algorithmic complications that exist, thus helping to leverage GenAI toward a more equitable world. Alongside this, longitudinal investigation of GenAI's long-term impacts on educational

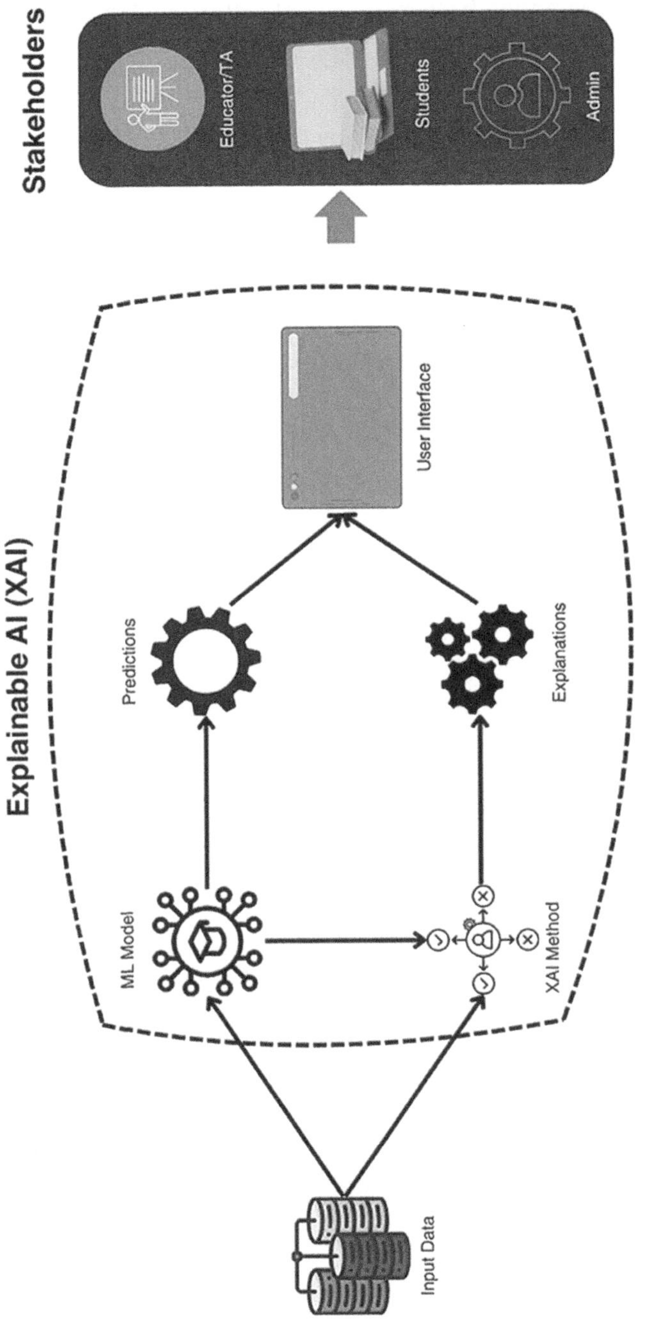

Source: Adapted from Clement et al., 2023.

Figure 9.2 Explanatory layer

assessment can assist in the further refining of GenAI/XAI systems, which leads the authors to hope for more transparent assessment. This is of utmost importance, given the evolving nature of GenAI and its potential impacts, both advantageous and otherwise. For instance, exploring how new developments in AI, such as self-supervised learning (Zhao et al., 2024), can positively impact the ability to understand and explain GenAI systems to stakeholders might mitigate some of the concerns.

The authors of this chapter are, admittedly, optimists by nature. But we see compelling reasons for hope that GenAI, deployed in higher education alongside an explanatory layer utilizing all that we know about how humans best learn, might lead us closer to a glass box of teaching, learning, and assessment: a giant step on the long path toward knowledge democratization.

Author Declaration: The authors declare that no generative artificial intelligence tools were used at any point in the writing of this chapter.

REFERENCES

Ahmad, N., Murugesan, S., & Kshetri, N. (2023). Generative Artificial Intelligence and the education sector. *Computer, 56*(6), 72–76. https://doi.org/10.1109/MC.2023.3263576.

Al Amin, M., & Greenwood, J. (2018). The examination system in Bangladesh and its impact: on curriculum, students, teachers and society. *Language Testing in Asia, 8*(1), 4. https://doi.org/10.1186/s40468-018-0060-9.

Anderson, L. W. (2018). A critique of grading: Policies, practices, and technical matters. *Education Policy Analysis Archives, 26*(49), 1–25. https://doi.org/https://doi.org/10.14507/epaa.26.3814.

Au, W. (2022). *Unequal by design: High-stakes testing and the standardization of inequality* (2nd ed.). Routledge.

Bandura, A. (1986). *Social foundations of thought and action*. Prentice-Hall.

Black, P., & Wiliam, D. (1998). *Inside the black box. Raising standards through classroom assessment*. GL Assessment.

Bloom, B. S. (1968). Learning for mastery. Instruction and Curriculum. Regional Education Laboratory for the Carolinas and Virginia, Topical Papers and Reprints, Number 1. *Evaluation Comment, 1*(2), n2. https://doi.org/https://eric.ed.gov/?id=eD053419.

Bloom, B. S. (1984). The 2 sigma problem: The search for methods of group instruction as effective as one-to-one tutoring. *Educational Researcher, 13*(6), 4–16. https://doi.org/10.3102/0013189x013006004.

Bucher, T. (2018). Neither black nor box: (Un)knowing algorithms. In *If … then: Algorithmic power and politics* (pp. 41–65). Oxford University Press. https://doi.org/10.1093/oso/9780190493028.003.0003.

Campbell, P. J. (2023). Demystifying the black box: from ignorance to observation to mechanism in cancer research. *European Journal of Epidemiology, 38*(12), 1265–1267. https://doi.org/10.1007/s10654-022-00935-9.

Chan, C. K. Y., & Hu, W. (2023). Students' voices on generative AI: Perceptions, benefits, and challenges in higher education. *International Journal of Educational*

Technology in Higher Education, *20*(1), 43. https://doi.org/10.1186/s41239-023-00411-8.

Clement, T., Kemmerzell, N., Abdelaal, M., & Amberg, M. (2023). XAIR: A systematic metareview of Explainable AI (XAI) aligned to the software development process. *Machine Learning and Knowledge Extraction*, *5*(1), 78–108. https://doi.org/https://doi.org/10.3390/make5010006.

Dewey, J. (1916). *Democracy and education*. Echo Library.

du Boulay, B. (2016). Recent meta-reviews and meta–analyses of AIED systems. *International Journal of Artificial Intelligence in Education*, *26*(1), 536–537. https://doi.org/https://doi.org/10.1007/s40593-015-0060-1.

Elzein, N. (2019). The demand for contrastive explanations. *Philosophical Studies*, *176*(5), 1325–1339. https://doi.org/10.1007/s11098-018-1065-z.

Frosst, N., & Hinton, G. (2017). *Distilling a neural network into a soft decision tree*. arXiv. https://doi.org/10.48550/arXiv.1711.09784.

Gambino, A., Fox, J., & Ratan, R. A. (2020). Building a stronger CASA: extending the computers are social actors paradigm. *Human–Machine Communication*, *1*, 71–85. https://doi.org/10.30658/hmc.1.5.

Goffman, E. (1967). *Interaction ritual: Essays in face-to-face behavior.* Routledge. https://doi.org/10.4324/9780203788387.

Guzzo, K. B., Nash, S. P., Manning, W. D., Longmore, M. A., & Giordano, P. C. (2015). Unpacking the "black box" of race–ethnic variation in fertility. *Race and Social Problems*, *7*(2), 135–149. https://doi.org/10.1007/s12552-014-9141-2.

Hattie, J. (2009). The black box of tertiary assessment: An impending revolution. In L. H. Meyer, S. Davidson, H. Anderson, R. Fletcher, P. M. Johnston, & M. Rees (Eds.), *Tertiary assessment & higher education student outcomes: Policy, practice & research* (Vol. 259, pp. 259–275). Ako Aotearoa National Centre for Tertiary Teaching Excellence.

Hillier, M. (2023, 22 July). A proposed AI literacy framework. *TECHE*. https://teche.mq.edu.au/2023/03/a-proposed-ai-literacy-framework/.

Holmes, W., & Tuomi, I. (2022). State of the art and practice in AI in education. *European Journal of Education*, *57*(4), 542–570. https://doi.org/https://doi.org/10.1111/ejed.12533.

Jonsson, A., & Svingby, G. (2007). The use of scoring rubrics: Reliability, validity and educational consequences. *Educational Research Review*, *2*(2), 130–144. https://doi.org/10.1016/j.edurev.2007.05.002.

Kenny, M., & Verge, T. (2016). Opening up the black box: Gender and candidate selection in a new era. *Government and Opposition*, *51*(3), 351–369. https://doi.org/10.1017/gov.2016.5.

Khosravi, H., Shum, S. B., Chen, G., Conati, C., Tsai, Y.-S., Kay, J., … Gašević, D. (2022). Explainable artificial intelligence in education. *Computers and Education: Artificial Intelligence*, *3*, 100074. https://doi.org/https://doi.org/10.1016/j.caeai.2022.100074.

Kulik, J. A., & Fletcher, J. D. (2016). Effectiveness of intelligent tutoring systems: A meta-analytic review. *Review of Educational Research*, *86*(1), 42–78. https://doi.org/https://doi.org/10.3102/0034654315581420.

Lado, R. (1957). *Linguistics across cultures: Applied linguistics for language teachers.* University of Michigan Press.

Lee, C.-J., Park, H.-J., & Lee, H. (2009). Shadow education systems. In G. Sykes, B. Schneider, & D. N. Plank (Eds.), *Handbook of education policy research.* Taylor & Francis Group. https://doi.org/10.4324/9780203880968.

Libbrecht, M. W., & Noble, W. S. (2015). Machine learning applications in genetics and genomics. *Nature Reviews Genetics, 16*(6), 321–332. https://doi.org/10.1038/nrg3920.

Lombrozo, T. (2006). The structure and function of explanations. *Trends in Cognitive Sciences, 10*(10), 464–470. https://doi.org/10.1016/j.tics.2006.08.004.

Meyer, J. G., Urbanowicz, R. J., Martin, P. C. N., O'Connor, K., Li, R., Peng, P.-C., … Moore, J. H. (2023). ChatGPT and large language models in academia: opportunities and challenges. *BioData Mining, 16*(1). https://doi.org/10.1186/s13040-023-00339-9.

Miller, T. (2019). Explanation in artificial intelligence: Insights from the social sciences. *Artificial Intelligence, 267*, 1–38. https://doi.org/10.1016/j.artint.2018.07.007.

OpenAI. (2024, 12 October). Learning to reason with LLMs. https://openai.com/index/learning-to-reason-with-llms/.

Palacio, S., Lucieri, A., Munir, M., Ahmed, S., Hees, J., & Dengel, A. (2021). XAI handbook: towards a unified framework for explainable AI. Proceedings of the IEEE/CVF International Conference on Computer Vision.

Reeves, B., & Nass, C. (1996). *The media equation: How people treat computers, television, and new media like real people* (Vol. 10). Cambridge University Press.

Ribino, P. (2023). The role of politeness in human–machine interactions: A systematic literature review and future perspectives. *Artificial Intelligence Review, 56*(1), 445–482. https://doi.org/10.1007/s10462-023-10540-1.

Samek, W., & Müller, K.-R. (2019). Towards explainable artificial intelligence. In W. Samek, G. Montavon, A. Vedaldi, L. K. Hansen, & K.-R. Müller (Eds.), *Explainable AI: interpreting, explaining and visualizing deep learning* (pp. 5–22). Springer. https://doi.org/10.1007/978-3-030-28954-6_1.

Shaw, J. (2004, Dec 2004). Demystifying the evaluation process for parents: Rubrics for marking student research projects. *Teacher Librarian, 32*(2), 16–19.

Slack, D., Hilgard, S., Jia, E., Singh, S., & Lakkaraju, H. (2020). Fooling LIME and SHAP: adversarial attacks on post hoc explanation methods. *Proceedings of the AAAI/ACM Conference on AI, Ethics, and Society* (pp. 180–186).

Smith, S., Sutherland, N., & Allen, D. (2024). Opening the black box of degree classification algorithms: towards a research agenda. *Teaching in Higher Education*, 1–11. https://doi.org/10.1080/13562517.2024.2302555.

Tanenbaum, A. S. (1988). *Computer Networks* (2nd ed.). Prentice-Hall, Inc.

Taras, M. (2009). Summative assessment: The missing link for formative assessment. *Journal of Further and Higher Education, 33*(1), 57–69. https://doi.org/10.1080/03098770802638671.

van Geel, M., Keuning, T., Frèrejean, J., Dolmans, D., van Merriënboer, J., & Visscher, A. J. (2019). Capturing the complexity of differentiated instruction. *School Effectiveness and School Improvement, 30*(1), 51–67. https://doi.org/10.1080/09243453.2018.1539013.

Von Hilgers, P. (2011). The history of the black box: The clash of a thing and its concept. *Cultural Politics, 7*(1), 41–58. https://doi.org/10.2752/175174311x12861940861707.

Vygotsky, L. S. (1978). *Mind in society: The development of higher psychological processes.* Harvard University Press.

Yu, C., & Helwig, E. J. (2022). The role of AI technology in prediction, diagnosis and treatment of colorectal cancer. *Artificial Intelligence Review, 55*(1), 323–343. https://doi.org/https://doi.org/10.1007/s10462-021-10034-y.

Zhang, K., & Aslan, A. B. (2021). AI technologies for education: Recent research & future directions. *Computers and Education: Artificial Intelligence*, *2*, 100025. https://doi.org/https://doi.org/10.1016/j.caeai.2021.100025.

Zhao, Z., Alzubaidi, L., Zhang, J., Duan, Y., & Gu, Y. (2024). A comparison review of transfer learning and self-supervised learning: Definitions, applications, advantages and limitations. *Expert Systems with Applications*, *242*, 122807. https://doi.org/https://doi.org/10.1016/j.eswa.2023.122807.

Zumbo, B. D., & Hubley, A. M. (2016). Bringing consequences and side effects of testing and assessment to the foreground. *Assessment in Education: Principles, Policy & Practice*, *23*(2), 299–303. https://doi.org/10.1080/0969594X.2016.1141169.

10. The pedagogical ethics: Navigating learning in a generative AI-augmented environment in a post-plagiarism era

Sarah Elaine Eaton and Mohammad Keyhani

INTRODUCTION

As generative artificial intelligence (GenAI) revolutionizes higher education, educators and students alike find themselves at a crossroads, grappling with unprecedented challenges and opportunities in the learning process. GenAI, which includes technologies capable of producing human-like text, images, and other content, is reshaping the landscape of academic work and prompting a fundamental rethinking of pedagogical approaches.

This chapter addresses the complex issues surrounding the ethical use of GenAI in educational settings, focusing on three interconnected key areas: (1) the reconceptualization of academic misconduct in light of AI-generated content, (2) the role of learner agency in AI-augmented environments, and (3) the development of authentic assessment strategies that account for GenAI capabilities. These areas represent critical points of tension where traditional educational practices intersect with emerging AI technologies.

By exploring these topics, we aim to provide educators and administrators with a nuanced understanding of the ethical implications of GenAI in education and offer practical strategies for navigating this new terrain. We conclude with a discussion of actionable steps that educators can take and examine the crucial role of institutional policies in shaping the responsible use of GenAI in higher education settings.

Readers will gain insights into the ethical considerations surrounding GenAI in education, develop strategies for fostering student agency in AI-augmented learning environments, and learn approaches to creating assessments that remain relevant and effective in the age of AI. Needless to say, our arguments will be most relevant to the types of assessment that are most impacted by generative AI, such as written assignments, and less relevant to forms of assessment that are less impacted, such as oral interview or presentations.

RETHINKING THE ROLE OF ASSESSMENT IN HIGHER EDUCATION

Education (in the Western world, at least) has long been considered to have begun with the ancient Greeks and undergone massive shifts through the Renaissance and later, during the Industrial Revolution (Boyd, 1975). Teaching, learning, assessment, and leadership (both in education and in business) have developed in the post-industrial era and have increasingly been viewed as complex and adaptive activities in which process is valued over product (Davis and Sumara, 2005; Uhl-Bien, 2007). However, students' submission of products of learning continues to persist as a normative part of assessment that has been difficult to shift.

In response to these evolving perspectives, the concept of authentic assessment has emerged as a promising approach to educational reform in increasingly complex times. Villarroel et al. (2018, p. 840) note that "authentic assessment aims to replicate the tasks and performance standards typically found in the world of work, and has been found to have a positive impact on student learning, autonomy, motivation, self-regulation and metacognition; abilities highly related to employability." However, developing and implementing authentic assessment may be easier said than done (Koh, 2017; Villarroel et al., 2018; Tai et al., 2018). Large class sizes often make it difficult to provide the individualized feedback and monitoring needed for complex authentic tasks, while online learning environments can present challenges in verifying student authorship and ensuring assessment security. Additionally, creating authentic assessment tasks that are both practically feasible within institutional constraints and truly representative of professional contexts demands significant time, expertise, and resources from educators.

The introduction of generative AI amplifies the imperative for authentic assessment in contexts where students are able to use this technology to produce the deliverables being assessed. Generative AI challenges traditional assessment methods with its ability to produce human-like responses to a wide range of prompts, from essays to problem-solving questions. This capability directly undermines the validity of many conventional assessment tools that rely on written outputs or standardized responses.

The fact that a large language model (LLM) can essentially do most of the work in many traditional forms of writing and question-answering that are used in assessments has prompted observers to announce the "end of the take-home essay" (Robin, 2023) or warn of an impending "homework apocalypse" (Mollick, 2024). The widespread panic about the possible negative impact of students being able to use LLMs to cheat or do their homework for them resulted in wholesale bans of generative AI tools such as ChatGPT in entire institutions, districts, or even countries as soon as these tools gained widespread adoption in 2023 (Bolici et al., 2024).

Although these concerns are valid, it is important to recognize that generative AI also presents opportunities for reimagining assessment. For instance, it could facilitate the creation of more dynamic, interactive, and personalized assessment experiences that better align with authentic assessment principles. Students could be tasked with critically evaluating AI-generated content, developing prompting strategies to solve complex problems, or collaborating with AI tools to complete projects in ways that mirror emerging workplace practices. Assessment tasks might involve students documenting their decision-making process when using AI tools, explaining why they accepted or rejected AI suggestions, or demonstrating how they integrated AI assistance with their own expertise to enhance their work quality. These approaches shift the focus from mere content production to higher-order skills such as critical analysis, strategic thinking, and professional judgment—competencies that are increasingly valuable in a world where AI tools are becoming ubiquitous in professional settings.

Generative AI requires a complete rethinking of the role of assessment in higher education. This technological shift demands innovative approaches that not only mitigate the risks of academic dishonesty but also leverage the potential of AI to enhance learning outcomes and better prepare students for a rapidly evolving workforce. As we move forward, the focus must be on developing assessment strategies that are resilient to AI-generated content while promoting critical thinking, creativity, and real-world problem-solving skills (Lee, 2025).

RECONCEPTUALIZING ACADEMIC CHEATING: LEARNING IN A POST-PLAGIARISM WORLD

Academic misconduct has long been framed through two primary lenses: as a moral issue relating to character development, or as a matter of academic literacy. Some scholars contend that individual values and morality are the foundation for academic integrity (e.g., Anderman and Murdock, 2006; Bertram Gallant, 2008; McCabe et al., 2012; Pavela et al., 2024; Rettinger, 2007). Others argue that academic integrity, and plagiarism in particular, is a matter of skill development, asserting that educators should focus on helping students develop the academic skills they need to succeed, rather than focusing on moral judgments (e.g., Howard, 1995; 2002; Jamieson, 2024; Robillard and Howard, 2008).

Challenging the "Plagiarism Plague" Narrative

More than two decades ago, Rebecca Moore Howard (2002, p. 47) cautioned against the adversarial approach to combating plagiarism: "In our stampede to fight what some call a 'plague' of plagiarism, we risk becoming the enemies rather than the mentors of our students; we are replacing the student–teacher relationship with the criminal–police relationship." Howard was writing about an increase in academic misconduct that some attributed to the popularization of the Internet, but she challenged the knee-jerk reaction to blame new technologies. Instead, she called for a closer critique of poor working conditions in higher education, such as increasing class sizes and professors' lack of interest or willingness to provide students with meaningful assessments.

Howard further noted the complexity of plagiarism:

> When a "plague" of plagiarism comes along and we believe academic integrity itself is under attack, things get even simpler. Encouraged by digital dualisms, we forget that plagiarism means many different things: downloading a term paper, failing to give proper credit to the source of an idea, copying extensive passages without attribution, inserting someone else's phrases or sentences—perhaps with small changes—into your own prose, and forgetting to supply a set of quotation marks. (p. 48)

The Impact of Large Language Models

The introduction of LLMs has brought with it a new wave of the 'plagiarism plague' narrative, with educators once again expressing frustration and blaming new technology for increased misconduct among students. This cycle of moral panic accompanying major technological advancements is a recurring pattern in education (Orben, 2020).

However, the challenge posed by LLMs goes beyond previous technological shifts. These AI models can generate human-like text that is often indistinguishable from student-written work, fundamentally challenging our traditional understanding of authorship and originality. This capability blurs the line between assistance and cheating, making it increasingly difficult to apply conventional definitions of plagiarism.

Towards a Post-plagiarism Era

The advent of generative AI necessitates a re-evaluation of how we define and approach academic integrity. Consider that definitions of plagiarism have remained relatively unchanged for the past several centuries and have not kept pace with technology (Eaton, 2021). The notion of working in a post-plagiarism era, in which writing is co-constructed between humans and GenAI (see Eaton, 2021, 2023), brings with it new possibilities and challenges.

This shift demands that we move beyond simplistic notions of 'copying' or 'originality' and towards a more nuanced understanding of knowledge creation and attribution in the age of AI. It requires us to develop new frameworks for assessing student work that account for the collaborative nature of AI-assisted writing while still valuing individual critical thinking and analysis.

Moving forward, educators and institutions are challenged to grapple with several key questions:

1. How do we redefine academic integrity in a world where AI can generate human-like text?
2. What skills should we prioritize in student assessments when factual recall and basic writing can be easily outsourced to AI?
3. How can we design assessments that authentically measure student learning while acknowledging the reality of AI assistance?

There are no easy answers to these questions, but addressing them is important to develop a more holistic and contemporary approach to academic integrity that prepares students for a future where collaboration with AI is likely to be the norm rather than the exception.

RE-ESTABLISHING AGENCY IN THINKING

A simplified way of understanding LLMs is that they are algorithms for predicting the next word in a text sequence. The technology has existed for decades but has recently shown surprising capabilities when scaled to enormous amounts of training data (Kaplan et al., 2020; Wolfram, 2023). Trained on vast amounts of human writing, these models can produce text that can surpass average or even high human intelligence on certain tasks (Katz et al., 2024). As a result, all human thinking can potentially become AI-assisted (Keyhani & Mohaghegh-Neyshabouri, 2025).

The Spectrum of AI Reliance

When co-thinking with an AI, there is a spectrum of reliance. In some contexts, it may be beneficial to let AI handle certain tasks. However, in educational settings where the goal is to improve students' capabilities, over-reliance on AI could be problematic. This mirrors the debate around calculators in math education: useful in practice, but not a replacement for learning fundamental skills. The analogy of a calculator helps us better link generative AI to previous technologies that appeared and suddenly 'just did it for you' instead of you having to do it yourself. When this occurs, the link between human agency and outcomes weakens. A useful framework to analyze this link is the culpable control model.

The Culpable Control Model

The model of culpable control in blame attribution theory (Alicke, 2000) provides a helpful framework for analyzing this issue. It posits that human agency and responsibility for an outcome consist of three links:

1. Mind-to-behavior
2. Behavior-to-consequence
3. Mind-to-consequence

When an LLM produces thinking and writing based on a user prompt, it weakens these linkages compared to traditional human thinking and writing, potentially diminishing the student's sense of involvement and responsibility for the outcome. To tackle this in educational settings, a useful rule of thumb is to search for mechanisms that consciously restrengthen the weakened link between human agency and outcomes. One such mechanism is the RRUYO rule.

The RRUYO Rule: Read and Revise Until You Own

We propose the RRUYO rule: Read and Revise Until You Own. This approach encourages students to interact deeply with AI-generated content, revising it until they truly feel ownership and responsibility for the work. There is a crucial distinction between blindly submitting AI-generated content and thoroughly engaging with it. Even in cases where the student ends up using large chunks of content produced by the AI, if the student has truly internalized it and feels a sense of ownership over it, this could be deemed acceptable. The larger the chunk is, the less likely it is that a student will be able to gain a sense of ownership and internalization without much editing and revision.

Redesigning Assessments for the AI Era

Along these lines, to address the decreased culpable control due to AI involvement, assessments need to be redesigned to emphasize:

1. Mental engagement: Encourage students to do the mental work of reading and revising AI-generated output until they feel genuine ownership and responsibility for the work.
2. Authentic contexts: Place the work in real-world contexts where students feel the weight of potential consequences. This aligns with the authentic assessment approach (Koh, 2017).

Some ways to achieve the above goals in practice could include:

1. Project-based assessments: Instead of traditional essays, assign projects where students must apply their knowledge to solve real-world problems, using AI as a tool but not as a substitute for critical thinking.
2. Reflection components: Include requirements for students to explain their thought process, including how they used AI and why they made specific revisions.
3. Peer-review processes: Implement peer-review stages where students critically evaluate each other's AI-assisted work, promoting deeper engagement with the material.
4. Iterative submissions: Allow for multiple submission rounds, encouraging students to refine their work based on feedback, demonstrating their growing ownership of the content.

Responsibility in the Age of GenAI

Although humans can delegate the task of writing to GenAI, we cannot delegate responsibility for the content. Assessments should be designed to make students fully aware of this responsibility. Humans remain accountable for the accuracy, truth, and validity of the content, regardless of whether AI assisted in its creation (Eaton, 2023).

As we navigate the integration of AI in education, our focus should shift from preventing AI use to fostering responsible and thoughtful AI collaboration. By redesigning assessments to emphasize mental engagement, authentic contexts, and clear responsibility, we can harness the power of AI while still promoting deep learning and critical-thinking skills essential for students' future success.

EMPHASIZING LEARNER AGENCY AND ETHICAL DECISION-MAKING IN LEARNING

In this section, we explore the concepts of learner agency and evaluative judgment. We begin with the theoretical and then conclude with practical strategies for educators.

Understanding Learner Agency

Learner agency refers to a person's sense of ownership over their own learning process. As Mercer (2011, p. 427) describes, it is "a complex dynamic system composed of a number of constituent components; each of which is itself a dynamic complex system. In particular, motivation, affect, and self-regulation emerge as the 'controlling' components of this learner's agentic system." This concept is crucial in understanding how students navigate their educational journey, especially in an AI-augmented environment.

Learner Agency and Ethical Decision-making

Learner agency is closely tied to an individual's ability to make decisions about their engagement in the learning process. This includes choices about whether to fully participate in learning activities or to take shortcuts, potentially engaging in academic misconduct (Anderman and Murdock, 2006; Rettinger, 2007). In the context of generative AI (GenAI), these decisions become even more complex and ethically charged.

GenAI: A Double-edged Sword for Learner Agency

GenAI tools present both opportunities and challenges for learner agency. Here, we share a few examples:

1. Augmentation vs. circumvention: High-agency students have control over their learning, including decisions about how to engage with GenAI tools. These tools can be used to augment the learning process, enhancing understanding and creativity. However, they can also be used to circumvent learning entirely, producing assignments or exam answers without genuine engagement.
2. Ethical decision-making: The availability of GenAI tools places a greater emphasis on students' ethical decision-making skills. They must constantly evaluate when and how to use these tools in ways that enhance rather than undermine their learning.
3. Shifting educator roles: In this new landscape, educators' roles shift towards guiding students in making better decisions about when, why, and how to use AI. This involves helping students develop critical-thinking skills to evaluate AI-generated content and understand its appropriate use.

These examples are intended to be illustrative rather than exhaustive. As GenAI continues to develop, more examples will emerge that show both opportunities and challenges for learner agency.

Cultivating Evaluative Judgment

To move beyond transactional approaches to learning and assessment in the age of GenAI, educators can focus on cultivating students' evaluative judgment (Bearman and Luckin, 2020; Fischer et al., 2024; Tai et al., 2018). Evaluative judgment refers to students' ability to make decisions about the quality of their own and others' work (Tai, 2018).

Bearman and Luckin (2020) argue that focusing on personal epistemology ("meta-knowing," p. 49) and evaluative judgment can help shift away from outdated assessment models. Instead, assessments can focus "on areas where humans think better than machines" (p. 49), emphasizing uniquely human cognitive skills.

Practical Strategies for Fostering Learner Agency and Evaluative Judgment

The development of learner agency and evaluative judgment opens exciting possibilities for reimagining education in the digital age. While these concepts might seem abstract at first glance, they come alive through thoughtful integration into everyday learning experiences. Here's how educators can create environments that nurture these essential capabilities:

Metacognitive reflection serves as a cornerstone for developing evaluative judgment. By incorporating regular reflection exercises, students gain insight into their learning processes, including their decisions around AI tool usage. These reflective practices help learners understand not just what they're learning, but how they are learning—a crucial distinction in an AI-enhanced educational landscape.

Ethical case studies offer rich territory for exploring the complexities of academic integrity in the digital age. When students engage with scenarios involving AI use in academic settings, they confront real-world dilemmas that challenge their assumptions and develop their ethical reasoning. These discussions naturally lead to critical examinations of algorithmic bias and how AI systems might inadvertently perpetuate societal inequalities, preparing students to be more thoughtful technology users.

Peer- and self-assessment activities create powerful opportunities for developing evaluative judgment. Through structured review processes, students learn to critically evaluate both traditional and AI-assisted work, developing a sophisticated understanding of quality across different contexts. This practice becomes particularly valuable when students consider how AI-generated content might be perceived differently across cultural contexts.

AI literacy workshops serve as crucial spaces for developing technical and critical awareness. Beyond teaching tool functionality, these workshops should explore the broader implications of AI systems, including their potential biases and limitations. Students learn to recognize how algorithms might reflect and amplify existing social inequalities, empowering them to use AI tools more thoughtfully and ethically.

Collaborative projects create natural opportunities for negotiating technology use in group settings. When students work together to determine appropriate AI tool usage, they encounter firsthand the challenges of balancing efficiency with creativity and technological assistance with independent thinking. These experiences prompt valuable discussions about ethical and effective AI integration across different cultural contexts.

Clear guidelines for AI use in coursework complete this framework. Rather than simple prohibitions, these policies should emphasize transparency and responsible use while acknowledging the complex interplay between technology, culture, and learning. This approach helps students develop a nuanced understanding of how to leverage AI tools while maintaining academic integrity and cultural sensitivity.

This integration of strategies creates a learning environment where students develop not just technical skills but the critical awareness and ethical judgment needed for thoughtful engagement with AI tools in their academic and professional lives.

Empowering Learners in the AI Era

By emphasizing learner agency and ethical decision-making, educators can prepare students to navigate the complexities of an AI-augmented learning environment. This approach not only addresses the immediate challenges posed by GenAI but also equips students with critical skills for lifelong learning and ethical technology use.

The focus on evaluative judgment and personal epistemology shifts the educational paradigm from mere knowledge acquisition to the development of higher-order thinking skills. In doing so, we can create a learning environment where AI serves as a tool for enhancement rather than a shortcut, fostering a generation of learners who are both technologically adept and ethically grounded.

PRACTICAL RECOMMENDATIONS FOR ETHICAL LEARNING IN GENAI-AUGMENTED LEARNING ENVIRONMENTS

A rapid scoping review by Moya et al. (2024) concludes that AI can be ethically incorporated into teaching, learning, and assessment. They recommend a four-step process for educators, which we unpack in more detail. Following that, we engage in a discussion of assessment validity in the context of GenAI, the connections between learner agency and evaluative judgment, and the pedagogical purpose of GenAI.

Moya et al.'s (2024) Four-step Process to Ethically Incorporate GenAI into Teaching, Learning, and Assessment

Step 1: Analyze the activity's intended learning outcomes

Key questions

- What, if any, are the embedded expectations for explicitly developing AI skills?
- Do the intended learning outcomes articulate an explicit intention to develop students' agency when using AI?

Practical example

In a first-year composition course, the initial essay assignment could focus on developing thesis statements and supporting arguments without AI. A later assignment could then allow AI for drafting and focus on peer review and revision, teaching students to critically evaluate AI-generated text.

Step 2: Examine the situation surrounding the learning activity

Key questions

- What do my students need?
- What is the disciplinary framework in which this activity is embedded?
- What type of learning am I planning?

Practical example

For a data analysis course, an instructor might use AI-assisted coding exercises in supervised lab sessions, allowing students to experiment with AI tools while providing guidance on their appropriate use.

Step 3: Review institutional policies related to AI and be sure to follow them

Key questions

- How does my institution define authorship, academic cheating, and plagiarism?
- What training, resources, or technical support are available?

Practical example
An instructor might organize a workshop with the academic integrity office to clarify AI-use policies and develop guidelines for students on how to properly cite AI-assisted work.

Step 4: Explore the capabilities and limitations of AI tools connected to the activity

Key questions
- What tasks can be effectively delegated to AI?
- What tasks can AI not do well for this learning task?
- How do I protect the validity of the assessment?

Practical example
In a critical-thinking course, an instructor might design an assignment where students use AI to generate arguments on a topic, then critically analyze and evaluate these arguments, highlighting the AI's strengths and limitations.

Assessment Validity in the Context of GenAI

Moving from Moya et al.'s (2024) four-step process, we note that Messick's (1989) framework for assessment validity remains relevant in the age of GenAI. The four elements of assessment validity can be applied to GenAI-augmented learning as follows:

1. Evidence support: Ensure that the assessment can differentiate between AI-generated content and student-generated insights.
2. Relevance and utility: Design assessments that measure skills valuable in an AI-augmented world, such as critical evaluation of AI outputs.
3. Credible rationale: Clearly communicate to students how and why AI tools are being incorporated into assessments.
4. Functional worth: Consider both intended outcomes (e.g., improved AI literacy) and unintended consequences (e.g., over-reliance on AI) of incorporating GenAI into assessments.

Connecting to Learner Agency and Evaluative Judgment

These practical recommendations align closely with our earlier discussions on learner agency and evaluative judgment. By following this four-step process, educators can:

- Foster learner agency by explicitly incorporating AI skills into learning outcomes (Step 1).
- Develop students' evaluative judgment by encouraging the critical examination of AI-generated content (Step 4).
- Promote ethical decision-making by clearly defining institutional policies on AI use (Step 3).

The Pedagogical Purpose of GenAI

A key takeaway from both the long-standing research on assessment validity and literature on ethical GenAI use is the importance of purposeful integration. Using GenAI in education should have a clear pedagogical rationale. It is not about using AI for the sake of novelty but about leveraging it to enhance learning outcomes, develop critical-thinking skills, and prepare students for an AI-augmented future.

As GenAI technology continues to evolve, these recommendations will likely need regular revision. Future considerations might include:

- Developing more sophisticated methods for detecting and evaluating AI-assisted work while protecting student privacy and academic freedom.
- Adapting curricula to include advanced AI literacy as a core competency across disciplines.
- Exploring the potential for personalized learning experiences facilitated by AI.

By applying these practical recommendations in a thoughtful and reflective way, educators can navigate the challenges of GenAI in education while harnessing its potential to enhance learning. This approach not only addresses immediate concerns about academic integrity but also prepares students for a future where AI collaboration will be an integral part of many professions. However, as the technology continues to evolve, educators will be challenged to return again and again to the steps we presented earlier. The same key message will still apply, though: the use of GenAI in education should have a clear pedagogical rationale.

The Role of Policy in AI and Education

The rapid popularization of ChatGPT has prompted schools and post-secondary institutions worldwide to focus on developing AI policies and revising academic misconduct guidelines. However, establishing educational policies is a complex and time-consuming process. As Ozga (2000, p. 1) aptly notes, educational policy is "struggled over, not delivered in tablets of stone to a grateful or quiescent population." This complexity stems partly from the lack of universally accepted definitions for policy, academic integrity, and ethical teaching and learning practices (Eaton, 2024; Ozga, 2000).

Historically, educational policies have been set by authorities who have limited contact with those affected by their implementation (Kowch, 2025). A more inclusive approach would involve educators and students in developing policies that impact their daily lives (Ozga, 2000). This raises the question: "Whose policy?" in the context of AI use in teaching and learning. Although government ministries and institutions can set overarching policies, academic departments and individual educators also play crucial roles in establishing guidelines and expectations for acceptable practices.

Effective policy implementation involves various challenges (Bretag et al., 2011a; 2011b; De Maio et al., 2020; Yorke et al., 2009):

1. Unclear definitions (e.g., "plagiarism", a concept for which there is no universal definition).
2. Inconsistent policies across subjects or institutions.
3. Insufficient resources for implementation.
4. Inadequate support for addressing policy breaches.

For policies to be effective, they must be supported by system-level resources and implemented in a manner deemed acceptable by those affected, including students and educators (Bretag et al., 2011a, 2011b). As of this writing, many questions remain about ethically incorporating AI into teaching, learning, and assessment. We argue that policy alone is insufficient to guide pedagogical decisions affecting student learning. Other factors discussed in this chapter, such as student agency, personal responsibility, and accountability, are at least as important as official policies in shaping practical aspects of education.

Although policies play a crucial role in addressing AI use in education, they must be developed collaboratively, implemented consistently, and supported by adequate resources. Moreover, they should be balanced with other pedagogical considerations to ensure effective and ethical integration of AI in educational settings. Finally, policies need to undergo regular cyclical review by policy-makers and interested parties to ensure that they remain up to date. The frequency of policy review may differ from one organization to the next; however, a regular policy review cycle of three to five years may be too long, given the rapid rate of development of AI. Institutions might instead consider revisiting policies every year to ensure they remain relevant.

CONCLUSIONS AND FUTURE DIRECTIONS: NAVIGATING THE AI-AUGMENTED EDUCATIONAL LANDSCAPE

The integration of GenAI into higher education represents a paradigm shift in teaching, learning, and assessment practices. In this chapter, we have explored various implications of AI-augmented environments, focusing on three critical areas: the reconceptualization of academic misconduct, the enhancement of learner agency, and the evolution of authentic assessment strategies.

Key Insights

To recap, here are some of the key points of this chapter:

- **Reconceptualizing academic misconduct**: The advent of GenAI necessitates a fundamental re-evaluation of traditional concepts such as plagiarism. The post-plagiarism era calls for a transition from punitive measures to proactive approaches that foster ethical AI use and critical-thinking skills (Eaton, 2023).
- **Cultivating learner agency**: In AI-augmented learning environments, student agency is paramount. Educators must prioritize the development of evaluative judgment and personal epistemology, empowering students to engage meaningfully with AI tools while maintaining intellectual autonomy (Keyhani & Mohaghegh-Neyshabouri, 2025).
- **Innovating assessment strategies**: Authentic assessment in the AI era should emphasize process over product and nurture higher-order thinking skills. The RRUYO (Read and Revise Until You Own) approach offers a promising framework for ensuring student accountability and genuine intellectual engagement.
- **Collaborative policy development**: Effective AI policies in education must be crafted through collaborative efforts involving educators, students, and administrators. Clear, consistent, and well-supported guidelines are essential for successful implementation and adaptation to rapidly evolving AI technologies.

As GenAI continues to advance, navigating the ethical dimensions of AI-augmented learning will remain a critical challenge. The focus can—and should—shift towards creating supervised and guided learning experiences that not only impart content knowledge but also enhance meta-cognitive skills and evaluative judgment. This approach becomes increasingly vital as AI's capability to perform various tasks expands.

Future Directions

To conclude this chapter, we offer these considerations for future directions in research, teaching, and learning:

Understanding cognitive development and learning

- How does sustained GenAI use in academic writing affect students' development of disciplinary thinking and writing capabilities?
- What are the cognitive implications of AI-assisted learning on students' long-term knowledge retention and transfer?
- How do different patterns of AI tool usage influence the development of critical thinking and evaluative judgment?

Pedagogical innovation and faculty development

- What pedagogical approaches most effectively integrate AI tools while preserving essential learning outcomes?
- How can we best support faculty in transitioning from traditional assessment methods to AI-aware authentic assessment practices?
- What professional development models most effectively prepare educators to leverage AI while maintaining their crucial role in student learning?

Cultural and ethical dimensions

- How do cultural differences influence the reception and effectiveness of AI-assisted learning approaches?
- What strategies best address algorithmic bias and equity concerns in AI-enhanced educational settings?
- How can institutions develop ethical frameworks for AI use that remain responsive to evolving technological capabilities?

Institutional transformation

- How are educator roles evolving as AI automates traditional teaching tasks, and what new forms of pedagogical expertise are emerging?
- What institutional structures best support the ethical integration of AI while preserving academic integrity?
- How can educational institutions balance innovation with their responsibility to ensure equitable access and outcomes?

Assessment and evaluation

- What assessment methods most effectively evaluate student learning in AI-enhanced environments?
- How can we measure the development of AI literacy and ethical judgment alongside traditional learning outcomes?

- What metrics best capture the impact of AI integration on student engagement and learning autonomy?

With these questions, we are just scratching the surface of what we need to study in the near future as generative AI starts to upend our world and technological innovation begins to become a defining feature of educational practice. We need to better understand how to harness AI's capabilities while preserving and enhancing the fundamental goals of education.

The journey ahead is complex but, with thoughtful implementation and a commitment to ethical practices, AI can become a powerful ally in cultivating a generation of learners who are not only knowledgeable but also critically engaged, ethically grounded, and prepared for the challenges of an AI-augmented world.

REFERENCES

Alicke, M. D. (2000). Culpable control and the psychology of blame. *Psychological Bulletin, 126*(4), 566–574. https://doi.org/10.1037/0033-2909.126.4.556

Anderman, E. M., & Murdock, T. B. (2006). Psychology of academic cheating: Introduction. In E. M. Anderman & T. B. Murdock (Eds.), *Psychology of Academic Cheating* (pp. 1–5). Elsevier Science & Technology.

Bearman, M., & Luckin, R. (2020). Preparing university assessment for a world with AI: Tasks for human intelligence. In M. Bearman, P. Dawson, R. Ajjawi, J. Tai, & D. Boud (Eds.), *Re-imagining university assessment in a digital world* (pp. 49–63). Springer International Publishing. https://doi.org/10.1007/978-3-030-41956-1_5

Bertram Gallant, T. (2008). Moral panic: The contemporary context of academic integrity [Article]. *ASHE Higher Education Report, 33*(5), 1–12.

Bolici, F., Varone, A., & Diana, G. (2024). Unpopular policies, ineffective bans: Lessons learned from ChatGPT prohibition in Italy. *Proceedings of the 32nd European Conference on Information Systems, 11*. https://aisel.aisnet.org/ecis2024/track04_impactai/track04_impactai/11

Boyd, W., & King, E. J. (1975). *The history of western education* (11th ed.). Rowman & Littlefield. https://archive.org/details/historyofwestern0000boyd_q3e5

Bretag, T., Mahmud, S., East, J., Green, M., & James, C. (2011a). Academic integrity standards: A preliminary analysis of the Academic integrity policies at Australian Universities. *Proceedings of AuQF 2011 Demonstrating Quality*, Melbourne. https://hdl.handle.net/10779/uow.27691431.v1

Bretag, T., Mahmud, S., Wallace, M., Walker, R., James, C., Green, M., East, J., McGowan, U., & Partridge, L. (2011b). Core elements of exemplary academic integrity policy in Australian higher education. *International Journal for Educational Integrity, 7*(2), 3–12. https://doi.org/10.21913/IJEI.v7i2.759

Davis, B., & Sumara, D. J. (2005). Challenging images of knowing: Complexity science and educational research. *International Journal of Qualitative Studies in Education, 18*(3), 305–321. https://doi.org/10.1080/09518390500082293

De Maio, C., Dixon, K., & Yeo, S. (2020). Responding to student plagiarism in Western Australian universities: The disconnect between policy and academic staff. *Journal*

of Higher Education Policy and Management, *42*(1), 102–116. https://doi.org/10.1080/1360080X.2019.1662927
Eaton, S. E. (2021). *Plagiarism in higher education: Tackling tough topics in academic integrity*. Bloomsbury.
Eaton, S. E. (2023). Postplagiarism: Transdisciplinary ethics and integrity in the age of artificial intelligence and neurotechnology. *International Journal for Educational Integrity*, *19*(1), 1–10. https://doi.org/10.1007/s40979-023-00144–1
Eaton, S. E. (2024). Comprehensive Academic Integrity (CAI): An Ethical Framework for Educational Contexts. In S. E. Eaton (Ed.), *Second Handbook of Academic Integrity* (pp. 1–14). Springer Nature Switzerland. https://doi.org/10.1007/978-3-031-54144-5_194
Fischer, J., Bearman, M., Boud, D., & Tai, J. (2024). How does assessment drive learning? A focus on students' development of evaluative judgement. *Assessment & Evaluation in Higher Education*, *49*(2), 233–245. https://doi.org/10.1080/02602938.2023.2206986
Howard, R. M. (1995). Plagiarisms, authorships, and the academic death penalty. *College English*, *57*(7), 788–806.
Howard, R. M. (2002). Don't police plagiarism: Just TEACH! *The Education Digest*, *67*(5), 46–49.
Jamieson, S. (2024). Patchwriting, plagiarism, pedagogy: Definitions and implications. In S. E. Eaton (Ed.), *Second Handbook of Academic Integrity* (pp. 433–449). Springer Nature Switzerland. https://doi.org/10.1007/978-3-031-54144-5_68
Kaplan, J., McCandlish, S., Henighan, T., Brown, T. B., Chess, B., Child, R., Gray, S., Radford, A., Wu, J., & Amodei, D. (2020). *Scaling laws for neural language models*. arXiv. https://doi.org/10.48550/arXiv.2001.08361
Katz, D. M., Bommarito, M. J., Gao, S., & Arredondo, P. (2024). GPT-4 passes the bar exam. *Philosophical Transactions of the Royal Society A: Mathematical, Physical and Engineering Sciences*, *382*, 1–17. https://doi.org/10.1098/rsta.2023.0254
Keyhani, M., & Mohaghegh-Neyshabouri, S. (2025). The rise of generative AI: Capabilities and potential for higher education. In S. Sabbaghan (Ed.), *Navigating Generative AI in Higher Education: Ethical, Theoretical and Practical Perspectives*. Edward Elgar.
Koh, K. H. (2017). Authentic Assessment. In *Oxford research encyclopedia of education*. Oxford University Press. https://oxfordre.com/education/display/10.1093/acrefore/9780190264093.001.0001/acrefore-9780190264093-e-22
Kowch, E. G. (2025). An innovation policy analysis of G10 nation strategic plans for AI leaders and researchers in higher education. In S. Sabbaghan (Ed.), *Navigating generative AI in higher education: Ethical, theoretical and practical perspectives*. Edward Elgar.
Lee, A. V. Y. (2025). The double-edged sword of generative AI in Assessment: efficiency versus homogenization. In S. Sabbaghan (Ed.), *Navigating Generative AI in Higher Education: Ethical, Theoretical and Practical Perspectives*. Edward Elgar.
McCabe, D. L., Butterfield, K. D., & Treviño, L. K. (2012). *Cheating in college: Why students do it and what educators can do about it*. Johns Hopkins University Press.
Mercer, S. (2011). Understanding learner agency as a complex dynamic system. *System*, *39*(4), 427–436. https://doi.org/10.1016/j.system.2011.08.001
Messick, S. (1989). Meaning and values in test validation: The science and ethics of assessment. *Educational Researcher*, *18*(2), 5–11. https://doi.org/10.3102/0013189x018002005

Mollick, E. (2024). *Co-intelligence: Living and working with AI.* Portfolio.

Moya, B. A., Eaton, S. E., Pethrick, H., Hayden, A. K., Brennan, R., Wiens, J., & McDermott, B. (2024). Academic integrity and artificial intelligence in higher education (HE) contexts: A rapid scoping review. *Canadian Perspectives on Academic Integrity*, *7*(3). https://doi.org/10.55016/ojs/cpai.v7i3

Orben, A. (2020). The Sisyphean cycle of technology panics. *Perspectives on Psychological Science*, *15*(5), 1143–1157. https://doi.org/10.1177/1745691620919372

Ozga, J. (2000). *Policy research in educational settings.* Open University Press.

Pavela, G., McDuff, D., & Coen, J. (2024). *Driving Plato's chariot: Lessons on student ethical development.* Is-Books.

Rettinger, D. A. (2007). Applying decision theory to academic integrity decisions. In E. M. Anderman & T. B. Murdock (Eds.), *Psychology of academic cheating* (pp. 141–167). Academic Press. https://doi.org/10.1016/B978-012372541-7/50011-5

Robillard, A. E., & Howard, R. M. (2008). Introduction: Plagiarisms. In R. M. Howard & A. E. Robillard (Eds.), *Pluralizing plagiarism: Identities, contexts, pedagogies* (pp. 1–7). Boynton/Cook Publishers. McNally Jackson.

Robin, C. (2023, August 24). The end of the take-home essay? How ChatGPT changed my plans for the fall. *Chronicle of Higher Education*, *70*(2). https://www.chronicle.com/article/the-end-of-the-take-home-essay

Tai, J., Ajjawi, R., Boud, D., Dawson, P., & Panadero, E. (2018). Developing evaluative judgement: Enabling students to make decisions about the quality of work. *Higher Education*, *76*(3), 467–481. https://doi.org/10.1007/s10734-017-0220-3

Uhl-Bien, M., Marion, R., & McKelvey, B. (2007). Complexity leadership theory: Shifting leadership from the industrial age to the knowledge era. *The Leadership Quarterly*, 18(4), 298–318. https://doi.org/https://doi.org/10.1016/j.leaqua.2007.04.002

Villarroel, V., Bloxham, S., Bruna, D., Bruna, C., & Herrera-Seda, C. (2018). Authentic assessment: Creating a blueprint for course design. *Assessment and Evaluation in Higher Education*, *43*(5), 840–854. https://doi.org/10.1080/02602938.2017.1412396

Wolfram, S. (2023). *What is ChatGPT doing ... and why does it work?* Wolfram Media.

Yorke, J., Lawson, K., & McMahon, G. (2009). Can we reliably determine intent in cases of plagiarism? *International Journal for Educational Integrity*, *5*(2). https://doi.org/10.21913/IJEI.v5i2.612

11. Challenges and misuses of generative AI and the quest for mitigation

Muhammad Abbas

INTRODUCTION

Generative artificial intelligence (GenAI) emerges as a cutting-edge technological advancement with the potential to significantly affect how knowledge is created, disseminated, and consumed. It provides assistance in a wide variety of tasks ranging from generating course material, writing essays or codes, and developing manuscripts, assignments, or projects (Abbas, 2023). In contemporary times, GenAI (e.g., ChatGPT or Meta AI) has become ubiquitous, accessible virtually to every individual. The paradigm has now shifted from a dichotomy of humans versus AI to a contrast between humans without AI compared to those equipped with it. Consequently, it appears that the integration of AI into educational frameworks is not merely advantageous but imperative. However, this ability of GenAI to transform the educational landscape also brings a host of challenges. Recent scholarly debates indicate that while GenAI may enhance educational experiences, it also poses risks related to academic integrity, learning, and the erosion of critical-thinking skills (Abbas et al., 2024; Chan, 2023).

Therefore, the importance of addressing the challenges and misuses of GenAI cannot be overstated. As educational institutions increasingly adopt AI-driven tools (Michel-Villarreal et al., 2023; Naujokaitytė, 2023), it is important to understand their impact on academia and provide plausible solutions to the challenges associated with their adoption. Issues such as plagiarism, where students might misuse GenAI to produce assignments or projects, threaten the integrity of academic achievements (Yang & Zhang, 2024). This poses a serious ethical and pedagogical challenge to the future of education. In addition, the degree of institutional readiness and access to advanced AI technologies has the potential to create a digital divide between nations (Eubanks, 2018; Noble, 2018). Such a digital divide may disproportionately affect developing countries, exacerbating existing socio-economic disparities and limiting

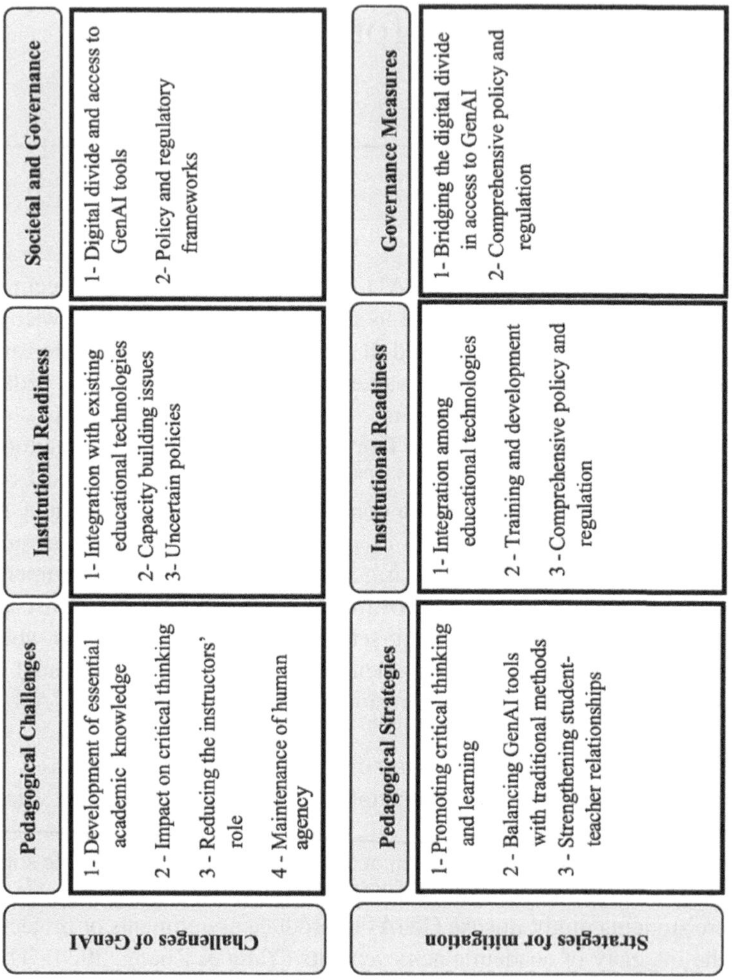

Source: Authors.

Figure 11.1 *Challenges of GenAI and mitigation strategies*

access to essential technological resources. This gap may impede their ability to harness the full potential of GenAI for economic growth, education, and innovation, further entrenching global inequality.

While GenAI offers transformative potential for higher education, its effective and ethical utilization requires a clear understanding and mitigation of the challenges related to academic integrity, teaching pedagogy, institutional readiness, and the potential digital divide within and across societies. This chapter discusses these challenges and potential mitigation strategies in detail. Addressing these challenges will help to ensure that the academic environment remains a place of genuine learning and intellectual growth. Similarly, it will protect students from becoming overly reliant on technology at the expense of developing critical-thinking skills. Finally, any mitigation initiatives directed at addressing institutional readiness and equal access to GenAI technologies for individuals, institutions, and societies will help to ensure that the potential of GenAI is equally harnessed by educational institutions across the globe.

This chapter is structured as follows. In the next section, I discuss the challenges for teaching pedagogies amid the GenAI boom and the corresponding mitigation strategies to improve those pedagogies. The third section covers the challenges and the strategies related to institutional readiness and support to harness effective utilization of GenAI in academia. The fourth section discusses the potential societal and governance issues posed by GenAI and the measures to address those issues. The final section provides conclusions and some future directions. In this way, this chapter aims to provide insights for educators, policy-makers, regulators, instructors, and students to help them in the responsible and effective integration of GenAI in higher education. This chapter does not cover the ethical challenges, as these issues and the corresponding mitigation strategies are discussed in detail by Eaton and Keyhani (2025) in Chapter 10 of this volume. Figure 11.1 summarizes these challenges and corresponding mitigation strategies.

PEDAGOGICAL CHALLENGES AND MITIGATION STRATEGIES

Pedagogical Challenges

Development of essential academic knowledge

A basic pedagogical challenge is the potential for students to become overly dependent on GenAI tools for their academic work. This dependence can hinder the development of essential academic skills such as writing, coding, research, and problem-solving. The convenience offered by GenAI might lead students to bypass traditional learning methods, resulting in a lack of foundational knowledge and skills. Also, overreliance on GenAI for academic tasks can lead to a superficial understanding of subjects. This is because GenAI-generated responses often lack the depth and context that are vital for a comprehensive grasp of complex topics. As a consequence, there is a risk of producing a generation of learners who are adept at using technology but lack a deeper understanding of the underlying essence of the subject. For example, preliminary evidence shows that extensive use of GenAI may lead to poor academic performance (Abbas et al., 2024).

Another related challenge is that GenAI, particularly ChatGPT, can produce content that appears plausible but may contain factual inaccuracies, logical inconsistencies, and even fake references (King & ChatGPT, 2023). GenAI has limitations in understanding context, which may lead to inaccuracies and misinformation (Marcus & Davis, 2019). This is particularly problematic in academic contexts where the reliability and accuracy of the information are paramount for students' academic learning and knowledge.

Impact on critical thinking

Another important challenge is that the use of GenAI in education may have unintended effects on students' critical-thinking skills (Abbas et al., 2024; Al-Zahrani, 2024; Peters et al., 2023). Relying heavily on GenAI for academic activities may encourage students to avoid deep cognitive engagement with course content because these tools offer a convenient means for cognitive offloading. Cognitive offloading refers to the process of using external aids or tools, such as ChatGPT, to handle tasks (e.g., generating ideas or completing assignments) that would otherwise require active mental effort, thereby reducing the need for personal intellectual involvement. Preliminary evidence indicates that excessive use of ChatGPT relates to deteriorated memory, poor cognitive abilities, and poor creative skills (Abbas et al., 2024; Farrokhnia et al., 2024).

Reducing the Instructors' Role

As the capabilities of GenAI are growing exponentially, there is a growing concern that GenAI may replace human tutors (Chan & Tsi, 2024). If this happens, GenAI's personalized approach would help to provide individualized learning but simultaneously limit student interactions and collaborative opportunities with instructors. Further, the introduction of GenAI in classrooms may alter the traditional methods of social interaction between students and instructors. As GenAI tools can provide instant feedback and assistance, it may reduce students' reliance on instructors. While this may allow instructors to focus on more complex instructional tasks, it can also lead to a significantly reduced role for teachers in the learning process, unless they adapt these technological advancements to revise their pedagogies (Lawless & Pellegrino,

2007). This potential reduction in the role of teachers or their replacement poses a significant challenge for educators (Yang & Zhang, 2024). For example, the shift in the teacher–student dynamics driven by GenAI could have cultural implications. In many collectivistic societies, education systems place a strong emphasis on hierarchical teacher–student relationships and face-to-face interaction – and the teachers are expected to demonstrate multiple roles. These roles extend beyond imparting subject knowledge to include mentoring students and offering moral and emotional guidance.

Therefore, the role of educators as facilitators, mentors, and role models is considered integral to the educational experience. The presence of a human teacher who can adapt to the emotional and intellectual needs of students, provide personalized support, and create a dynamic classroom environment is irreplaceable. Ignoring this aspect when educational processes become overly automated can lead to a depersonalized education system where the nuances of human interaction and mentorship are lost (Chan & Hu, 2023).

Maintenance of human agency

Human agency refers to individuals' capacity to make their own choices independently and take responsibility for their actions. This agency is fundamental to education as it forms the foundation of creativity, freedom to pursue goals, and moral responsibility. However, this power may diminish due to the growing reliance on GenAI. With the excessive use of GenAI, students might unconsciously depend heavily on these tools, which can reduce their sense of independence. The content generated by GenAI is sometimes misleading, and this information can lead students to make wrong decisions. Moreover, GenAI threatens human agency by undermining independent thought, encouraging dependency, and influencing human choices in ways that might not be consistent with personal or societal values. For example, in one instance, a Florida teen's interaction with an AI chatbot allegedly influenced his decision to take his life, highlighting concerns over the platform's lack of safeguards and its impact on vulnerable users (NBC News, 2024).

Pedagogical Strategies

Promoting critical thinking and learning

To foster critical thinking and creativity, educators may want to encourage students not to rely too heavily on GenAI tools, using them, rather, as supplementary resources. Specifically, assignments, projects, and other assessment methods should be devised in a way that promotes analytical reasoning, problem-solving, and original thinking among students. Such initiatives may help to ensure students' personal insights and reflections on the subject (Sabbaghan, 2023).

To enhance critical-thinking skills among students, assignments may be designed in a way that encourages them to think critically. The first strategy can be designing an assignment that cannot be completed using GenAI. For example, assignments could include personalized reflections on a topic, detailed analysis of local issues, or incorporating fieldwork observations or personal interviews, which demand unique and context-specific inputs beyond the capabilities of GenAI. However, given the fact that such fieldwork may be challenging or not relevant in some subjects, another approach may be to ask students to complete assignments using GenAI and then identify inaccuracies in those outputs (e.g., wrong answers, biases, logical inconsistencies). This will help students think critically and develop their ability to assess the content quality. Another approach may be to ask students to compare outputs generated by GenAI with those available in textbooks and identify the differences. Furthermore, students may be asked to generate responses from GenAI to propose initial solutions on any topic and then refine those solutions based on their own critical thinking and research.

Balancing GenAI tools with traditional methods

Maintaining a balance between GenAI tools and traditional learning methods is crucial for effective learning. While GenAI can streamline certain tasks, the traditional methods, such as face-to-face discussions, hands-on group projects, and exercises, are irreplaceable for developing foundational skills and personality. Instructors should create curricula that blend GenAI assistance with conventional pedagogical practices to optimize students' learning and skill development (Bucea-Manea-Ţoniş et al., 2022). The use of multiple pedagogical approaches, such as collaborative group work, case-based learning, experiential activities, and reflective thinking exercises, can ensure that students engage deeply with the material while leveraging the strengths of both GenAI and traditional methods.

Strengthening student–teacher relationships

Related to the previous point, the introduction of GenAI in education should not undermine the essential student–teacher relationship. Instead, educators may use GenAI to enhance their interactions with students rather than replace them. GenAI can be leveraged to handle administrative tasks, freeing up teachers' time for more personalized interactions and mentorship. For example, GenAI can assist with study plans, assignment creation, grading, scheduling, and analysis, allowing teachers to focus more on providing individualized support and fostering meaningful connections with students.

Moreover, GenAI can be used to supplement teacher–student communication in innovative ways. For instance, platforms such as Duolingo, Codecademy, Khanmigo, or Grammarly can be employed to help students learn more effectively. However, students would be required to give classroom presentations on what they learned from these digital platforms. This will allow teachers to assess whether students have effectively learned from these platforms. It may also ensure that students use these digital platforms in a more cognizant way, as they will be expected to present their learning in the classroom and demonstrate their grasp of the material and the practical application of their skills. Ultimately, this approach may help to ensure seamless GenAI integration while preserving meaningful teacher–student interaction.

INSTITUTIONAL READINESS: CHALLENGES AND MEASURES

Challenges for Institutional Readiness

Integration with existing educational technologies

Integrating GenAI with existing educational technologies poses a key challenge for educational institutions. Many institutions already use a variety of digital tools and platforms for teaching and administration, such as campus management systems or learning management systems. Introducing GenAI into the educational ecosystem requires seamless integration to avoid technical issues and user frustration. The integration process can be complicated due to potential technical incompatibilities between GenAI tools and existing educational technologies. Educational tools often vary in their technical foundations, including different data formats, language protocols, software architectures, and many other challenges, which include infrastructure and data privacy concerns, especially in developing countries. For example, educational settings in developing countries have limited access to cutting-edge technologies and limited capacity and resources to digitize their educational technology infrastructure (Mannuru et al., 2023), which can impact the quality of education. These disparities can create significant challenges to achieving smooth integration, requiring careful planning and substantial investments in infrastructure to ensure compatibility and efficient operation of GenAI technologies.

Capacity building issues

Capacity building of instructors and students is another crucial challenge in the effective implementation of GenAI. Educational institutions, especially in low-income countries, may lack the necessary expertise and support to integrate AI technologies effectively (Kim et al., 2022). Luckin (2017) highlights the importance of professional development for educators and the need for institutional policies that support the effective implementation of any technology. Instructors may lack sufficient expertise and motivation to use GenAI tools in their pedagogies for several reasons. For example, they may experience low efficacy and low commitment to use GenAI due to limited training in these tools, exacerbated by the absence of institutional support for skill development. Time constraints and the additional workload of integrating GenAI into existing curricula may also discourage the adoption of these tools. Moreover, concerns about the reliability of GenAI outputs and ambiguity of ethical implications may further reduce motivation. Without capacity-building initiatives, even the most advanced GenAI tools cannot be utilized to their full potential.

Uncertain policies

The rapid development and deployment of GenAI technologies have outpaced the establishment of clear guidelines to regulate the use of these tools in academic institutions. Therefore, uncertain policies present another significant challenge for the ethical use of GenAI in higher education (Chan & Hu, 2023). This lack of well-defined policies leads to confusion among students and instructors regarding the appropriate and ethical use of GenAI. Without clear guidelines, students may misuse the technology, inadvertently compromising academic integrity or violating intellectual property rights. Furthermore, inconsistent policies across different departments or institutions can create an uneven playing field, where some students might benefit from more liberal use of GenAI, while others are restricted. This uncertainty also hinders the integration of GenAI into curricula and assessment methods, as educators may be unsure about the boundaries regarding the ethical use of GenAI.

Institutional Readiness Measures

Integration among educational technologies

Effective integration of GenAI tools with existing educational technologies requires seamless interoperability and user-friendly interfaces. Upgrading technical infrastructure is crucial to achieving these goals, particularly in resource-limited settings, to ensure compatibility between GenAI tools and existing systems. Further, effective use of GenAI tools may require substantial investments in hardware and software (Bozkurt et al., 2023). Institutions should also establish support systems, such as help desks and technical assistance teams, to address any challenges that arise during GenAI adoption. Educational institutions should invest in scalable GenAI solutions that can be easily integrated with learning management systems, virtual classrooms, and other digital platforms. One way to do this is to collaborate with the developers of GenAI tools, such as OpenAI. For example, many universities, including University of Oxford, University of Pennsylvania, and Arizona State University, are collaborating with OpenAI to implement ChatGPT Enterprise on their campuses (OpenAI, 2023). In the same vein, providing technical training to educators to use these integrated systems proficiently will also enhance their effectiveness.

Training and development

Training and development programs are pivotal for ensuring that support staff, instructors, and students are well prepared to leverage the full potential of GenAI tools in educational settings. Support staff require targeted training to manage and maintain the GenAI infrastructure, ensuring seamless functionality and troubleshooting. Workshops and certification programs can be organized to equip them with the necessary technical skills to deploy and facilitate the use of GenAI for academic purposes. Instructors, as the primary users of GenAI in the classroom, need comprehensive training on both the technical and pedagogical aspects of GenAI. Professional development sessions should focus on integrating GenAI into lesson planning, assessment design, and student engagement strategies (Al-Zahrani, 2024). Similarly, students must be guided on using GenAI tools effectively and responsibly to enhance their learning experiences and on the potential consequences of any misuse of GenAI. Orientation sessions and workshops can introduce students to these tools, highlighting their role in fostering critical thinking, problem-solving, research skills, and the boundary conditions.

Institutions can also encourage peer-learning initiatives where experienced team members mentor others, fostering a collaborative learning environment. These capacity-building initiatives may also include training on understanding the limitations and the ethical use of GenAI. These programs should also focus on raising awareness, learning-oriented teaching practices, training faculty on data privacy and bias, and fostering a culture of preparedness and continuous learning using GenAI tools (Kurtz et al., 2024).

Comprehensive policies and regulations

Finally, a comprehensive policy and regulatory framework for governing the use of GenAI in higher education is essential (Duah & McGivern, 2024). Policy-makers should collaborate with educators, technologists, and ethicists to develop guidelines that address issues such as data privacy, academic integrity, copyrights, exam preparation and assessments, reporting of GenAI usage in academic tasks, and authorship for scholarly works. Also, higher education institutions need to develop and communicate comprehensive policies that provide clear guidelines on the ethical and responsible use of GenAI. Such policies would need continuous revisions as the potential capabilities of GenAI are evolving over time. Furthermore, each institution may constitute a specialized GenAI ethics committee to enforce the institutional values, ethical standards, regulatory requirements, and best practices in GenAI usage.

SOCIETAL CHALLENGES AND MITIGATION STRATEGIES

Societal and Governance Issues

Digital divide and access to GenAI tools

The digital divide presents a significant long-term societal challenge in the adoption of GenAI. Although ChatGPT may be an exception, not all students and institutions have equal access to other forms of GenAI, which may exacerbate existing educational inequalities. Even with ChatGPT, users often need to subscribe to access advanced features or versions, which can be cost-prohibitive for many, particularly in developing countries.

In contrast to the developed countries, where digital literacy is higher and access to technology is available, allowing users to more effectively utilize GenAI's potential, developing countries often struggle with the lack of technology infrastructure, training, and financial resources to support the effective implementation of advanced technologies in education. This may lead to an exacerbated digital divide across nations, where students in developing countries might be unable to fully harness the benefits of GenAI due to inadequate technology infrastructure, limited access to the internet and devices, and a lack of digital literacy training. As a result, these students may fall further behind their counterparts in developed nations, perpetuating inequality in educational opportunities and outcomes. Therefore, it is critical to address these disparities to ensure that all students have access to GenAI technologies in order to prevent a digital divide (Song, 2024).

Policy and regulatory frameworks

The development of a comprehensive policy and regulatory framework is essential to guide the ethical use of GenAI in higher education (Duah & McGivern, 2024). Although many educational institutions, publishers, funding agencies, and the Committee on Publication Ethics (2023) have developed guidelines on the use and reporting of GenAI in academic works, especially in scholarly studies, we still lack a clear regulatory framework on the use of GenAI and the detection of any misuse.

Similarly, governments worldwide are striving to regulate AI technologies to balance innovation with public safety and ethical concerns, with the European Union taking the lead by implementing the first comprehensive AI Act to oversee systems such as ChatGPT (Tribune, 2024). That said, each country is trying to develop its own regulatory framework for AI, which may vary significantly from those of other countries depending on cultural, economic, and technological contexts. This lack of global uniformity can create challenges such as cross-border legal conflicts, inconsistent ethical standards, and difficulties in complying with multiple regulatory systems.

Societal Measures

Bridging the digital divide in access to GenAI

Addressing the digital divide is crucial to ensure that all students have equal access to GenAI technologies across societies (Song, 2024). Governments and higher education institutions must invest in infrastructure and other relevant resources to provide access to GenAI tools and appropriate training. To address these issues, potential solutions may include government subsidies, particularly in developing countries, for GenAI literacy programs aimed at equipping students and educators with the resources and skills to effectively use GenAI tools. Such programs could focus on making GenAI technologies accessible in under-resourced schools and institutions. Moreover, partnerships with technology companies could be established to offer free or discounted access to GenAI tools to ensure that financial constraints do not hinder students' ability to benefit from these advancements. These initiatives would not only mitigate the impact of the digital divide but also promote equitable opportunities for students across the globe to engage with and benefit from GenAI.

Comprehensive Policy and Regulation

Finally, a globally uniform and comprehensive regulatory framework for governing the use of GenAI in higher education is essential (Duah & McGivern, 2024). These frameworks can be developed and implemented at three levels. First, at the global level, a uniform regulatory framework is critical to avoid challenges related to cross-border legal conflicts, inconsistent ethical standards, and difficulties in complying with multiple regulatory systems. Second, at the country level, governments and regulators should collaborate with educators, technologists, and ethicists to develop guidelines that address issues related to data privacy, academic integrity, reporting, and authorship. Finally, at the institutional level, higher education institutions need to develop and communicate comprehensive policies that provide clear guidelines on the responsible use of GenAI by instructors and students. These regulatory frameworks should aim to address issues related to the use of GenAI for academic tasks (e.g., research projects, books, applications). In addition, such policies would need continuous revisions as the potential capabilities of GenAI are evolving over time.

CONCLUSION

As the capabilities of GenAI are rapidly evolving, it has strong potential to redefine the academic landscape, offering unprecedented opportunities for innovation in teaching, learning, and research. However, these benefits come with many challenges that need to be addressed before educational institutions can utilize the full potential of GenAI. In this chapter, I have discussed some core challenges and proposed workable solutions to governments, regulators, educational institutions, and instructors for the effective use of GenAI in educational settings.

The key pedagogical challenges of GenAI adoption in education revolve around overreliance on GenAI-driven learning, which may undermine critical thinking. Additionally, the educators' lack of familiarity with GenAI tools may hinder effective integration into teaching practices. To address these challenges, a balanced approach is needed, where GenAI complements rather than replaces traditional teaching methods. Moreover, professional development programs can empower educators with the skills to leverage GenAI in ways that foster deeper learning, engagement, and cognitive development among students. Further, institutions must promote awareness of GenAI's limitations and risks in educational contexts. Moreover, integrating GenAI literacy and ethics into the curriculum can empower students to use these technologies responsibly.

Similarly, institutional readiness-related challenges involve the lack of digital infrastructure and resources required to support GenAI adoption, as well as resistance from educators and administrators who are unfamiliar with or not comfortable with GenAI. Institutions may lack the relevant capabilities or funding to effectively integrate GenAI with other educational technologies. I propose investing in GenAI-friendly infrastructure and fostering a culture of openness to technological innovation as potential solutions. Furthermore, institutional leadership must prioritize resource allocation, training initiatives, and partnerships with technology providers to ensure smooth adoption and long-term sustainability.

At the societal and government levels, challenges include regulatory and policy gaps, as well as concerns about the role of GenAI in employment and equal access to quality education. Governments must develop comprehensive policies that address GenAI governance, ensuring equitable access to these learning tools across diverse socio-economic groups. Collaborative efforts between policy-makers, educational institutions, and industry can pave the way for inclusive and ethical GenAI integration in education.

Looking forward, several critical areas warrant further investigation. First, understanding the impact of GenAI on student learning outcomes is essential.

While personalized GenAI-driven learning may boost engagement, it is vital to ensure that it fosters deeper cognitive and collaborative skills rather than superficial understanding. Longitudinal studies tracking the academic trajectories of students who make extensive use of GenAI could provide valuable insights into its long-term effects on students' learning. Second, the evolving role of educators in AI-powered classrooms will be transformative. As GenAI takes on more administrative and instructional functions, such as assistance in marking, course planning, content generation, and assessments, educators will need to shift their focus toward improving teaching pedagogies to facilitate experiential learning, critical thinking, mentoring, and ethical guidance. Research exploring how this transition affects teaching practices and the teacher–student relationship will be crucial.

Finally, ethical considerations surrounding the use of GenAI in education must be explored further in order to understand its long-term moral consequences for students. Issues such as data privacy, academic integrity, algorithmic bias, and the potential for fostering dependency on GenAI tools raise important questions about its responsible use. Developing robust and unified ethical policies will be critical to ensuring that GenAI usage benefits all students without incurring significant risks.

REFERENCES

Abbas, M. (2023). Uses and misuses of ChatGPT by academic community: An overview and guidelines. *SSRN Electronic Journal*. https://doi.org/10.2139/ssrn.4402510.

Abbas, M., Jam, F. A., & Khan, T. I. (2024). Is it harmful or helpful? Examining the causes and consequences of generative AI usage among university students. *International Journal of Educational Technology in Higher Education*, *21*(10), 1–22. https://doi.org/10.1186/s41239-024-00444-7.

Al-Zahrani, A. M. (2024). Unveiling the shadows: Beyond the hype of AI in education. *Heliyon*, *10*(9), e30696. https://doi.org/10.1016/j.heliyon.2024.e30696.

Bozkurt, A., Junhong, X., Lambert, S., Pazurek, A., Crompton, H., Koseoglu, S., … & Romero-Hall, E. (2023). Speculative futures on ChatGPT and generative artificial intelligence (AI): A collective reflection from the educational landscape. *Asian Journal of Distance Education*, *18*(1), 53–130. http://doi.org/10.5281/zenodo.7636568.

Bucea-Manea-Ţoniş, R., Kuleto, V., Gudei, S. C. D., Lianu, C., Lianu, C., Ilić, M. P., & Păun, D. (2022). Artificial intelligence potential in higher education institutions enhanced learning environment in Romania and Serbia. *Sustainability*, *14*(10), 5842. https://doi.org/10.3390/su14105842.

Chan, C. K. Y. (2023). A comprehensive AI policy education framework for university teaching and learning. *International Journal of Educational Technology in Higher Education*, *20*(1), 1–25. http://doi.org/10.1186/s41239-023-00408-3.

Chan, C. K. Y., & Hu, W. (2023). Students' voices on generative AI: Perceptions, benefits, and challenges in higher education. *International Journal of Educational*

Technology in Higher Education, *20*(1), 43. http://doi.org/10.1186/s41239-023-00411-8.
Chan, C. K. Y., & Tsi, L. H. (2024). Will generative AI replace teachers in Higher Education? A study of teacher and student perceptions. *Studies in Educational Evaluation*, *83*, 101395. https://doi.org/10.1016/j.stueduc.2024.101395.
Committee on Publication Ethics (COPE). (2023, February 13). *Authorship and AI tools*. COPE: Committee on Publication Ethics. https://publicationethics.org/cope-position-statements/ai-author.
Duah, J. E., & McGivern, P. (2024). How generative artificial intelligence has blurred notions of authorial identity and academic norms in higher education, necessitating clear university usage policies. *The International Journal of Information and Learning Technology*, *41*(2). https://doi.org/10.1108/IJILT-11-2023-0213.
Eaton, S. E., & Keyhani, M. (2025). The pedagogical ethics: Navigating learning in a generative AI-augmented environment. In S. Sabbaghan (Ed.), *Navigating generative AI in higher education: Ethical, theoretical and practical perspectives*. Edward Elgar.
Eubanks, V. (2018). *Automating inequality: How high-tech tools profile, police, and punish the poor*. St. Martin's.
Farrokhnia, M., Banihashem, S. K., Noroozi, O., & Wals, A. (2024). A SWOT analysis of ChatGPT: Implications for educational practice and research. *Innovations in Education and Teaching International*, *61*(3), 460–474. https://doi.org/10.1080/14703297.2023.2195846.
Kim, J., Lee, H., & Cho, Y. H. (2022). Learning design to support student-AI collaboration: Perspectives of leading teachers for AI in education. *Education and Information Technologies*, *27*(5), 6069–6104. http://doi.org/10.1007/s10639-021-10831-6.
King, M. R., & ChatGPT. (2023). A conversation on artificial intelligence, chatbots, and plagiarism in higher education. *Cellular and Molecular Bioengineering*, *16*, 1–2. https://doi.org/10.1007/s12195-022-00754-8.
Kurtz, G., Amzalag, M., Shaked, N., Zaguri, Y., Kohen-Vacs, D., Gal, E., Zailer, G., & Barak-Medina, E. (2024). Strategies for integrating generative AI into higher education: Navigating challenges and leveraging opportunities. *Education Sciences*, *14*(5), 503. https://doi.org/10.3390/educsci14050503.
Lawless, K. A., & Pellegrino, J. W. (2007). Professional development in integrating technology into teaching and learning: Knowns, unknowns, and ways to pursue better questions and answers. *Review of Educational Research*, *77*(4), 575–614. https://doi.org/10.3102/0034654307309921.
Luckin, R. (2017). *Enhancing learning and teaching with technology: What the research says*. UCL Institute of Education Press.
Mannuru, N. R., Shahriar, S., Teel, Z. A., Wang, T., Lund, B. D., Tijani, S., Pohboon, C. O., Agbaji, D., Alhassan, J., Galley, J., Kousari, R., Ogbadu-Oladapo, L., Saurav, S. K., Srivastava, A., Tummuru, S. P., Uppala, S., & Vaidya, P. (2023). Artificial intelligence in developing countries: The impact of generative artificial intelligence (AI) technologies for development. *Information Development*. https://doi.org/10.1177/02666669231200628.
Marcus, G., & Davis, E. (2019). *Rebooting AI: Building artificial intelligence we can trust*. Vintage.
Michel-Villarreal, R., Vilalta-Perdomo, E., Salinas-Navarro, D. E., Thierry-Aguilera, R., & Gerardou, F. S. (2023). Challenges and opportunities of generative AI for

higher education as explained by ChatGPT. *Education Sciences*, *13*(9), 856. https://doi.org/10.3390/educsci13090856.

Naujokaitytė, G. (2023, October 24). *Universities ready to take up generative artificial intelligence, but say guidelines are needed. Science|Business.* https://sciencebusiness.net/news/universities/universities-ready-take-generative-artificial-intelligence-say-guidelines-are.

NBC News. (2024, November 30). *Character.AI lawsuit: Florida teen's death raises questions about chatbot safety.* NBC News. https://www.nbcnews.com/tech/characterai-lawsuit-florida-teen-death-rcna176791.

Noble, S. U. (2018). *Algorithms of oppression: How search engines reinforce racism.* New York University Press. https://doi.org/10.18574/nyu/9781479833641.001.0001.

OpenAI. (2023). *Introducing ChatGPT-EDU.* https://openai.com/index/introducing-chatgpt-edu/.

Peters, M. A., Jackson, L., Papastephanou, M., Jandrić, P., Lazaroiu, G., Evers, C. W., Cope, B., Kalantzis, M., Araya, D., Tesar, M., Mika, C., & Fuller, S. (2023). AI and the future of humanity: ChatGPT-4, philosophy and education – critical responses. *Educational Philosophy and Theory*, *56*(9), 828–862. https://doi.org/10.1080/00131857.2023.2213437.

Sabbaghan, S. (2023). *Crafting AI terms of use for higher education.* University of Calgary. https://dx.doi.org/10.11575/PRISM/41675.

Song, N. (2024). Higher education crisis: Academic misconduct with generative AI. *Journal of Contingencies and Crisis Management*, *32*(1), e12532. https://doi.org/10.1111/1468–5973.12532

Tribune. (2024). Governments race to regulate AI tools. https://tribune.com.pk/story/2449657/governments-race-to-regulate-ai-tools.

Yang, J., & Zhang, H. (2024). Development and challenges of generative artificial intelligence in education and art. *Highlights in Science, Engineering and Technology*, *85*, 1334–1347. https://doi.org/10.54097/vaeav407.

12. From student artificial intelligence (AI) literacy to AI competency: Essential skills for the next generation

Thomas K. F. Chiu

INTRODUCTION

There is a global drive to incorporate artificial intelligence (AI) into higher education in order to educate the next generation and cultivate future citizens, making sure students have both AI literacy and competency (Delcker et al., 2024; Laupichler et al., 2022; Mikalef et al., 2023; Southworth et al., 2023). This drive is supported by the nationwide projects advocating AI education for all (Chiu et al., 2022; Schiff, 2022). All students should have strong AI literacy (Chiu, 2023; Chiu et al., 2024a; Huang, 2021; Long & Magerko, 2020)—that is, they should be able to explain how AI technologies work and the effects they have on society, and have the ability to use them effectively in ethical and responsible ways in a variety of contexts (Chiu et al., 2024a; Long & Magerko, 2020). This literacy emphasizes knowledge and skills. However, it may not align with the way students utilize generative artificial intelligence (GenAI) in their education and professions because GenAI is different from traditional AI.

GenAI technologies such as ChatGPT and Claude enable students to interact with them, unlike other AI technologies (e.g., translation tools, spam filters, image classifiers). They can produce essays, photographs, videos, and other digital content, and their technologies are becoming increasingly powerful and intrusive in education. Their accessibility to students and teachers is having a disruptive effect on higher education (Bates et al., 2020; Chiu, 2024b; O'Dea, 2024; Laupichler et al., 2022; Southworth et al., 2023), as students may use them to improve their learning or complete assignments without understanding. As a result, the effects of GenAI on learning may be positive or negative (Chan & Lee, 2023; Chiu, 2024b). Using GenAI goes beyond AI literacy; students must be responsible, ethical, confident, and skilled in order to get the benefits of GenAI during their learning, which is viewed as AI competency (Chiu et al., 2024a; Sanusi et al., 2022; UNESCO, 2024).

The early conversations regarding AI for non-engineers in higher education studies center on students' AI literacy and include identifying what AI literacy is (Long & Magerko, 2020), designing curriculum to foster AI understanding (Huang, 2021; Southworth et al., 2023), and outlining AI competency for non-computer science undergraduate students (Tenório & Romeike, 2023). Researching a single definition of AI literacy is difficult owing to continually changing technical, cultural, and societal learning environments (Chiu et al., 2024a; Long & Magerko, 2020), but it often emphasizes knowledge and skills such as understanding how AI processes data, recognizing how human actions contribute to AI bias, and learning how to develop machine learning models (Chiu et al., 2022). Recent research on promoting AI literacy emphasizes the curriculum design approach (Laupichler et al., 2022; Southworth et al., 2023), which has been criticized for its narrow focus on skills, lack of authenticity, failure to account for different sociocultural contexts in technology use, and ineffectual, oversimplified design (Falloon, 2020; Zhao et al., 2021). Transitioning from AI literacy to AI competency is also essential (Delcker et al., 2024; Falloon, 2020; Zhao et al., 2021). AI competency extends beyond AI literacy and involves applying AI knowledge in a beneficial and confident way, and actively engaging in continuous AI learning (Chiu et al., 2024a), so that higher education students with strong AI competencies are able to learn and collaborate with GenAI (Delcker et al., 2024; Kong et al., 2021). However, student AI competency is understudied (Chiu et al., 2024a), and how to effectively cultivate AI competency is also unclear. Accordingly, the purpose of this study is to present both a framework for student AI competency in higher education and suggestions on how to nurture it at the institution, teacher, and student levels.

LITERATURE REVIEW

The Definition of AI Literacy for Non-engineers

Long and Magerko (2020) defined AI literacy as "the abilities to critically evaluate AI technologies; communicate and collaborate effectively with AI; and use AI as a tool online, at home, and in the workplace." The links between this and other forms of literacy are quite close. For example, digital literacy is viewed as the capacity of an individual to locate, assess, produce, and convey information through the use of digital tools (Borthwick & Hansen, 2017), which is a prerequisite for AI literacy because AI is a type of digital tool. Mathematical literacy is the ability of a person to create, use, and understand mathematics in different situations (Jackson et al., 2021), which pertains to the fundamental understanding of AI, including machine learning. Data literacy is the ability to read, comprehend, evaluate, and generate shared data as information (Chiu et al., 2024a), which is also very important for AI literacy, as learning from and with data is the core idea of AI. Computational literacy involves using coding and computational tools to develop and explain solutions to problems (Burke et al., 2016). Non-engineering students are generally not AI developers or AI researchers, but they can learn about AI without learning programming. This supports the idea that data is the new coding for AI. Moreover, Chiu and colleagues (2024a) define AI literacy as "an individual's ability to clearly explain how AI technologies work and impact society, as well as to use them in an ethical and responsible manner and to effectively communicate and collaborate with them in any setting. It focuses on knowing (i.e., knowledge and skills)." This definition is aligned with Long and Magerko's (2020) definition, which explicitly mentions the ethics and impact of AI. The definitions emphasize AI knowledge and abilities and may not align with how students use AI in their studies and careers (i.e., AI competency).

What is AI Competency?

AI literacy and AI competency are distinct concepts (Chiu et al., 2024a; Janssen et al., 2013). AI literacy is technical knowledge; AI competency goes beyond technical knowledge and includes confidence, wellbeing, and productivity, but less research exists on its definition (Chiu et al., 2024a). To use AI in their education and careers, students must gain AI competency (Kong et al., 2021), which involves utilizing AI in a responsible, rational, and healthy manner; demonstrating knowledge of legal, moral, and ethical issues, including privacy and security; understanding AI's societal impact; and maintaining a balanced attitude towards AI, while adopting a mindset focused on technological innovations (Chiu et al., 2024a; Falloon, 2020; Janssen et al., 2013). Students foster their AI competency within a broader sociocultural context and will face a significant challenge in using AI effectively and responsibly in their professional careers and lifelong learning, which means that they must cultivate an awareness and concern for the broader implications of AI use and its impacts (Chiu et al., 2024a; Zhao et al., 2021). The concept of competency requires continuous updating to adapt to advancements in AI technologies and applications, considering the evolving nature of these technologies (Falloon, 2020; Janssen et al., 2013; Zhao et al., 2021), which means that students must consistently assess their existing knowledge, abilities, and needs, and, when necessary, engage in continuous learning to adapt to the rapidly evolving educational and professional landscape shaped by AI. This requires a positive attitude and confidence toward AI (Chiu et al., 2024b). As a result, AI competency should include a self-reflective mindset, interest in further learning, and informed beliefs about the role and impact of AI in society.

Studies proposing a student AI competency framework are aligned with the AI competency concept being discussed here. For example, the United Nations Educational, Scientific and Cultural Organization (UNESCO) drafted an AI competency framework for school students that included the definition: "the knowledge, skills, and attitudes students should acquire to understand and actively engage with AI in a safe and ethical manner in school and beyond" (UNESCO, 2024). The framework includes four major components: human-centered mindset, ethics of AI, AI techniques and applications, and AI system design. In each component, there are three levels: understand, apply, and create. The framework is still under development and each component lacks clear descriptions. Chiu et al. (2024a, p. 4) defined AI competency as "an individual's confidence and ability to clearly explain how AI technologies work and impact society, as well as to use them in an ethical and responsible manner and to effectively communicate and collaborate with them in any setting. They should have the confidence and ability to self-reflect on their AI understanding in order to continue learning." The focus of this definition is on how effectively individuals use AI for their own benefit. It comprises five major components: technology (how AI works); impact (how AI affects individuals and society); ethics (the moral and ethical implications of AI); collaboration (the use of AI for communication and collaboration in any context); and self-reflection (witnessing and evaluation of AI understanding). Chiu et al. (2024a) differentiated AI competency from AI literacy by emphasizing ethics, attitudes, confidence, a self-reflective mindset, and foundational beliefs about AI's role, value and impact in society.

Tenório and Romeike (2023) suggest an AI competency framework for non-computer-science undergraduate students. Their framework focuses solely on assessing the knowledge and skill needs of the students. The nine recommended topics in the framework are: computers, the basics of AI, AI capabilities, multidisciplinary AI, data, machine learning, advanced machine learning, human–AI interaction, and responsible AI. The framework concerns AI learning topics, making it focused on AI literacy rather than AI expertise. Overall, however, these studies agree that AI competency should include knowledge, skills, attitudes, foundational beliefs about AI's role and impact in society, and a self-reflective mindset.

Research Gap

To the best of our knowledge, despite the need for a clear framework to cultivate student AI competency, one does not yet exist in higher education. As intimated above, literacy and competency are related but different concepts in educational research (Chiu et al., 2024a; Janssen et al., 2013). However, they have often been used interchangeably in the literature (e.g., Long & Magerko, 2020; Tenório & Romeike, 2023), and it is necessary to clarify their meanings because the healthy, ethical, and productive integration of GenAI tools into education and the workplace requires strong AI competency. Therefore, it is necessary to propose an AI competency framework and investigate how to foster it.

THIS STUDY AND METHOD

Research Goal

This study aims to introduce an AI competency for non-engineering students in higher education and provide recommendations for developing this ability. Students' AI competency relates to their use of AI to enhance their learning and professional pursuits. Students' perspectives are essential for comprehending this new competency. Hence, we exchanged ideas on fostering competency and co-designed the framework with experienced GenAI students.

Participants

A total of 16 student participants was involved in this study at a university in Hong Kong. They studied in different faculties, including social science, education, and science, across different years of study. The student group consisted of seven males and nine females ranging from 18 to 21 years of age. They all used large language models (LLMs) in their learning tasks, which included addressing disciplinary problems, finishing projects, and composing essays. Another crucial participant was a researcher with expertise in educational technology and AI education for non-engineering students.

Research Design and Procedure

This study used a co-design approach to develop a framework for student AI competency and provide recommendations for fostering it. Five higher education educators and researchers engaged in an iterative co-design process that encompassed data collection, analysis, and design. The researcher and student participants helped establish the framework by outlining the needs for students to use AI in learning and future careers in a healthy, responsible, and ethical way.

Prior to the co-design process, the researcher conducted a two-hour workshop with the student participants on the pedagogy of utilizing GenAI (see Chiu, 2024a), UNESCO's (2024) AI competency framework for educators and students, and the definitions of AI literacy and competency from Chiu et al. (2024a) and Long and Magerko (2020). Three cycles of data collection occurred in which all the students participated. During each cycle, the researcher had a one-hour meeting with the students to get their perspectives. The students were divided into four groups of four, in which they stayed for all the cycles, to review and revise the previous cycle's framework. Together, the researchers and students developed a framework for student AI competency in higher education and suggested activities to cultivate this competency.

Reliability and Validity of the Research Design and Analysis

In each cycle, the student participants in the groups shared their individual ideas about the form of the framework. At the end of the meeting, the researchers consolidated their ideas using an agreement of 80%. This agreement is considerably reliable (Ahmadi et al., 2023). Student ideas that reached the agreement level were indicated as final. In the last cycle, all participants (100%) reached a consensus about the final framework and agreed that the activities could nurture their AI competency. This indicates the high reliability of the analysis. We discuss the validity of this qualitative design and analysis through the framing of six separate aspects (Cypress, 2017; Leung, 2015):

1. **Appropriateness:** We used the framework and definition of AI competency discussed in the literature review in the first cycle of the co-design process. These were well-recognized frameworks and definitions in the field. Moreover, the leading researcher has designed and delivered AI and education for non-engineering students, and has published 27 Scopus articles related to AI and education. The other researchers are experienced instructors in higher education. The student participants used AI to support their learning and work. This shows that the materials, researchers, and participants used for gathering data were suitable for the co-design process and research context.
2. **Triangulation:** We recruited students with different majors to avoid individual (subject) biases and provide a more diverse view.
3. **Credibility:** Qualitative research's credibility is determined by the researcher's competency in the co-design process. Using a qualitative design, the researcher has experience researching, designing, and teaching AI in different regions.
4. **Ethical procedures:** All the participants understood their rights and gave consent.
5. **Transferability:** The participants' majors were diverse, providing a wide range of data.

6. **Respondent validation:** This study was supported by the frameworks and definitions discussed in the literature review. Therefore, the reliability and validity of the research design and analysis are high.

The Development of the Proposed Framework

In the first cycle, an AI competency framework for K-12 students based on UNESCO's (2024) framework was presented for discussion; see Table 12.1. Tables 12.2a and b show the results of the first cycle. AI literacy, beliefs, interests, attitudes, learning with AI, and AI for careers were added to the framework. AI ethical principles and AI impact were rephrased. In the second cycle, all the added and rephrased items reached the agreement level, and life-long learning for AI was added. In the third cycle, the added item reached the agreement level, and AI knowledge and application were rephrased. Following the third cycle, all the student participants cast their votes to indicate their approval of the proposed framework and activities.

Table 12.1 *AI competency framework for student discussions in cycle 1*

Aspects	Understanding	Applying	Creating
Human-centered mindset	Human agency	Human accountability	Citizenship in the era of AI
Ethics of AI	Embodied ethics	Safe and responsible use	Ethics by design
AI techniques and applications	AI foundations	Application skills	Creating AI tools
AI system design	Problem scoping	Architecture design	Iteration and feedback loops

Note: This table outlines the initial AI competency framework presented for discussion during the first co-design cycle. The framework includes four aspects:1. Human-Centered Mindset: Focusing on human agency, accountability, and citizenship in the AI era.2. Ethics of AI: Covering embodied ethics, safe and responsible use, and ethics by design.3. AI Techniques and Applications: Including foundational knowledge, application skills, and creating AI tools.4. AI System Design: Addressing problem scoping, architecture design, and iteration with feedback loops.

*Table 12.2a AI competency framework for student discussions in cycle 2: AI literacy+**

Aspects	Understanding	Applying	Creating
AI techniques and applications	AI foundations	Application skills	Create AI tools
AI ethical principles#*	Understand key AI ethical principles	Apply ethical principles to evaluate AI applications	Design a set of AI ethical principles for a context
AI impact#*	Understand the personal and societal impact of AI	Discuss the impact of AI with others	Evaluate impacts of an AI application

*Table 12.2b AI competency framework for student discussions in cycle 2: beliefs, interest, and attitudes+**

Aspects	Understanding	Applying	Creating
Learning with AI+*	Identify appropriate AI applications for learning	Apply appropriate AI applications to complete a learning task	Regulate their learning with appropriate AI applications (self-regulated learning with AI)
AI for careers+*	Identify appropriate AI applications for careers	Apply appropriate AI applications to complete their careers	Evaluate or create AI applications for their careers

Note: + new idea after the first cycle; # rephrased ideas after the first cycle; * agreed idea in the second cycle. This table presents the revised AI competency framework after the second co-design cycle, incorporating new and rephrased ideas:AI Literacy: Emphasizes understanding AI foundations, applying skills, and creating tools.AI Ethical Principles: Explores understanding ethical principles, applying them to evaluate AI, and designing principles for specific contexts.AI Impact: Focuses on understanding AI's societal and personal impact, discussing it, and evaluating AI applications.Beliefs, Interests, and Attitudes: Added as a new focus area to encourage positive engagement with AI.Learning with AI: Highlights identifying, applying, and self-regulating AI tools for learning.AI for Careers: Covers identifying, applying, and creating AI tools relevant to professional tasks.

THE PROPOSED AI COMPETENCY FRAMEWORK FOR STUDENTS

Table 12.3a and Table 12.3b shows the results of the analysis—the proposed

Table 12.3a The proposed AI competency framework and essential skills for students: AI literacy

Aspects	Understanding	Applying	Creating
AI knowledge and application	Understand how AI processes data	Apply an AI application to complete a task effectively	Develop an AI application
AI ethical principles	Understand key AI ethical principles	Apply ethical principles to evaluate AI applications	Design a set of AI ethical principles for a context
AI impact	Understand the personal and societal impacts of AI	Discuss the impact of AI with others	Evaluate impacts of an AI application

Table 12.3b The proposed AI competency framework and essential skills for students: beliefs, interest, and attitudes

Aspects	Understanding	Applying	Creating
Learning with AI	Identify appropriate AI applications for learning	Applying appropriate AI applications to complete a learning task	Regulate their learning with appropriate AI applications (self-regulated learning with AI)
AI for careers	Identify appropriate AI applications for careers	Apply appropriate AI applications to complete their careers	Evaluate or create AI applications for their careers
Lifelong learning for AI	Understand the latest development of AI	Share the latest development of AI with others	Develop a strong self-reflective mindset towards AI

Note: This table represents the finalized AI competency framework, structured into six aspects, each with three levels of understanding, applying, and creating:AI Knowledge and Application: From understanding AI processes to developing AI applications.
AI Ethical Principles: From understanding to designing ethical guidelines for AI.AI Impact: From understanding AI's societal effects to predicting impacts of new applications.Learning with AI: From identifying tools to self-regulating learning with AI.AI for Careers: From identifying tools for careers to creating relevant AI solutions.Lifelong Learning for AI: From understanding AI advancements to fostering a self-reflective mindset.

AI competency framework for students in higher education. This framework is the last step in the co-design process (i.e., the last cycle), which was confirmed by all the student participants. It contains six aspects: (a) AI knowledge and application; (b) AI ethical principles; (c) AI impact; (d) learning with AI; (e) AI for careers; and (f) lifelong learning for AI. The first three aspects are more related to AI literacy—i.e., knowledge and skills; the other aspects concern beliefs about using AI, interest in further learning, and attitudes toward AI. In each aspect, there are three levels driven by Bloom's Taxonomy (Krathwohl, 2002): understanding, applying, and creating. These indicate the order of thinking and are also necessary abilities for lifelong learning. These levels also indicate how well students understand AI competencies. Not every student is expected to achieve the top level.

The following discussion relates to each of the aspects in the framework.

1. **AI knowledge and application:** Students are expected to possess fundamental knowledge and practical skills in AI. At the understanding level, students should comprehend the concepts of AI, data processing in AI, and task completion by AI. At the applying level, students should use an AI tool to accomplish a basic task. This level is associated with data literacy (Long & Magerko, 2020). At the creating level, students should develop a simple AI application. This aspect is in line with the worldwide effort to advocate for AI education for everyone (Chiu et al., 2022; Schiff, 2022). Several AI curricula for non-professionals include these knowledge and skills, which form the basis of the other five aspects of AI competency. This is supported by the progress of AI educational technologies. Previously, it was difficult for individuals without professional expertise to develop AI applications. Utilizing user-friendly educational technologies for AI such as Google Teachable Machine and HuskyLens, students may design and create a basic AI tool, such as those using machine learning, without needing to acquire complex coding knowledge and skills. They just need to gather and analyze sets of data for the creation. In other words, user-friendly educational technologies for AI reduce the entrance barriers to machine learning development. However, creating robust and meaningful AI applications necessitates considerable knowledge beyond mere data collection and analysis.**Examples for practitioners:** Art students can leverage machine learning to identify the style of a painting, while language students can develop machine learning models to analyze and determine the emotional tone of a text.

   Examples for practitioners: Art students can leverage machine learning to identify the style of a painting, while language students can develop machine learning models to analyze and determine the emotional tone of a text.

2. **AI ethical principles:** Ethical knowledge, being abstract, is approached in a more concrete manner through AI ethical principles in the framework. Students with a certain degree of ethical understanding should familiarize themselves with established AI ethical guidelines, such as those outlined by IBM (2022) and UNESCO (2022). Students at the applying level should be capable of ethical reasoning and using ethical principles to evaluate AI applications, while those at the creating level should be able to formulate and implement a new set of ethical rules for a different setting. Students should gain an understanding of how culture and religion can affect ethical principles (ÓhÉigeartaigh et al., 2020). This aspect is consistent with the fundamental elements of the AI curriculum as outlined by Chiu et al. (2022) and Schiff (2022), and also the definitions of AI literacy (Chiu et al., 2024a; Long & Magerko, 2020).

   Examples for practitioners: Economics students can use the ethical principles to evaluate how ethical an AI application is; biology students can create their own ethical guidelines for the use of AI in scientific research.
3. **AI impact:** This aspect is closely connected to the daily lives of students and their environment. Students should comprehend the impacts of AI on individuals and society (understanding level), engage in discussions about these impacts (applying), and be capable of evaluating the limitations and predicting the effects of new AI applications (creating). This aspect is considered part of the fundamental knowledge and skills set of AI literacy, as discussed in earlier studies (Chiu et al., 2022; Chiu et al., 2024a; Long & Magerko, 2020). It requires strong critical-thinking skills. In this approach, we explicitly incorporate the concept of prediction at the creating level. Predicting the impact of an emerging technology is crucial to preventing chaos (Sangiorgio et al., 2021). **Examples for practitioners:** Law students can explore how AI impacts the development of intellectual property and privacy; psychology students can discuss how AI affects the cognitive development of young children and the emotions of citizens.

   Examples for practitioners: Law students can explore how AI impacts the development of intellectual property and privacy; psychology students can discuss how AI affects the cognitive development of young children and the emotions of citizens.
4. **Learning with AI:** The primary goal of higher education students is studying. AI technologies provide students with enhanced learning opportunities through interactions between humans and computers (Chiu, 2024a, 2024b). Students may use LLMs (e.g., ChatGPT) for feedback, answers, and suggestions, as well as GenAI for multimodal tools such as text-to-images, text-to-speech, and text-to-video to quickly generate posters, photographs, animations, and videos to enhance their learning experience. AI

can serve as an alternative intelligence and multimedia-generating tool. Students should possess the knowledge and skills to recognize suitable AI applications for their learning at the understanding level, apply appropriate AI applications to complete learning tasks at the applying level, and use AI applications for self-regulated learning at the creating level. This aspect advocates for meaningful learning outcomes by highlighting the significance of self-regulated learning using AI technologies. This is aligned with studies on future research recommendations for GenAI in higher education (Chiu, 2024a, 2024b; Wang & Lin, 2023). **Examples for practitioners:** Higher education teachers may consider including learning with AI in the learning outcomes of their course—for example, using GenAI to create learning material (education students), using GenAI to analyze data related to the elderly (social worker students), and using GenAI to get feedback on their essay (any students).

Examples for practitioners: Higher education teachers may consider including learning with AI in the learning outcomes of their course—for example, using GenAI to create learning material (education students), using GenAI to analyze data related to the elderly (social worker students), and using GenAI to get feedback on their essay (any students).

5. **AI for careers:** Higher education institutions should equip students for their future professions, where they may be required to collaborate with AI (Chiu, 2024b). For example, cashiers use image recognition to identify items for customers, while teachers use AI to forecast student attrition rates and identify giftedness. In this aspect, students are expected to recognize suitable AI applications for their careers (understanding), utilize these applications to accomplish necessary activities in their future careers (applying), and evaluate or develop AI applications relevant to their careers (creating). This framework encourages higher education instructors to contemplate the future skills needed by students that are supported by studies on how AI transforms higher education (Bates et al., 2020; Chiu, 2024b; Southworth et al., 2023).

   Examples for practitioners: Higher education teachers may consider including learning with AI in the learning outcomes of programs—for example, using GenAI to design presentation slides and videos, draft cover letters and curriculum vitae for job applications, and draft reports for some analyses. Students should be aware of the limitations of working with GenAI.
6. **Lifelong learning for AI:** AI is an emerging and disruptive domain. Unlike other traditional disciplines (e.g., mathematics, language), its knowledge and skills are evolving. Students should keep updating their knowledge of AI by reading related articles, taking courses, and discussing AI topics with others. In this aspect, at the understanding level, students should

understand the latest developments in AI; at the applying level, students should share the latest developments in AI with others; at the creating level, students should develop a strong self-reflective mindset towards AI. This aspect is aligned with the concept of competency discussed in the literature review (Chiu et al., 2024a; Falloon, 2020; Janssen et al., 2013; Zhao et al., 2021). It also highlights the importance of a self-reflective mindset. Graduate students should have the confidence and ability to self-reflect on their AI understanding for further learning. Individuals with stronger self-reflective mindsets are more likely to keep reviewing their AI knowledge and identify areas and needs for further learning.

Examples for practitioners: Higher education teachers can ask students to explain how their AI products work and how to advance their work. This learning approach reminds students that AI products can be improved, fostering a self-reflective mindset.

Overall, this framework is a result of a co-design process between teacher–researchers and students. This process took both educator and student perspectives into account, ensuring the voices of various stakeholders were heard. It offers relevant concepts for institutions, educators, and students to develop student AI competency. Through the co-design process, both educators and students gain a deeper understanding of AI competency. Practically, educators can comprehend what AI competencies their students need when integrating AI in teaching, while students can identify the areas they need to improve for AI competency. This co-design approach promotes a broader understanding of AI competency instead of focusing only on technical AI literacy. These insights will help educators effectively develop and arrange learning programs and activities to enhance students' competencies as outlined in the framework and discussed in the next section.

USING THE FRAMEWORK TO CULTIVATE STUDENT AI COMPETENCY

Foundation Courses for AI Literacy (Institution and Teacher Levels)

The first three aspects in the framework are directly tied to AI literacy and focus on knowledge and skills, which are best developed through a well-structured approach. AI knowledge and application may be covered in a foundational university course, while AI ethical principles and impact can be incorporated into courses that encourage discussions, debates, and projects. The last three aspects pertain more to the student experience. Using a course format to develop these qualities is not recommended, as they are better suited for assignment integration. The course may explicitly state that these are learning objectives.

Self-assessment of Student AI Competency (Institution and Student Levels)

We suggest that institutions develop self-learning and self-assessment platforms for student AI competency development. In the self-learning platform, we can create videos and tasks to discuss content related to the understanding level in the framework. Applying and creating levels should be fostered through student-centered learning activities. Peer learning and sharing culture can be used to develop these two levels—e.g., online discussions, proposal writing sharing, prototype creation, and online presentations. Moreover, we recommend that institutions use the framework to develop online self-assessment tests. They can utilize scenario-based or task-based methods to build the test for each aspect of the framework, making it more authentic. Students can use the test to evaluate their AI competency and enhance their self-reflective mindset.

Interdisciplinary and Collaborative Approach (Institution and Teacher Levels)

Ideally, cultivating student AI competency in higher education requires the engagement of all faculty members and an interdisciplinary strategy (Falloon, 2020). It should not be considered an exclusive duty or the expertise of only one or two instructors (Chiu et al., 2024b; Falloon, 2020). For successful implementation of an interdisciplinary approach, every teaching faculty member must consistently understand the full scope and definition of the six aspects of the framework. Interdisciplinary approaches are not common, and it is challenging to alter the inflexible discipline-based structure of institutions (Falloon, 2020). Therefore, we suggest that a collaborative approach to student AI competency be adopted such that professionals from different departments collaborate within the framework to determine how each component could be integrated into discipline-specific curricula. For example, engineering and science faculties could teach AI knowledge and application; law faculty could teach AI ethical principles; humanities and social sciences faculties could teach AI impact; and other faculties can teach learning with AI, AI for careers, and lifelong learning for AI by redesigning course objectives.

Overall, AI will enforce changes to both the essential skills higher education students need for lifelong learning and careers and the ways in which institutions and educators design their curricula and courses. Although changing the rigid structure of higher education institutions is challenging, we recommend institutions and educators discuss how higher education should transform to fit the needs of their students.

CONCLUSIONS, LIMITATIONS, FUTURE RESEARCH DIRECTION

This chapter presents a student AI competency framework in higher education aimed at promoting the transition from AI literacy to AI competency. This framework is essential for operating effectively, healthily, securely, ethically, and morally in contexts that are increasingly influenced by AI. It underscores the importance of this framework for students' learning and future career prospects, fostering a mindset and aptitude for lifelong learning. Research on AI education is still in its early phases. More empirical studies are required to develop a comprehensive understanding of AI competency and practices for fostering it. The framework may require revision to include new technology, findings, society's expectations, and culture. We urge scholars in education, psychology, and engineering to collaborate on interdisciplinary research to develop a more comprehensive knowledge of AI competency. Finally, we hope educators can use our co-designed framework consisting of six aspects—AI knowledge and application, AI ethical principles, AI impact, learning with AI, AI for careers, and lifelong learning for AI—to foster students' AI competency from behavioral, cognitive, affective, and agentic perspectives.

REFERENCES

Ahmadi, A., Noetel, M., Parker, P., Ryan, R. M., Ntoumanis, N., Reeve, J., … & Lonsdale, C. (2023). A classification system for teachers' motivational behaviours recommended in self-determination theory interventions. *Journal of Educational Psychology, 115*(8), 1158–1176. https://doi.org/10.1037/edu0000783.

Bates, T., Cobo, C., Mariño, O., & Wheeler, S. (2020). Can artificial intelligence transform higher education? *International Journal of Educational Technology in Higher Education, 17,* 1–12. https://doi.org/10.1186/s41239-020-00218-x.

Borthwick, A., & Hansen, R. (2017). Digital literacy in teacher education. Are teacher educators competent? *Journal of Digital Learning in Teacher Education, 33*(2), 46–48. https://doi.org/10.1080/21532974.2017.1291249.

Burke, Q., O'Byrne, W. I., & Kafai, Y. B. (2016). Computational participation: Understanding coding as an extension of literacy instruction. *Journal of Adolescent & Adult Literacy, 59*(4), 371–375. https://doi.org/10.1002/jaal.496.

Chan, C. K. Y., & Lee, K. K. (2023). The AI generation gap: Are Gen Z students more interested in adopting generative AI such as ChatGPT in teaching and learning than their Gen X and millennial generation teachers? *Smart Learning Environments, 10*(1), 60. https://doi.org/10.1186/s40561-023-00269-3.

Chiu, T. K. F. (2023). The impact of Generative AI (GenAI) on practices, policies and research direction in education: A case of ChatGPT and Midjourney. *Interactive Learning Environments*, 1–17. https://dx.doi.org/10.1080/10494820.2023.2253861.

Chiu, T. K. F. (2024a). A classification tool to foster self-regulated learning with ChatGPT by applying self-determination theory from a teacher perspective. *Education Tech Research Dev*, *72*, 2401–2416. https://doi.org/10.1007/s11423-024-10366-w.

Chiu, T. K. F. (2024b). Future research recommendations for transforming higher education with Generative AI. *Computer & Education: Artificial Intelligence*, *6*, 100197. https://doi.org/10.1016/j.caeai.2023.100197.

Chiu, T. K. F., Meng, H., Chai, C. S., King, I., Wong, S., & Yeung, Y. (2022). Creation and evaluation of a pre-tertiary artificial intelligence (AI) curriculum. *IEEE Transactions on Education*, *65*(1), 30–39. https://doi.org/10.1109/TE.2021.3085878.

Chiu, T. K. F., Ahmad, Z., Ismail, M., & Sanusi, I. T. (2024a). What are artificial intelligence literacy and competency? A comprehensive framework to support them. *Computers & Education Open*, *6*, 100171. https://doi.org/10.1016/j.caeo.2024.100171.

Chiu, T. K. F., Falloon, G., Song, Y. J., Wong, V. W. L., Zhao, Li, & Ismailov, M., (2024b) A self-determination theory approach to teacher digital competence development. *Computers & Education*, *24*, 105017. https://doi.org/10.1016/j.compedu.2024.105017.

Cypress, B. S. (2017). Rigor or reliability and validity in qualitative research: Perspectives, strategies, reconceptualization, and recommendations. *Dimensions of Critical Care Nursing*, *36*(4), 253–263. https://doi.org/10.1097/DCC.0000000000000253.

Delcker, J., Heil, J., Ifenthaler, D., Seufert, S., & Spirgi, L. (2024). First-year students AI-competence as a predictor for intended and de facto use of AI-tools for supporting learning processes in higher education. *International Journal of Educational Technology in Higher Education*, *21*(1), 18. https://doi.org/10.1186/s41239-024-00452-7.

Falloon, G. (2020). From digital literacy to digital competence: The teacher digital competency (TDC) framework. *Educational technology research and development*, *68*(5), 2449–2472. https://doi.org/10.1007/s11423-020-09767-4.

Huang, X. (2021). Aims for cultivating students' key competencies based on artificial intelligence education in China. *Education and Information Technologies*, *26*(5), 5127–5147. https://doi.org/10.1007/s10639-021-10530-2.

IBM (2022). *Everyday Ethics for Artificial Intelligence*. IBM. https://www.ibm.com/watson/assets/duo/pdf/everydayethics.pdf.

Jackson, C., Mohr-Schroeder, M. J., Bush, S. B., Maiorca, C., Roberts, T., Yost, C., & Fowler, A. (2021). Equity-oriented conceptual framework for K-12 STEM literacy. *International Journal of STEM Education*, *8*, 1–16. https://doi.org/10.1080/19477503.2022.2150462.

Janssen, J., Stoyanov, S., Ferrari, A., Punie, Y., Pannekeet, K., & Sloep, P. (2013). Experts' views on digital competence: Commonalities and differences. *Computers & Education*, *68*, 473–481. https://doi.org/10.1016/j.compedu.2013.06.008.

Kong, H., Yuan, Y., Baruch, Y., Bu, N., Jiang, X., & Wang, K. (2021). Influences of artificial intelligence (AI) awareness on career competency and job burnout. *International Journal of Contemporary Hospitality Management*, *33*(2), 717–734. https://doi.org/10.1108/IJCHM-07-2020-0789.

Krathwohl, D. R. (2002). A revision of Bloom's taxonomy: An overview. *Theory Into Practice*, *41*(4), 212–218. https://doi.org/10.1207/s15430421tip4104_2.

Laupichler, M. C., Aster, A., Schirch, J., & Raupach, T. (2022). Artificial intelligence literacy in higher and adult education: A scoping literature review. *Computers and*

Education: Artificial Intelligence, *3*, 100101. https://doi.org/10.1016/j.caeai.2022.100101.

Leung, L. (2015). Validity, reliability, and generalizability in qualitative research. *Journal of Family Medicine and Primary Care*, *4*(3), 324–327. https://doi.org/10.4103/2249-4863.161306.

Long, D., & Magerko, B. (2020, April). What is AI literacy? Competencies and design considerations. In *Proceedings of the 2020 CHI conference on human factors in computing systems* (pp. 1-16).

Mikalef, P., Islam, N., Parida, V., Singh, H., & Altwaijry, N. (2023). Artificial intelligence (AI) competencies for organizational performance: A B2B marketing capabilities perspective. *Journal of Business Research*, *164*, 113998. https://doi.org/10.1016/j.jbusres.2023.113998.

O'Dea, X. (2024). Generative AI: is it a paradigm shift for higher education? *Studies in Higher Education*, *49*(5), 811–816. https://doi.org/10.1080/03075079.2024.2332944.

ÓhÉigeartaigh, S. S., Whittlestone, J., Liu, Y., Zeng, Y., & Liu, Z. (2020). Overcoming barriers to cross-cultural cooperation in AI ethics and governance. *Philosophy & technology*, *33*, 571–593. https://doi.org/10.1007/s13347-020-00402-x.

Sangiorgio, M., Dercole, F., & Guariso, G. (2021). Forecasting of noisy chaotic systems with deep neural networks. *Chaos, Solitons & Fractals*, *153*, 111570. https://doi.org/10.1016/j.chaos.2021.111570.

Sanusi, I. T., Olaleye, S. A., Agbo, F. J., & Chiu, T. K. F. (2022). The role of learners' competencies in artificial intelligence education. *Computers and Education: Artificial Intelligence*, *3*, 100098. https://doi.org/10.1016/j.caeai.2022.100098.

Schiff, D. (2022). Education for AI, not AI for education: The role of education and ethics in national AI policy strategies. *International Journal of Artificial Intelligence in Education*, *32*(3), 527–563. https://doi.org/10.1007/s40593-021-00270-2.

Southworth, J., Migliaccio, K., Glover, J., Reed, D., McCarty, C., Brendemuhl, J., & Thomas, A. (2023). Developing a model for AI Across the curriculum: Transforming the higher education landscape via innovation in AI literacy. *Computers and Education: Artificial Intelligence*, *4*, 100127. https://doi.org/10.1016/j.caeai.2023.100127.

Tenório, K., & Romeike, R. (2023, November). AI competencies for non-computer science students in undergraduate education: Towards a competency framework. In *Proceedings of the 23rd Koli Calling International Conference on Computing Education Research* (pp. 1–12). https://doi.org/10.1145/3631802.3631829.

UNESCO (2022). *Recommendation on the ethics of artificial intelligence*. https://unesdoc.unesco.org/ark:/48223/pf0000381137_eng.

UNESCO (2024, May 8). *AI competency frameworks for school students and teachers*. https://www.unesco.org/en/digital-education/ai-future-learning/competency-frameworks.

Wang, C. Y., & Lin, J. J. (2023). Utilizing artificial intelligence to support analyzing self-regulated learning: A preliminary mixed-methods evaluation from a human-centered perspective. *Computers in Human Behavior*, *144*, 107721. https://doi.org/10.1016/j.chb.2023.107721.

Zhao, Y., Llorente, A. M. P., & Gómez, M. C. S. (2021). Digital competence in higher education research: A systematic literature review. *Computers & Education*, *168*, 104212. https://doi.org/10.1016/j.compedu.2021.104212.

13. An innovation policy analysis of G10 nations' strategic plans for future AI leaders and researchers in higher education

Eugene G. Kowch

INTRODUCTION

National AIS (Artificial Intelligence Strategies) today exist in a turbulent and emergent policy ecosystem where interconnected, relational partnerships are essential in a constant-flux edosystem of AI innovation, economic drivers, organizational learning, and AI hype. Here, we analyze AI strategic policy (including generative AI) within the world's top ten producing nations: USA, China, Germany, Japan, India, United Kingdom, France, Brazil, Italy, and Canada (Statista, 2024). To describe the G10 AI policy environment, we use a *complexity* approach to describe AI strategy enablers and constraints and to characterize existing policy approaches, legislation, and regulatory efforts (Uhl-Bien et al., 2007; Innes et al., 2018). Because AI is an innovation shaping both the process and products from institutional activities such as education (Kowch, 2021), we adopt the Policy Innovation Framework (Diercks et al., 2019) to analyze individual and collective AI strategies. To interpret *power* and *organizational* dynamics incentivized by AIS plan implementation, we utilize the Complex Adaptive Systems (CAS) approach (Uhl-Bien et al., 2007), taking a systemic change lens to interpret AI higher education leadership and organizations' adaptability (Kowch, 2018; 2023). We incorporate Policy Networks and Community Frameworks (Klijn et al., 2015) alongside Policy Design (Howlett, 2024) and Dynamic Adaptive Systems Theory to interpret these AI strategic plan governance and power implications and, finally, we offer specific governance and higher education organization/institution implications for higher education leaders and policy makers.

THE G10 AI POLICY ECOSYSTEM TODAY

This section explores two significant policy environment factors influencing the G10 nations' AI strategy policy-making efforts: learning, and financial resources. We then briefly analyze the current G10 national AI policy-maker approaches, legislation, regulation, and policy-making constraints and enablers to conclude with AI policy-making factors that have been found to influence higher education leaders and scholars.

Major AI Policy Ecosystem Influences

Learning is essential in leading university technology-enhanced education ecosystems. When instructors, professors, and learners face unpredictable innovations, system leaders know that collective (organizational) learning about artificial intelligence and its impacts matters. At a minimum, we must develop new cognitive tools (i.e., ways to think critically as we learn) and content (i.e., AI and computational literacy) for us all (Aoun, 2017). Once the technology matures, AI will be a game-changer for instructors and students, helping instructors do what they do best and freeing them up to focus on what matters most (Gates, 2024).

As Li (2023) notes, even AI science professors and senior researchers are continually learning about AI due to the rapid evolution of deep learning, which feels like an entirely new field each year. This underscores an imperative for higher education leaders to recognize and to prioritize ongoing transdisciplinary, adaptable education organization and networked learning processes that can evolve alongside advancements in AI. We know from technology innovation leadership theory that AI, understood as a "black box," cannot sustain the trust of policy communities (Gardner et al., 2021; Kowch, 2013; Tweedie & Sharmi, 2025).

Investment is another significant influence on AI strategic policy. Enormous rivers of financial investments flow into the national and international AI ecosystems today, with nearly one trillion USD invested from existing G10 national AI strategic plan directions (OECD.AI, 2024) since 2019 and these plans will soon be updated. Educators must be more involved in that. Figure 13.1 displays venture capitalist investment in AI totaling USD 750 billion in the G10 countries (OECD.AI, 2024).

Meanwhile, G10 governments are investing billions in higher education systems, too. As demonstrated below, those investments fuel industries and universities incentivized by national AI strategic policies to join with universities and governments. Nearly a trillion USD (*The Economist*, 2024) has poured into industry partnerships focused on AI development (mostly

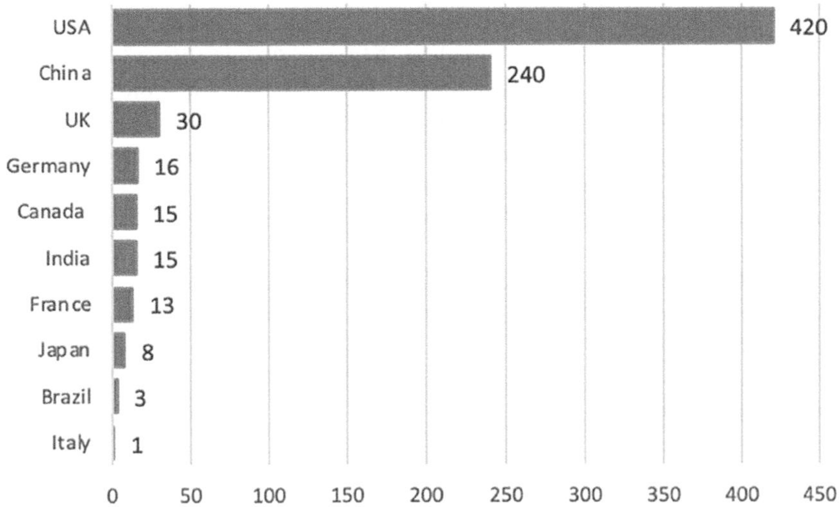

Figure 13.1 *Distribution of G10 nations' venture capital investments in AI (billions USD)*

computing technology), impacting higher education as a place for talent and research; however, humanities faculties are barely involved in the process so far. Meanwhile, about 80% of the G10 national AI strategies are over five years old, so we expect these plans to be updated soon. The following sections examine how AIS planners have set their AI innovation agendas, arguing that educators and humanities experts must be more significant actors in future AIS update processes. AI investors are becoming more uneasy about their returns on AI investment (*The Economist*, 2024) in an intensifying global AI policy and political environment (Coeckelbergh, 2022).

G10 AI POLICY-MAKING APPROACHES, LEGISLATION, REGULATION, AND GUIDELINES

We coded G10 nations as follows: (a) regulation approaches are either *ex-ante* (regulators predict and prevent risk in advance) or *ex-post* (regulators use evidence to assess and respond to risk); (b) deregulation approaches (i.e., they prefer guidelines instead of regulations); and (c) policy implementation approaches from a power perspective – *centralized* or mostly government control (Wu et al., 2018) vs *decentralized* or mostly AI legislation institutional/partnership control. China is an example of an ex-ante AI regulation approach because it regulates AI algorithm development in the public domain (China State Council, 2017). In contrast, the UK, for example, prefers AI guideline provision over regulations (Comunale & Manera, 2024). All nations have a data security act or similar legislation. However, without comprehensive national or state-level AI legislation, innovation (including AI) regulations and guidelines are inefficient because enforceable regulations and guidelines require superordinate or umbrella legislation as part of a coherent legal support system (Calderini et al., 2023). Educators must soon become part of the AI strategic planning process.

Table 13.1 summarizes the G10 policy-making approaches to comprehensive AI legislation, AI Acts, and AI regulation using a policy design analytical framework (Howlett, 2024).

Implementation

No G10 nation has comprehensive AI legislation. The European Union is not a member of the G10, although several of its member states are and it has a new AI Act (European Commission 2021) that is influencing member states' policies through a combination of approaches, while also providing funding for specific AI initiatives. Italy has taken the lead by beginning to draft its own AI Act in alignment with this directive.

Japan, Brazil, France, Germany, Canada, Italy, and the UK take a more arm's-length policy and regulation approach, having developed flexible AI use guidelines that are easy to adapt to the context. The decentralized USA approach places responsibility for AI planning on targeted AI partnerships that achieve particular policy and technical outcomes, while countries such as Japan, Germany, and the UK take a "light touch" to AI regulation in an attempt not to constrain innovation while empowering economic growth possibilities in a context where the AI industry may pursue more far-reaching research than would be possible under stricter regulatory conditions (Calderini et al., 2023).

AIS Policy-making Enablers and Constraints

The following UK AI Strategic Plan passage represents most G10 AI strategic plans' (funded) objectives, being focused on the economy:

> Much like James Watt's 1776 steam engine, AI is a "general-purpose" technology with many possible implications. We expect it to transform the whole economy. (Secretary of State for Digital, Culture, Media and Sport, 2021, p. 16)

Among AI policy-making enablers is social hype, which drives a lot of AI investment and policy as people aspire to achieve personal, institutional,

Table 13.1 *G10 national government approaches to AI legislation, regulation, and Strategies-*

G10 nations	AI legislation: has AI legislation (Act)	AI legislation: has a regional AI legislation (Act)	AI legislation: has a data security act	AI regulation: general approach/ regulations	AI regulation: deregulation approach/ guidelines	AI strategic policy implementation/ organizations: centralized/ government-led	AI strategic policy implementation/ Organization: decentralized/ AI R&D centers/ (triple-helix partnerships)
USA	No	No	✓	Ex-post	No	No	✓
China	No	No	✓	Ex-ante	No	✓	No
Germany[1]	No	No	✓	Ex-ante	✓	No	✓
Japan	No	No	✓	Ex-ante	✓	No	✓
India	No	No	✓	Ex-ante	✓	✓	No
UK	No	No	✓	Ex-ante	✓	No	✓
France[1]	No	No	✓	Ex-ante	✓	No	✓
Brazil	No	No	✓	Ex-post	No	No	No
Italy[1]	No	No	✓	Ex-ante	✓	No	✓
Canada[2]	No	No	✓	Ex-ante	✓	No	✓

Note: [1] EU countries are part of the EU AI Act. While this legislation informs national policy, it is new (European Commission 2021). Existing EU national policies are presently independent. [2] Canada has an Artificial Intelligence and Data Act (AIDA) in the parliamentary approval process (Government of Canada, 2025). This table summarizes the policy approaches of G10 nations concerning AI legislation and regulation. Key insights include: Some countries, such as China, adopt an ex-ante regulatory approach, emphasizing preventive measures; the UK and Japan prefer deregulation, focusing on flexible guidelines to encourage innovation; all G10 nations have Data Security Acts, but comprehensive national AI legislation is generally lacking.

industrial, and national utility improvements in a contemporary "gold rush" or "space race" (see Figure 13.1) fueled by reasonable and irrational expectations that go beyond the current capabilities of foundational AI science – indeed, some voice unrealistic dreams of God-like AI tools (Li, 2023; Hogarth, 2023). These factors could become higher education AI system constraints if AI falls short of popular ideals.

Constraints also shape AI policy making. First, IMF researchers have recently documented a profound disconnect between AI strategic policy and policy research, warning that much AI regulation is designed without policy research evidence (Comunale & Manera, 2024). Meanwhile, AI intellectual property is closely guarded by competing companies and partnerships, limiting innovation sharing and networked ecosystem AI learning (OECD.AI, 2024) – so it is not surprising, then, to find that most G10 AI plans express a desire to improve AI science transparency. AI risk is also a significant constraint for G10 policy makers attempting, in all cases, to balance risk and opportunity (Mohanty & Sahu., 2024).

G10 AI Strategic Plans and Policies in Higher Education Contexts: Challenges for AI Integration

The G10 strategic policies significantly impact higher education institutions (see Table 13.2), a context about which surprisingly little research has been carried out. This study finds that G10 universities exist in the AIS agenda as institutions providing "talent development education". However, when we follow the funding, we see mostly university chairs in computer science research and development (R&D) and triple-helix partnerships operating with enormous nationally funded incentives and often implementing AI plans within research super-centers. By contrast, little research reports on AI learning. In higher education, national AIS objectives such as AI talent development, recruitment and retention, skill building, and language reskilling dominate. An overall focus on fundamental science research drives funding, with relatively minor AI-focused (doctoral, master's) programs cultivating AI talent and research super-labs. Yet, there is a notable absence of research on how higher education institutions are organizing themselves, pedagogically and administratively, to meet these evolving national AI goals. This includes a paucity of research examining the organization and leadership of these enormous R&D complexes. This is an issue of particular significance because national AI plans allocate over 9 billion USD to higher education systems through a competitive process run mostly by new national R&D centre partnerships (Figure 13.2). Table 13.2 shows that national research centers and chairs, a robust economic agenda, and a global scientific AI policy-making network are emerging from the AISs.

Table 13.2 *G10 nation AI strategies (AIS): priority sectors, actor features, institutions and governance*

Nation	Innovation policy paradigm[a]	Agenda type	Priority AI sectors[c]	Value[b]	Disciplinary backgrounds: AIS expert advisory groups – science (%)	Disciplinary backgrounds: AIS expert advisory groups – humanities (%)	Disciplinary backgrounds: AIS expert advisory groups – gov (%)	Research & governance: features – new/AI centres (#)	Research & governance: features – new/AI chairs (#)	Research & governance: features – authority	Research & governance: features – organization[ef]
UK	IS	Economic	IT, IND, Gov	Safety	86	24[d]	86	28	28	Gov/DSIT Ministry	I
Germany	IS	Economic	IT, IND, Labor	Safety	–	–	–	–	–	Gov/DFKI Research Centre	I
USA	IS	Economic	IT, IND, INF	Safety	67	33	33	37	37	Gov/NSF Research Centre	I
Canada	IS	Economic	IT, IND, Hlth	Growth	59[e]	41[e]	0	–	3	Gov CIFAR/ Ministries	I
France	IS	Economic	IND, Hlth, Def	Safety	100	0	0	–	4	Gov/ MHERI Ministry	I
Japan	IS	Economic	IT, IND, Educ	Growth	53	47	47	–	3	Gov/CSTI Research Centre	I
China	IS	Economic	IT, IND, Def	Growth	81	19	19	–	–	Gov/3 Ministries	C?

Nation	Innovation policy paradigm[a]	Agenda type	Priority AI sectors[c]	Value[b]	Disciplinary backgrounds: AIS expert advisory groups – science (%)	Disciplinary backgrounds: AIS expert advisory groups – humanities (%)	Disciplinary backgrounds: AIS expert advisory groups – gov (%)	Research & governance: features – new/AI centres (#)	Research & governance: features – new/AI chairs (#)	Research & governance: features – authority	Research & governance: features – organization[ef]
Italy	IS	Economic	IT, IND, Gov	Growth	100	0	0	–	5	Gov/ Ministries	C (Gov)
India	T	Social	Hlth, IND, IND2	Growth	–	–	–	–	–	Gov/NITI Ayog Centre+	C?
Brazil	IS	Economic	IT, IND, Gov	Safety	–	–	–	–	–	Gov/MSTI/ Ministry	C/Gov

Note. A dash (–) indicates insufficient or unavailable data. [a] *ST = Science & Technology, IS = innovation systems, T = transformational innovation (Diercks et al., 2019).* [b] *OECD:* Safety = robustness, security & safety; Growth = inclusive growth, sustainable development & well-being; H = human rights and democratic values, including fairness and privacy, T = transparency and explainability, A = accountability (OECD. AI, 2024) [c] IT = information technology/computer science; IND = industry; IND2 = food industry; INF = infrastructure (IT); Hlth = healthcare; Educ = education; Gov = government; Labor = Labor; Def = defense [d] In 2023, the UK replaced its AI statutory body comprised of 67% science and 33% humanities actors (Prime Minister Johnson, 2021) with one comprised of 86% science and 24% humanities actors (Prime Minister Sunak), creating a higher concentration of defense and computer science actors. [e] In 2019, Canada formed its Artificial Intelligence (AIS) Advisory Body from 100% Science to 59% science and 41% Humanities personnel. [f] I = institutionalized; a semi-autonomous organization or with government ministry oversight; C = centralized; a government-directed entity or office. This table outlines the primary sectors targeted by G10 AI strategies, such as computer science research, healthcare, and economic development. It identifies the dominant actors involved (e.g., government, industry, academia) and notes the governance models employed, typically emphasizing economic over social agendas.

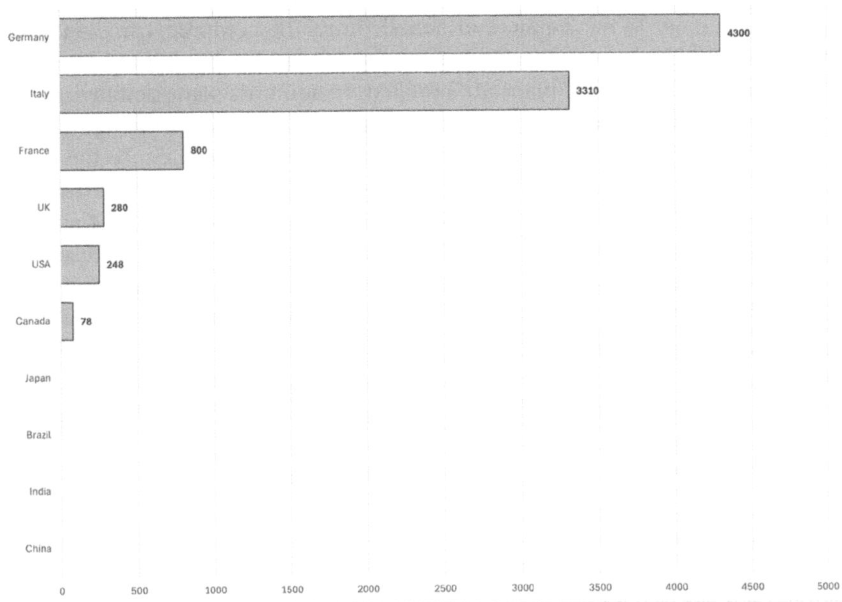

Source: Authors.

Figure 13.2 *G10 national government AI strategic plan investments in higher education (millions USD)*

Detailed findings later in the chapter offer strong evidence that state and industry incentives are provided from these research centers to partnered applicants (Diercks et al., 2019) who apply for a range of fundamental AI research or talent development programming (e.g., new AI doctoral programs). In this way, thousands of doctoral positions have been funded by universities in France, Germany, the UK, the US, and Canada to help integrate foundational AI science into economic and other sectors. Additionally, nationwide university and K-12 AI literacy programs, encompassing mathematics, data science, computing, and AI, have been funded in the UK, Italy, and Germany (UKRI, 2024), significantly impacting existing university programs. These substantial investments in foundational AI research enable universities to expand their AI foundational science research capabilities, attract top talent, and develop specialized AI literacy programs that meet national strategic objectives.

In some AISs, the university is merely a human resource site for locating research. In these situations, university leadership is far from autonomous when AI funding flows from AIS plans. An absence of specific AIS funding data from China, India, Japan, and Brazil limits the comprehensive analysis of global G10 AI investments.. Therefore, greater transparency in AI planning is essential when these AI plans are updated. In addition, some countries have added chairs, programs, and all sorts of AI funding since their (aging) AI strategic plans (not within the scope of this chapter) were written, so the numbers in Table 13.2 represent minimums. From available information, the UK, Germany, USA, Canada (CIFAR, 2017), and France have created financial incentives and research institutes to allocate competitive funds for AI research, most of it in fundamental AI (computer science) research and industry-related challenge projects involving combinations of university professors, graduate students, and industry researchers. A good policy evaluation study is needed to evaluate the full impact of AI strategies' enormous impacts on universities in terms of leadership, institutional development, and perhaps academic freedom.

Consolidated Analysis of G10 AI Innovation Policies

This section summarizes findings from our detailed analysis of G10 AI national strategic plans, examining three policy categories: (1) objectives, (2) sectors, actors, and norms, and (3) policy logic (Wu et al., 2018). Additionally, we apply Diercks et al.'s (2019) Innovation Policy Framework, which incorporates organizational and governance analyses, distinguishing between economic and social agenda in innovation in funded AIS implementation contexts. We analyze each nation's AI objectives, policy authors, values, and implementation strategies, focusing on higher education's role across countries, as outlined in Table 13.2. This approach identifies aspects of higher education involvement in AISs that may benefit from more contemporary policy paradigm shifts (Calderini et al., 2023).

Following Diercks et al. (2019), we categorize AIS policy agendas into economic (focusing on growth, competitiveness, and jobs) and social (including national prestige and societal challenges) policy agenda types. Economic agenda policies emphasize positive innovation outcomes, while social agenda policiesconsider both positive and negative impacts across sectors. We analyzed each G10 AIS by coding for themes across objectives, sectors, actors, norms, and policy logic. This process extends Diercks et al.'s framework by incorporating Howlett's (2024) governance modes and Complex Adaptive Systems (CAS) theory (Uhl-Bien et al., 2007) to provide a more comprehensive and integrated innovation policy analysis. Additionally, we examined policy mixes to assess nations' transformational potential through a combination of economic and social strategies embedded in their AIS (Rogge & Reichardt, 2016; Baldwin et al., 2024).

Agenda setting

Strategic plans are a policy-making tool used by governments to manage social actors (Howlett, 2024). They are, by definition, technocratic, corporate approaches to policy design that began in the 1960s (Howlett, 2024). These plans aim to balance economic and social development through informational strategies, ideally (Wu et al., 2018). As agenda-setting policies, G10 AI strategic plans are informational tools (Hood, 1986) that can be either *substantive* (with suggestions for alternative ways to achieve the goal) or *procedural* (defining the objectives and the means to achieve them), and we found most to be substantive. The primary service or implementation mechanisms of most G10 strategic plans provide nations with operational objectives, subsidies, grant incentives and advice from expert advisory bodies. This said, some plans do not identify funding linked to action instruments or include transparent budgets (India, Japan, and Canada, for example), making their clear objectives good indicators of policy paradigm choice but poor indicators of contemporary innovation policy-design thinking (Howlett, 2024). The adoption of a policy strategy with clear objectives but without the simultaneous adoption of a set of instruments can be understood as an attempt to set the agenda for upcoming changes in the instrument mix (Rogge & Reichardt, 2016).

Policy objectives

All G10 AISs are early-stage agenda-setting documents (Wu et al., 2018) focused on AI science and knowledge production (70% of countries) and reflect an innovation systems (IS) policy approach (Diercks et al., 2019). Most AISs (80%) use discretionary issue windows – policy opportunities opened by the political priorities of government leaders – rather than broad societal demand. Exceptions include Germany and the USA, where public pressure has played a more direct role in shaping AI nation strategy. Although 90% of AISs align economic agendas and consider social pressure for AI, emphasizing growth and competitiveness, they also mention education and social development without corresponding funding - indicating a gap between objectives and resource allocation. There are many signals from the business, science, and policy-making communities that AI should be regarded as a key enabling technology and that lasting investment in applications should be undertaken or facilitated (Federal Government of Germany, 2018).

As Figure 13.3 indicates, 70% of the G10 countries share common objectives related to AI science and knowledge production, establishing what Diercks et al. (2019) define as an information systems (IS) policy paradigm. In this innovation policy paradigm, academics lean towards a narrower understanding of knowledge building (fundamental AI research) via partnership members forming the classical triple helix: academia, industry, and government. Since several countries outline strategic objectives without detailing specific

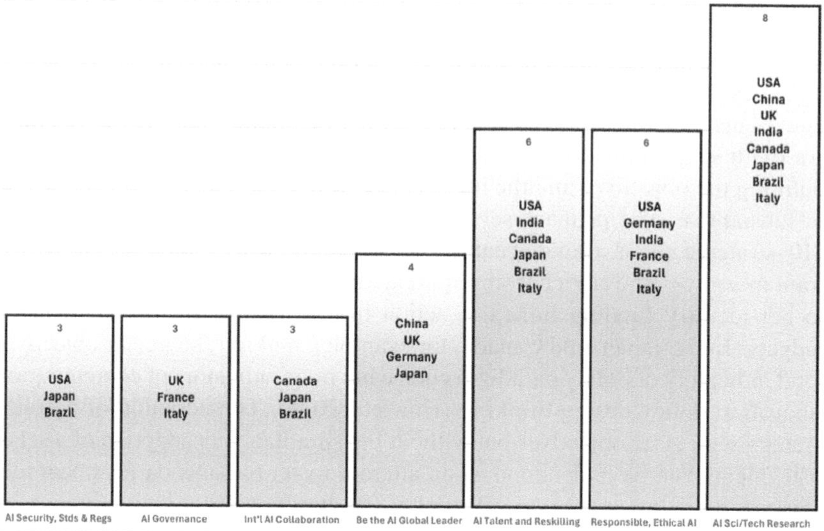

Source: Authors.

Figure 13.3 *Frequency of national AI strategy objectives by category: G10*

governance plans, resource allocation, or funding mechanisms to achieve these objectives (Barzelay, 2001), we conducted a deeper analysis. We verified the coherence between AI strategy goals and investments, classifying each nation's primary AI strategy objective as economic, social, or both, using the framework proposed by Diercks et al. (2019). We examined the funds allocated to align with the stated main goals and identified a gap between the goals and the funding instruments. Our analysis revealed that 90% of the G10 AI strategic plans are primarily oriented toward achieving an economic agenda through AI. Meanwhile, while all G10 AI strategies include extensive rhetoric emphasizing education and social development, only limited funding was aligned with these objectives.

Policy domain/sectors, actors, and norms

Figure 13.4 illustrates that G10 AI strategies predominantly focus on industry (38%) and the IT sectors (31%), which together account for 69% of the

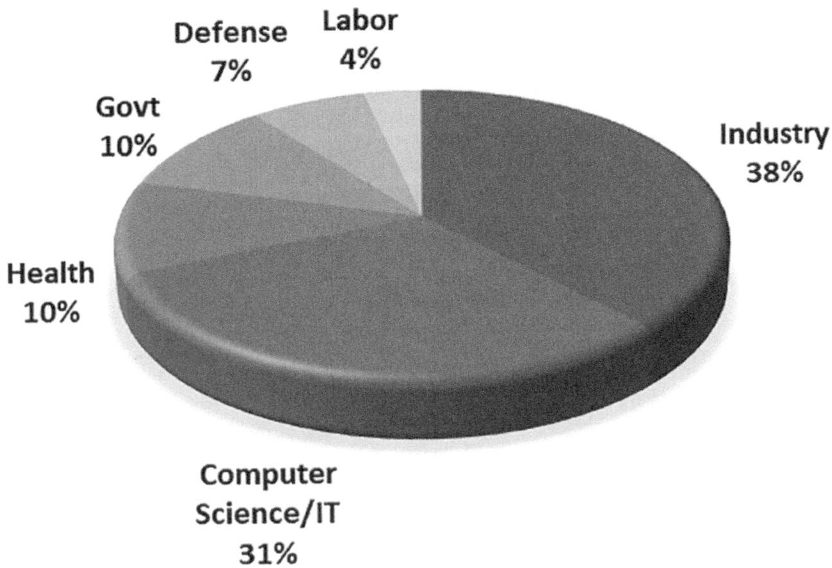

Source: Authors.

Figure 13.4 G10 AI strategic policy: distribution of priority sectors

prioritized sectors. In contrast, society-oriented sectors, including labor, defense, public administration, and healthcare, make up only 30% of the focus. This narrow focus aligns with the economic objectives of 70% of AISs but contrasts with the mixed policy making seen during the COVID-19 pandemic. Expert advisory councils, predominantly from scientific and technical backgrounds, drive these strategies, with minimal representation from social or humanities disciplines.

A few countries' AIS strategy councils or lead group experts were not identified in policy (Brazil, India, Germany), so we assumed the prime actors were government agents. Figure 13.5 shows the distribution of AIS expert advisor disciplinary backgrounds: most are in science, as expanded upon below.

The original national artificial intelligence strategic plans in Canada, France, and Italy were developed by expert advisory committees composed entirely of members from the computer science discipline (CIFAR, 2017; MHERI, 2021; MSTI, 2021). China has established a two-tier system of experts to guide its AI strategy. The Ministry of Education Technology AI Expert Group (China State Council, 2017) oversees the Working Group (PRC Ministry of Science and Technology, 2020). Of the Expert Group members, 48% are computer science

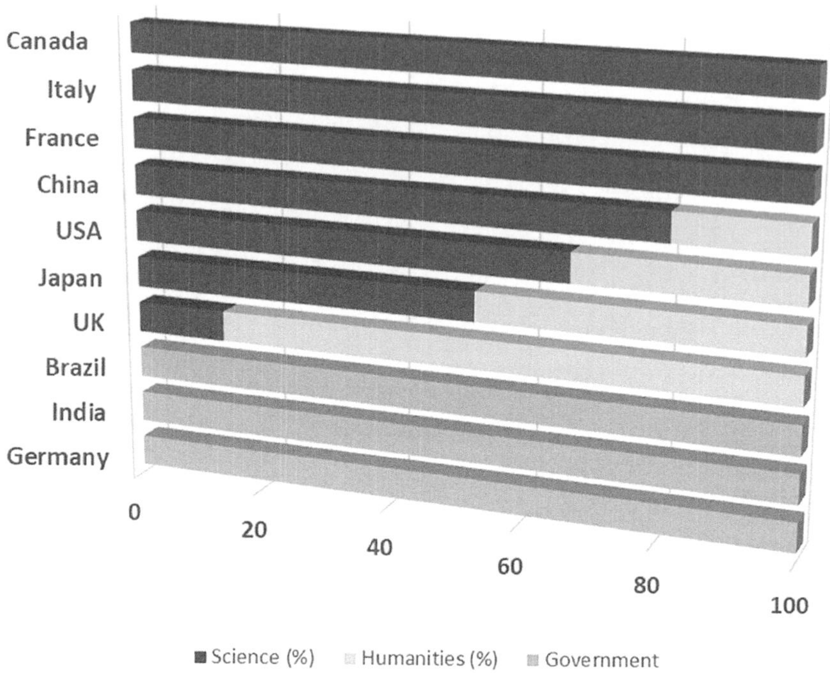

Source: Authors.

Figure 13.5 *Distribution of national AI strategy expert advisory disciplinary backgrounds*

experts and 33% are industry representatives, making up an economic focus of 81%. Additionally, 11% of the members come from defense and 8% from healthcare, contributing to a social focus of 19%. Meanwhile, the 15-member Working Group includes 85% computer science experts and features the only education specialist (in instructional design) among the G10 nations, representing 15% of its composition. Scholars or education professionals comprise less than 1% of the advisory bodies across the G10. The entire education sector (higher education and schools) is, in fact, absent.

Values play a crucial role in AI strategy and innovation policy making, becau they address national concerns about fostering responsible AI use and design within a climate of trust. In coding each nation's G10 strategy to identify AI norms we utilized the OECD AI principles (OECD.AI, 2024): (1) inclusive growth, sustainability, and wellness, (2) human rights and democratic values,

(3) transparency and explainability, (4) robustness, security, and strategy, and (5) accountability. Germany, the UK, Brazil, the USA, and France value principle 1 (inclusive growth, sustainability, and wellness). When we align the AIS national objectives with delivery mechanisms to achieve the objectives, we see that most effort and resources are allocated to setting up prominent AI research institutes and centers where the agenda is primarily scientific and economic research focused on the growth part of principle 1. When we align policy goals with implementation and resource strategies we can see that India, Japan, China, Italy, and France also value principle 1. Next, we analyze the organizations and governance models set up by AI national strategies to provide a better understanding of understand the innovation policy approaches shaping AIS implementation structures and organizations.

Governance

All G10 AISs employ a Corporate Governance mode policy making approach (Howlett, 2024), characterized by technocratic control, target setting, and the provision of grants and subsidies. Expert advisory committees, drive policy design and implementation with members primarily from scientific and technical backgrounds, This governance approach tends to be bureaucratic,lacking accountability measures that limit its transformative potential as innovaton policy.

Coding across the G10 AISs, we found the following results per policy making approach: corporate governance (100%), control form (plans) (100%), targets, grants, and subsidy resources (100%). Corporate governance policy aims to manage significant actor activity and control the social and economic development rate by setting targets and providing grants and subsidies for implementation; it often uses a privileged specialist advisory committee (Howlett, 2024). All available data in this analysis indicatesthat expert specialist advisory committees consistently play a central role in shaping policy content and guiding subsequent stages of the policy cycle. However, corporate structures, in the absence of accountability measures and supporting research, are prone to over-bureaucratization and processes delays, making them a less effective avenue for transformative policy direction (Wu et al., 2018). We also found minimal incentives for policy research and dearth of plan evaluations in the AI strategic plans, likely because few policy or education discipline actors are on the expert committees.

By contrast, network governance modes promote organized inter-actor activity and emphasize collaborative partnerships with an aim toward self-organizing economic- and social-actor relational structures involving a network of government and non-government actors. Policy networks implement policy through network brokerage activities spanning institutional boundaries (Howlett, 2024). Design approaches to innovation itself in the context of G10

AI need to change as nations update these (now-dated) AIS plans by using more contemporary, mixed innovation policy approaches weighted more toward network governance and policy research to inform AI policy making and strategies (Howlett, 2024; Schot & Steinmueller, 2018).

Policy paradigms and organization

Another complex dynamic that allows self-regulating adaptive organizations and governance groups to thrive in innovation settings is policy mixing, where policies across sectors are designed to interact and create results more significant than the sum of the parts. Policy mixing involves understanding how different policies interact and influence each other across various sectors within a policy ecosystem (Kern & Rogge, 2018). Further *in situ* studies could shed light on this complex phenomenon. In G10 AISs, we did not find evidence of a newer policy-mixing theory, and only two of the ten G10 countries (Germany, Japan) suggested or considered contemporary policy mixing, with no empirical evidence.

Policy paradigm

According to Diercks et al. (2019), economic innovation policy objectives aim to build and commercialize a knowledge base around specific technologies. This reflects a science-and-technology-driven approach (S&T), often resembling a "space race" mentality – where the primary goal is to be the first to develop and sell new technologies or innovations. As highlighted in Table 13.2, the IS paradigm reflects a relatively narrow understanding among G10 nations in which AI is part of a mindset geared toward "the commercialization of science" with an emphasis on "economic utility." Within this framework, all citizens are positioned primarily as consumers of innovation (in this case, AI). In S&T policy paradigms, the innovation process is primarily driven by academic and industry actors, with government playing a limited or supporting role. In contrast IS paradigms are based on a "triple helix" model, where academia, industry, and government are all seen as central, interdependent actors within a broader innovation ecosystem. In the S&T policy paradigm, society's role is passively adopting new inventions from science and technology. In contrast, in the IS policy paradigm the public participates in AI-related demand and supply. The commercialization of science by policy leaders taking an S&T paradigm approach led to the space race 60 years ago; for example, industrial and economic benefits were realized before any social impacts because the paradigm ignored initial deep innovation potentials from the activity that can impact the entire ecosystem.

Using Diercks et al.'s (2019) innovation policy framework, we discovered that 90% of the G10 countries are employing an IS paradigm as they create AI strategies. Germany and the UK are closest to moving to a transformational paradigm, blending societal and economic challenges in the future AI agenda. India has a perfectly compatible plan for transformational policy development and AI. However, the governance and mechanisms for this remain too unclear in the existing plan, and follow-up research is required. Figure 13.6 demonstrates that 90% of AIS objectives are economic agenda when matched with policy implementation mechanisms and governance and organization objectives, hinting at a narrow policy network understanding of AI innovation.

As most AISs include reskilling and AI talent development initiatives, the IS paradigm does not view citizens as merely passive adopters of newly commercialized technologies. Instead, they are positioned as active consumers, engaging with and utilizing these innovations. Hence, the uses of AI matter, as a linear adoption model is set aside in these plans in favour of market forces becoming part of R&D. This shift towards demand-side economics occurs in a healthy entrepreneurial climate, with patent laws and financial access matters rising proportionately. At the same time, academics remain within triple-helix research partnerships, where economic sensibilities play a crucial role, tending to narrow the policy agenda.

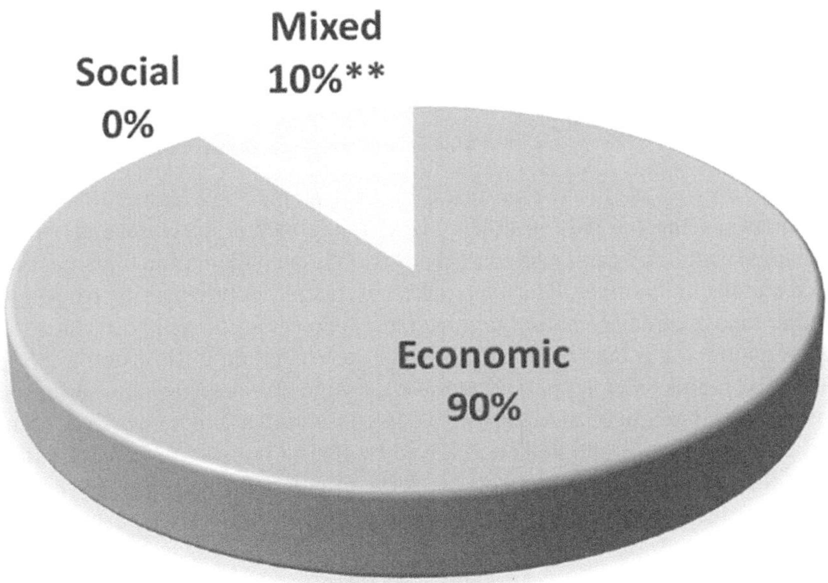

Source: Authors.

Figure 13.6 G10 AI strategic policy: distribution of agenda by type

Among the G10 nations, we found that 80% of AISs were initiated by internal government political actors, while in the USA and Germany (20%), governments developed policies in response to pressures from other issues spilling over into the AI discourse. These pressures included "many signals from the business, science, and policy-making communities that AI should be regarded as a key enabling technology and that lasting investment in applications should be undertaken or facilitated" (Federal Government of Germany, 2018, p. 4). The most interesting AI innovation policy frame comes from the transformational India AI strategy (Rogge & Reichardt, 2016; Ossenbrink et al., 2019), which outlines science and social development before disclosing governance and organization details (NITI Aayog, 2018). Uniquely, the India plan goals include a mixed policy agenda focused on grand challenges presented by ministries to research partnerships to improve healthcare, agriculture, education, smart cities, and intelligent mobility (NITI Aayog, 2018). Although weak in instrumentation and funding details linking plans to implementation, this promising plan opens doors for many sectors to collaborate beyond AI science development. Before this policy is updated, a good research study showing results from the plan could inform many other nations updating their AISs so that AI innovation strategic goals can be directed toward meaningful national transformation beyond the economic and science sectors (Kowch, 2013; Henry, 2021).

IMPLICATIONS FOR HIGHER EDUCATION LEADERS AND RESEARCHERS

To our surprise, we discovered that G10 AI strategies provide funding mechanisms (nearing the trillion dollar mark) for foundational science primarily aimed at economic gain, while largely overlooking challenges in higher education and the humanities. This focus stems from an IS policy-making paradigm, rather than the transformative approach that scholars argue will be essential for a groundbreaking innovation such as AI (Diercks et al., 2019; Kowch, 2021). We also found older IS policy approaches with non-design policy mindsets limiting the breadth of actors in the policy communities and networks charting AI futures, which could be better served by taking innovation transformation and complex adaptive ecosystem leadership and policy-making approaches that can include education and other disciplinary knowledge for systemic change (Innes & Booher, 2018).

Over the last five years, substantial AI investments in partnerships involving universities as innovation hubs have primarily driven R&D focused on advancing AI science, rather than fostering university learning initiatives such as programming for students, professors, and staff or integrating AI into learning partnerships. As a result, AI foundational science has evolved to where AI image recognition and large language models are stable and proliferating in all sectors of life (Li, 2023). Meanwhile, a lack of AI strategic plan research creates a significant gap between AI plan goals and measured results/evaluations (Comunale & Manera, 2024) during this "gold rush."

By analyzing the G10 national strategic plan contexts, objectives, actors, and sectors with their policy logics, this chapter offers readers plenty of context for individual AI innovation leadership and research opportunities in universities. In anticipation of critical AIS updates necessary at the national level, our study finds that nations should expedite the preparation of teams to generate fresh aligned meso-level (provincial, state) and micro-level AI strategies by involving a balance of economic and science experts. Inclusion in AI strategy design remains inadequate. Only about 10% of G10 expert advisory networks involve humanities faculties such as education, social work, law, arts, and culture. This exclusion limits AI policies' ethical and social dimensions, leading to less comprehensive strategies.

AI means reskilling and new skilling. Higher education leaders and scholars in the future will work in networks to co-evolve innovative AI policy making and implementation across the sectors, particularly in terms of organization and governance policy and operations integrated with graduate students, professors, and industry and social sector professionals. Research opportunities abound for critical studies necessary to improve AI centers, learning programs, leadership, and governance across traditional disciplinary boundaries and within institutions. Education is part of the solution in dealing with deepfakes. It also plays a vital role in equipping individuals and institutions to guide, shape, and influence the development and use of widely adopted technologies that attract significant public attention. AI literacy programs such as those in Japan, for example, can inform elementary, secondary, undergraduate, and graduate students, higher education leaders, and policy makers. Without new literacy approaches, our teams will not know how to change and lead universities in the coming AI age (Aoun, 2017). A vast opportunity exists for combinations of education policy, philosophy, and law teams to become involved in forming the AI legislation and developing AI regulations aligned with guidelines on ethics and practice across sectors, universities, and industries. We therefore offer actionable recommendations, grounded in our analysis, for higher education leaders and researchers reviewing and renewing AI strategic national policy.

ACTIONABLE RECOMMENDATIONS

To conclude, we offer the following eight recommendations and action steps for leaders and researchers engaging in higher education AI.

1. National AI strategy renewal leaders must include more humanities sector expertise to form policy networks of diverse disciplines spanning social and economic domains. Education expertise, while necessary for AI strategies with so much going into "talent and skills," is not at the table other than in the form of university administrators (leaders) who may have science backgrounds. Higher education leaders should form coalition networks with faculty representatives from humanities disciplines to advocate for inclusion in national AI policy discussions. These coalition networks, spanning traditional university administrative and academic chambers, should develop white papers outlining the ethical and societal implications of generative AI and proposing concrete policy recommendations.
2. Provincial (and state) governments and universities should begin preparing renewed AI strategies in alignment with federal AI policies and in concert with potential partners. University researchers can help different sectors and institutions create their own AI policies. Higher education leaders can begin AI literacy and AI planning task forces, involving other institutions and communities by using a policy network approach and proposing grand challenges for systemic change focused on both economic and social contexts. More evidence-based research should inform the work.
3. AI will require new kinds of university and institutional leader and new kinds of public administration familiar with policy mixing and post-economic policy agenda national policymaking. Transdisciplinary research to evaluate AI's goal attainments will offer solid evidence for next-generation strategies. Networks of researchers should study the new AI institutions, degree programs, fundamental AI research processes, organizations, governance, and education systems to create similar evidence for leaders, organizers, and policy makers at national, provincial (state), and institutional levels. Higher education leadership can incentivize AI research conducted by transdisciplinary teams from all faculties and disciplines. New leadership in higher education programs focusing on innovation policy and learning science must generated anduse evidence-based (new) research utilizing policy-mix and policy-design/ecosystem thinking for the next round of G10 AISs.
4. Some research resources should be reallocated from institutional ethics guideline creation for some of these other recommendations until AI Acts and Regulations with more deep innovative knowledge of AI are in place (Kowch, 2021). While managing AI-involved practice is essential, leading this means shifting emphases until the technology becomes better known and explainable. Higher education leadership can work with law, policy, and education leadership scholars to connect with state and national AI legislation with the aim of conducting more research, gathering more

evidence for AI legislation creation at the state and national level, and making AI more transparent and trustworthy as part of human capital development in all education systems.
5. Japan's AI strategy affords AI literacy programs for the next generation of primary, secondary, baccalaureate, and graduate students. Existing STEM enhancements (USA, Germany) and STEAM (India) might not build people's capacity to realize the strategy objectives over time, however. We are all learning as AI develops. Higher education leaders worldwide can connect their education faculties with others to research and draft AI literacy strategies for K-12, college, university, and industry contexts, learning from Japan and the UK as exemplars.
6. AI strategies should be developed based on evidence and grand challenges that advance fundamental AI science research while solving social and economic problems (Diercks et al., 2019). This requires advanced policy theoretical learning and training for policy makers, institutional leaders, and public administrators. New doctoral programs merging law, business, AI engineering, and education could help ensure that the next round of updated national AIS plans is transformative.
7. Education scholars and leaders should be more engaged and funded to assess the impact of, design improvements for, and co-develop systemic changes through the AI literacy and degree programs proliferating today. Learning sciences, culture, leadership, policy, and governance research opportunities abound in the vast new institutes, doctoral programs, and K-12 programs funded by the current AI boom. Higher education leaders in education faculties should form collaborative AI networks across government, industry, and education systems to describe, learn about, and draft policy around AI technology with learning science and education leadership in mind.

As ecosystem change thinkers, education-technology leadership scholars know that building up our knowledge and networking capacities while renewing institutions through good research can drive the AI future in a proactive way beyond merely managing our organizations as they respond to an endless series of novel apps placed before us.

The future holds significant promise for higher education leaders and researchers who engage in transformative, transdisciplinary AI strategy and policy networks empowered by more contemporary innovation policy thinking. However, updating current AI strategies (AISs) will require sustained effort to gain access to existing policy processes – processes that are often dominated by education administrators in high-level roles who lack formal training in educational leadership or pedagogy.

REFERENCES

Aoun, J. (2017). *Robot-proof higher education in the age of artificial intelligence.* MIT Press. https://doi.org/10.7551/mitpress/11456.001.0001.

Baldwin, C. Y., Bogers, M. L. A. M., Kapoor, R., & West, J. (2024). Focusing the ecosystem lens on innovation studies. *Research Policy, 53*(3), 104949. https://doi.org/10.1016/j.respol.2023.104949.

Barzelay, M. (2001). *The new public management.* University of California Press. https://doi.org/10.1525/9780520925274.

Calderini, M., Fia, M., & Gerli, F. (2023). Organizing for transformative innovation policies: The role of social enterprises. Theoretical insights and evidence from Italy. *Research Policy, 52*(7), 104818. https://doi.org/10.1016/j.respol.2023.104818.

China State Council. (2017). *A next generation artificial intelligence development plan.* (New America, Trans) https://airuniversity.af.edu/Portals/10/CASI/documents/Translations/2021-03-02%20China's%20New%20Generation%20Artificial%20Intelligence%20Development%20Plan-%202017.pdf?ver=N2TtRVNODYyWR0yGHuK_cA%3d%3d.

CIFAR. Canadian Institute for Advanced Research. (2017). *Pan-Canadian artificial intelligence strategy.* https://perma.cc/E5PF-LDL2.

Coeckelbergh, M. (2022). Earth, technology, language: A contribution to holistic and transcendental revisions after the artifactual turn. *Foundations of Science*, 27,259–270. https://doi.org/10.1007/s10699-020-09730-9.

Comunale, M., & Manera, A. (2024). *The economic impacts and the regulation of AI: A review of the academic literature and policy actions.* IMF Working Paper, 065. https://doi.org/10.5089/9798400268588.001.

Diercks, G., Larsen, H., & Steward, F. (2019). Transformative innovation policy: Addressing variety in an emerging policy paradigm. *Research Policy, 48*(4), 880–894. https://doi.org/10.1016/j.respol.2018.10.028.

European Commission. (2021). Proposal for a regulation of the European parliament and of the council laying down harmonised rules on Artificial Intelligence (Artificial Intelligence Act) and amending certain Union legislative acts, Pub. L. No. COM(2021) 206 final.

Federal Government of Germany. (2018, November). *Artificial Intelligence Strategy of the German Federal Government. Update.* https://www.ki-strategie-deutschland.de/files/downloads/Fortschreibung_KI-Strategie_engl.pdf.

Gardner, A., et al. (2021). Ethical funding for trustworthy AI: Proposals to address the responsibilities of funders to ensure that projects adhere to trustworthy AI practice. *AI and Ethics, 2*(2), 227–291. https://doi.org/10.1007/s43681-021-00069-w.

Gates, B. (2024, September 11). My trip to the frontier of AI education. *GatesNotes.* https://www.gatesnotes.com/My-trip-to-the-frontier-of-AI-education.

Government of Canada (2025, January 31). *The Artificial Intelligence and Data Act (AIDA) – Companion document.* Innovation, Science and Economic Development. https://ised-isde.canada.ca/site/innovation-better-canada/en/artificial-intelligence-and-data-act-aida-companion-document.

Henry, A. (2021). *Platform and collective intelligence: Digital ecosystem of organizations.* John Wiley & Sons, Incorporated. https://doi.org/10.1002/9781119808367.

Hogarth, I. (2023, April 22). We must slow down the race to God-like AI [USA Region]. *Financial Times*. https://www.ft.com/content/03895dc4-a3b7-481e-95cc-336a524f2ac2.

Hood, C. (1986). *The tools of government*. Chatham.

Howlett, M. (2024). *Designing public policies: Principles and instruments* (3rd ed.). Routledge. https://doi.org/10.4324/9781003343431.

Innes, J. E., & Booher, D. E. (2018). *Planning with complexity: An introduction to collaborative rationality for public policy* (2nd ed.). Routledge. https://doi.org/10.4324/9781315147949.

Kern, F., & Rogge, K. S. (2018). Harnessing theories of the policy process for analysing the politics of sustainability transitions: A critical survey. *Environmental innovation and societal transitions*, *27*, 102-117.

Klijn, E.H., Koppenjan, J., Spekkink, W., & Warsen, R. (2015). Governance Networks in the Public Sector (1st ed.). Routledge. https://doi.org/10.4324/9781315887098.

Kowch, E. (2013). Conceptualizing the essential qualities of complex adaptive leadership: Networks that organize and learn. *International Journal of Complexity in Leadership and Management*, *2*(3), 162–184. https://doi.org/10.1504/ijclm.2013.057549.

Kowch, E. (2018, December 18). *Readying smart education ecosystems to thrive with Artificial Intelligence (AI): A systemic change approach*. [Keynote Address]. 2018 Smartshow EXPO National Conference and Summit, Beijing, China.

Kowch, E. (2021). Leading transformation with digital innovations in schools and universities: Beyond adoption. In D. Ifenthaler, S. Hofhues, M. Egloffstein, & C. Helbig (Eds.), *Digital transformation of learning organizations* (pp. 145–168). Springer Nature. https://doi.org/10.1007/978-3-030-55878-9_9.

Kowch, E. G. (2023). Systems thinking and change: A section introduction. In J. M. Spector, B. B. Lockee, & M. D. Childress (Eds.), *Learning, design, and technology: An international compendium of theory, research, practice, and policy* (pp. 1481–1494). Springer International Publishing. https://doi.org/10.1007/978-3-319-17461-7_133.

Li, F.-F. (2023). *The World I See*. Flatiron Books. https://doi.org/10.5860/crl.85.5.794.

MHERI (Minister of Higher Education, Research and Innovation). (2021, November). *The national strategy for research in artificial intelligence – 2nd phase*. https://minefi.hosting.augure.com/Augure_Minefi/r/ContenuEnLigne/Download?id=334FD34F-7844-497E-9551-79EDFF3B2EEF&filename=1645%20-%20DP%20-%20Strat%C3%A9gie%20Nationale%20pour%20l%27IA%202%C3%A8me%20phase.pdf.

MSTI (Ministry of Science, Technology and Innovations). (2021). *Strategic plan on artificial intelligence*. https://docs.italia.it/italia/mid/programma-strategico-nazionale-per-intelligenza-artificiale-en-docs/en/bozza/the-strategic-programme-on-artificial-intelligence-anchoring-principles-and-goals.html#.

Mohanty, A., and Sahu, S. (2024, February). *India's AI strategy: Balancing risk and opportunity. [Carnegie India Commentary]*. Carnegie Endowment for International Peace. https://carnegieindia.org/posts/2024/02/indias-ai-strategy-balancing-risk-and-opportunity?lang=en.

NITI Aayog (National Institution for Transforming India). (2018). *National strategy for artificial intelligence*. https://niti.gov.in/sites/default/files/2021-02/NationalStrategy-for-AI-Discussion-Paper.pdf.

OECD.AI. (2024). *Database of national AI policies*. OECS. https://oecd.ai.

Ossenbrink, J., Finnsson, S., Bening, C. R., & Hoffmann, V. H. (2019). Delineating policy mixes: Contrasting top-down and bottom-up approaches to the case of energy-storage policy in California. *Research Policy, 48*(10), 103582. https://doi.org/10.1016/j.respol.2018.04.014.

PRC Ministry of Science and Technology (MST). (2020). *Notice regarding the establishment of the Ministry of Education AI Technology Expert Group.* (The Center for Security and Emerging Technology, Trans). https://cset.georgetown.edu/publication/notice-of-the-office-of-the-ministry-of-education-regarding-the-establishment-of-the-ministry-of-education-ai-technology-innovation-expert-group/.

Rogge, K. S., & Reichardt, K. (2016). Policy mixes for sustainability transitions: An extended concept and framework for analysis. *Research Policy, 45*(8), 1620–1635. https://doi.org/10.1016/j.respol.2016.04.004.

Schot, J., & Steinmueller, W. E. (2018). Three frames for innovation policy: R&D, systems of innovation and transformative change. *Research Policy, 47*(9), 1554–1567. https://doi.org/10.1016/j.respol.2018.08.011.

Secretariat of Council of Science, Technology and Innovation. (2022) *AI Strategy 2022*. https://www8.cao.go.jp/cstp/ai/aistratagy2019en.pdf.

Secretary of State for Digital, Culture, Media and Sport. (2021). *National AI Strategy.* https://assets.publishing.service.gov.uk/media/614db4d1e90e077a2cbdf3c4/National_AI_Strategy_-_PDF_version.pdf.

Statista. (2024). *The 20 countries with the largest gross domestic product (GDP) in 2024* [data set]. https://www.statista.com/statistics/268173/countries-with-the-largest-gross-domestic-product-gdp/.

The Economist (2024, July 2). What happened to the artificial-intelligence revolution? https://www.economist.com/finance-and-economics/2024/07/02/what-happened-to-the-artificial-intelligence-revolution.

Tweedie, M. G., & Sharmi, S. T. (2025). Transparency and the "black box" dilemma. In S. Sabbaghan (Ed.), *Navigating generative AI in higher education: Ethical, theoretical, and practical perspectives*. Edward Elgar.

Uhl-Bien, M., Marion, R., & McKelvey, B. (2007). Complexity leadership theory: Shifting leadership from the industrial age to the knowledge era. T*he Leadership Quarterly, 18*(4), 298–318. https://doi.org/10.1016/j.leaqua.2007.04.002.

UKRI (United Kingdom Research and Innovation). (2024, July 24). *UKRI artificial intelligence centres for doctoral training*. https://www.ukri.org/who-we-are/our-vision-and-strategy/tomorrows-technologies/how-we-work-in-ai/ukri-artificial-intelligence-centres-for-doctoral-training/.

Wu, X., Ramesh, M., Howlett, M., & Fritzen, S. (2018). *The public policy primer: Managing the policy proces*s (2nd ed.). Routledge. https://doi.org/10.4324/9781315624754.

14. Collaborative approaches: Bridging the gap between generative AI developers and educators

Rita Detrick and Jinhee Kim

INTRODUCTION

The technological ecosystem has recently been defined by rapid advancements in generative artificial intelligence (GenAI), which has been marked by its ability to identify and build connections within vast amounts of data to produce new and original content. While AI has existed for decades, GenAI represents a breakthrough that makes AI accessible to users of all technological skill levels and is quickly establishing itself as a general-purpose technology that can be broadly used and applied in various ways. This has opened the door to unprecedented opportunities and applications to enhance learning efficiency, customize educational supports and learning experiences, and automate administrative tasks for educators, researchers, and students (Wang et al., 2023; Zhang et al., 2023). Even so, we are aware that we must remain vigilant to the array of challenges that GenAI presents. This includes but is not limited to students' academic integrity (Ng et al., 2021), reliance on AI technologies, devaluation of human expertise, decrease or loss of interpersonal interaction in the learning process, the redefining of roles and responsibilities of human educators, and the potential for bias and discrimination in AI algorithms (Kim & Cho, 2023; Kooli, 2023). As discussed by Tweedie and Sharmi (2025), the lack of transparency and accountability in AI systems also adds to the complexity of navigating the ever-shifting technological ecosystem within higher education settings.

The integration of GenAI into higher education is not merely an issue of accommodating technological advancement; instead, it is a paradigm shift in the educational model and landscape that challenges educators and leaders to revisit what, why, and how we teach, learn, and assess. It calls the education community to establish the long-term goals and visions of AI in Higher Education (AIHED) in order to answer why, what, and how well AI acknowledges and incorporates the varied beliefs and values of education, reflecting on the long-term implications for both contemporary and future learner needs and contexts (Kim, 2024; Miao & Holmes, 2023). In support of this aim, many researchers claim that intersectoral collaboration is critical to supporting the capacity-building of AIHED and allowing prompt identification of and engagement with the key challenges of AIHED. Through intersectoral collaboration, stakeholders can plan a system-wide curriculum that leverages ongoing and cumulative benefits of AIHED and mitigates the associated risks, validates AI systems on their ethical and pedagogical appropriateness for education, and provides timely advice on the iterative updates of regulations and policies (Kim, 2024; Miao & Holmes, 2023). This requires an innovative approach that encourages the co-evolution of knowledge to create a common language for different stakeholders around AIHED.

This chapter aims to explore and outline the dynamic value of intersectoral collaboration (i.e., public sector, private sector, academicians, and community) in AIHED, examine barriers to intersectoral collaboration, and offer several recommendations for possible supportive strategies to enhance multi-sectoral collaboration for AIHED.

COLLABORATIVE DESIGN AND IMPLEMENTATION OF AIHED

Human-centered design is imperative to ensuring that AIHED truly serves the intended audience, keeping human values at its core so that it can serve as a collaborative tool that enhances human abilities in a positive way (Miao & Holmes, 2023). Such design practices ensure that the technology's engineers can access multi-disciplinary perspectives and that AI-powered educational technology (ed-tech) tools are optimized for integration into education.

In this regard, participatory design and co-design processes are key to ensuring a human-centered approach by actively engaging multiple stakeholders from across sectors. Specifically, academia can work together with developers and instructional designers to create GenAI solutions that meet the needs of both educators and students. Using participatory and co-design processes will ensure human-centered AI-powered solutions by fostering a deeper understanding of user needs and challenges and encouraging ongoing feedback through iterative testing and design (Nicholson et al., 2022). Generally, participatory design emphasizes the involvement of end-users, such as students and educators, from the initial design phase of a product. Co-design can go slightly further by encouraging the involvement of other stakeholders, such as researchers or experts. These strategies facilitate communication between product developers, users, and experts to identify user needs and desires, ensuring full consideration of the educational context in which solutions will be applied (Axelsson et al., 2021).

Both strategies lend themselves to intersectoral and multi-stakeholder collaboration, where the public sector, private sector, academicians, and the community can work together to identify general best practices and coordinate on policy in an impactful manner, enabling the use of AI-powered tools as a standard practice. Encouraging multi-stakeholder involvement starting at the design phase will be beneficial all the way through implementation and beyond. Several AI developers are already setting an example in implementing this strategy. For example, the AI-powered writing assistance tool Grammarly maintains a research team that engages educational institutions and experts to enhance their products continuously. A recent publication shared by the company highlights a strategic partnership between Grammarly, the University of Minnesota, and the University of Virginia to develop and test a text revision system, referred to as "Read, Revise, Repeat (R3)" (Du et al., 2022). The project demonstrates an iterative co-design process that builds upon previous research conducted by the team in the area of text revision and infuses the expertise of linguistic experts, resulting in a system that was reported to be effective in assisting with revisions. This success can be attributed to the collaborative efforts of Grammarly and academic researchers and represents a partnership trend with the international academic community through research (i.e., Yermilov et al., 2023; Du et al., 2022).

Kim et al. (2022) envision AI as collaborative and interactive educational support that can augment educator and student skills and capabilities across the learning environment and process. This vision, draws from the Student–AI Collaboration (SAC) model (Kim et al., 2022), shown in Figure 14.1. It comprises three components that will frame the discussion in this chapter: curriculum, human–AI interaction, and the learning environment.

Although this model illustrates collaboration between students and AI, these components are also highly relevant to intersectoral collaboration and the framing of related opportunities for collaboration. Considering that the use and application of AIHED can be extremely broad, this model can help guide the conversation about where collaborative relationships can enhance AI development and instructional design for AI-assisted learning. Adopting a holistic approach, as outlined in the SAC model, helps identify all relevant stakeholders in AI use and develop targeted plans to address specific aspects of AI integration in higher education. This approach minimizes the risk of overburdening educators and students by ensuring that stakeholders are engaged at the appropriate time and within the right context for each initiative or project.

Such collaboration brings together diverse stakeholders to share their perspectives on AIHED while promoting a sense of common purpose and creating champions for the adoption and implementation of technology in the

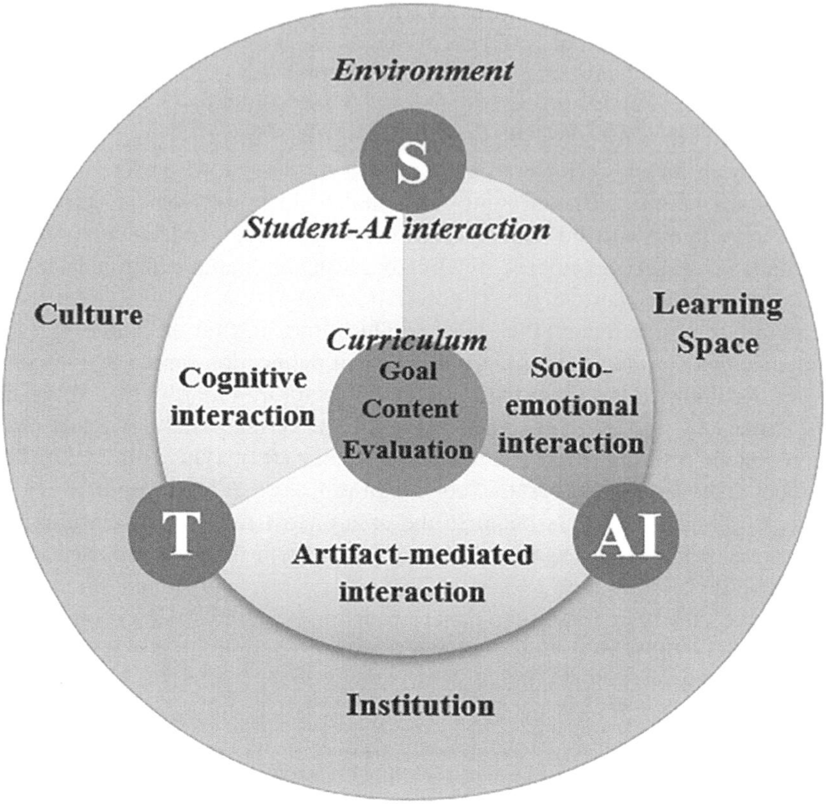

Source: Adapted from Fig. 1 in Kim et al., 2022.

Figure 14.1 Student–AI Collaboration (SAC) model

classroom. We will showcase how the three dimensions of the SAC model (Kim et al., 2022) – curriculum, human–AI collaboration, and environment – support diverse forms of intersectoral collaboration in higher education and can be used as a framing device to enable the development of a targeted approach to partnership development in order to strategically address specific applications of AIHED. For example, focusing on collaborations to support the curriculum can lead to professional development for educators that help ensure that the use of AIHED reflects pedagogical theory and best practices that complement educators' expertise while providing the necessary scaffolding to increase AI literacy. Collaborations emphasizing human–AI interaction can result in research partnerships that explore how AI can partner with educators and learners to shape and enhance learning processes. Finally, focusing on the larger learning environment allows for targeted problem-solving related to identifying the infrastructure needs and cultural shifts required to address issues such as the automation of routine tasks or personalization of learning. Leveraging the SAC model as a framework for examining intersectoral collaboration lends itself to developing a holistic strategy for implementing AIHED and emphasizes that successful implementation necessitates shared responsibility across diverse stakeholders for scalability and sustainability.

Curriculum-Related

The curriculum is vital to the overall learning environment in higher education, representing the intended instructional plan and learning objectives of any given course. It speaks not only to the expertise and intent of the individual educator but also to the values and norms of the institution at large. While GenAI presents the risk of encroaching on the intellectual property rights of human creators and potentially providing false or misleading content (Ding et al., 2023), educators also find opportunities for GenAI to impact their curriculum development and design by generating instructional materials, sequencing learning, and identifying learning strategies, ultimately saving them valuable time in their planning process (Arora, 2021). For example, GenAI is being leveraged to aid in the creation of open educational resources to accelerate open educational practices, with some researchers envisioning a future where, rather than spending time on developing materials such as textbooks, educators will instead become adept at writing prompts to produce content more interactively (Bozkurt, 2023). To support this type of use of GenAI, OpenAI, the creators of ChatGPT, have collaborated explicitly with researchers across academia to provide recommendations on developing prompts to support the creation of their *Teaching with AI* resource (OpenAI, 2023), which includes guidance on developing lesson plans and creating opportunities for formative assessment.

In line with this, higher education institutions and the private sector (e.g., ed-tech tool developers) can build collaborative relationships to ensure the accuracy and appropriateness of the information they generate or recommend, thus enhancing pedagogical practice. For instance, the University of Florida (UF) has been investing in AI and implementing it into the curriculum across the entire campus as a result of intersectoral collaboration between the university and the technology company NVIDIA (Southworth et al., 2023). The goal of the collaboration is to enable students to become part of an AI-literate workforce, and the impact of this goal has been the provision of resources allowing faculty and staff at the university to become more knowledgeable about AI so that they can implement it into their teaching and research (Southworth et al., 2023).

Curriculum development presents ample opportunity for collaboration between developers and education stakeholders to shape tool development through a deeper understanding of the context in which the tools will be used. UF has demonstrated how an institution-wide curriculum can incorporate learning both with and about AI. Such collaborations fuel and sustain feedback loops between the private ed-tech sector and the educators and learners they hope to engage through the practical application of participatory and co-design principles and values. This sort of engagement with AIHED systems' end-users then serves to uncover additional wants and needs to inform further development. The developers of the AI-powered graphic design tool Canva actively engaged educators through surveys, conferences, and their online *Canva for Teachers* community to understand how educators perceive and use AI in the classroom, revealing that, while most respondents were excited about the prospect of AI, many were unsure how to integrate AI into their classroom practices (Wilmot, 2023). The findings reported by Canva are consistent with similar surveys conducted by the AI Education Project (aiEDU, 2023) and the EdWeek Research Center (Langreo, 2024). Both surveys revealed that while many educators are aware of AI and may be curious or even eager to use it in the classroom, some face challenges in understanding AI and integrating it effectively into their teaching practices. Similarly, Uzumcu and Acilmis (2024) have shown comparable findings among pre-service teachers, many of whom were unsure whether they had used AI prior to participating in a study on AI use. Canva tied these results to the release of related resources meant to assist in closing the AI knowledge gap for educators, including targeted outreach both online and within schools to provide teachers with training on their product. Through the relationship Canva has established with educators globally, they can tailor their AI development and messaging to address teacher concerns such as privacy or the risk of generating content inappropriate for learners. This ongoing relationship between OpenAI and Canva and the educator community showcases the value of intersectoral collaboration practices that provide educators, students, community members, and others with a mechanism to participate in the ongoing development of AIHED technology to support curriculum development.

Human (Students & Teacher)–AI Interaction-Related

More than a piece of software or a tool, AI acts as a learning agent that can enrich the learning experience and complement the educator's role through interaction with the student, resulting in a transformative change in education (Kim & Cho, 2023; Kim, 2024). Human–AI interaction within the context of AIHED encompasses cognitive and socio-emotional interactions between educators and AI, students and AI, and all three, through interfaces and/or hardware (Kim et al., 2022) such as ChatGPT for writing or DALL-E for image generation. The interactions that take place between human users and AI can serve to either promote or hinder learning; therefore, it is vital that private-sector stakeholders actively work to understand these interactions to optimize the learning process while minimizing related risks.

To this end, developing pedagogically relevant AIHED technologies that support educationally meaningful interaction between students and AI is crucial and should be prioritized by intersectoral collaboratives. Current research demonstrates that many students actively use AI; however, this use includes simply copying content generated by GenAI into their assignments, which leads to accusations of cheating or plagiarism (Črček & Patekar, 2023). Additionally, risks associated with decreased interactions between humans and overreliance on AI, leading to less diversity of thought, have also been identified (Miao & Holmes, 2023). While this has led some classrooms or institutions to attempt to ban AI use in the educational setting (Klein, 2024), many educators and students remain optimistic regarding the potential to benefit from student–AI interactions in the learning environment. Educators have expressed that they believe AI can be leveraged to expose students to multiple viewpoints (Memmert et al., 2023), promote self-efficacy, and augment or build skills such as critical thinking, creativity, and problem-solving (Kim, 2024; Kim et al., 2022). These possibilities have been supported by students themselves, who, in student-focused research, have expressed a preference for AI tools that act as instructional support and help to scaffold their learning and provide storytelling elements that can help promote their creative thinking as they approach a task (Kim & Lee, 2023).

Realizing the potential benefits of AIHED to promote systems that enable positive interactions between educators, learners, and AI necessitates collaborative approaches, both technological and within instructional development, as commercially driven GenAI solutions may only partially meet the needs of educators and their students due to a lack of understanding of the on-the-ground experience of learning participants and a lack of expertise in relevant pedagogy. Communication loops between AI developers, learners, and educators promote the creation of tools and systems that can serve the various roles that educational stakeholders are eager for AI to fulfill. For instance, AIHED is positioned as an educational resource that can influence the learning ecosystem in at least two capacities. The first is through *Learning with AI*, which is to use AI as a direct teaching tool, as experienced through adaptive learning management systems or intelligent tutoring systems (Holmes et al., 2019). The second is through *Learning about AI,* which includes teaching and learning about AI, rather than with it (Baker & Smith, 2019). In other words, areas for potential collaboration related to human–AI interactions can also be framed in two ways: AI development and instructional design for AI-assisted learning. Working directly with education stakeholders will enable the resulting technologies to be built in a pedagogically informed manner intuitive to educators and students, making AI-powered education technology accessible to a wider audience within the education ecosystem.

Environment-Related

The integration of GenAI in the educational domain through learning analytics and related technologies is fueling ed-tech innovation to support the creation of personalized classroom learning environments that are adaptive to student needs and abilities. These personalized experiences can meet the needs of a wide range of students and educators by automating routine tasks such as tracking student engagement or progress through a course and grading assignments (Kim, 2023). Through its ability to process and make connections within large datasets, AI can support the creation of unique student profiles that lend themselves to generating custom learning paths that promote concept or task mastery (Kim, 2023). In addition, AI can further support tasks such as proofreading written work, generating personalized assessments, or providing immediate feedback on assignments (Cardona et al., 2023). All of this lends itself to the transformation of traditional classrooms and online learning environments.

However, changes to the educational environment can lead to risks and challenges. Introducing these technologies may lead to over-automation within the classroom and threaten the role of the human educator in areas such as decision-making, pacing, and goal-setting. Additionally, the automation and personalization described above require AI-powered technology to access large quantities of data to detect patterns, generate content, or make decisions. This leads to data-related concerns, including about privacy, security, and discrimination (Cardona et al., 2023). For example, since AI detects patterns in data it could inadvertently reinforce or perpetuate human biases (Ng et al., 2021). As an alternative example, the data required to enable custom learning solutions for students includes the collection of those students' personal information and, simply as a result of the nature of current technology, there is a risk of a data leak or hacking incident that could lead to student data and privacy being exposed. Even beyond the risk of negligence or ill intent, data privacy laws and regulations vary by jurisdiction, which could lead to data being lawfully exposed in a manner a student user may not be comfortable with (Wang et al., 2023). The injection of these technologies into education requires an understanding of potential data concerns and the most appropriate level of automation across tasks and contexts. This understanding will minimize potential risks to enhance the learning process and environment rather than harm it (Kim & Lee, 2023). This is most readily achievable through multi-stakeholder collaboration and reflection within the educational ecosystem and across sectors.

IDENTIFYING AND OVERCOMING BARRIERS TO INTERSECTORAL COLLABORATION: STRATEGIES FOR SUCCESS

Thus far, we have discussed both challenges and opportunities presented by GenAI in education, emphasizing the role of intersectoral collaboration in ensuring that AI services and tools are developed to effectively meet the needs of the educational community. The components discussed above represent a host of possibilities for the future of AIHED, revealing new areas and possibilities for intersectoral collaboration and suggesting a discussion agenda to better structure AIHED and intersectoral collaboration to advance AIHED. AI usage is not yet widespread enough throughout academia to consider it a foregone conclusion that it will be adopted and implemented routinely, and AI developers must employ human-centered design practices that incorporate ongoing feedback loops with educators and other stakeholders to meet end-users' needs in a pedagogically sound way. However, as important as intersectoral collaboration is to facilitating these ideals, forming such a collaboration can face many barriers. In this section, we will identify a few of those barriers and some strategies for addressing them.

Barrier One: Communication

The first challenge results from the potential for communication gaps between the AI developers and the educators participating in collaborative work. These gaps can stem from multiple areas, such as differences in priorities, organizational missions, and cultures or understandings of technology. For example, while developers will likely represent a private, for-profit entity that is prioritizing knowledge exploitation for profitability and scalability, educators will represent an institution and their students with an eye toward knowledge-building and sound pedagogical practices (O'Dwyer et al., 2023). However, this is not an insurmountable issue for burgeoning intersectoral collaborative partnerships and can be addressed through an alignment of the competing priorities of stakeholders. Such alignment can be achieved by building trust between partners, which can be enhanced through transparent policies and shared governance within the partnership across stakeholders (Kowch, 2025).

An additional example of a communication gap can be seen in the form of institutional policies on AI in the learning environment. Globally, some institutions have implemented policies that seek to limit GenAI use due to fears that students will use such tools to cheat or plagiarize, resulting in an inconsistent approach to guidance about AI for education across higher education that can limit the formation of intersectoral collaborations. Many countries are still deciding how to approach AI guidance and regulation and who should own the implementation and enforcement of it. In a 2023 report by the Organization for Economic Cooperation and Development (OECD), only two out of 18 countries had any GenAI-specific regulation pending approval, while only nine had published non-binding guidance on the topic (Vidal et al., 2023). Such fears can be negotiated through shared knowledge, understanding, and guidance related to AIHED, such as the AI competency framework proposed previously in this volume comprising six key elements, including AI knowledge and application; AI ethical principles; AI impact; learning with AI; AI for careers; and lifelong learning for AI. Empowering educators with this common foundation to build their AI literacy enables them to effectively adapt pedagogical frameworks to adequately account for the existence or use of GenAI.

Barrier Two: Access to Resources

The second challenge to forming a successful intersectoral collaboration is access to resources. Resources can include people, funding, time, information, or training, among other things. This can pose a particular problem for higher education institutions, which often have budget restrictions that limit their ability to invest in new technologies and rapidly scale them across their curriculum. Funding issues can be overcome in several ways, such as through government grants and other funding mechanisms. Institution alumni associations can also be a source of funding (Awasthy et al., 2020), as can the industry partners themselves. For example, in the UF use case shared earlier in this chapter, the industry partner NVIDIA helped offset costs by providing technology resources that set the stage for implementing their campuswide AI curriculum. These resources included the launch of a supercomputer called HiPerGator that, at the time of launch, was the "22nd most powerful system in the world" (Southworth et al., 2023). HiPerGator supports teaching, research, and learning to prepare students for a world where AI familiarity and skills will be required.

From the perspective of human resources, participating in successful intersectoral collaborations requires higher education institutions to have faculty or staff available to actively engage in the collaborative work in addition to their existing duties while also, ideally, sharing the collaboration's vision and having some familiarity with the industry being partnered with to build trust and increase the likelihood of success (Awasthy et al., 2020). Likewise, the industry partners need to have the capacity to be able to successfully absorb and make use of the knowledge provided by their academic partners, requiring that they have personnel capable of facilitating that knowledge transfer in a meaningful way (Awasthy et al., 2020). To ensure this, both higher education institutions and industry partners looking to form an intersectoral collaboration in support of furthering AIHED must be deliberate when selecting the appropriate stakeholders to actively engage in these efforts so that the collaboration benefits from the right mix of subject-matter experts, intermediaries, champions, and management who are committed to actively participating. Returning to UF, recognizing the need to ensure the right resources are available to ensure the success of their AI initiatives, the university invested in over 100 new hires across all their colleges (Southworth et al., 2023). The University of Cambridge, as an additional example, has formed a partnership with Microsoft to support research related to AI innovation, which provides a forum for academic stakeholders to provide feedback on AI prototypes. To enable this partnership, Cambridge and Microsoft established a joint lab that is further supported by the United Kingdom government, with funding to support researchers, students, and interns to allow for ideas to be easily exchanged between Microsoft and the university (University of Cambridge, 2019).

Barrier Three: Keeping Up with GenAI

The final challenge is that higher education stakeholders have not yet fully considered the full impact of GenAI on education. This is partly due to the rapid pace at which GenAI in education is developing. While widespread accessibility and the innovations that accessibility enables are positive, institutions struggle to keep up and provide leadership to faculty and students on the appropriate use of GenAI in education. This can perpetuate negative attitudes, reactive policies, and communication gaps, discussed earlier, as users struggle to keep up with the changes. This becomes a crucial consideration when planning intersectoral collaboration because it signals that such partnerships cannot occur at a single point in time, or else existing insights, recommendations, or guidelines stemming from initial collaborative activities may become outdated. Rather, successful intersectoral collaborations require open and ongoing communication to ensure that such advances continue incorporating multi-stakeholder insights from educators. However, this introduces hurdles related to maintaining partner commitment and interest, pointing to a need to develop collaborations with sustainability in mind (O'Dwyer et al., 2023) so that technology designers can continue to iteratively improve their current products, create training and resources to optimize their use, and plan for future needs.

Addressing Barriers

Outlining the barriers to effective intersectoral collaboration through the lens of the SAC model clarifies the necessary steps for developing a strategic plan that supports successful collaboration. First, as discussed earlier in this chapter, a key benefit of leveraging a framework such as the SAC model is that it helps collaborators define the scope of their collaboration or initiative. AIHED is a massive topic area that can easily span numerous use cases across the curriculum, human–AI interactions, and the educational environment. Setting clear parameters for the intended collaboration will increase the likelihood of success.

Second, it is essential to develop a clear communication plan and disseminate shared definitions to aid collaborators in understanding expectations and facilitate a shared understanding of what is being discussed. These practices can be amplified and strengthened by providing collaborators with multiple means of interaction and feedback (O'Dwyer et al., 2023). For instance, Stanford University is a proactive example of enabling multi-stakeholder communication through its Human-Centered Artificial Intelligence Institute, where it actively engages students, faculty, and staff in the design process through courses, workshops, student affinity groups, and feedback sessions (https://hai.stanford.edu/).

Third, it is essential to establish clear expectations for each stakeholder's role, including guidance on how and when they should contribute, to prevent overburdening participants. Building strategic partnerships can also help mitigate resource constraints by introducing new funding, materials, or subject-matter expertise. However, roles and relationships within these partnerships must be clearly defined to set expectations for post-partnership scenarios. For example, if an industry partner provides an institution with access to a tool during a research collaboration, the institution must decide whether it will continue using the tool after the collaboration ends and plan accordingly. Additionally, both parties must clarify data ownership and access after the partnership concludes.

Finally, as GenAI is rapidly advancing, it is essential to empower collaborators with the means to stay up to date with the technology so they can continue to contribute in a meaningful way. One possible strategy for addressing this issue is to engage students and instructors as co-designers in developing AI solutions. For example, one study on the process of democratizing learning design through collaborative practices engaged college students, lecturers, and researchers from across disciplines at a Spanish university in the co-design of a chatbot that aimed to support self-regulated learning (SRL) (Gazulla et al., 2023). To capture feedback and ideas from these various stakeholders, the designers held workshops where participants could freely contribute their thoughts and express their needs (Gazulla et al., 2023). Having such a diverse group expressing ideas can lead to challenges relating to issues such as developing common understandings, defining requirements, navigating schedules, and other barriers to successful collaboration. The chatbot design team addressed these challenges by creating opportunities to provide brief feedback outside of more in-depth sessions or discussions, creating a space to prioritize stakeholder feedback where participants felt safe in providing diverse perspectives, describing their attitudes toward technology, and negotiating opposing viewpoints (Gazulla et al., 2023).

CONCLUSION

Integrating GenAI into higher education presents both opportunities and challenges. It requires a paradigm shift in the educational model and landscape that challenges educators and leaders to reconsider how we teach, learn, and assess. Intersectoral collaboration is crucial to supporting the capacity-building of AIHED. Thoughtful intersectoral collaboration provides opportunities for the public, private sector, academicians, and the community to collaborate and provide feedback on GenAI solutions. Human-centered design, participatory design, and co-design processes are essential for ensuring that AI-powered educational technology solutions are optimized for integration into education and meet the needs of educators and students. These practices directly lead to keeping humans in the loop so that human dignity, ethics, and empowerment can be prioritized in designing these tools and systems (Cardona et al., 2023).

Through these collaborative processes, stakeholders can identify general best practices based on actual usage and feedback from human educators and learners to coordinate policy and guidelines effectively. Collaboration and interaction between stakeholders will be key to creating a common understanding among different stakeholders around AIHED and addressing the key challenges effectively to overcome resistance to AIHED. To support these goals, developers can implement multiple feedback mechanisms to establish a continuous feedback loop. This can include user testing, pilots, focus groups, co-design workshops with educators and students, and surveys. Additionally, educators and institutions can form or join existing learning communities or professional learning communities, begin to experiment with AI within their lesson planning, and involve students in AI exploration in the classroom. This will enable the use of AI-powered tools in education as a standard practice rather than an inconsistent trend.

REFERENCES

aiEDU. (2023). *Pulse survey report.* https://www.aiedu.org/pulse.

Arora, V. (2021). *Artificial intelligence in schools: A guide for teachers, leaders, and technology administrators*. Routledge. https://doi.org/10.4324/9781003183235.

Awasthy, R., Flint, S., Sankarnarayana, R., & Jones, R. L. (2020). A framework to improve university–industry collaboration. *Journal of Industry-University Collaboration*, *2*(1), 49–62. https://doi.org/10.1108/JIUC-09-2019-0016.

Axelsson, M., Oliveira, R., Racca, M., & Kyrki, V. (2021). Social robot co-design canvases: A participatory design framework. *ACM Transactions on Human-Robot Interaction*, *11*(1), 1–39. https://doi.org/10.1145/3472225.

Baker, T. and Smith, L. (2019, February 19) *Educ-AI-Tion rebooted?* Exploring the future of artificial intelligence in schools and colleges. https://www.nesta.org.uk/report/education-rebooted/.

Bozkurt, A. (2023). Generative artificial intelligence (AI) powered conversational educational agents: The inevitable paradigm shift. *Asian Journal of Distance Education*, *18*(1). Retrieved from https://asianjde.com/ojs/index.php/AsianJDE/article/view/718.

Cardona, M. A., Rodriguez, R. J., & Ishmael, K. (2023). *Artificial intelligence and the future of teaching and learning*. Office of Educational Technology. https://www2.ed.gov/documents/ai-report/ai-report.pdf.

Črček, N., & Patekar, J. (2023). Writing with AI: University students' use of ChatGPT. *Journal of Language and Education*, *9*(4), 128–138. https://doi.org/10.17323/jle.2023.17379.

Ding, L., Li, T., Jiang, S., & Gapud, A. (2023). Students' perceptions of using ChatGPT in a physics class as a virtual tutor. *International Journal of Educational Technology in Higher Education*, *20*(1), 63–18. https://doi.org/10.1186/s41239-023-00434-1.

Du, W., Kim, Z. M., Raheja, V., Kumar, D., & Kang, D. (2022). *Read, Revise, Repeat: A System Demonstration for Human-in-the-loop Iterative Text Revision*. arXiv. https://doi.org/10.48550/arxiv.2204.03685.

Gazulla, E. D., Martins, L., & Fernández-Ferrer, M. (2023). Designing learning technology collaboratively: Analysis of a chatbot co-design. *Education and Information Technologies*, *28*. https://doi.org/10.1007/s10639-022-11162-w.

Holmes, W., Bialik, M., & Fadel, C. (2019). *Artificial intelligence in education promises and implications for teaching and learning*. Center for Curriculum Redesign.

Kim, J. (2023). Leading teachers' perspective on teacher-AI collaboration in education. *Education and Information Technologies*, *29*, 8693–8724. https://doi.org/10.1007/s10639-023-12109-5.

Kim, J. (2024). Types of teacher-AI collaboration in K-12 classroom instruction: Chinese teachers' perspective. *Education and Information Technologies*, *29*, 17433–17465. https://doi.org/10.1007/s10639-024-12523-3.

Kim, J., & Cho, Y. H. (2023). My teammate is AI: Understanding students' perceptions of student–AI collaboration in drawing tasks. *Asia Pacific Journal of Education*, 1–15. https://doi.org/10.1080/02188791.2023.2286206.

Kim, J., & Lee, S. S. (2023). Are two heads better than one? The effect of student–AI collaboration on students' learning task performance. *TechTrends*, *67*, 365–375. https://doi.org/10.1007/s11528-022-00788-9.

Kim, J., Lee, H., & Cho, Y. H. (2022). Learning design to support student–AI collaboration: Perspectives of leading teachers for AI in education. *Education and Information Technologies*, *27*(5), 6069–6104. https://doi.org/10.1007/s10639-021-10831-6.

Klein, A. (2024). Does your district ban ChatGPT? Here's what educators told us. *Education Week*. https://www.edweek.org/technology/does-your-district-ban-chatgpt-heres-what-educators-told-us/2024/02.

Kooli, C. (2023). Chatbots in education and research: A critical examination of ethical implications and solutions. *Sustainability*, *15*(7), 5614.

Kowch, E. (2025). An innovation policy analysis for higher education generative AI leaders and researchers. In S. Sabbaghan (Ed.), *Navigating generative AI in higher education: Ethical, theoretical and practical perspectives*. Edward Elgar.

Langreo, L. (2024). Most teachers are not using AI. Here's why. *Education Week*. https://www.edweek.org/technology/most-teachers-are-not-using-ai-heres-why/2024/01.

Memmert, L., Tavanapour, N., & Bittner, E. (2023). Learning by doing: Educators' perspective on an illustrative tool for AI-generated scaffolding for students in conceptualizing design science research studies. *Journal of Information Systems Education*, *34*(3), 279–292. https://aisel.aisnet.org/jise/vol34/iss3/3.

Miao, F., & Holmes, W. (2023). *Guidance for generative AI in education and research*. UNESCO. https://doi.org/10.54675/EWZM9535.

Ng, D. T. K., Leung, J. K. L., Chu, S. K. W., & Qiao, M. S. (2021). Conceptualizing AI literacy: An exploratory review. *Computers and Education: Artificial Intelligence*, *2*, 100041. https://doi.org/10.1016/j.caeai.2021.100041.

Nicholson, R., Bartindale, T., Kharrufa, A., Kirk, D., & Walker-Gleaves, C. (2022). Participatory design goes to school: Co-teaching as a form of co-design for educational technology. *CHI '22: Proceedings of the 2022 CHI Conference on Human Factors in Computing Systems*, 1–17. https://doi.org/10.1145/3491102.3517667.

O'Dwyer, M., Filieri, R., & O'Malley, L. (2023). Establishing successful university–industry collaborations: barriers and enablers deconstructed. *The Journal of Technology Transfer*, *48*(3), 900–931. https://doi.org/10.1007/s10961-022-09932-2

OpenAI. (2023, August 31). *Teaching with AI*. https://openai.com/index/teaching-with-ai/.

Southworth, J., Migliaccio, K., Glover, J., Glover, J., Reed, D., McCarty, C., Brendemuhl, J., & Thomas, A. (2023). Developing a model for AI across the curriculum: Transforming the higher education landscape via innovation in AI literacy. *Computers and Education. Artificial Intelligence*, *4*, 100127. https://doi.org/10.1016/j.caeai.2023.100127.

Tweedie, M. G., & Sharmi, S. T. (2025). Transparency, assessment and the "Black Box" dilemma. In S. Sabbaghan (Ed.), *Navigating generative AI in higher education: Ethical, theoretical and practical perspectives*. Edward Elgar.

University of Cambridge. (2019, October 18). *UK government backs University of Cambridge and Microsoft mission to build better AI*. Department of Engineering. https://www.eng.cam.ac.uk/news/uk-government-backs-university-cambridge-and-microsoft-mission-build-better-ai.

Uzumcu, O., & Acilmis, H. (2024). Do innovative teachers use AI-powered tools more interactively? A study in the context of diffusion of innovation theory. *Technology, Knowledge and Learning*, *29*(2), 1109–1128. https://doi.org/10.1007/s10758-023-09687-1.

Vidal, Q., Vincent-Lancrin, S., & Yun, H. (2023). Emerging governance of generative AI in education. In *OECD Digital Education Outlook 2023: Towards an Effective Digital Education Ecosystem*. OECD Publishing. https://doi.org/10.1787/2a73a245-en.

Wang, T., Lund, B. D., Marengo, A., Pagano, A., Mannuru, N. R., Teel, Z. A., & Pange, J. (2023). Exploring the potential impact of artificial intelligence (AI) on international students in higher education: Generative AI, chatbots, analytics, and international student success. *Applied Sciences*, *13*(11), 6716. https://doi.org/10.3390/app13116716.

Wilmot, J. (2023, October 23). *Canva's AI in education study: Teachers embrace power of AI*. Canva. https://www.canva.com/newsroom/news/ai-education-survey/.

Yermilov, O., Raheja, V., & Chernodub, A. (2023). *Privacy- and utility-preserving NLP with anonymized data: A case study of pseudonymization*. arXiv. https://doi.org/10.48550/arxiv.2306.05561.

Zhang, H., Lee, I., Ali, S., DiPaola, D., Cheng, Y., & Breazeal, C. (2023). Integrating ethics and career futures with technical learning to promote AI literacy for middle school students: An exploratory study. *International Journal of Artificial Intelligence in Education*, *33*(2), 290–324.

15. Charting a human-centered path for generative AI in higher education

Soroush Sabbaghan

INTRODUCTION

Throughout this book, we have explored how generative artificial intelligence (GenAI) can reshape the landscape of higher education, influencing teaching, learning, and research. We have highlighted GenAI's potential to refine research methods, tailor educational experiences, and simplify administrative tasks. Nevertheless, there are ethical issues that come with such advancements, such as bias, academic integrity, authorship, and data privacy. These challenges remind us of the complexities involved in deploying AI. We also considered the shifts in teaching methods required to integrate GenAI effectively, stressing the importance of flexible instructional design and new approaches to assessment that encourage critical thinking. Additionally, we have emphasized the importance of developing AI literacy and skills among both educators and students, along with the need for strong policy frameworks and collaborative efforts. Although each chapter has provided unique insights, this final chapter aims to bring these perspectives together into a more integrated and human-centered vision for the future of higher education with GenAI.

In examining the role of GenAI in education, it is important to recognize that technology should serve human needs and values. This chapter highlights the necessity of adopting a human-centered approach when integrating GenAI into higher education. We must design educational systems that prioritize well-being, equity, and the development of essential skills such as critical thinking, creativity, and ethical reasoning. By focusing on the learner, we ensure that technological advancements support and enhance the educational process rather than hinder it. This approach ensures that GenAI is implemented in a way that aligns with our core values and educational goals, fostering an environment where technology and human-centric principles work together to create meaningful learning experiences.

In applying Human-Centered Design (HCD) to GenAI in higher education, the needs, preferences, and limitations of end-users must guide every step of the design process (Giacomin, 2014; Maguire, 2001). Although HCD encompasses various principles (Magalhães, 2018; Tosi, 2020), this chapter focuses on four key components: Inclusivity, Contextual Awareness, Adaptive Processes, and Collaborative Participation. We begin by summarizing main insights from earlier chapters, highlighting recurring themes and concerns. We then introduce a framework for integrating HCD into GenAI in higher education, outlining actionable steps and offering real-world examples. Finally, we propose practical recommendations for educators, institutions, policy-makers, and technology developers, encouraging a shared effort to shape a future in higher education that balances innovation with human values.

SYNTHESIS OF KEY INSIGHTS FROM PREVIOUS CHAPTERS

The Transformative Potential of GenAI

GenAI presents significant opportunities to enhance various aspects of higher education. In Chapter 2, Keyhani and Mohaghegh-Neyshabouri (2025) explore how large language models (LLMs) are reshaping teaching, learning, research, and academic administration. The potential for personalized learning experiences is a recurring theme; for example, in Chapter 4 Brown and Roberts (2025) demonstrate how GenAI tools are capable of adapting to individual student needs and providing customized support. Additionally, as discussed in Chapter 3, GenAI can perform advanced statistical and qualitative analyses, accelerating the pace of discovery and enabling new methodologies in research (Farrokhnia et al., 2025). Moreover, GenAI can simplify administrative tasks, allowing educators to dedicate more time to teaching and engaging with students, as highlighted in Chapter 2. Chapter 5, by Baidoo-Anu et al. (2025), further emphasizes GenAI's capability to automate tasks such as question generation and feedback provision in assessments. These capabilities indicate that GenAI has the potential to create a more efficient and effective educational system, enhancing both academic and administrative functions.

Recognizing the diverse learning needs of students is essential in creating an inclusive educational environment. By providing personalized learning pathways and adaptive feedback, GenAI can accommodate students with varying backgrounds, abilities, and learning preferences (Al-Zahrani, 2025; Baidoo-Anu et al., 2025; Keyhani & Mohaghegh-Neyshabouri, 2025). This approach fosters more inclusive and equitable educational experiences, ensuring that all students have the opportunity to succeed. Additionally, GenAI can generate content in multiple formats and languages, which may enhance accessibility for students with disabilities and those from diverse linguistic backgrounds (Farrokhnia et al., 2025). Chapter 4 further discusses how GenAI supports experiential learning and open education practices (Brown & Roberts, 2025). Through these applications, GenAI contributes to creating an educational environment that accommodates and enriches the learning experiences of all students.

Ethical and Epistemological Challenges

Although we recognize the significant benefits of GenAI, we must also address the substantial ethical and epistemological challenges it presents. Chapters 8, 10, and 11 highlight concerns about bias in GenAI algorithms, which could reinforce existing inequalities if not properly managed (Lee, 2025; Abbas, 2025; Eaton & Keyhani, 2025). Academic integrity is another crucial issue. Kumar (2025), in Chapter 7, and Eaton and Keyhani (2025), in Chapter 10, discuss the potential for students to misuse GenAI tools for plagiarism or other forms of academic dishonesty. Additionally, Kumar (2025) questions the traditional notion of authorship and notes that the collaborative nature of human–AI interactions in writing underscore the need for new models of attribution and responsibility. Data privacy also remains a key concern, with Al-Zahrani (2025) emphasizing the importance of protecting student data and ensuring its ethical use. Addressing these challenges is essential to ensure that GenAI supports rather than undermines the foundational values of higher education.

In Chapter 9, Tweedie and Sharmi (2025) address the "black box" problem, which describes the lack of transparency in certain GenAI systems and the difficulty in understanding how they produce their results. Baidoo-Anu et al. (2025) point out that this opacity raises important issues related to accountability and trust, particularly in high-stakes settings such as assessments. Eaton and Keyhani (2025) emphasize the necessity of ethical frameworks and transparent GenAI practices to ensure that GenAI is employed responsibly and in ways that reflect educational values. Furthermore, Kumar (2025), drawing from Eaton's (2023) notion of post-plagiarism, advocates for a redefinition of academic integrity in the age of AI. Together, these discussions highlight the critical need for clarity and ethical considerations in the deployment of GenAI within educational contexts.

Pedagogical Shifts and Instructional Design

As we incorporate GenAI into higher education, we must embrace significant changes in our teaching methods and rethink our roles as educators. In Chapter 4, Brown and Roberts (2025) introduce a responsive instructional design approach, highlighting the necessity for educators to comprehend the interconnections within a learning system and to implement deliberate changes to their instructional strategies. Al-Zahrani (2025), in Chapter 6, suggests that educators must transition from being content providers to becoming facilitators of learning, guiding students in the effective and ethical use of GenAI tools. Additionally, Lee (2025), in Chapter 8, emphasizes the importance of prioritizing higher-order thinking skills, such as critical analysis, problem-solving, and creativity, especially in a context where GenAI can perform many routine tasks. These shifts are essential to ensure that our educational practices evolve alongside technology, fostering environments where students can thrive and think deeply in an AI-supported environment.

Lee (2025) emphasizes the importance of active learning methodologies and authentic assessment practices. He argues that these approaches are crucial for ensuring students engage deeply with the material, rather than simply absorbing information passively. By fostering active participation, students can develop the skills they need to thrive in a GenAI-driven world. Lee proposes using interactive presentations, project-based learning, and personalized portfolios as effective strategies to enhance student engagement and promote meaningful learning experiences. Throughout Chapters 5 and 8, the recurring emphasis is on moving beyond traditional assessment methods (Baidoo-Anu et al., 2025) and the embrace of more authentic and personalized approaches (Lee, 2025). These emphases highlight the imperative for educational institutions to adopt these progressive practices.

The Importance of AI Literacy and Competency

The effective integration of GenAI in higher education requires a strong foundation of AI literacy for both educators and students. In Chapter 3, Farrokhnia et al. (2025) highlight the importance of educators developing the ability to critically assess and utilize GenAI tools within their teaching practices. This means not only understanding what these tools can and cannot do but also recognizing how they influence learning outcomes. Similarly, in Chapter 12, Chiu (2025) emphasizes the importance for students to go beyond basic technical skills and gain a thorough understanding of AI. This framework includes areas such as AI knowledge and application, ethical principles, societal impact, learning with AI, career applications, and lifelong learning. It suggests that students should be able to understand, apply, and create with AI to operate ethically and effectively in AI-driven environments. Chiu also points out that developing AI literacy involves more than just technical proficiency; it requires the ability to critically evaluate the ethical, social, and cultural implications of AI. This comprehensive understanding is central for responsible and informed engagement with AI in all areas of life.

Policy and Governance Considerations

The integration of GenAI in higher education requires a thoughtful approach to policy and governance frameworks. In Chapter 13, Kowch (2025) examines the AI strategies of the G10 nations and finds that they prioritize economic growth and computer science, often overlooking the humanities and education sectors. This observation highlights the need for more inclusive and diverse policy approaches that address the wider impacts of AI in education. Kowch emphasizes the importance of aligning strategic goals with the allocation of resources to ensure that AI policies are effectively implemented. Additionally, international cooperation is vital to address the global challenges and opportunities that AI presents in the educational landscape. Lee (2025), in Chapter 8, further argues that policies must ensure equitable access to AI resources and training. This is essential to guarantee that all students and educators can benefit from these technologies, addressing the digital divide and preventing the exclusion of marginalized communities. Moreover, the creation of clear ethical guidelines for AI use in education is a vital policy issue, a point that both Al-Zahrani (2025) and Eaton and Keyhani (2025) reinforce. By developing robust ethical frameworks, we can ensure that the deployment of GenAI in education respects the rights and dignity of all learners.

The Need for Collaboration

The successful integration of GenAI in higher education relies heavily on effective collaboration among various partners. In Chapter 14, Detrick and Kim (2025) highlight the need for partnerships between GenAI developers and educators to develop educational technologies that are focused on human needs. This approach involves participatory design processes, actively engaging both educators and students in the creation and assessment of AI tools. Open communication and transparency are essential to ensuring that these AI tools align with educational objectives and uphold ethical standards (Tweedie & Sharmi, 2025). Moreover, collaboration should extend beyond educators and developers to include policy-makers, researchers, and other stakeholders, promoting a comprehensive and inclusive strategy for AI integration. Detrick and Kim (2025) conclude that cross-sector collaboration is important to address the complex challenges and opportunities that GenAI presents in education. Additionally, maintaining ongoing dialogue and feedback loops is important to continuously improve and adapt AI tools to meet the evolving needs of the educational community (Lee, 2025). By collaborating across different sectors, we can ensure that the adoption of GenAI enhances our educational systems in meaningful and responsible ways.

A HUMAN-CENTERED DESIGN FRAMEWORK FOR GENAI IN HIGHER EDUCATION

The Core Principles Revisited: The Necessity of a Human-centered Approach

Building upon the benefits and challenges discussed in the preceding chapters, it is clear that a human-centered approach is essential for integrating GenAI in higher education. Figure 15.1 outlines four guiding principles—Inclusivity, Contextual Awareness, Adaptive Processes, and Collaborative Participation—that directly address the ethical, educational, and practical issues identified.

In our commitment to inclusivity, it is important to design GenAI tools that address the diverse needs of all learners, including those from under-represented or marginalized communities. Chapters in this book have highlighted the importance of equitable access, showing how biases in AI systems and uneven distribution of resources can disadvantage certain groups (Abbas, 2025; Al-Zahrani, 2025; Eaton & Keyhani, 2025). By developing GenAI solutions that consider varied cultural backgrounds, learning preferences, abilities, and socioeconomic conditions, educational institutions can help prevent the deepening of existing inequalities. Understanding the context in which GenAI operates is also central. Developers and institutions must recognize

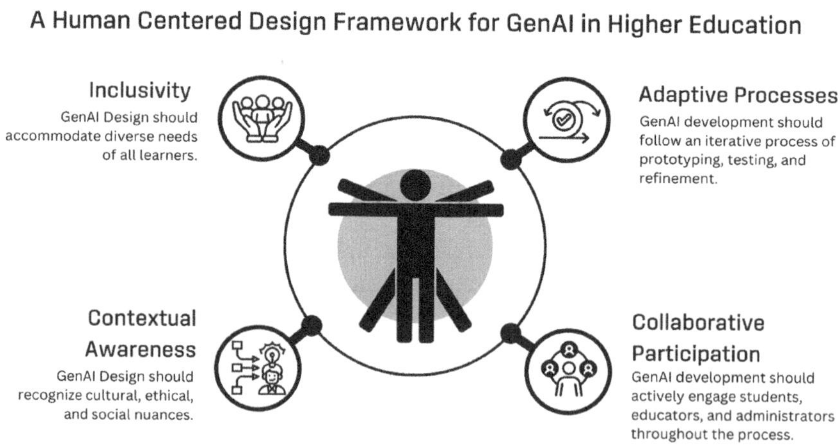

Source: Authors.

Figure 15.1 *A human-centered design framework for GenAI in higher educations*

the cultural, ethical, and social factors that shape different educational settings. Case studies and analyses in the preceding chapters have shown that applying AI tools without this understanding may result in unforeseen and negative impacts (Abbas, 2025; Chiu, 2025; Lee, 2025). By embedding GenAI within the broader framework of institutional values, societal norms, and learner goals, educators can achieve outcomes that are equitable, respectful, and meaningful. Adopting an adaptive processes approach is important given the constantly evolving nature of both AI technology and educational environments. Throughout the chapters, we have seen how challenges such as algorithmic bias and concerns about academic integrity require continuous improvement based on real-world feedback. An iterative cycle of prototyping, testing, and adjusting ensures that GenAI remains effective and ethical, fostering ongoing enhancements in usability and overall impact. Engaging users is a key component of successful GenAI implementation. It is important to involve students, educators, and administrators at every stage of development and deployment. The lessons learned indicate that, when partners are not heard, even well-intentioned innovations can lead to friction or fail to meet actual needs. By collaborating with users from the beginning and maintaining that partnership, developers and institutions can ensure that GenAI tools genuinely enhance learning, support teaching, and fit smoothly into the everyday realities of academic life. By integrating these fundamental principles into policies, teaching methods, and practical applications, institutions can ensure that GenAI tools align with human values, uphold academic integrity, and provide equitable access for all learners. This comprehensive approach ensures that GenAI contributes positively to higher education, creating an environment where every student has the opportunity to thrive.

Applying the Core Principles in Practice

As we integrate GenAI into higher education, we ground our efforts in the essential principles of human-centered design: Inclusivity, Contextual Awareness, Adaptive Processes, and Collaborative Participation. These principles go beyond theoretical ideas; they offer clear, practical guidance that directs our design process. The sections that follow will explain how each principle is implemented in practice, guiding actions, shaping processes, and achieving desired outcomes.

1. Inclusivity in GenAI Design:
   - **Action:** Conduct thorough research to identify the diverse needs and challenges of all potential users, particularly those from

under-represented groups. This includes understanding varying levels of digital literacy and accessibility requirements.
   - **Process:** Ensure that the design process involves diverse voices and perspectives from the outset. Use inclusive language, provide multiple modes of engagement, and actively seek out and address potential biases in the design.
   - **Outcome:** Develop GenAI tools and practices that are accessible, equitable, and adaptable to the needs of all learners and educators, regardless of their background or abilities. This includes considering accessibility standards (e.g., WCAG) and offering content in multiple formats and languages.
2. Contextual Awareness in GenAI Integration:
   - **Action:** Ground the design in a holistic understanding of the cultural, ethical, and social contexts in which GenAI will be used.
   - **Process:** Conduct thorough research to understand the specific needs and challenges of different educational settings and user groups. Consider the broader societal implications of AI and the potential impact on different communities.
   - **Outcome:** Create GenAI tools and practices that are respectful, responsive, and relevant to the specific contexts in which they are used. This includes considering ethical implications and ensuring that the technology is used in a way that promotes equity and social justice.
3. Adaptive Processes in GenAI Development:
   - **Action:** Adopt a cyclical approach to design, moving through stages of prototyping, testing, and refinement.
   - **Process:** Start with low-fidelity prototypes to quickly gather initial feedback. Continuously evaluate and refine the design based on user feedback and real-world performance. Be prepared to make significant changes to the design based on what is learned from each iteration.
   - **Outcome:** Create GenAI tools that are continuously improving, adaptable, and responsive to the evolving needs of users. This process ensures that the final product is not only functional but also effective and user-friendly.
4. Collaborative Participation in GenAI Implementation:
   - **Action:** Actively involve users at every stage of the design and implementation process.
   - **Process:** Employ a variety of collaborative participation methods, such as surveys, interviews, focus groups, and co-design workshops. Ensure that feedback is collected from a diverse range of users and that their voices are heard and valued.

- **Outcome:** Develop GenAI tools and practices that are user-centered and meet the needs of the educational community. This approach fosters a sense of ownership and ensures that the final product is relevant and effective.

Examples of Human-centered Design in Action

Let's consider the development of a GenAI-powered academic writing assistant specifically designed for graduate students, with a particular focus on supporting them in adhering to APA 7th edition formatting and style guidelines. This example will illustrate how each of the core HCD principles can be applied in a practical scenario.

Inclusivity in Action: The design process begins with a commitment to inclusivity. Recognizing that graduate students come from diverse backgrounds, the development team conducts initial research to understand the varied needs of their target users. They discover that some students may have visual impairments, others may have varying levels of familiarity with APA 7th edition, and some might struggle with the nuances of academic writing conventions. To address these diverse needs, the writing assistant is designed with several key features. It incorporates adjustable font sizes and screen reader compatibility to ensure accessibility for students with visual impairments. It provides clear, concise explanations of APA 7th edition guidelines, avoiding complex jargon that might be confusing for those less familiar with academic writing. Furthermore, the tool is designed to be adaptable, allowing users to customize the interface and settings to suit their individual preferences. This ensures that the tool is not only functional but also welcoming and supportive for all graduate students. The team also actively seeks feedback from students from under-represented groups to identify and address any potential biases or barriers to access, focusing on issues related to usability and clarity of guidance.

Contextual Awareness in Action: The design of the writing assistant should be rooted in a contextual awareness of the unique challenges faced by graduate students. The team recognizes that these students are often working under pressure, juggling multiple responsibilities, and facing high expectations for their academic writing. Therefore, the writing assistant is designed to be intuitive and user-friendly, minimizing the learning curve and allowing students to quickly integrate it into their workflow. The team also acknowledges the ethical considerations related to AI and academic integrity. The tool is designed to promote ethical writing practices, providing recommendations on improving academic writing. Critically, the tool includes a reference system where, for every AI-generated suggestion or recommendation, the student can click a link that takes them directly to the relevant section of the official APA 7th edition guidelines or a reputable academic resource. This allows students to verify the AI's recommendations and develop a deeper understanding of academic writing conventions. It is crucial to emphasize that the AI does not provide any original thought or content; it solely checks for adherence to APA 7th edition style guidelines and provides recommendations for improvement. This ensures that students remain the authors of their work and that they are actively engaged in the writing process. The team also considers the different disciplinary contexts in which graduate students work, ensuring that the tool is relevant and applicable across a wide range of academic fields.

Adaptive Processes in Action: The development of the writing assistant follows adaptive processes. Initially, the team creates a low-fidelity prototype featuring a text input area where students can paste their writing. The AI then analyzes the text sentence by sentence, providing recommendations for corrections to improve compliance with the APA 7th edition style. For example, if a student writes, "The study showed that … ", the AI might suggest "The study demonstrated that … " to adhere to more formal academic language. If a student uses a direct quote without proper attribution, the AI will label this and provide a link to the relevant APA guidelines. This initial prototype is tested with a small group of graduate students from diverse disciplines. Careful analysis of their feedback reveals that, although students appreciate the sentence-by-sentence feedback, they sometimes want more context or explanation for the suggested changes. The development team revises the prototype accordingly, adding a feature that provides a brief explanation for each recommendation, along with a link to the relevant APA 7th edition guidelines. This revised prototype is then tested with a larger group of students, and the feedback loop continues. The iterative process continues through several cycles, with each iteration incorporating user feedback and leading to a more refined and effective tool. The team also continuously monitors the tool's performance and adapts to changes in APA guidelines, ensuring that the tool remains up to date and reliable.

Collaborative Participation in Action: Collaborative participation is central to the entire design process. The development team actively involves graduate students at every stage, from initial concept development to final implementation. They conduct focus groups and co-design workshops to gather feedback on students' needs and preferences. They also employ user surveys to collect data on the tool's usability and effectiveness. These engagement activities indicate that students value the tool's ability to catch errors in APA 7th edition formatting and style but emphasize that they need to be in control of the final output. In response, the team designs the tool so that the user is responsible for accepting or rejecting each of the AI's recommendations. The AI provides suggestions, but the student makes the final decision, ensuring accountability for the quality and style of the work. The team also establishes a feedback mechanism within the tool, allowing students to provide ongoing feedback and suggestions for improvement, which directly informs future iterations. This continuous engagement ensures that the writing assistant remains user-centered and responsive to the evolving needs of graduate students.

By applying these four core principles throughout the design process, the resulting GenAI-powered academic writing assistant is not only technologically advanced but also deeply human-centered, meeting the diverse needs of graduate students, supporting their academic integrity, empowering them in their academic journey, and ensuring they remain accountable for their work.

Addressing Potential Challenges

Adopting a human-centered design approach for GenAI in higher education involves addressing several important challenges to ensure these technologies are integrated both responsibly and effectively. One major obstacle is the need for diverse and multidisciplinary teams. Developing and implementing GenAI tools requires expertise from areas such as education, computer science, ethics, and the social sciences. This diversity should extend beyond different academic disciplines to include individuals from varied cultural, socioeconomic, and experiential backgrounds. Another significant challenge is ensuring that all voices are heard and respected, especially those from marginalized communities. Historically, technology development has been shaped by a narrow range of perspectives, leading to tools that may not meet the needs of all users (An & Oliver, 2021). A human-centered approach necessitates actively seeking out and incorporating the viewpoints of those who have been traditionally excluded from the design process. This can be achieved through various engagement methods, including focus groups, interviews, and co-design workshops, to ensure that every voice is acknowledged and valued. By addressing these challenges, we can create GenAI tools that are more inclusive and effective, ultimately enhancing the educational experience for all students.

Sustaining funding and support for research and development that emphasizes inclusivity and equity presents a significant challenge (Gardner et al., 2022). Developing GenAI tools that are accessible, equitable, and effective for all users requires a long-term commitment to investment and innovation (Kumar et al., 2024). Additionally, it is essential to cultivate a culture that values experimentation and views setbacks as opportunities to learn and grow. The chapters in this book have illustrated that integrating GenAI into higher education is a complex and dynamic process, inevitably accompanied by obstacles and setbacks. Therefore, it is important to build an environment that encourages trying new approaches, embraces learning from failures, and is dedicated to continuous improvement. By fostering such a culture, we can better navigate the challenges of GenAI integration and ensure that our educational practices evolve in meaningful and equitable ways.

RECOMMENDATIONS

Recommendations for Educators

Educators play a critical role in the successful integration of generative artificial intelligence (GenAI) in higher education. To effectively navigate this evolving landscape, educators should adopt an approach that leverages GenAI to personalize educational experiences and accommodate diverse student needs (Giannakos et al., 2024). This approach involves deploying GenAI tools to develop flexible materials and provide personalized support, ensuring that these technologies enhance rather than undermine critical thinking, creativity, and ethical reasoning skills (Abbas, 2025). We should design activities that encourage students to evaluate information, generate innovative ideas, and consider the ethical implications of GenAI (Al-Zahrani, 2025; N. Wang et al., 2024). Promoting AI literacy is also essential, helping students understand how these systems operate and their broader impact on society (Kumar, 2025). This includes discussions on potential biases, algorithmic fairness, and privacy protocols (Eaton & Keyhani, 2025; Zhai, 2024). Furthermore, educators need to develop new literacies and competencies specific to AI technologies. This means learning how to effectively integrate AI tools into their teaching practices while maintaining educational integrity (Mao et al., 2024), as well as fostering students' ability to engage meaningfully with AI tools while preserving their intellectual autonomy (Chiu, 2025; Eaton & Keyhani, 2025). This includes avoiding over-reliance on automated systems and fostering a balanced environment where technology and human insight coexist productively. Al-Zahrani (2025) highlights that traditional teaching methods differ significantly from those needed in an era dominated by generative AI, requiring a fundamental shift in pedagogical approaches. For example, educators should encourage students to develop evaluative judgment and personal epistemology, enabling them to assess the quality of their own and others' work. Lastly, Detrick and Kim (2025) emphasize that educators should actively participate in the design and evaluation of GenAI-powered educational practices, providing valuable insights to ensure these tools meet the needs of both students and educators.

Recommendations for Institutions

In addressing the integration of GenAI in higher education, it becomes evident that the rapid advancement of AI technology has outpaced the development of clear guidelines, resulting in confusion and inconsistent practices, as Abbas (2025) points out in Chapter 11. Kowch (2025) echoes this sentiment, emphasizing the need for transparent governance and responsible AI frameworks. Additionally, Tweedie and Sharmi (2025) highlight the black box challenge, advocating for the use of Explainable AI (XAI) to make GenAI systems more transparent and understandable. Therefore, educational institutions must establish clear policies that ensure the ethical and responsible use of GenAI, addressing critical areas such as data privacy and academic integrity. These policies should be transparent, regularly reviewed, and flexible enough to adapt to the continuous evolution of AI technologies. Eaton and Keyhani (2025) stress the importance of ethical frameworks that focus on inclusivity and the preservation of human skills. In line with this, institutions should prioritize the inclusion of AI ethics courses within their curricula. Moreover, it is essential for institutions to guarantee that all students and faculty have equal access to GenAI technologies and the necessary training to utilize them effectively. This involves providing resources to support those who may be disadvantaged by socio-economic factors, as highlighted by Abbas (2025). Higher education institutions must also develop clear guidelines for the use of AI learning resources and generative interfaces, addressing concerns related to academic integrity and establishing standards for the appropriate use of AI tools in coursework, as emphasized by Eaton and Keyhani (2025). Lee (2025) advocates for revising assessment strategies to encourage higher-order thinking skills. Similarly, Eaton and Keyhani (2025) point out the need for authentic assessment methods that take GenAI capabilities into account. Consequently, institutions should move away from traditional assessments that focus on memorization and instead adopt approaches that promote critical thinking, problem-solving, creativity, and real-world application. This includes methods such as project-based learning, interactive presentations, and personalized portfolios. Furthermore, institutions must invest in training programs that equip educators and staff with the skills to effectively incorporate GenAI tools into their teaching, research, and administrative tasks. These programs should also emphasize AI literacy, ethics, and responsible technology use, as noted by Chiu (2025). Professional development should explore how these technologies can be used in ways that enhance the educational experience without detracting from it, as suggested by Hosseini et al. (2024). This involves creating opportunities for creative and innovative applications of AI in teaching and learning contexts.

Recommendations for Policy-makers

As we integrate GenAI into education, we must establish clear and transparent guidelines supported by strong regulatory frameworks. This means refining data collection methods, ensuring labeling accuracy, and enhancing algorithmic documentation to eliminate any ambiguities (Al-Zahrani, 2025; H. Wang et al., 2024). We need to develop policies that address data privacy, academic integrity, copyright, and the ethical use of GenAI, ensuring these policies are regularly updated to keep up with technological advancements (Abbas, 2025; Eaton & Keyhani, 2025). Additionally, creating detailed guidelines to manage copyright and intellectual property concerns is essential. Policy-makers should strive to create regulations that protect creators' rights while encouraging the innovative use of AI-generated content (Akpan et al., 2024). Furthermore, it is important for policy-makers to stay informed about emerging trends in AI and education to anticipate future challenges and opportunities. This requires continuous learning and adaptation to ensure that educational policies remain relevant and effective in a constantly evolving technological landscape (Mao et al., 2024).

Recommendations for Developers

In envisioning the role of GenAI in higher education, it is important to ground development and implementation efforts in human-centered design. Engaging educators, students, and other partners in the co-design process ensures that their feedback and insights drive continuous improvements (Brown & Roberts, 2025; Detrick & Kim, 2025). By positioning human expertise at the center, AI tools enhance—rather than replace—interactive learning experiences and pedagogical decision-making. Equally important is the promotion of AI literacy and the emphasis on ethical usage. Developing training programs focused on prompt engineering, bias detection, and responsible application (Chiu, 2025; Keyhani & Mohaghegh-Neyshabouri, 2025; Lee, 2025) empowers learners and instructors to navigate GenAI critically. This knowledge helps users understand the strengths and limitations of GenAI, reducing the risk of over-reliance and ensuring that these tools are used wisely. Transparency in GenAI systems is another key factor that benefits both educators and students. Providing clear explanations of how AI outputs are generated (Tweedie & Sharmi, 2025) demystifies the technology, allowing users to identify biases and inaccuracies while building trust and accountability. Collaboration also plays a significant role in how GenAI is incorporated into classroom settings. Designing platforms that encourage peer learning, shared projects, and the collective creation of knowledge maintains the social aspects of education (Chiu, 2025). In these human–AI partnerships, GenAI serves as a support tool, facilitating dynamic interactions between learners and instructors rather than replacing them. Finally, maintaining a commitment to continuous improvement is essential. Establishing feedback loops, regularly evaluating outcomes, and staying updated with the latest research and technological advancements ensures that GenAI tools remain effective and aligned with the evolving needs of education (Detrick & Kim, 2025).

CONCLUSION

As we incorporate GenAI into higher education, we must remember that technology, no matter how advanced, is a means to support our goals, values, and educational objectives. The chapters in this book have highlighted the potential of GenAI—from customizing learning experiences to improving administrative efficiency—but they have also revealed the ethical, teaching, and policy challenges that necessitate a focus on people-centered approaches. Moving forward requires continuous development, experimentation, and flexibility. As GenAI advances, our teaching practices, regulatory policies, and collaborative strategies must also evolve. Educational institutions can adopt flexible processes, encourage active participation, and establish clear governance to maintain academic integrity and ensure fairness, making sure that GenAI enhances rather than disrupts our fundamental educational goals. As educators, our responsibility is to equip students with the critical, creative, and ethical skills needed to navigate environments rich in AI. Meanwhile, technology developers should create inclusive and transparent systems that respect students' dignity and privacy. Policy-makers, for their part, need to design regulations that promote responsible AI use, ensure equitable access to resources, and prioritize student well-being in higher education. Ultimately, creating a cohesive ecosystem that brings together educators, institutions, policy-makers, and developers will foster an environment that values human agency, upholds ethical standards, and provides equal learning opportunities for everyone. Although significant challenges remain, there is every reason to believe that, with thoughtful leadership and collaborative effort, GenAI can do more than just enhance education—it can drive meaningful transformation. The GenAI era calls on us to address its complexities with hope and resolve, confident that, when guided by human-focused principles, this powerful technology can lead to a future where higher education is more accessible, inclusive, and deeply human.

REFERENCES

Abbas, M. (2025). Challenges and misuses of generative AI and the quest for mitigation. In S. Sabbaghan (Ed.), *Navigating generative AI in higher education: Ethical, theoretical, and practical perspectives*. Edward Elgar.

Akpan, I. J., Kobara, Y. M., Owolabi, J., Akpan, A. A., & Offodile, O. F. (2024). Conversational and generative artificial intelligence and human–chatbot interaction in education and research. *International Transactions in Operational Research, 32*(3), 1251–1281. https://doi.org/10.1111/itor.13522.

Al-Zahrani, A. M. (2025). The future landscape: Predictions and prospects for generative AI in academia. In S. Sabbaghan (Ed.), *Navigating generative AI in higher education: Ethical, theoretical, and practical perspectives.* Edward Elgar.

An, T., & Oliver, M. (2021). What in the world is educational technology? Rethinking the field from the perspective of the philosophy of technology. *Learning, Media and Technology, 46*(1), 6–19. https://doi.org/10.1080/17439884.2020.1810066.

Baidoo-Anu, D., Asamoah, D., & Monsurat, R. (2025). Innovative applications of generative artificial intelligence in classroom assessment: A scoping review. In S. Sabbaghan (Ed.), *Navigating generative AI in higher education: Ethical, theoretical, and practical perspectives.* Edward Elgar.

Brown, B., & Roberts, V. (2025). Responsive instructional design using GenAI and digital skill development framework. In S. Sabbaghan (Ed.), *Navigating generative AI in higher education: Ethical, theoretical, and practical perspectives.* Edward Elgar.

Chiu, T. K. F. (2025). From student artificial intelligence (AI) literacy to AI competency: Essential skills for the next generation. In *Navigating generative AI in higher education: Ethical, theoretical, and practical perspectives.* Edward Elgar.

Detrick, R., & Kim, J. (2025). Collaborative approaches: Bridging the gap between generative AI developers and educators. In S. Sabbaghan (Ed.), *Navigating generative AI in higher education: Ethical, theoretical, and practical perspectives.* Edward Elgar.

Eaton, S. E. (2023). Postplagiarism: Transdisciplinary ethics and integrity in the age of artificial intelligence and neurotechnology. *International Journal for Educational Integrity, 19*(1), 23, s40979-023-00144–1. https://doi.org/10.1007/s40979-023-00144-1.

Eaton, S. E., & Keyhani, M. (2025). The pedagogical ethics: Navigating learning in a generative AI-augmented environment in a post-plagiarism era. In S. Sabbaghan (Ed.), *Navigating generative AI in higher education: Ethical, theoretical, and practical perspectives.* Edward Elgar.

Farrokhnia, M., Soleimani, S., & Noroozi, O. (2025). Generative AI in higher education: Transformative tools for research, teaching, and assessment. In S. Sabbaghan (Ed.), *Navigating generative AI in higher education: Ethical, theoretical, and practical perspectives.* Edward Elgar.

Gardner, A., Smith, A. L., Steventon, A., Coughlan, E., & Oldfield, M. (2022). Ethical funding for trustworthy AI: Proposals to address the responsibilities of funders to ensure that projects adhere to trustworthy AI practice. *AI and Ethics, 2*(2), 277–291. https://doi.org/10.1007/s43681-021-00069-w.

Giacomin, J. (2014). What Is Human Centred Design? *The Design Journal, 17*(4), 606–623. https://doi.org/10.2752/175630614X14056185480186.

Giannakos, M., Azevedo, R., Brusilovsky, P., Cukurova, M., Dimitriadis, Y., Hernandez-Leo, D., Järvelä, S., Mavrikis, M., & Rienties, B. (2024). The promise and challenges of generative AI in education. *Behaviour & Information Technology,* 1–27. https://doi.org/10.1080/0144929X.2024.2394886.

Hosseini, M., Bahrami, V., & Dikilitaş, K. (2024). From research reading and doing to research use: Tracking trajectories of becoming research-informed second language teachers. *System, 125,* 103445. https://doi.org/10.1016/j.system.2024.103445.

Keyhani, M., & Mohaghegh-Neyshabouri, S. (2025). The rise of generative AI: Capabilities and potential for higher education. In S. Sabbaghan (Ed.), *Navigating generative AI in higher education: Ethical, theoretical, and practical perspectives.* Edward Elgar.

Kowch, E. (2025). An innovation policy analysis of G10 nations' strategic plans for future AI leaders and researchers in higher education. In S. Sabbaghan (Ed.), *Navigating generative AI in higher education: Ethical, theoretical, and practical perspectives*. Edward Elgar.

Kumar, R. (2025). Rethinking authorship in a generative AI-driven academic world. In S. Sabbaghan (Ed.), *Navigating generative AI in higher education: Ethical, theoretical, and practical perspectives*. Edward Elgar.

Kumar, S., Verma, A. K., & Mirza, A. (2024). Digital revolution, artificial intelligence, and ethical challenges. In S. Kumar, A. K. Verma, & A. Mirza, *Digital transformation, artificial intelligence and society* (pp. 161–177). Springer Nature Singapore. https://doi.org/10.1007/978-981-97-5656-8_11.

Lee, A. V. Y. (2025). The double-edged sword of generative AI for assessment: efficiency versus homogenization. In S. Sabbaghan (Ed.), *Navigating generative AI in higher education: Ethical, theoretical, and practical perspectives*. Edward Elgar.

Magalhães, R. (2018). Human-centred organization design. *The Design Journal*, *21*(2), 227–246. https://doi.org/10.1080/14606925.2018.1426940.

Maguire, M. (2001). Methods to support human-centred design. *International Journal of Human-Computer Studies*, *55*(4), 587–634. https://doi.org/10.1006/ijhc.2001.0503.

Mao, J., Chen, B., & Liu, J. C. (2024). Generative artificial intelligence in education and its implications for assessment. *TechTrends*, *68*(1), 58–66. https://doi.org/10.1007/s11528-023-00911-4.

Tosi, F. (2020). From user-centred design to human-centred design and the user experience. In F. Tosi, *Design for ergonomics* (Vol. 2, pp. 47–59). Springer International Publishing. https://doi.org/10.1007/978-3-030-33562-5_3.

Tweedie, M. G., & Sharmi, S. T. (2025). Transparency, assessment and the "black box" dilemma. In S. Sabbaghan (Ed.), *Navigating generative AI in higher education: Ethical, theoretical, and practical perspectives*. Edward Elgar.

Wang, H., Dang, A., Wu, Z., & Mac, S. (2024). Generative AI in higher education: Seeing ChatGPT through universities' policies, resources, and guidelines. *Computers and Education: Artificial Intelligence*, *7*, 100326. https://doi.org/10.1016/j.caeai.2024.100326.

Wang, N., Wang, X., & Su, Y.-S. (2024). Critical analysis of the technological affordances, challenges and future directions of Generative AI in education: A systematic review. *Asia Pacific Journal of Education*, *44*(1), 139–155. https://doi.org/10.1080/02188791.2024.2305156.

Zhai, X. (2024). Transforming teachers' roles and agencies in the era of generative AI: Perceptions, acceptance, knowledge, and practices. *Journal of Science Education and Technology*. https://doi.org/10.1007/s10956-024-10174-0.

Index